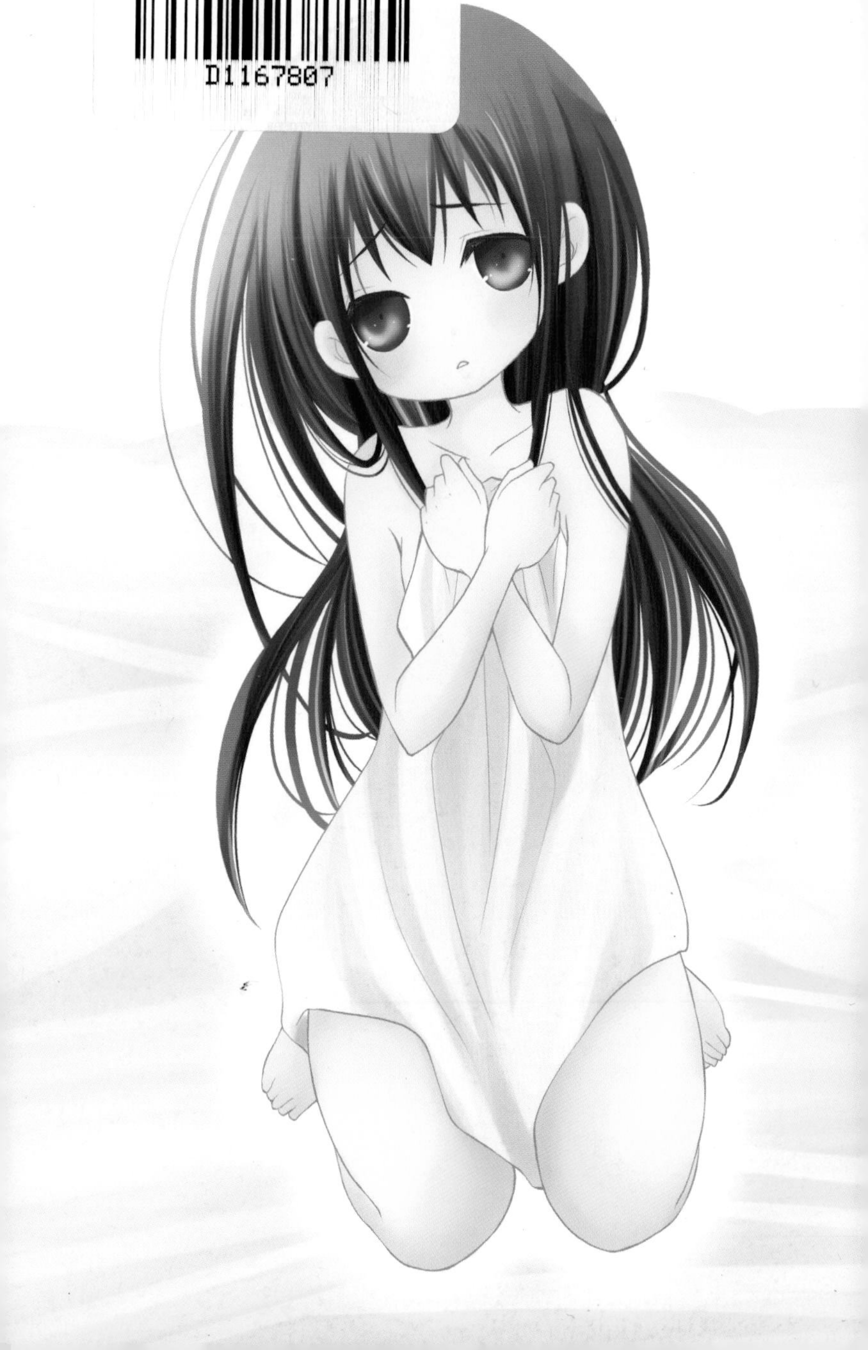

[Ani-Imo]

Big Brother becomes Little Sister;
Little Sister becomes Big Brother.

Ani-Imo

$$\left(4\right)$$

[Ani-Imo]
Big Brother becomes
Little Sister;
Little Sister becomes
Big Brother.

Haruko
Kurumatani

CHARACTERS

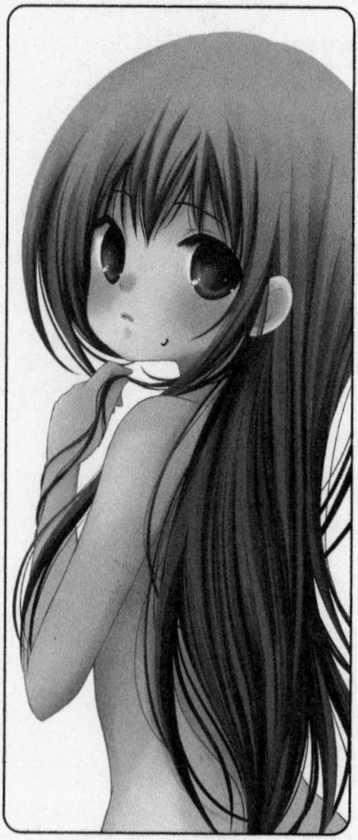

Youta Koizumi

A first-year in high school. Has Hikaru's body but is in fact Youta on the inside. Hikaru is his precious little sister, but he can't accept how she feels about him.

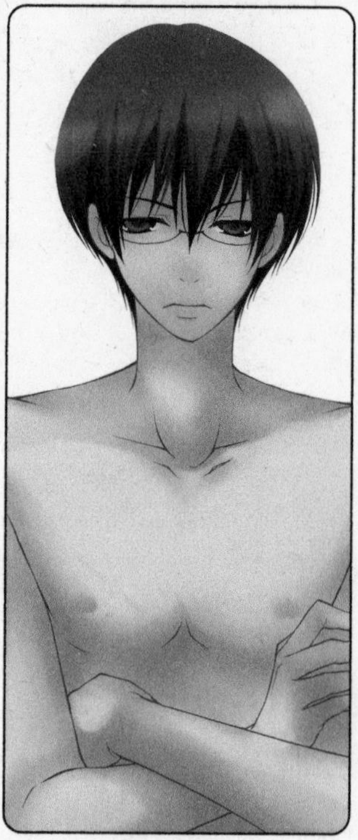

Hikaru Koizumi

A first-year in high school. Outwardly appears to be Youta but is Hikaru on the inside. Her feelings for her brother are very serious and only became all the more so when they switched bodies.

Kakeru Mayama

Has Yurika's body but is Mayama on the inside. A ditzy classmate who can't accept reality for what it is.

Yurika Oda

Has Mayama's body but is Yurika on the inside. Hikaru and Youta's classmate. She is Yurika-sama, the merciless lesbian.

Chisato Ichijou

Hikaru and Youta's doctor. Sadistic and brutal at heart. Despite this, he has taken an interest in the Koizumi siblings.

S T O R Y

I'm Youta Koizumi.
One day, I switched bodies with my precious little sister, whom I've protected my whole life!!!!!
Before I could recover from the shock, my once adorable little sister went completely sadistic on me, and I fell for her ploy to get me to go out with her. But in the bath, we almost made it to the next base, and I deeply regretted having taken Hikaru's feelings so lightly before......Then the lesbian babe Oda-san and our innocent, clueless classmate Mayama switched bodies too! Amid all the chaos, Hikaru had a sudden change of attitude and declared that she wasn't going to lay a finger on me. Could this be the start of her getting over me? On our day off from school, I followed Hikaru while she went out on the town with Mayama (in Yurika's body) and found myself tailing them to a love hotel!! Yurika (in Mayama's body) suddenly showed up and dragged me into the same love hotel with her!!!!?

CONTENTS

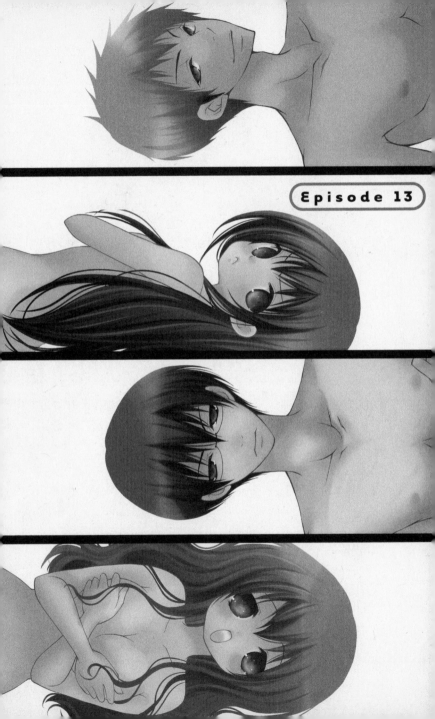

Episode 13

THIS IS YOUTA KOIZUMI'S...
...FIRST TIME IN A LOVE HOTEL. ♡
PLEASE BE GENTLE, OKAY...?
*DRAMATIZATION.

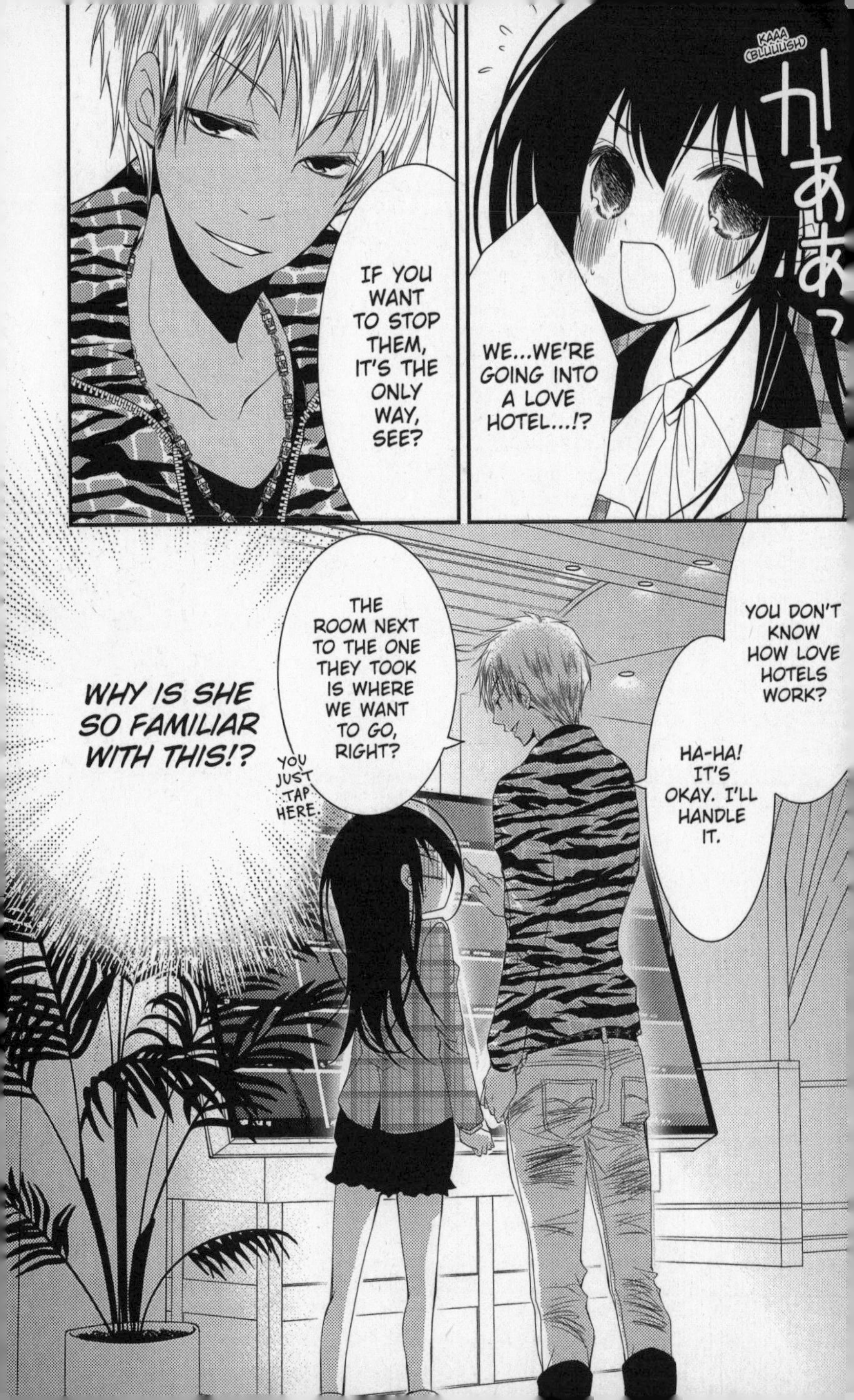
KAAA (BLUUUSH)
WE...WE'RE GOING INTO A LOVE HOTEL...!?
IF YOU WANT TO STOP THEM, IT'S THE ONLY WAY, SEE?
YOU DON'T KNOW HOW LOVE HOTELS WORK?
HA-HA! IT'S OKAY. I'LL HANDLE IT.
THE ROOM NEXT TO THE ONE THEY TOOK IS WHERE WE WANT TO GO, RIGHT?
YOU JUST TAP HERE.
WHY IS SHE SO FAMILIAR WITH THIS!?

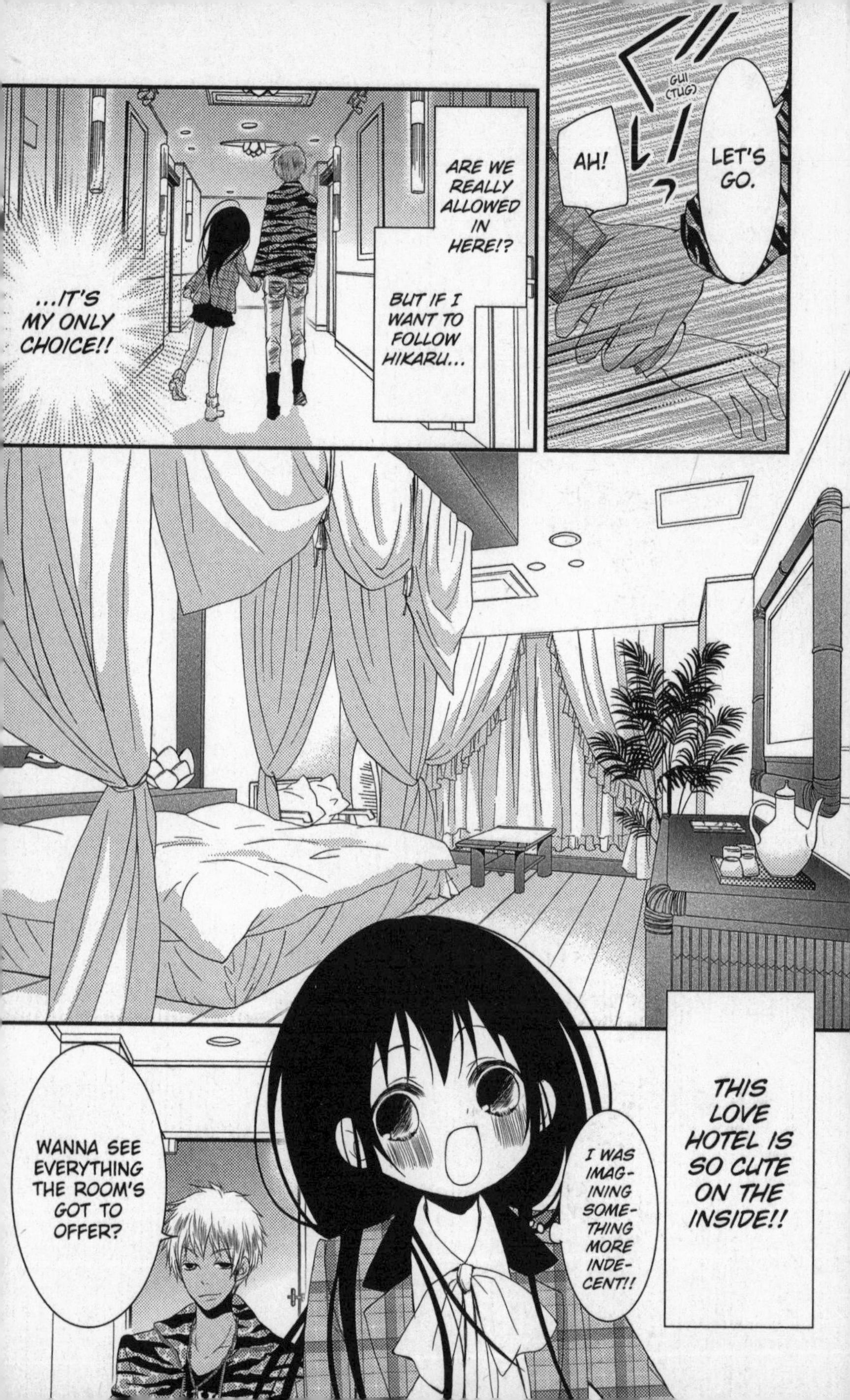
LET'S GO.
GUI (TUG)
AH!
ARE WE REALLY ALLOWED IN HERE!?
BUT IF I WANT TO FOLLOW HIKARU...
...IT'S MY ONLY CHOICE!!
THIS LOVE HOTEL IS SO CUTE ON THE INSIDE!!
I WAS IMAG-INING SOME-THING MORE INDE-CENT!!
WANNA SEE EVERYTHING THE ROOM'S GOT TO OFFER?

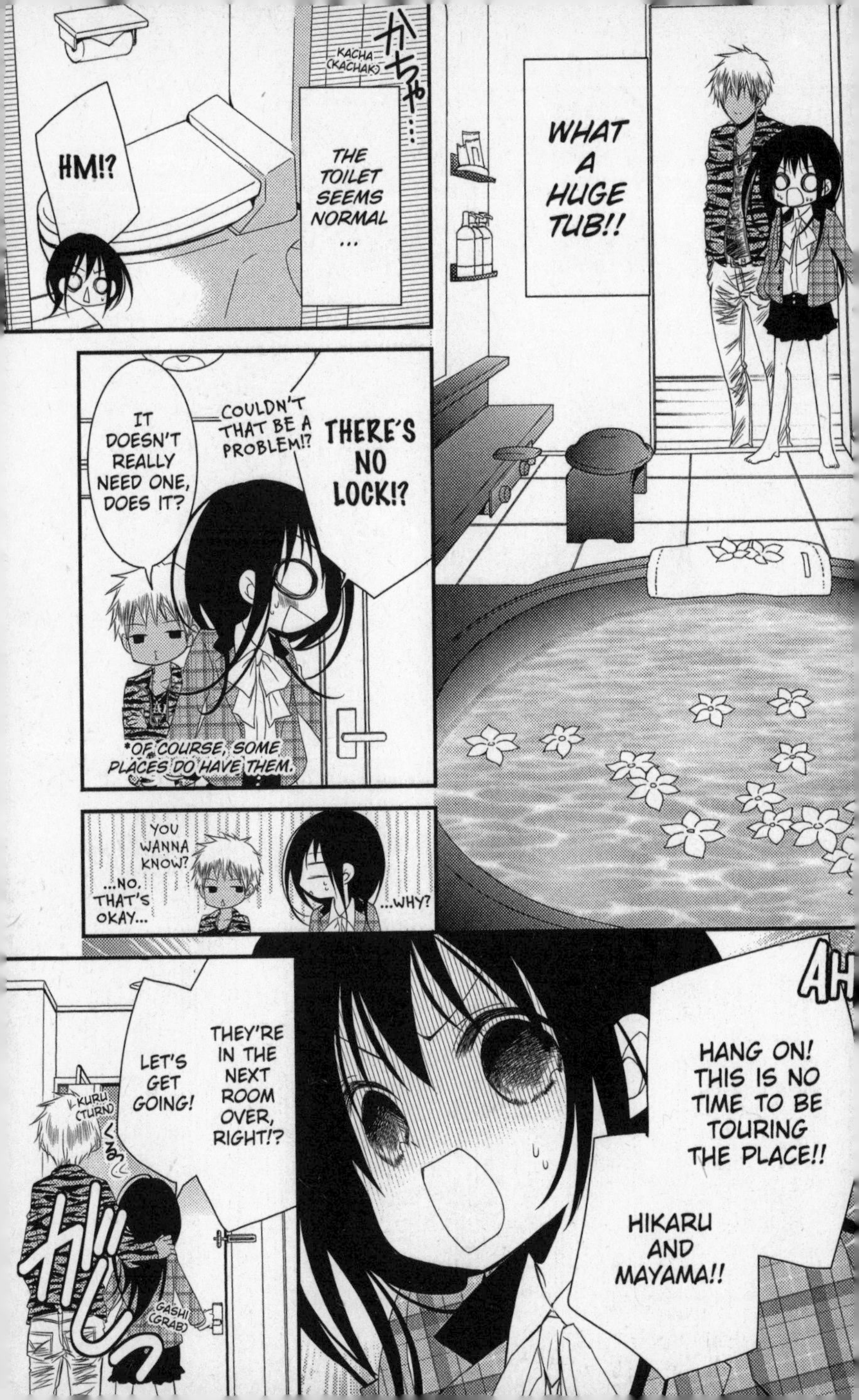
WHAT A HUGE TUB!!
かちゃ…
KACHA (KACHAK)
THE TOILET SEEMS NORMAL...
HM!?
THERE'S NO LOCK!?
COULDN'T THAT BE A PROBLEM!?
IT DOESN'T REALLY NEED ONE, DOES IT?
*OF COURSE, SOME PLACES DO HAVE THEM.
...WHY?
YOU WANNA KNOW?
...NO. THAT'S OKAY...
AH
HANG ON! THIS IS NO TIME TO BE TOURING THE PLACE!!
HIKARU AND MAYAMA!!
THEY'RE IN THE NEXT ROOM OVER, RIGHT!?
LET'S GET GOING!
くる
KURU (TURN)
ガシっ
GASHI (GRAB)

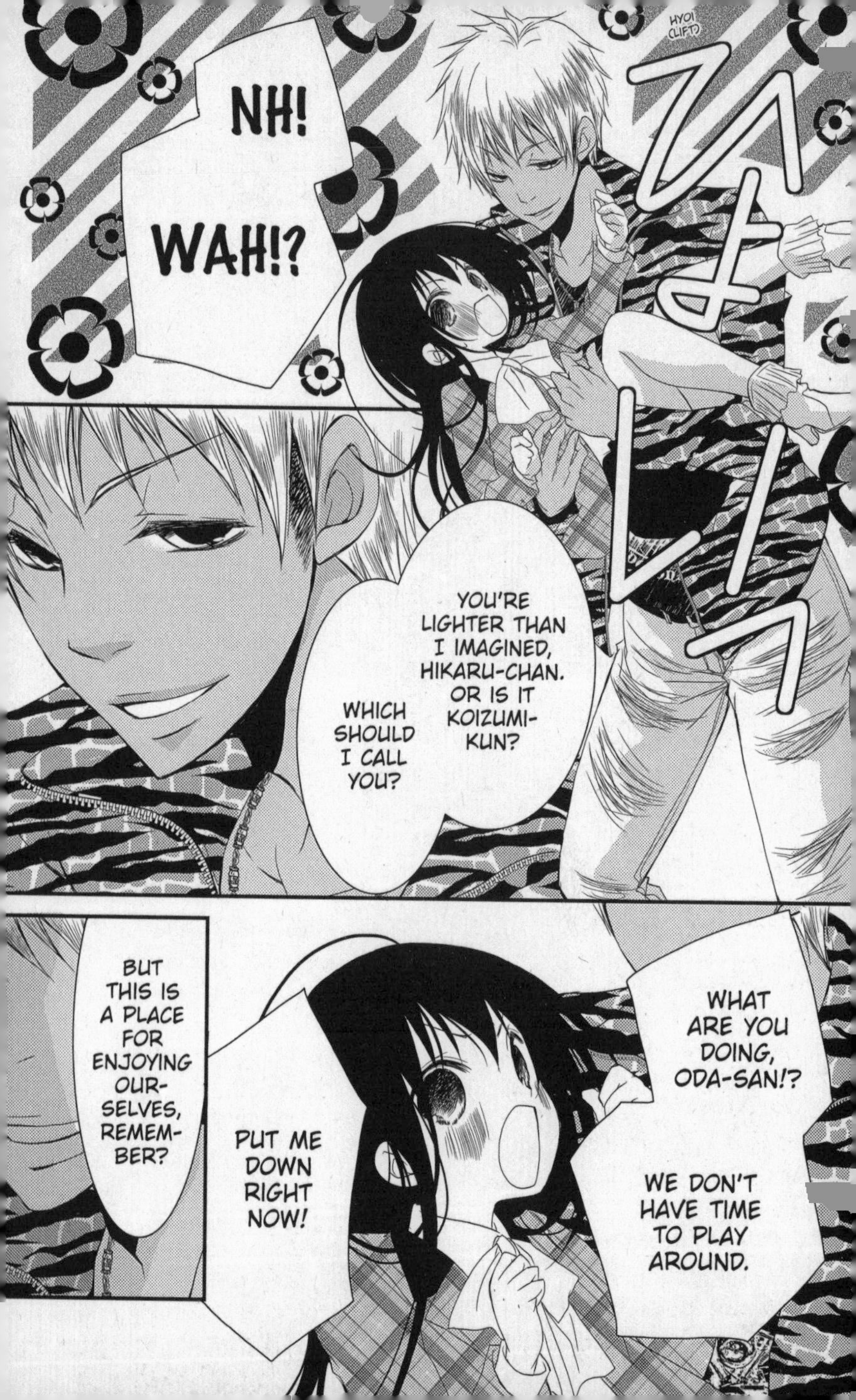
HYOI (LIFT)
NH!
WAH!?
YOU'RE LIGHTER THAN I IMAGINED, HIKARU-CHAN. OR IS IT KOIZUMI-KUN?
WHICH SHOULD I CALL YOU?
WHAT ARE YOU DOING, ODA-SAN!?
WE DON'T HAVE TIME TO PLAY AROUND.
PUT ME DOWN RIGHT NOW!
BUT THIS IS A PLACE FOR ENJOYING OUR-SELVES, REMEM-BER?

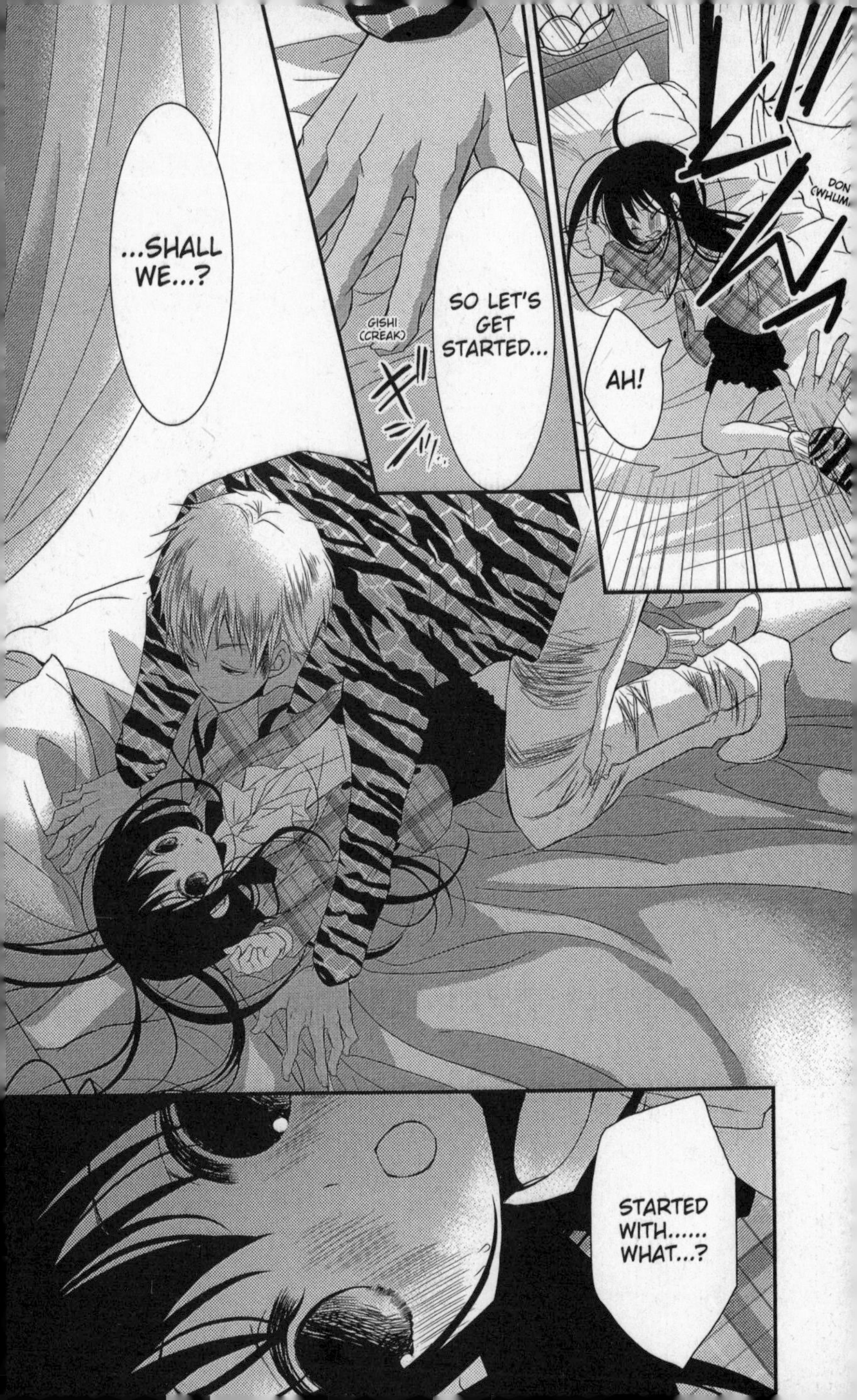
DON (WHUM
AH!
GISHI (CREAK)
SO LET'S GET STARTED...
...SHALL WE...?
STARTED WITH...... WHAT...?

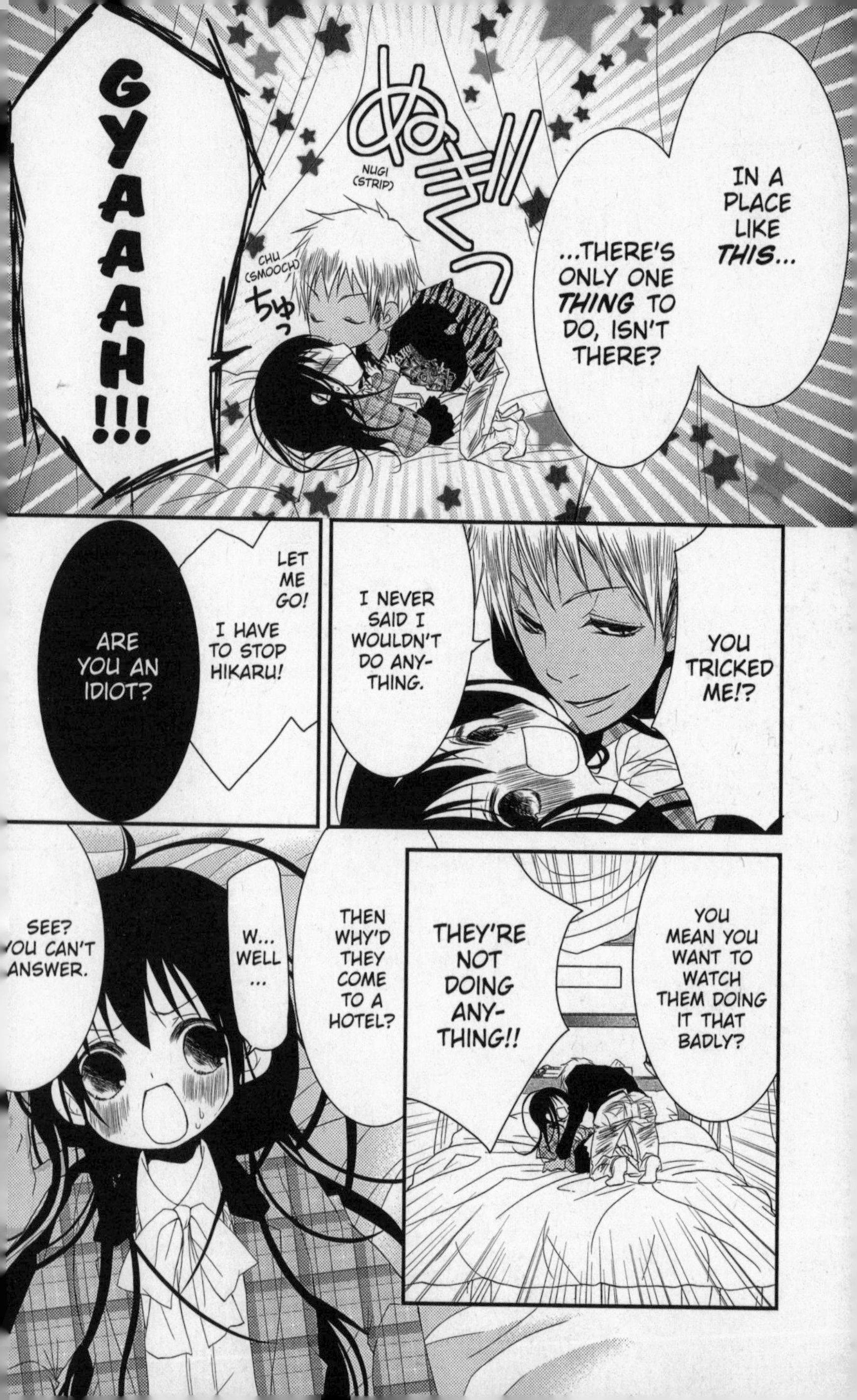
IN A PLACE LIKE *THIS*...
...THERE'S ONLY ONE *THING* TO DO, ISN'T THERE?
ぬぎっ
NUGI (STRIP)
ちゅっ
CHU (SMOOCH)
GYAAAAH!!!
YOU TRICKED ME!?
I NEVER SAID I WOULDN'T DO ANY-THING.
LET ME GO!
I HAVE TO STOP HIKARU!
ARE YOU AN IDIOT?
YOU MEAN YOU WANT TO WATCH THEM DOING IT THAT BADLY?
THEY'RE NOT DOING ANY-THING!!
THEN WHY'D THEY COME TO A HOTEL?
W... WELL ...
SEE? YOU CAN'T ANSWER.

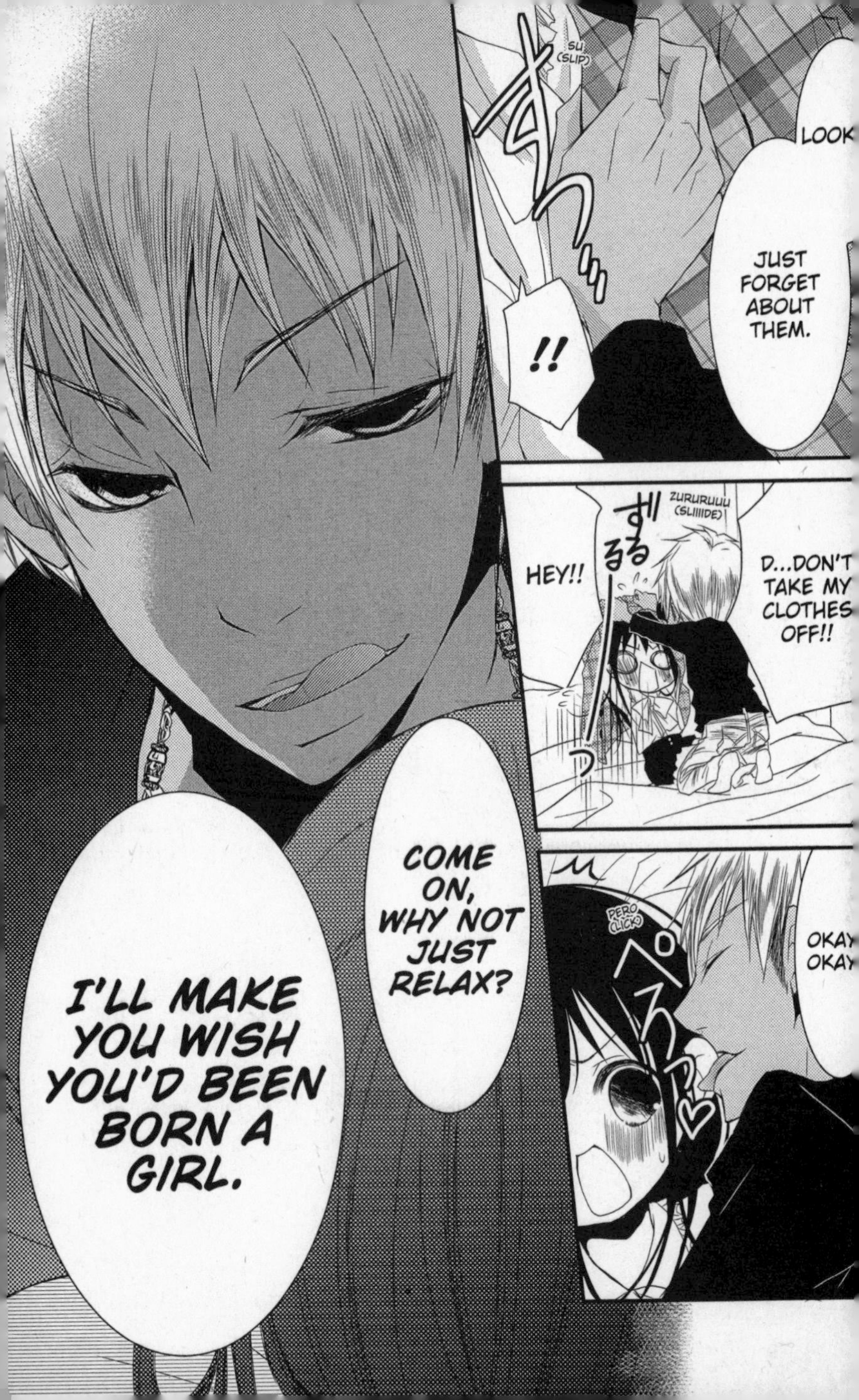

LOOK
JUST FORGET ABOUT THEM.
SU (SLIP)
!!
D...DON'T TAKE MY CLOTHES OFF!!
ZURURUUU (SLIIIIDE)
HEY!!
OKAY OKAY
PERO (LICK)
COME ON, WHY NOT JUST RELAX?
I'LL MAKE YOU WISH YOU'D BEEN BORN A GIRL.

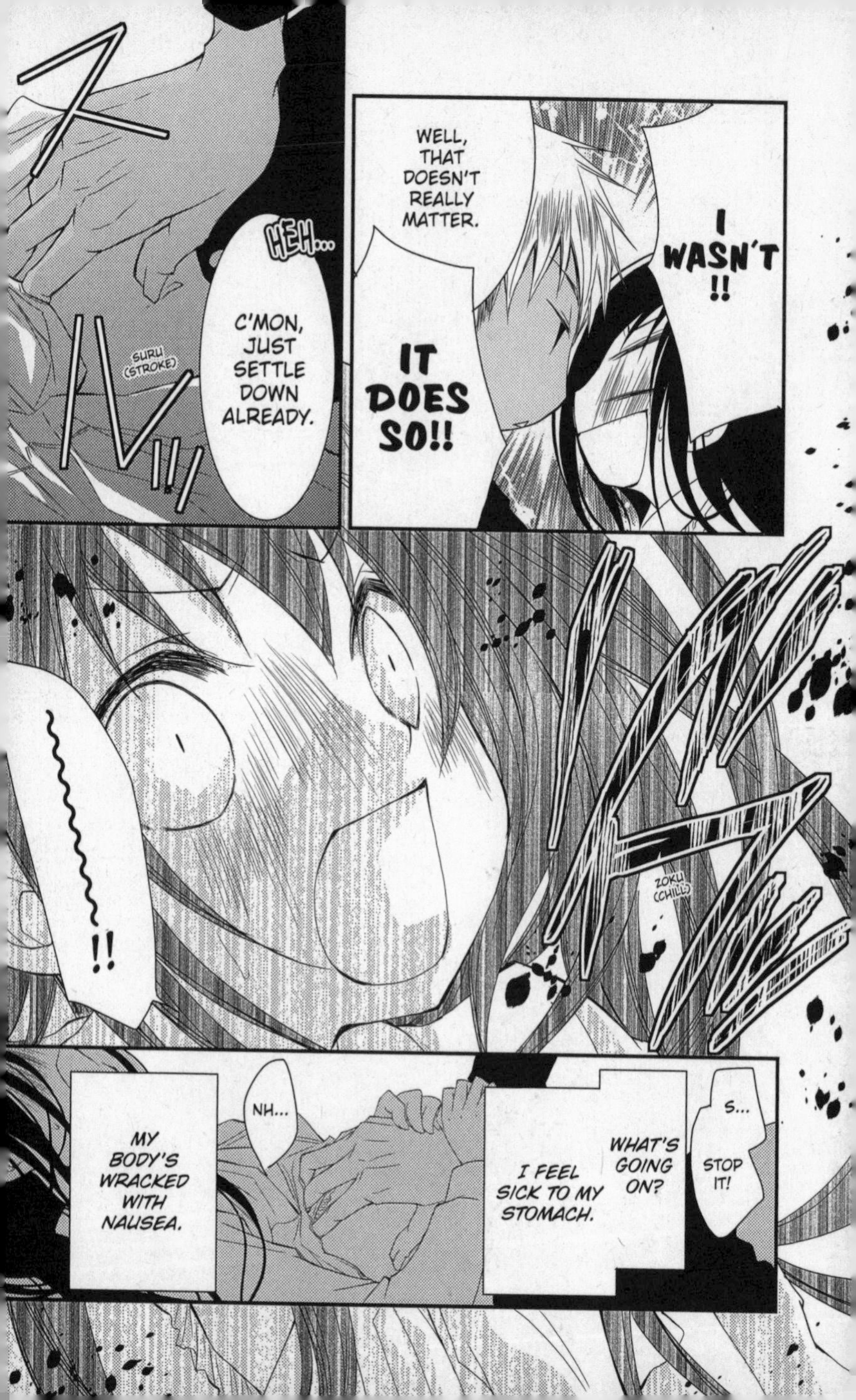
I WASN'T!!
WELL, THAT DOESN'T REALLY MATTER.
IT DOES SO!!
HEH...
C'MON, JUST SETTLE DOWN ALREADY.
SURU (STROKE)
ZOKU (CHILL)
~~!!
S...
STOP IT!
WHAT'S GOING ON?
I FEEL SICK TO MY STOMACH.
NH...
MY BODY'S WRACKED WITH NAUSEA.

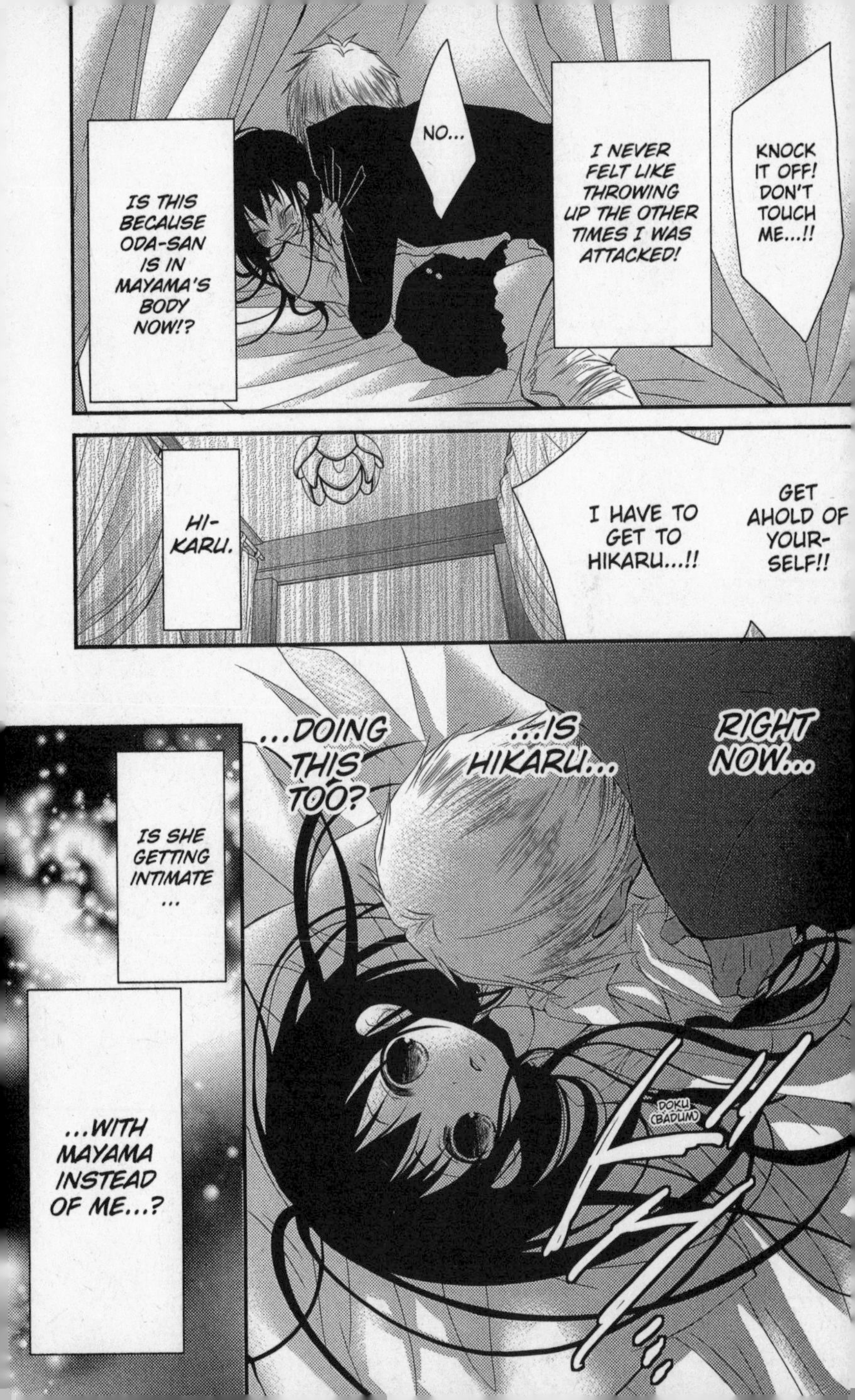
KNOCK IT OFF! DON'T TOUCH ME...!!
I NEVER FELT LIKE THROWING UP THE OTHER TIMES I WAS ATTACKED!
NO...
IS THIS BECAUSE ODA-SAN IS IN MAYAMA'S BODY NOW!?
GET AHOLD OF YOUR-SELF!!
I HAVE TO GET TO HIKARU...!!
HI-KARU.
RIGHT NOW...
...IS HIKARU...
...DOING THIS TOO?
DOKU (BADUM)
IS SHE GETTING INTIMATE ...
...WITH MAYAMA INSTEAD OF ME...?

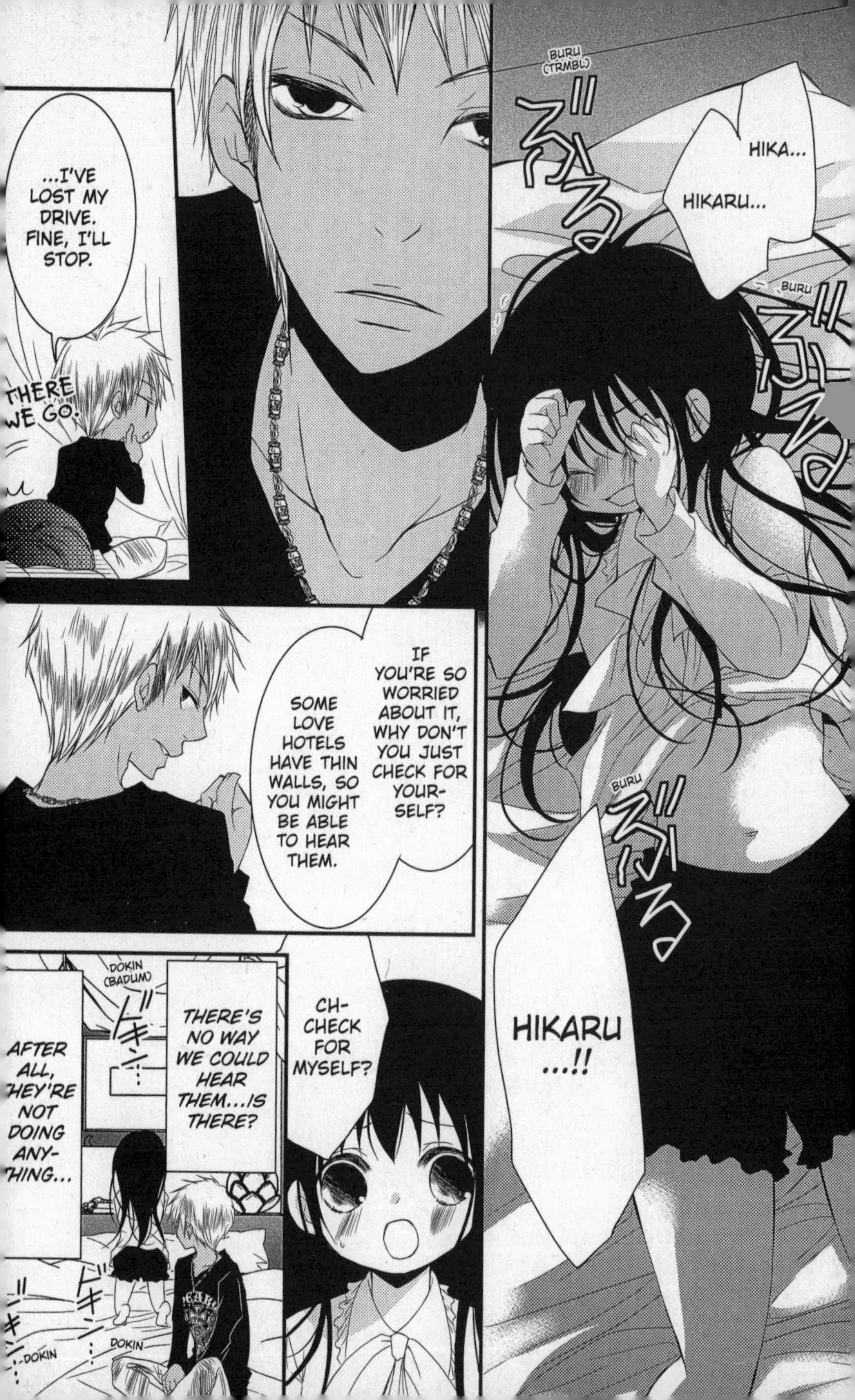
BURU (TRMBL)
HIKA... HIKARU...
BURU
BURU
HIKARU ...!!
...I'VE LOST MY DRIVE. FINE, I'LL STOP.
THERE WE GO.
IF YOU'RE SO WORRIED ABOUT IT, WHY DON'T YOU JUST CHECK FOR YOUR-SELF?
SOME LOVE HOTELS HAVE THIN WALLS, SO YOU MIGHT BE ABLE TO HEAR THEM.
CH-CHECK FOR MYSELF?
DOKIN (BADUM)
THERE'S NO WAY WE COULD HEAR THEM...IS THERE?
AFTER ALL, HEY'RE NOT DOING ANY-HING...
DOKIN
DOKIN

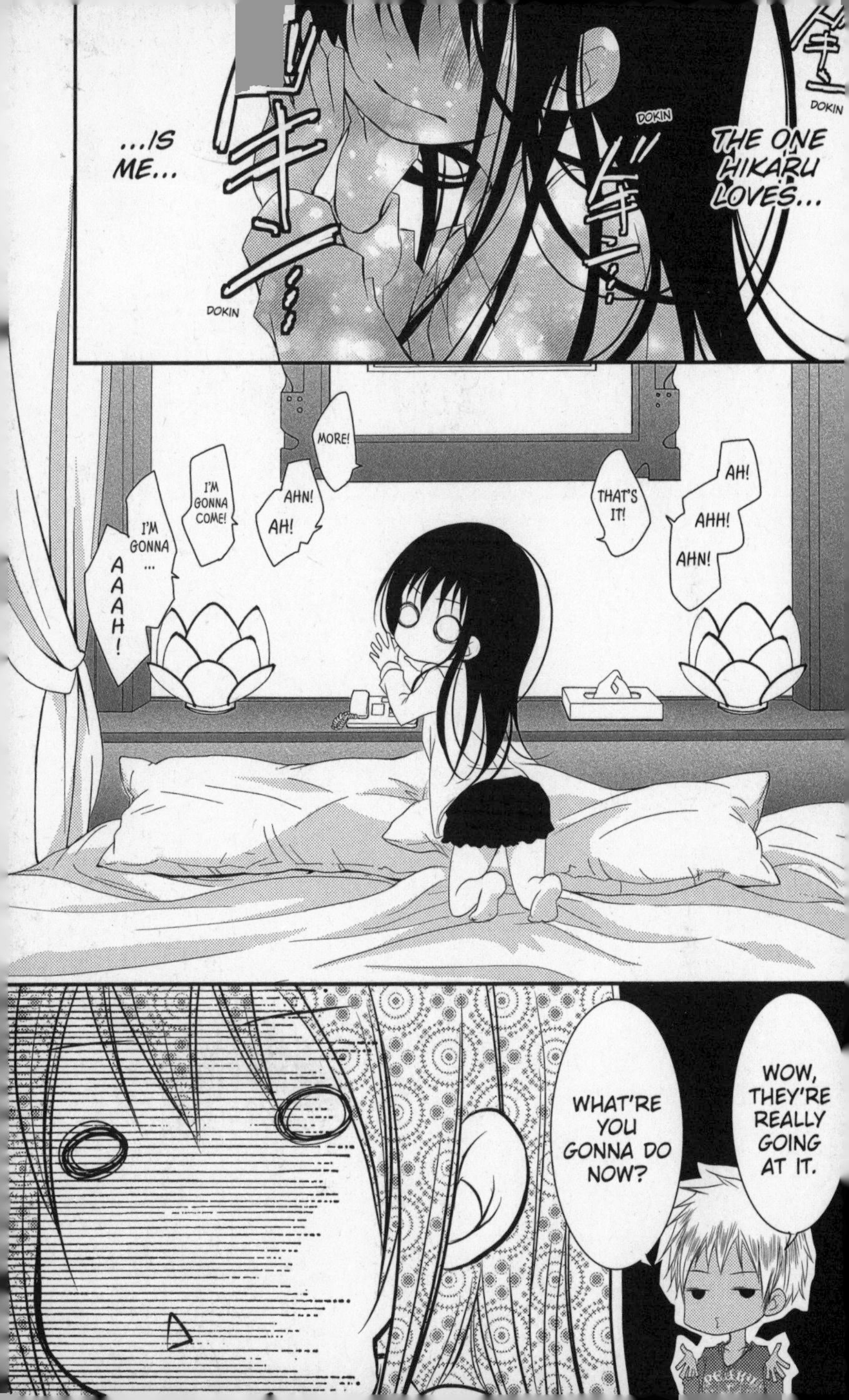
DOKIN
THE ONE HIKARU LOVES...
DOKIN
...IS ME...
DOKIN
AH! AHH! AHN!
THAT'S IT!
MORE!
AHN! AH!
I'M GONNA COME!
I'M GONNA ...
AAAAH!
WOW, THEY'RE REALLY GOING AT IT.
WHAT'RE YOU GONNA DO NOW?

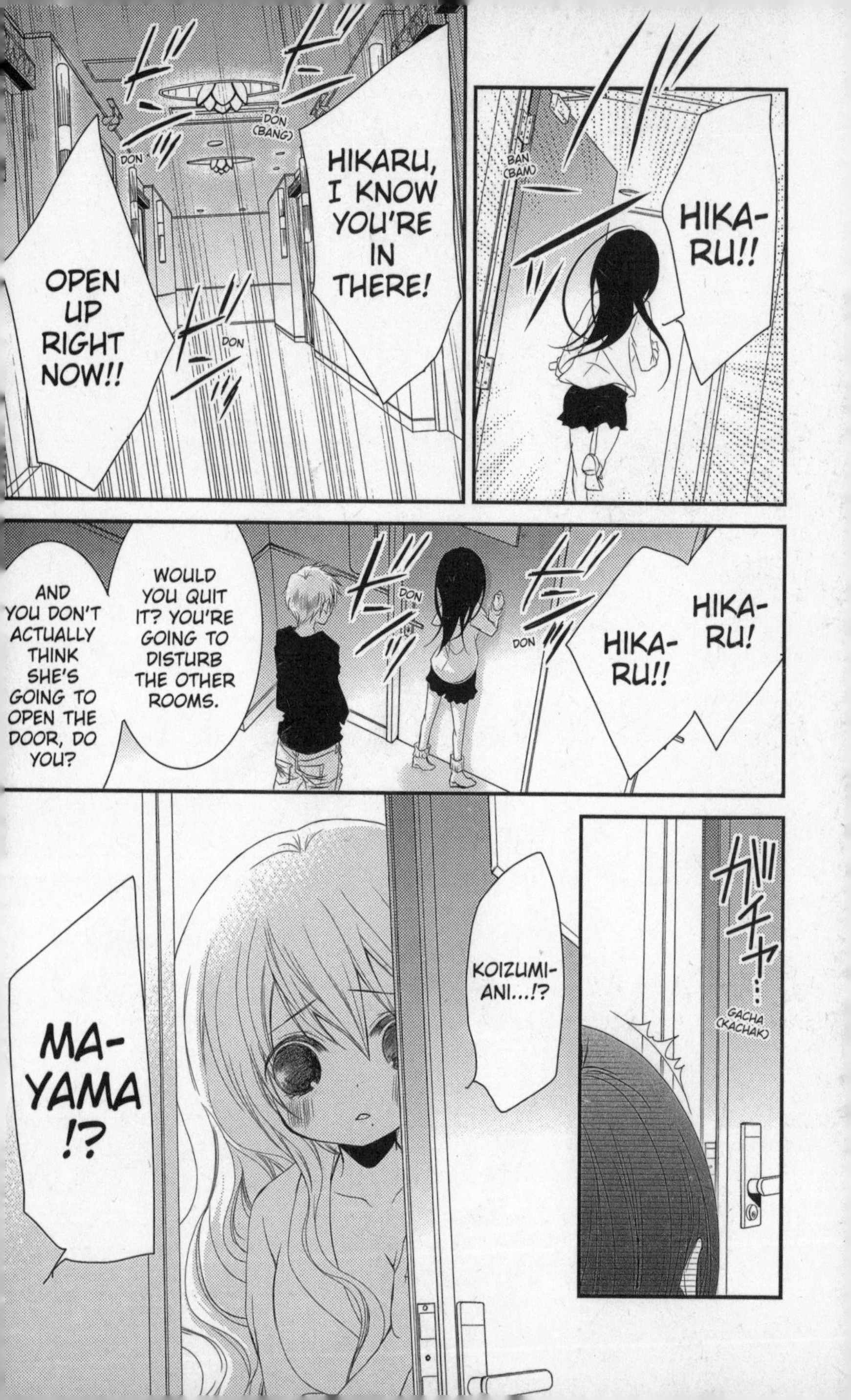
BAN (BAM)
HIKA-RU!!
DON (BANG)
HIKARU, I KNOW YOU'RE IN THERE!
DON
OPEN UP RIGHT NOW!!
DON
HIKA-RU!
HIKA-RU!!
DON
DON
WOULD YOU QUIT IT? YOU'RE GOING TO DISTURB THE OTHER ROOMS.
AND YOU DON'T ACTUALLY THINK SHE'S GOING TO OPEN THE DOOR, DO YOU?
ガチャ…
GACHA (KACHAK)
KOIZUMI-ANI...!?
MA-YAMA!?

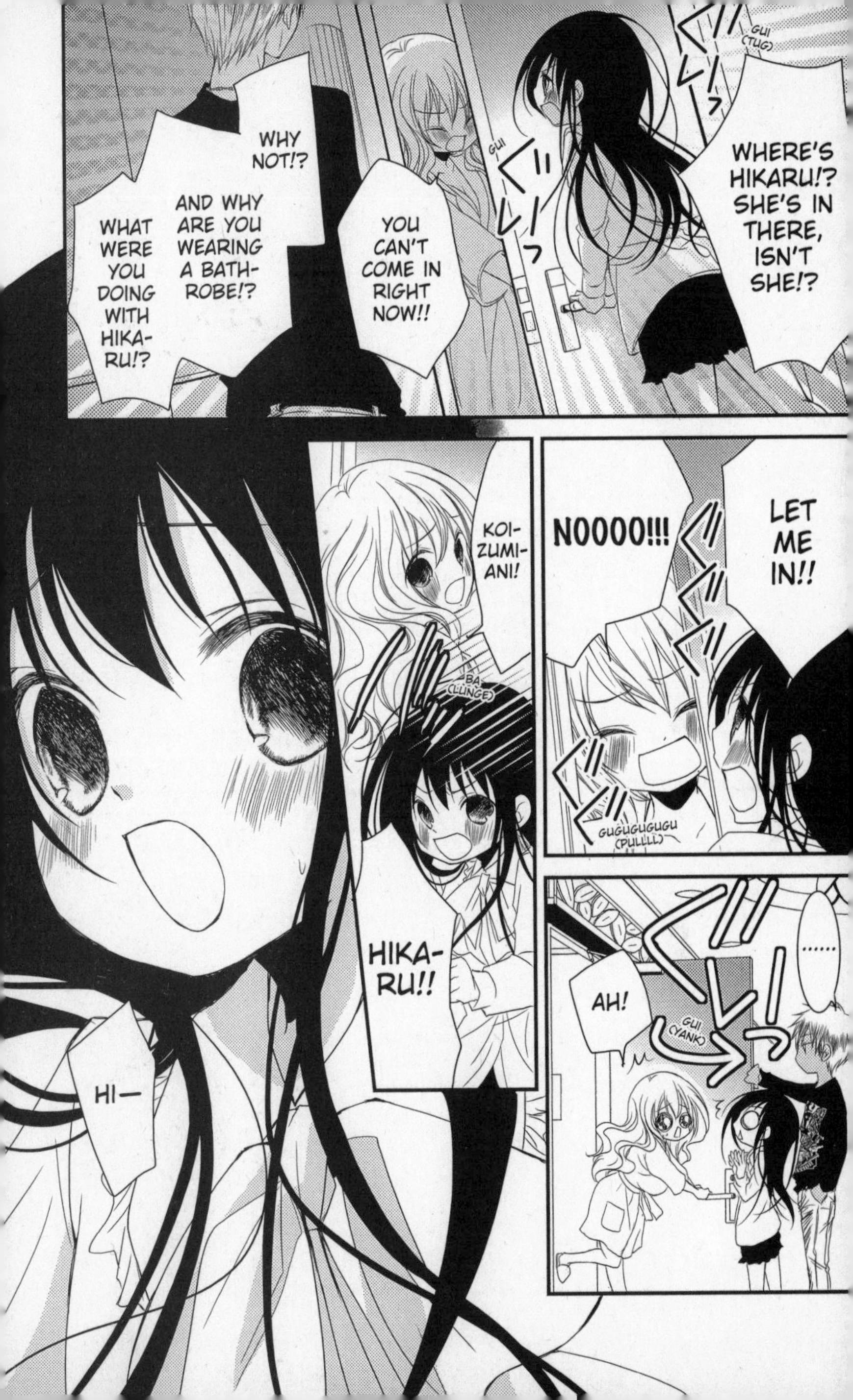
GUI (TUG)
WHERE'S HIKARU!? SHE'S IN THERE, ISN'T SHE!?
GUI
YOU CAN'T COME IN RIGHT NOW!!
WHY NOT!?
AND WHY ARE YOU WEARING A BATH-ROBE!?
WHAT WERE YOU DOING WITH HIKA-RU!?
LET ME IN!!
NOOOO!!!
GUGUGUGUGU (PULLLL)
......
AH!
GUI (YANK)
KOI-ZUMI-ANI!
BA (LUNGE)
HIKA-RU!!
HI—

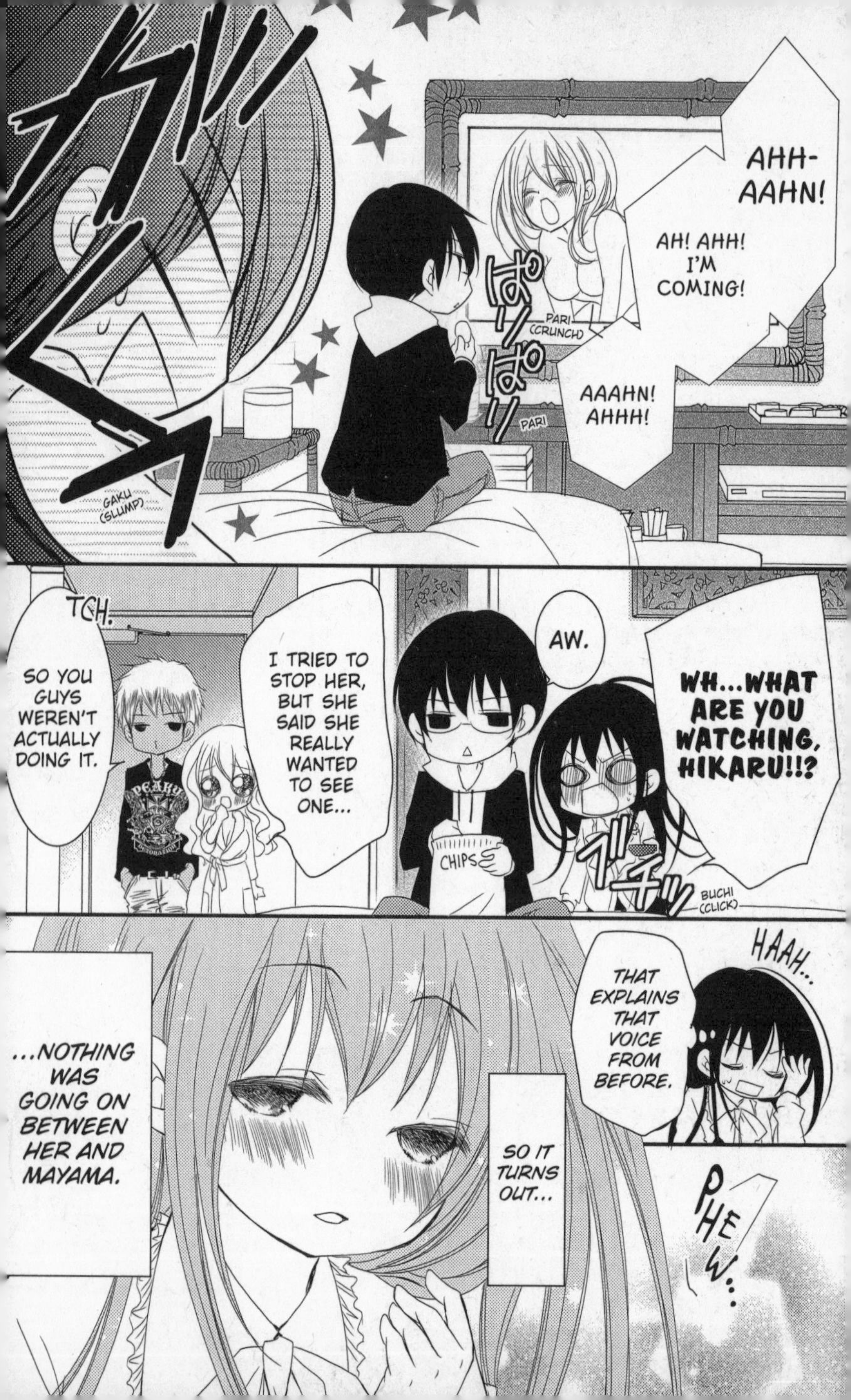
AHH-AAHN!
AH! AHH! I'M COMING!
AAAHN! AHHH!
PARI (CRUNCH)
PARI
GAKU (SLUMP)
WH...WHAT ARE YOU WATCHING, HIKARU!!?
BUCHI (CLICK)
AW.
CHIPS
I TRIED TO STOP HER, BUT SHE SAID SHE REALLY WANTED TO SEE ONE...
TCH.
SO YOU GUYS WEREN'T ACTUALLY DOING IT.
HAAAH...
THAT EXPLAINS THAT VOICE FROM BEFORE.
PHEW...
SO IT TURNS OUT...
...NOTHING WAS GOING ON BETWEEN HER AND MAYAMA.

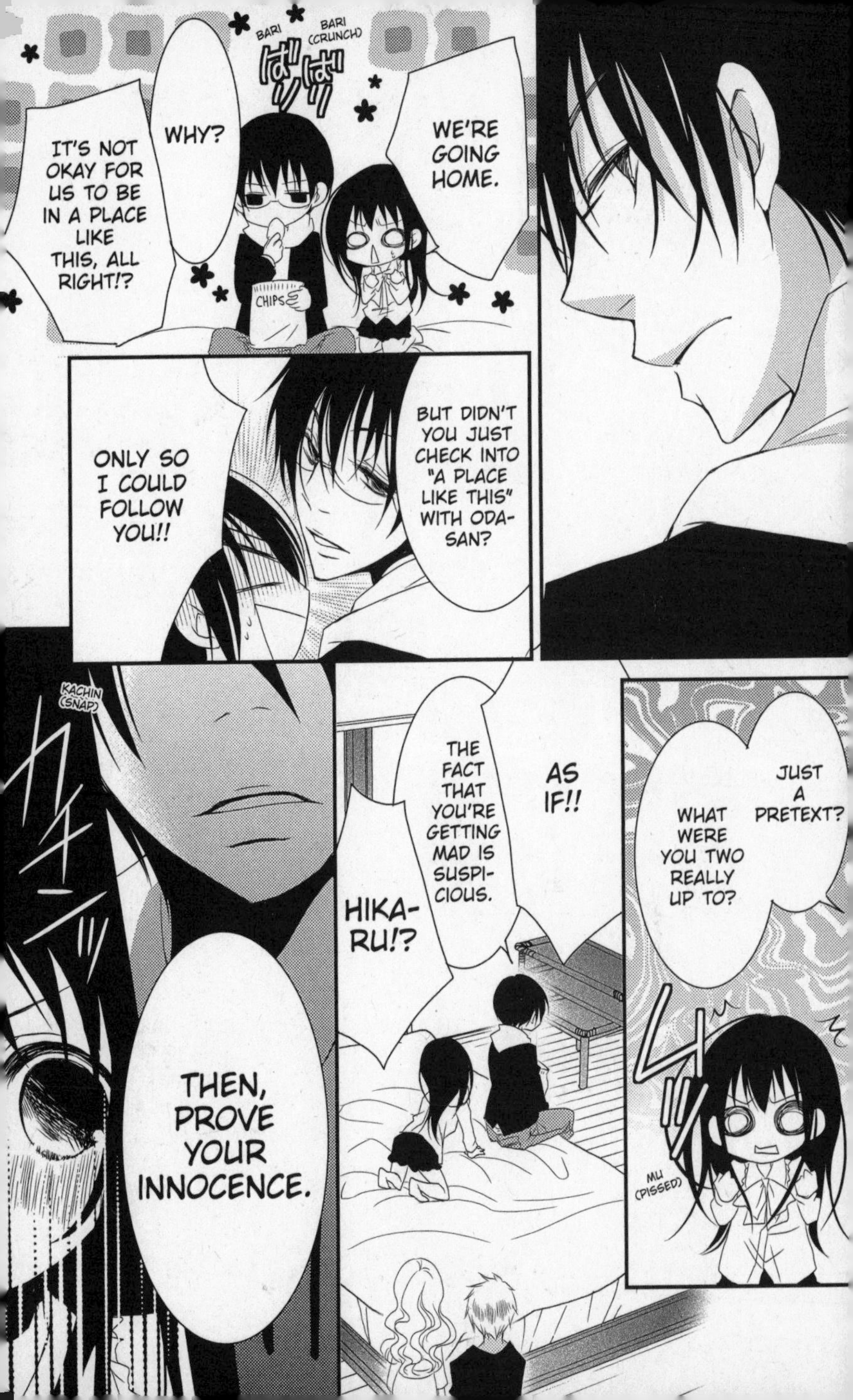
WE'RE GOING HOME.
BARI BARI (CRUNCH)
WHY?
IT'S NOT OKAY FOR US TO BE IN A PLACE LIKE THIS, ALL RIGHT!?
CHIPS
BUT DIDN'T YOU JUST CHECK INTO "A PLACE LIKE THIS" WITH ODA-SAN?
ONLY SO I COULD FOLLOW YOU!!
JUST A PRETEXT? WHAT WERE YOU TWO REALLY UP TO?
MU (PISSED)
AS IF!!
THE FACT THAT YOU'RE GETTING MAD IS SUSPICIOUS.
HIKARU!?
KACHIN (SNAP)
THEN, PROVE YOUR INNOCENCE.

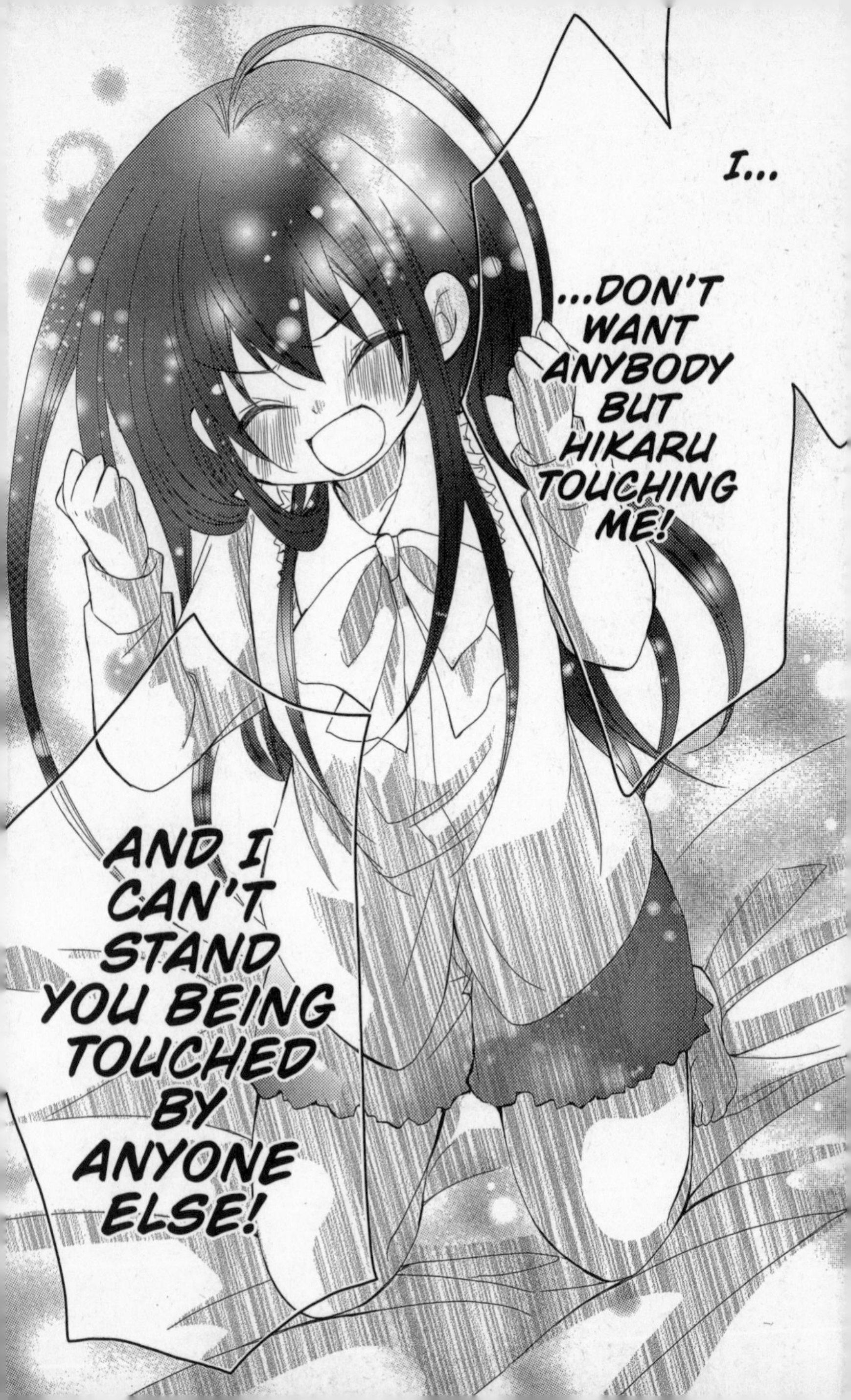
I...
...DON'T WANT ANYBODY BUT HIKARU TOUCHING ME!
AND I CAN'T STAND YOU BEING TOUCHED BY ANYONE ELSE!

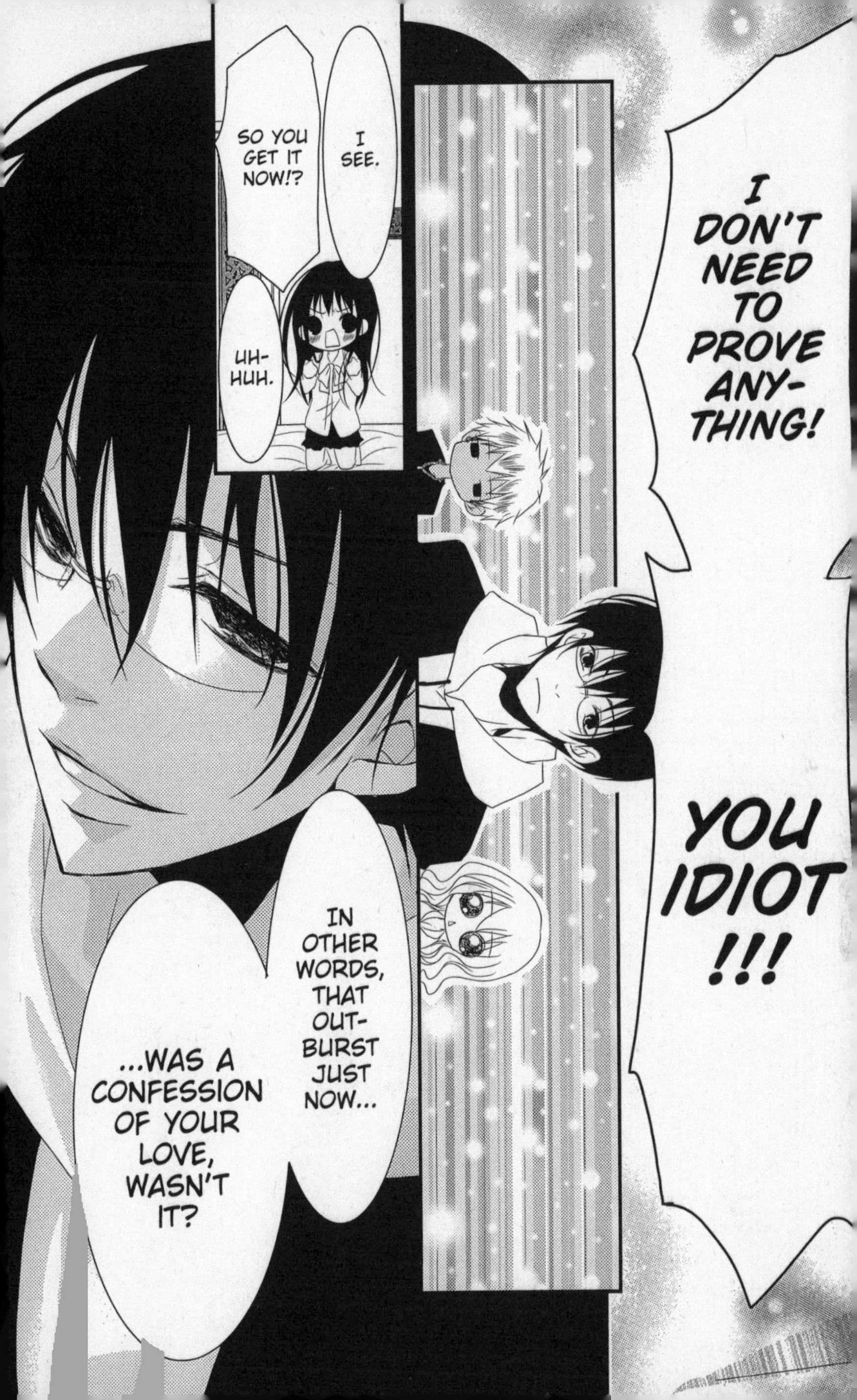
I DON'T NEED TO PROVE ANY-THING!
YOU IDIOT!!!
I SEE.
SO YOU GET IT NOW!?
UH-HUH.
IN OTHER WORDS, THAT OUT-BURST JUST NOW...
...WAS A CONFESSION OF YOUR LOVE, WASN'T IT?

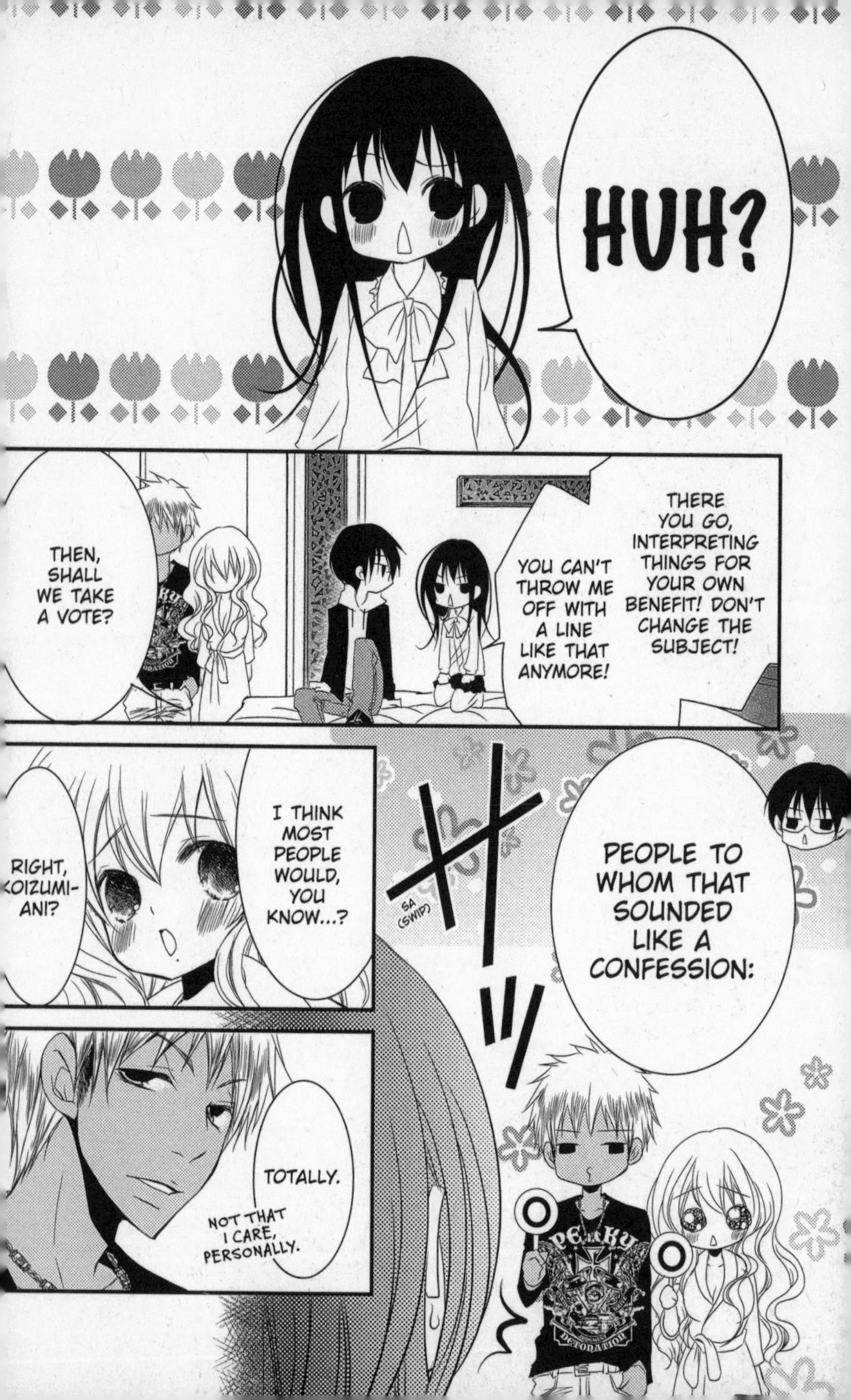
HUH?
THERE YOU GO, INTERPRETING THINGS FOR YOUR OWN BENEFIT! DON'T CHANGE THE SUBJECT!
YOU CAN'T THROW ME OFF WITH A LINE LIKE THAT ANYMORE!
THEN, SHALL WE TAKE A VOTE?
PEOPLE TO WHOM THAT SOUNDED LIKE A CONFESSION:
SA (SWIP)
I THINK MOST PEOPLE WOULD, YOU KNOW...?
RIGHT, KOIZUMI-ANI?
TOTALLY.
NOT THAT I CARE, PERSONALLY.

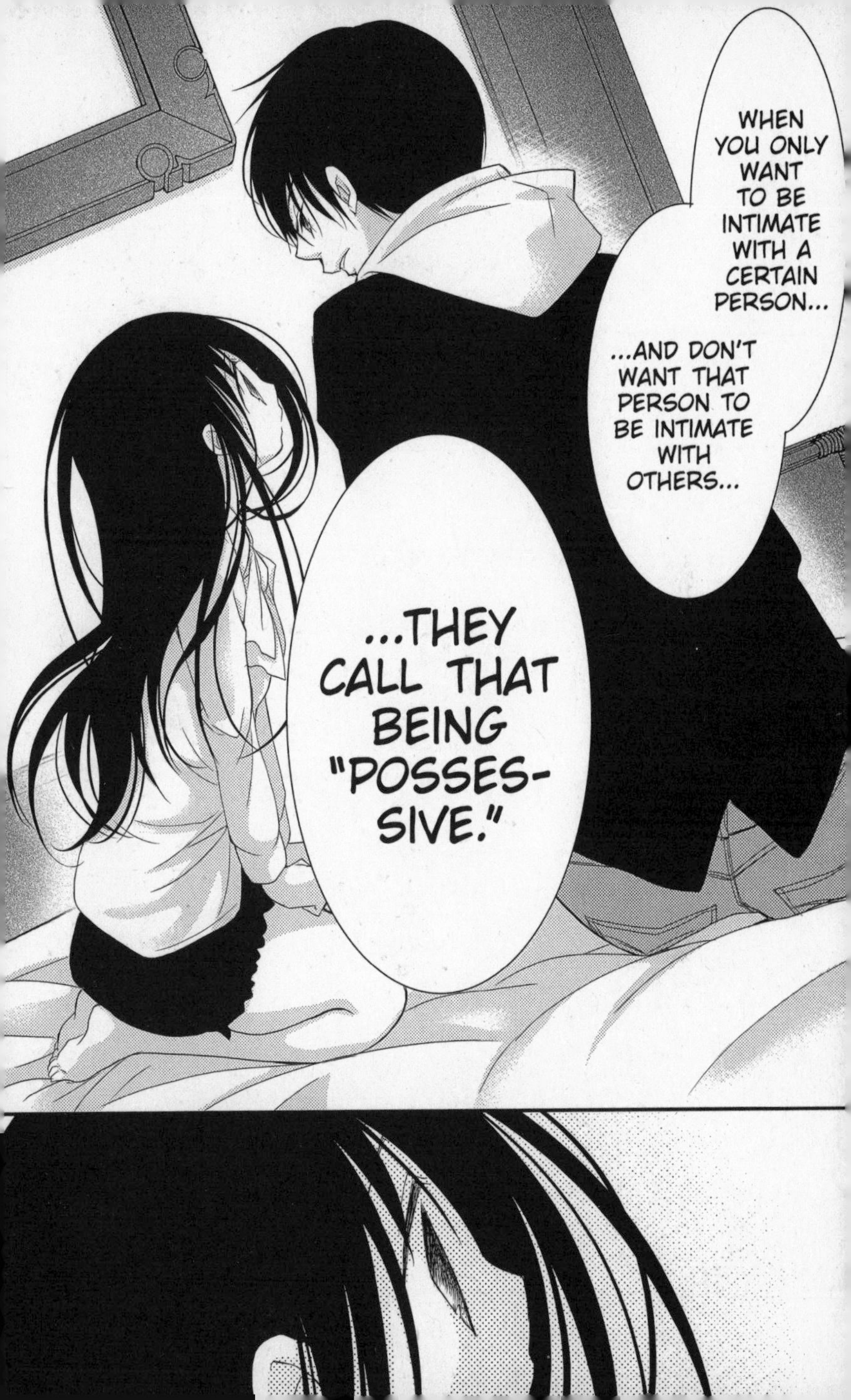
WHEN YOU ONLY WANT TO BE INTIMATE WITH A CERTAIN PERSON...
...AND DON'T WANT THAT PERSON TO BE INTIMATE WITH OTHERS...
...THEY CALL THAT BEING "POSSES-SIVE."

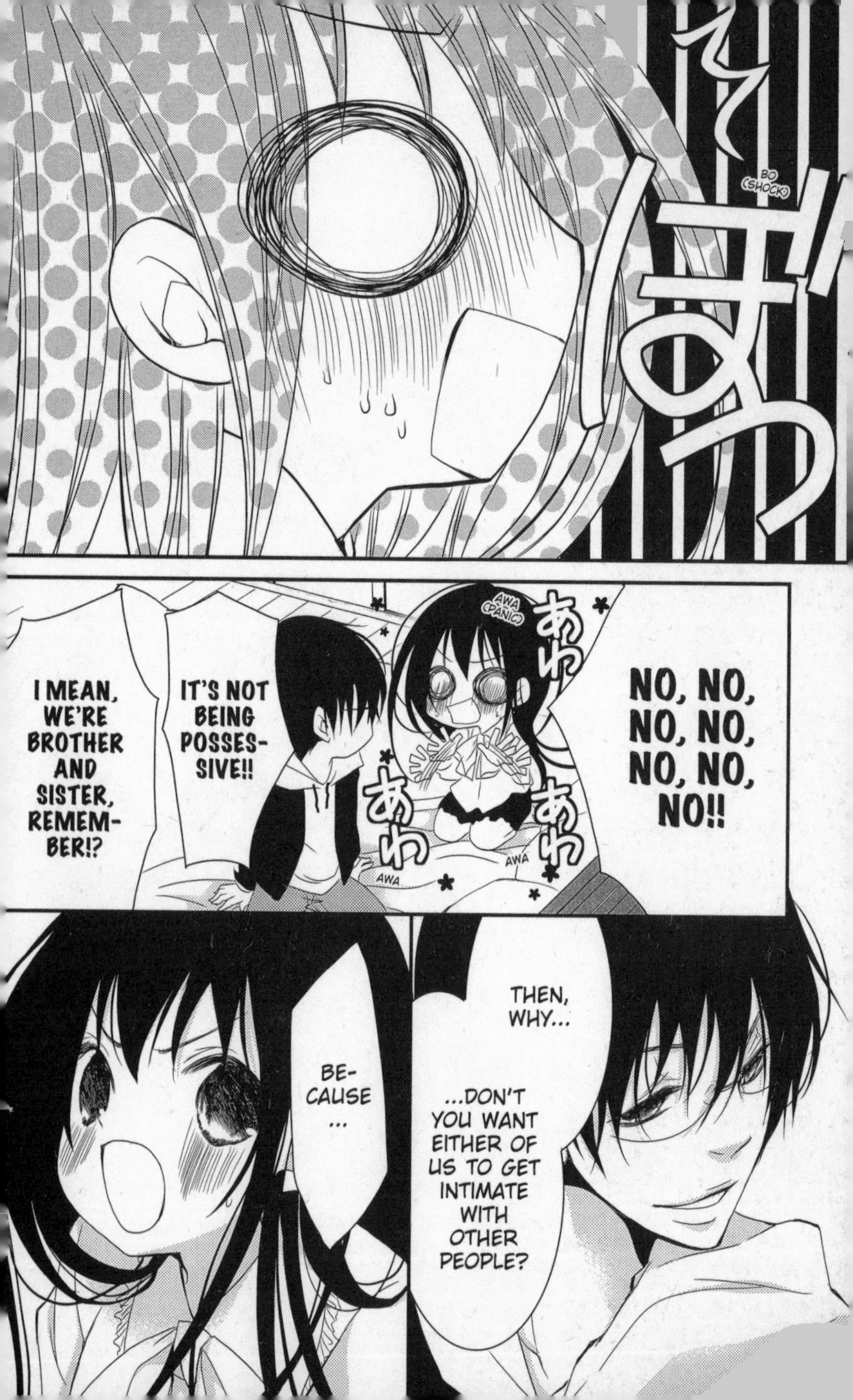
BO (SHOCK)
NO, NO, NO, NO, NO, NO, NO!!
AWA (PANIC)
AWA
AWA
IT'S NOT BEING POSSESSIVE!!
I MEAN, WE'RE BROTHER AND SISTER, REMEMBER!?
THEN, WHY...
...DON'T YOU WANT EITHER OF US TO GET INTIMATE WITH OTHER PEOPLE?
BECAUSE ...

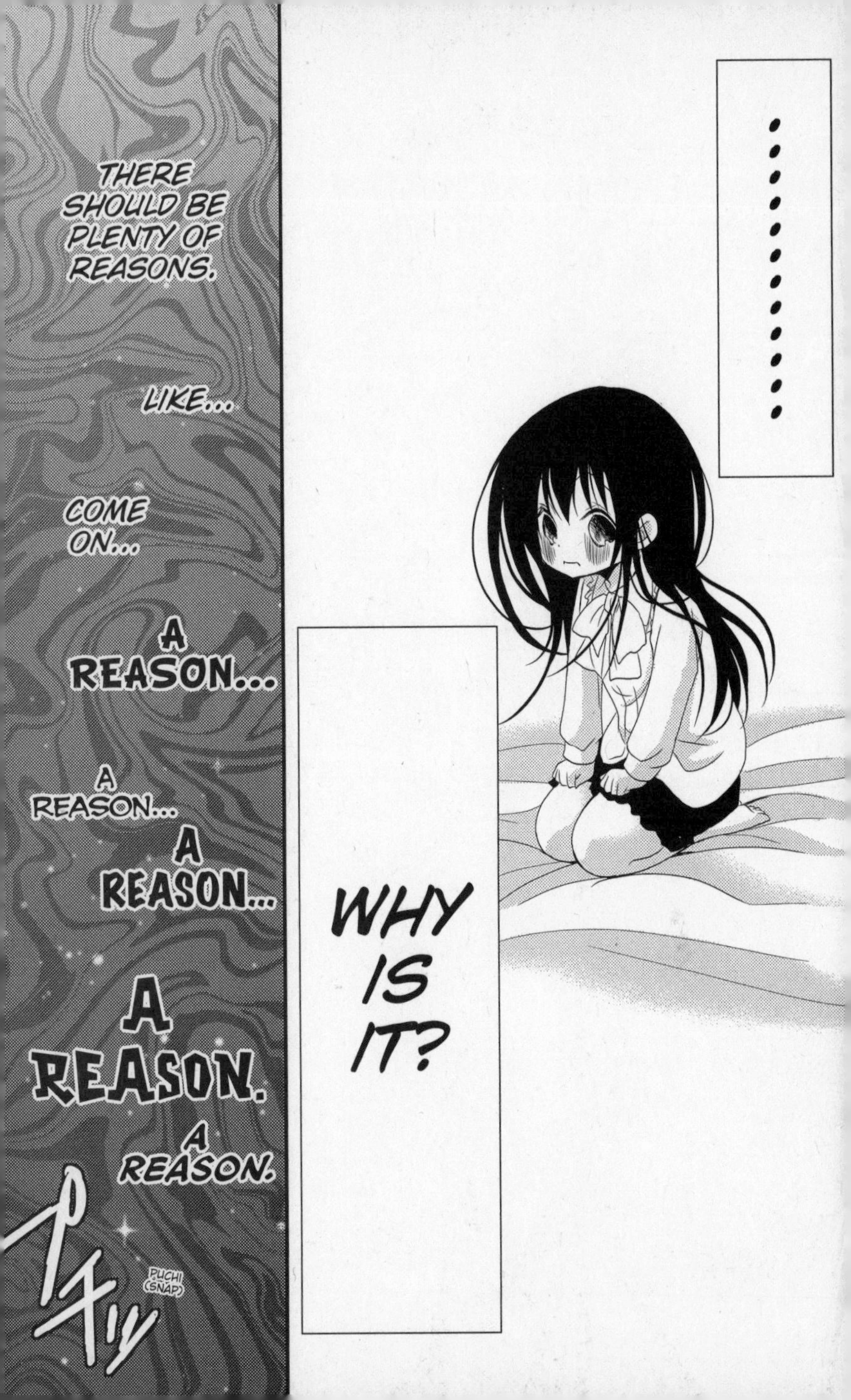
....
WHY IS IT?
THERE SHOULD BE PLENTY OF REASONS.
LIKE...
COME ON...
A REASON...
A REASON...
A REASON...
A REASON.
A REASON.
プチッ
PUCHI (SNAP)

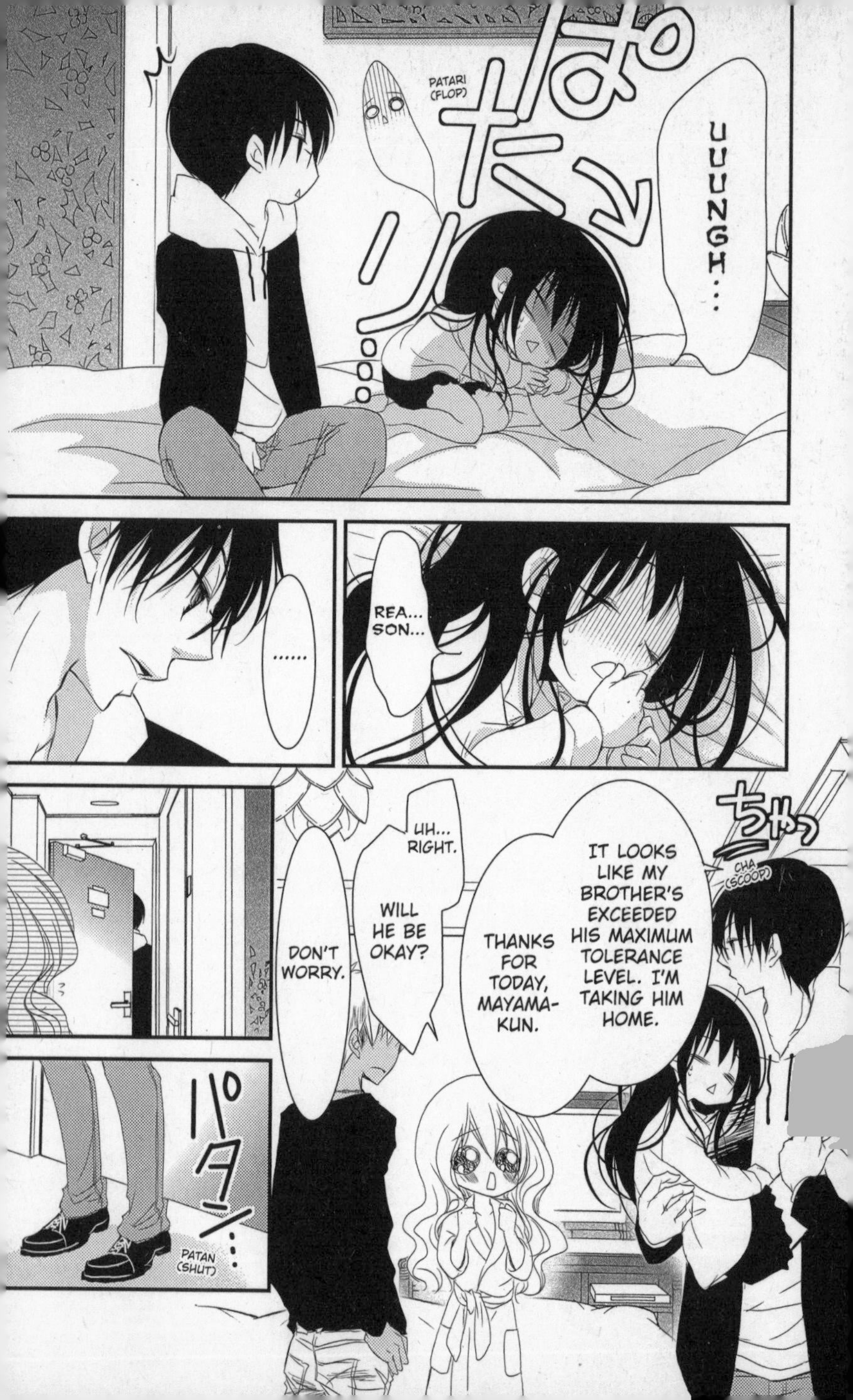

PATARI (FLOP)
UUUNGH...
REA... SON...
......
ちゃっ
CHA (SCOOP)
IT LOOKS LIKE MY BROTHER'S EXCEEDED HIS MAXIMUM TOLERANCE LEVEL. I'M TAKING HIM HOME.
THANKS FOR TODAY, MAYAMA-KUN.
UH... RIGHT.
WILL HE BE OKAY?
DON'T WORRY.
パタン…
PATAN (SHUT)

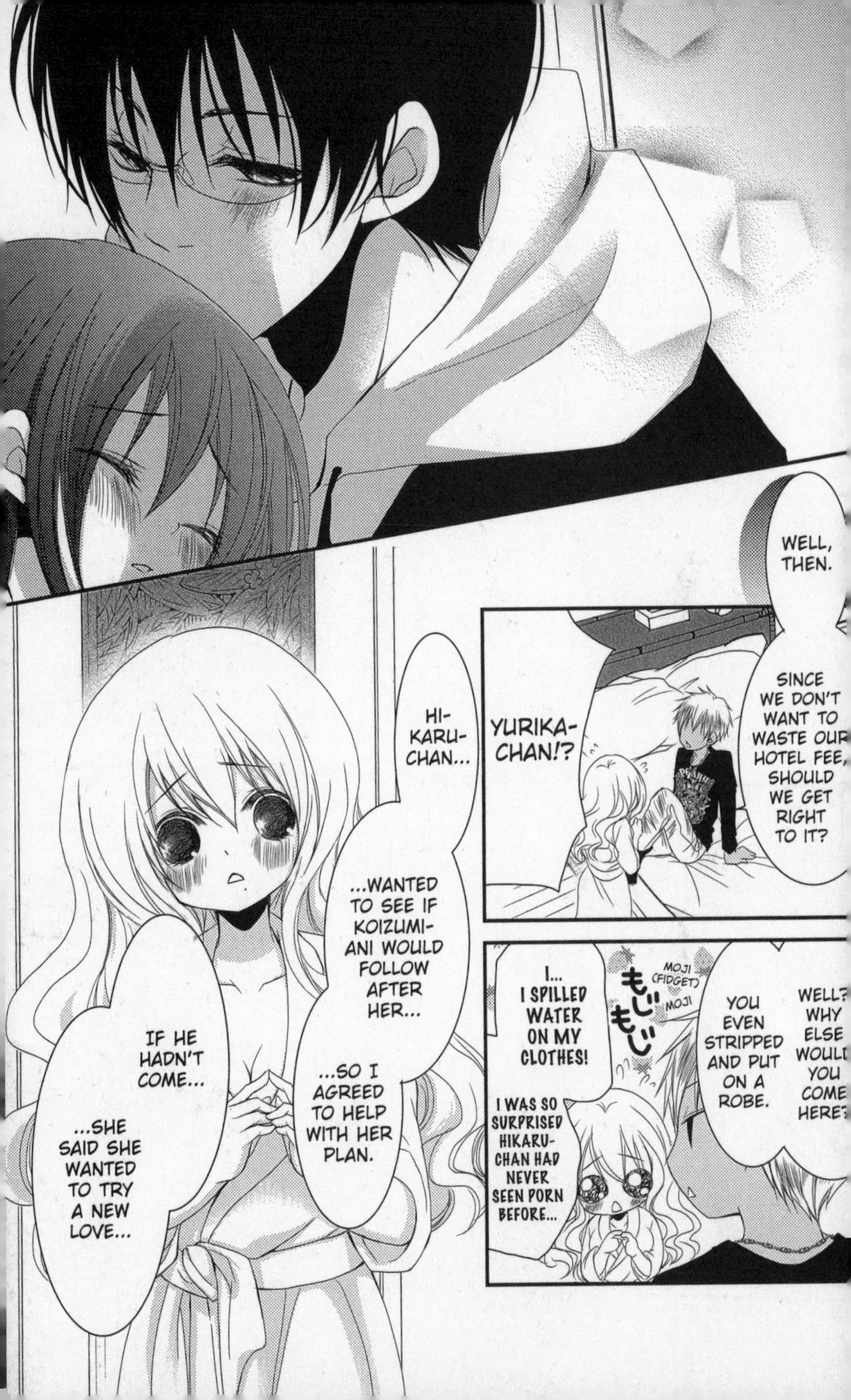
WELL, THEN.
SINCE WE DON'T WANT TO WASTE OUR HOTEL FEE, SHOULD WE GET RIGHT TO IT?
YURIKA-CHAN!?
WELL? WHY ELSE WOUL YOU COME HERE?
YOU EVEN STRIPPED AND PUT ON A ROBE.
I... I SPILLED WATER ON MY CLOTHES!
もじもじ
MOJI (FIDGET) MOJI
I WAS SO SURPRISED HIKARU-CHAN HAD NEVER SEEN PORN BEFORE...
HI-KARU-CHAN...
...WANTED TO SEE IF KOIZUMI-ANI WOULD FOLLOW AFTER HER...
...SO I AGREED TO HELP WITH HER PLAN.
IF HE HADN'T COME...
...SHE SAID SHE WANTED TO TRY A NEW LOVE...

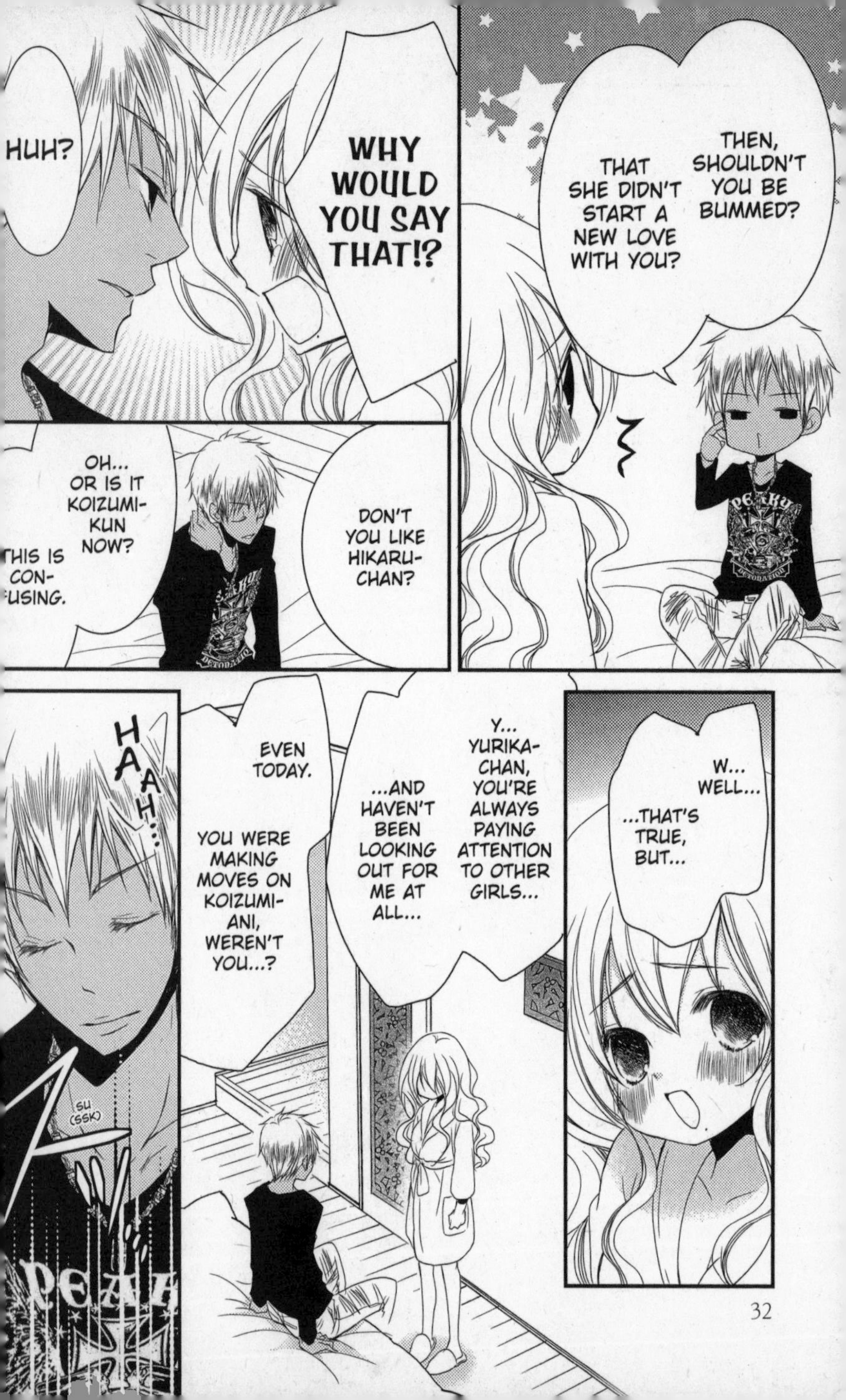
THEN, SHOULDN'T YOU BE BUMMED?
THAT SHE DIDN'T START A NEW LOVE WITH YOU?
WHY WOULD YOU SAY THAT!?
HUH?
DON'T YOU LIKE HIKARU-CHAN?
OH... OR IS IT KOIZUMI-KUN NOW?
THIS IS CON-FUSING.
W... WELL...
...THAT'S TRUE, BUT...
Y... YURIKA-CHAN, YOU'RE ALWAYS PAYING ATTENTION TO OTHER GIRLS...
...AND HAVEN'T BEEN LOOKING OUT FOR ME AT ALL...
EVEN TODAY.
YOU WERE MAKING MOVES ON KOIZUMI-ANI, WEREN'T YOU...?
HAAAH...
SU (SSK)

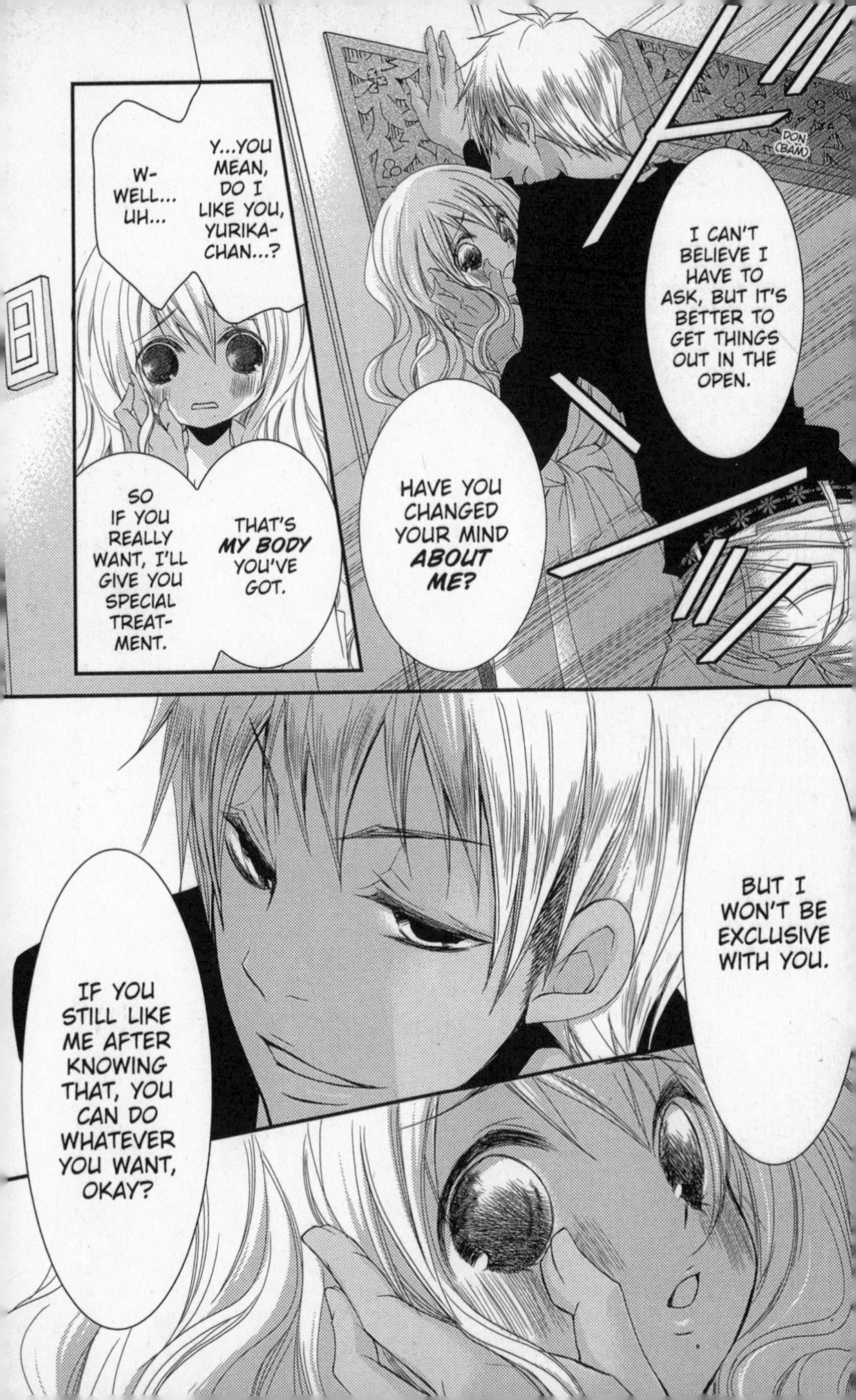
DON (BAM)
I CAN'T BELIEVE I HAVE TO ASK, BUT IT'S BETTER TO GET THINGS OUT IN THE OPEN.
HAVE YOU CHANGED YOUR MIND ***ABOUT ME?***
Y...YOU MEAN, DO I LIKE YOU, YURIKA-CHAN...?
W-WELL... UH...
THAT'S ***MY BODY*** YOU'VE GOT.
SO IF YOU REALLY WANT, I'LL GIVE YOU SPECIAL TREAT-MENT.
BUT I WON'T BE EXCLUSIVE WITH YOU.
IF YOU STILL LIKE ME AFTER KNOWING THAT, YOU CAN DO WHATEVER YOU WANT, OKAY?

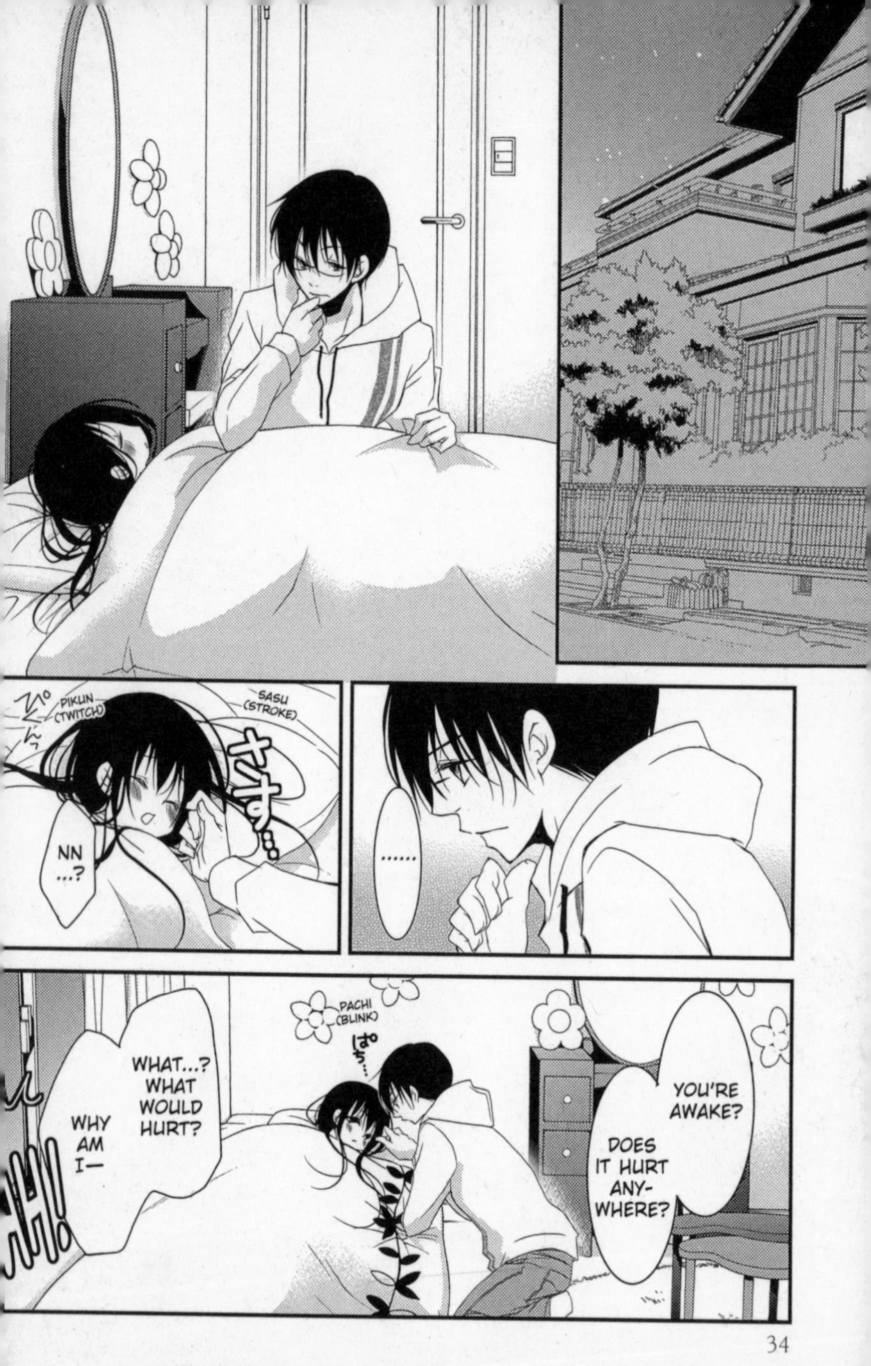
......
SASU (STROKE)
さす…
PIKUN (TWITCH)
ぴくん
NN ...?
YOU'RE AWAKE?
DOES IT HURT ANY-WHERE?
PACHI (BLINK)
ぱち…
WHAT...? WHAT WOULD HURT?
WHY AM I—

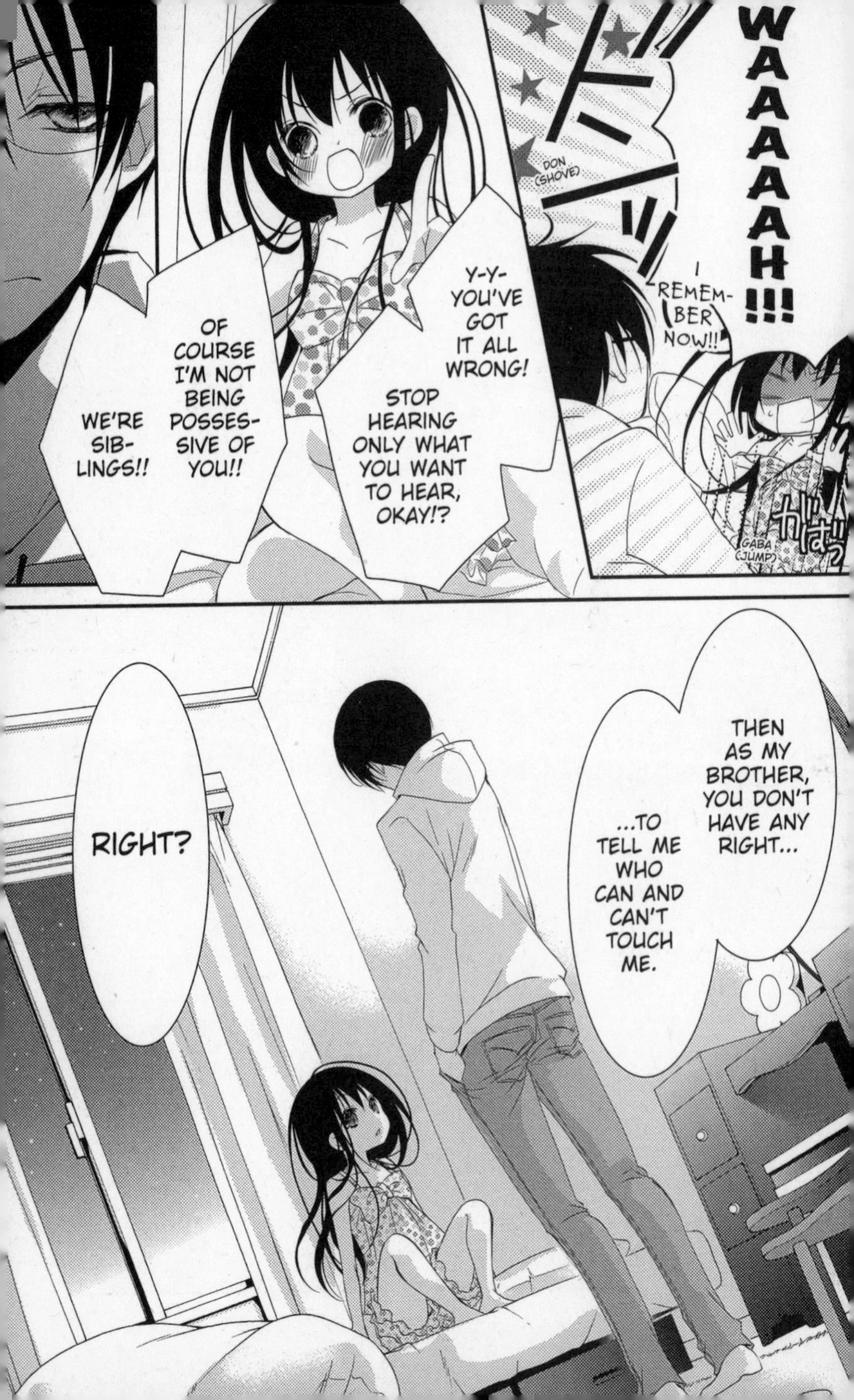
WAAAAAH!!!
I REMEM-BER NOW!!
DON (SHOVE)
がばっ
GABA (JUMP)
Y-Y-YOU'VE GOT IT ALL WRONG!
STOP HEARING ONLY WHAT YOU WANT TO HEAR, OKAY!?
OF COURSE I'M NOT BEING POSSES-SIVE OF YOU!!
WE'RE SIB-LINGS!!
THEN AS MY BROTHER, YOU DON'T HAVE ANY RIGHT...
...TO TELL ME WHO CAN AND CAN'T TOUCH ME.
RIGHT?

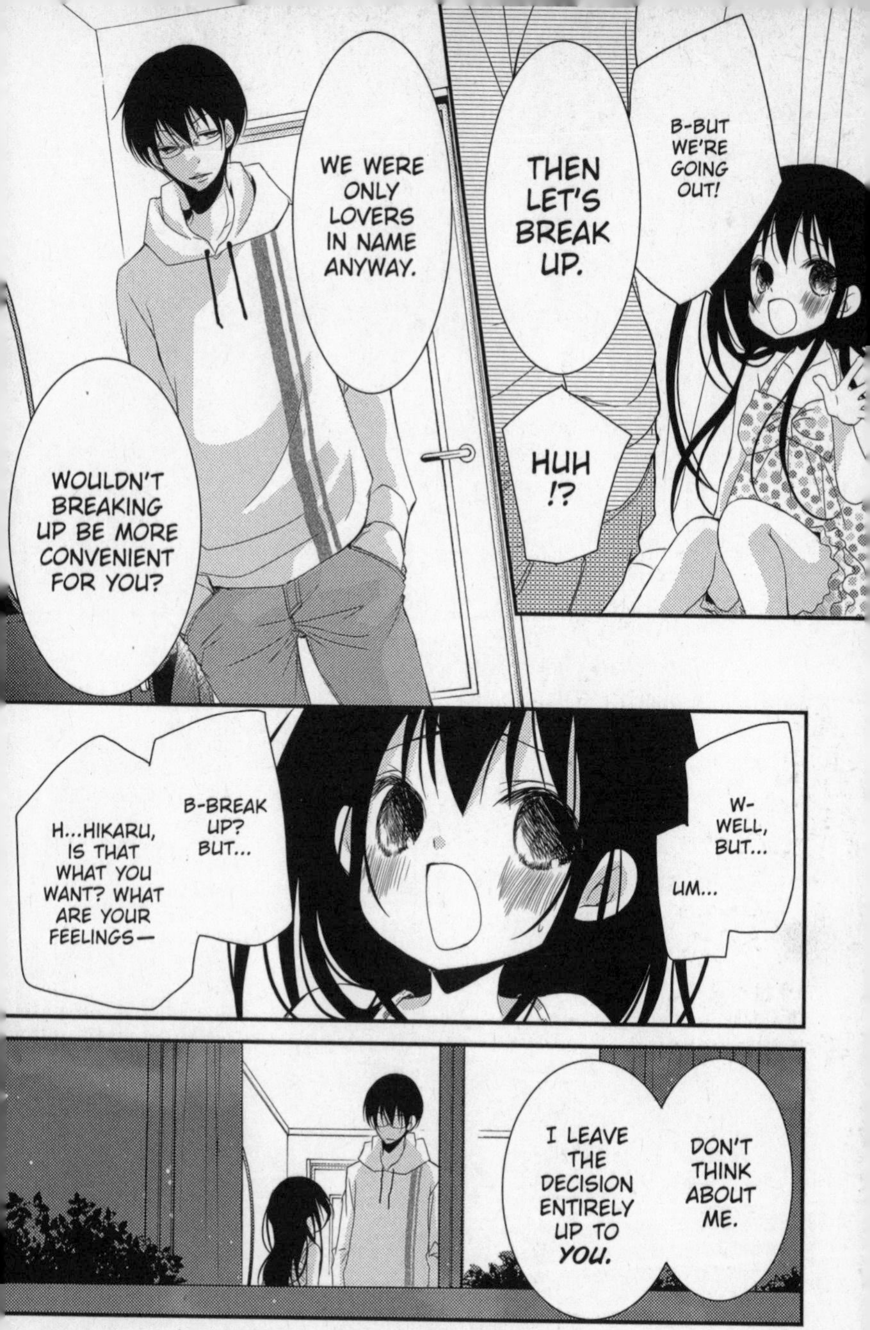
B-BUT WE'RE GOING OUT!
THEN LET'S BREAK UP.
HUH!?
WE WERE ONLY LOVERS IN NAME ANYWAY.
WOULDN'T BREAKING UP BE MORE CONVENIENT FOR YOU?
W-WELL, BUT...
UM...
B-BREAK UP? BUT...
H...HIKARU, IS THAT WHAT YOU WANT? WHAT ARE YOUR FEELINGS—
DON'T THINK ABOUT ME.
I LEAVE THE DECISION ENTIRELY UP TO YOU.

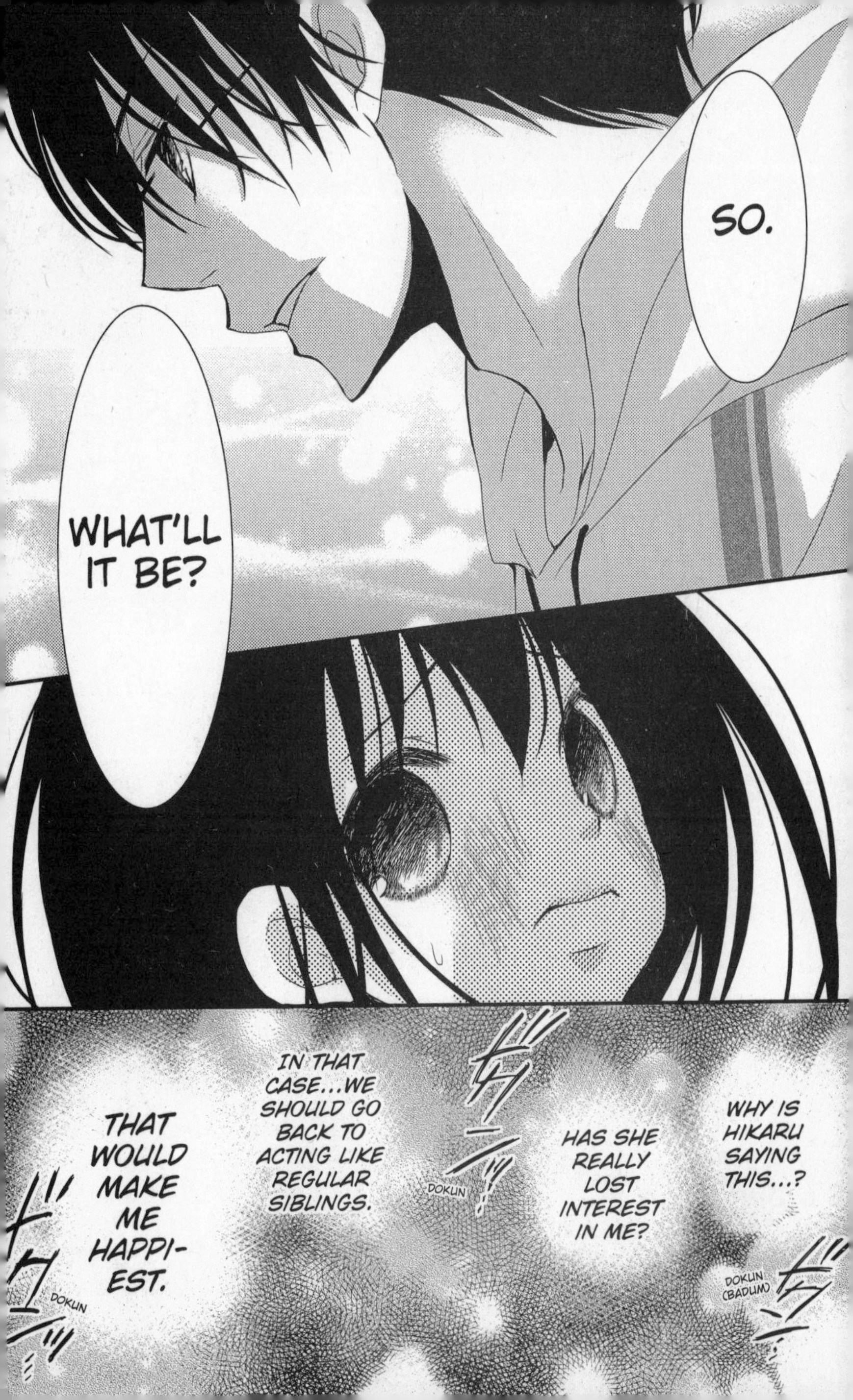
SO.
WHAT'LL IT BE?
WHY IS HIKARU SAYING THIS...?
DOKUN (BADUM)
HAS SHE REALLY LOST INTEREST IN ME?
DOKUN
IN THAT CASE...WE SHOULD GO BACK TO ACTING LIKE REGULAR SIBLINGS.
THAT WOULD MAKE ME HAPPI-EST.
DOKUN

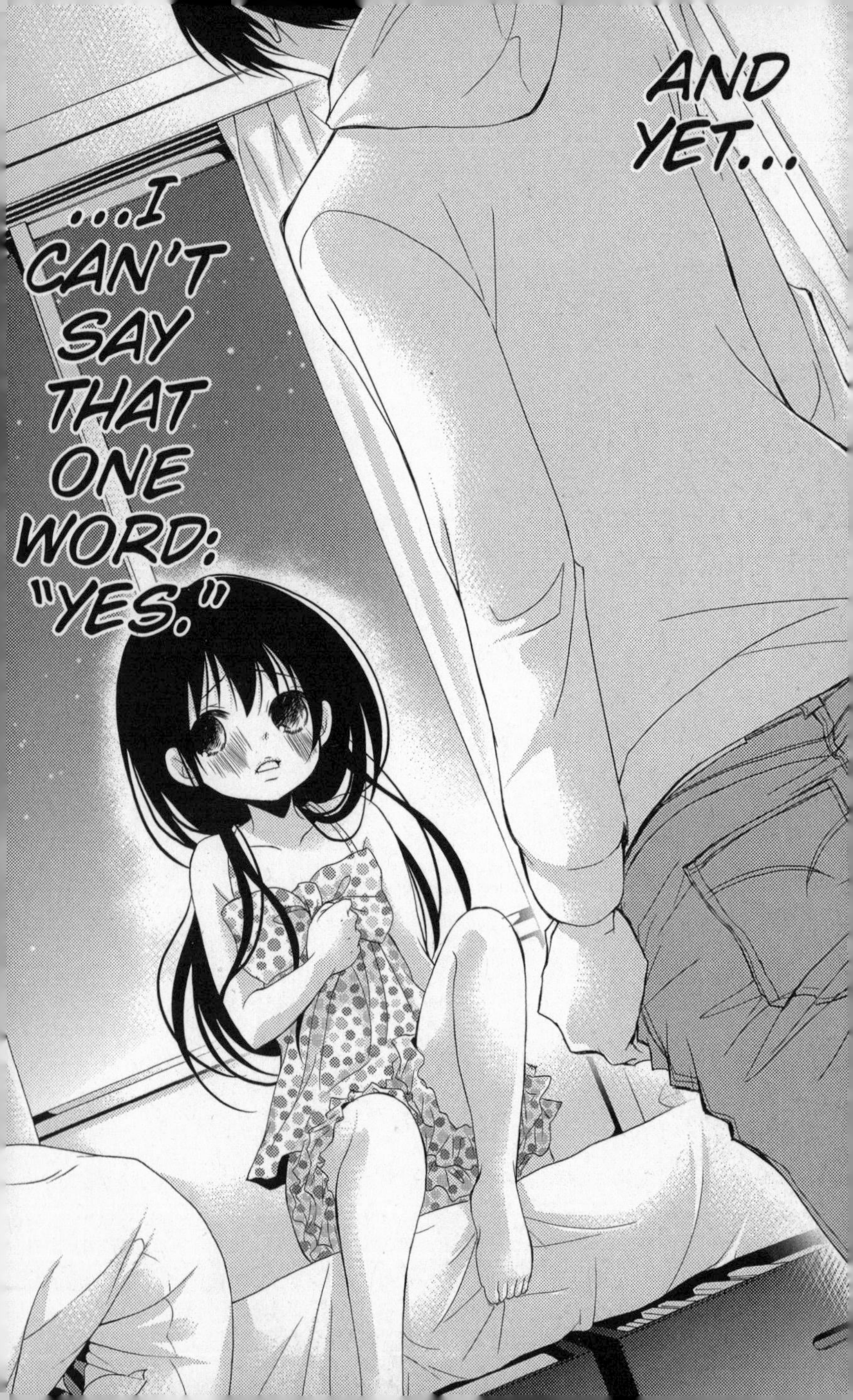
AND YET...
...I CAN'T SAY THAT ONE WORD: "YES."

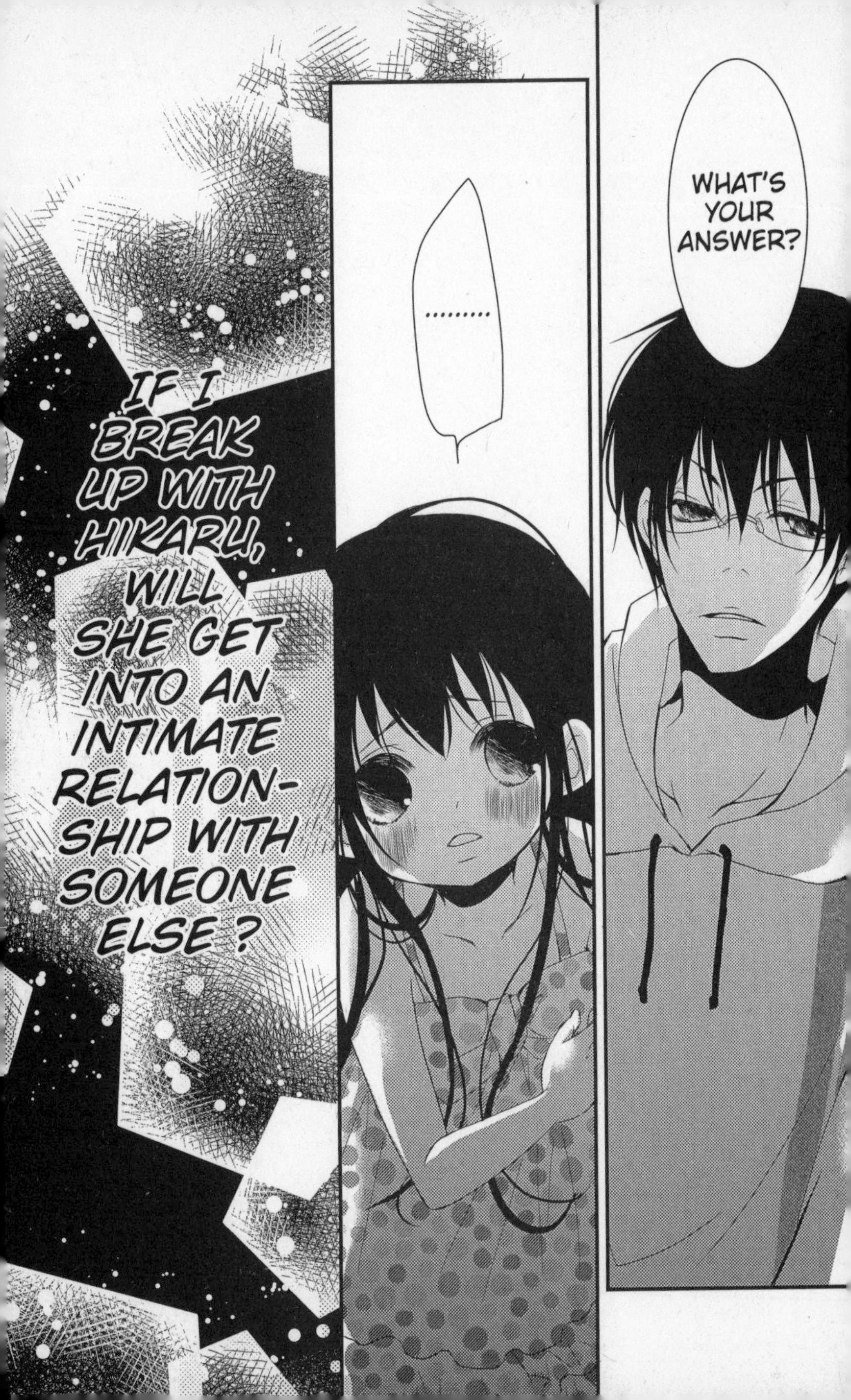
WHAT'S YOUR ANSWER?
....
IF I BREAK UP WITH HIKARU, WILL SHE GET INTO AN INTIMATE RELATION-SHIP WITH SOMEONE ELSE ?

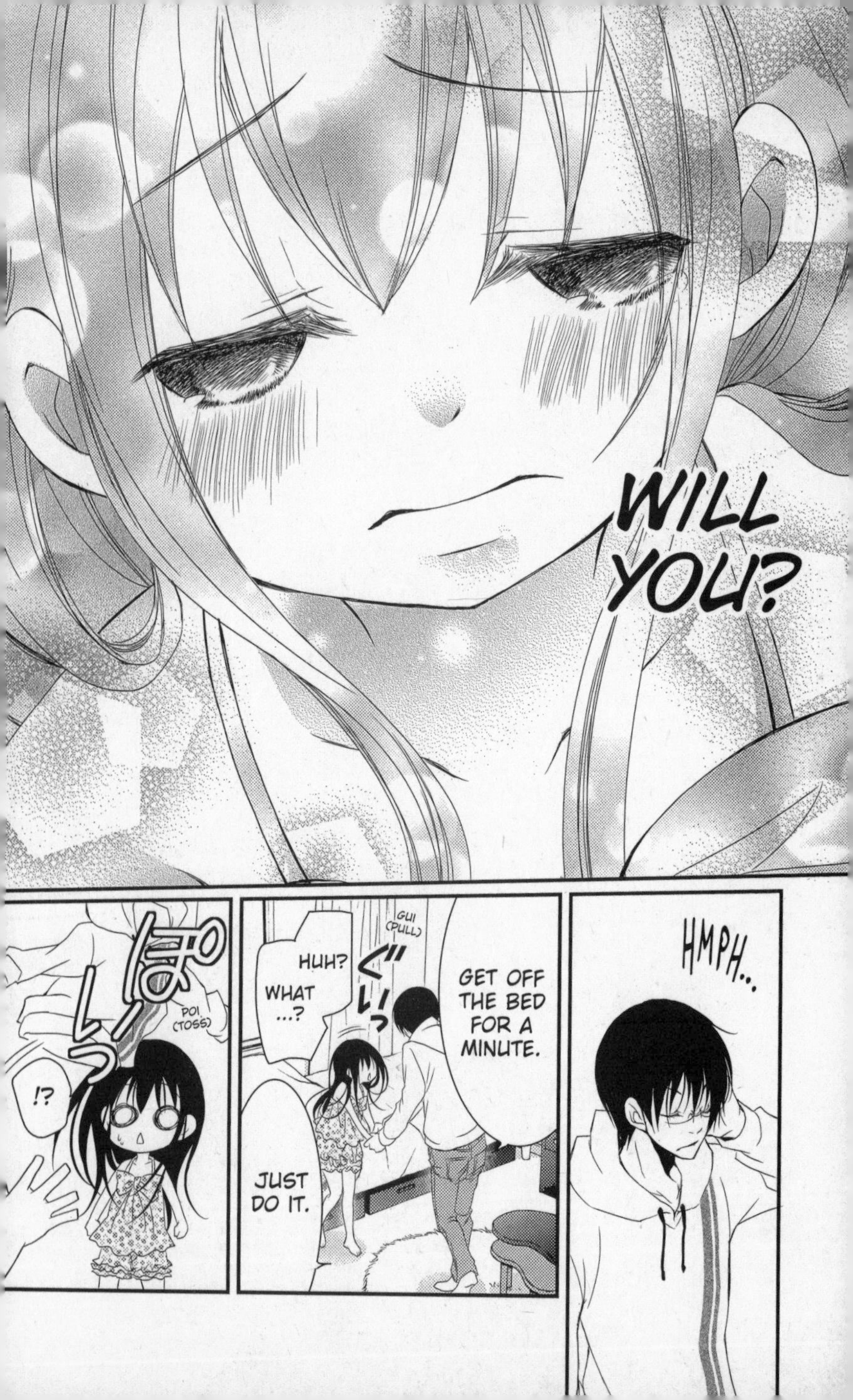
WILL YOU?
HMPH...
GET OFF THE BED FOR A MINUTE.
GUI (PULL)
ぐいっ
HUH? WHAT ...?
JUST DO IT.
ぽいっ
POI (TOSS)
!?

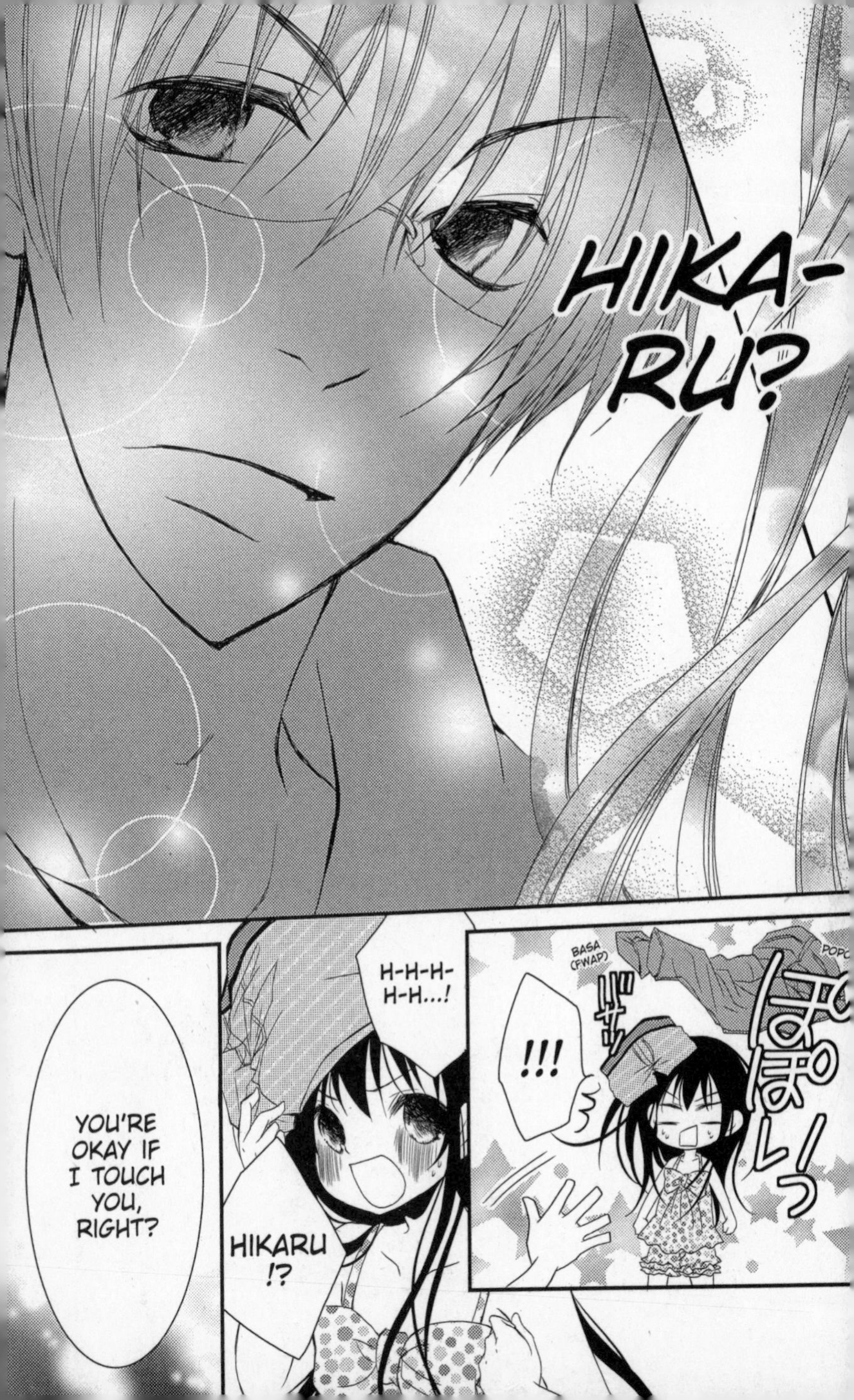
HIKA-
RU?
POPO
BASA
(FWAP)
バサッ
!!!
H-H-H-
H-H...!
HIKARU
!?
YOU'RE
OKAY IF
I TOUCH
YOU,
RIGHT?

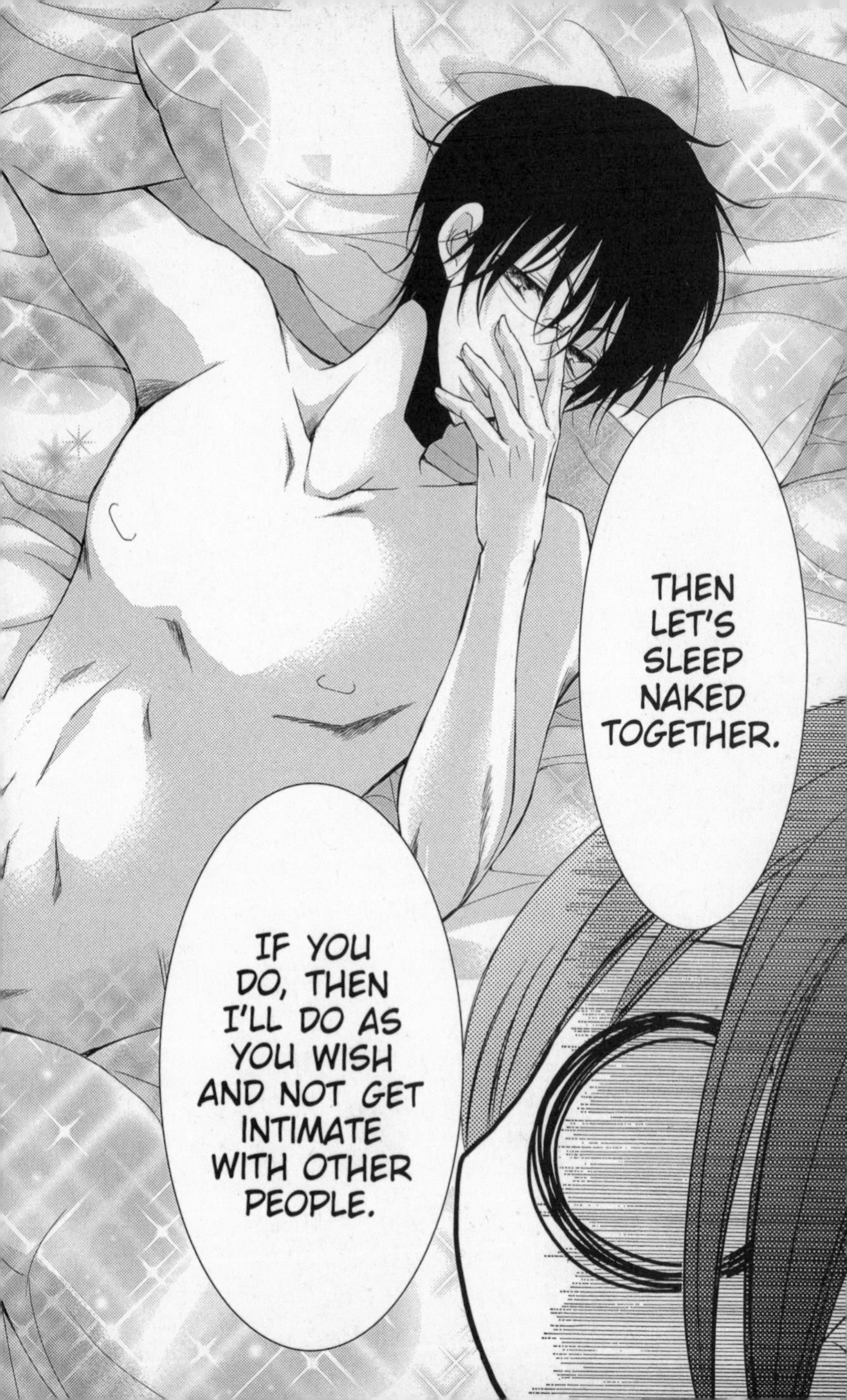
THEN LET'S SLEEP NAKED TOGETHER.
IF YOU DO, THEN I'LL DO AS YOU WISH AND NOT GET INTIMATE WITH OTHER PEOPLE.

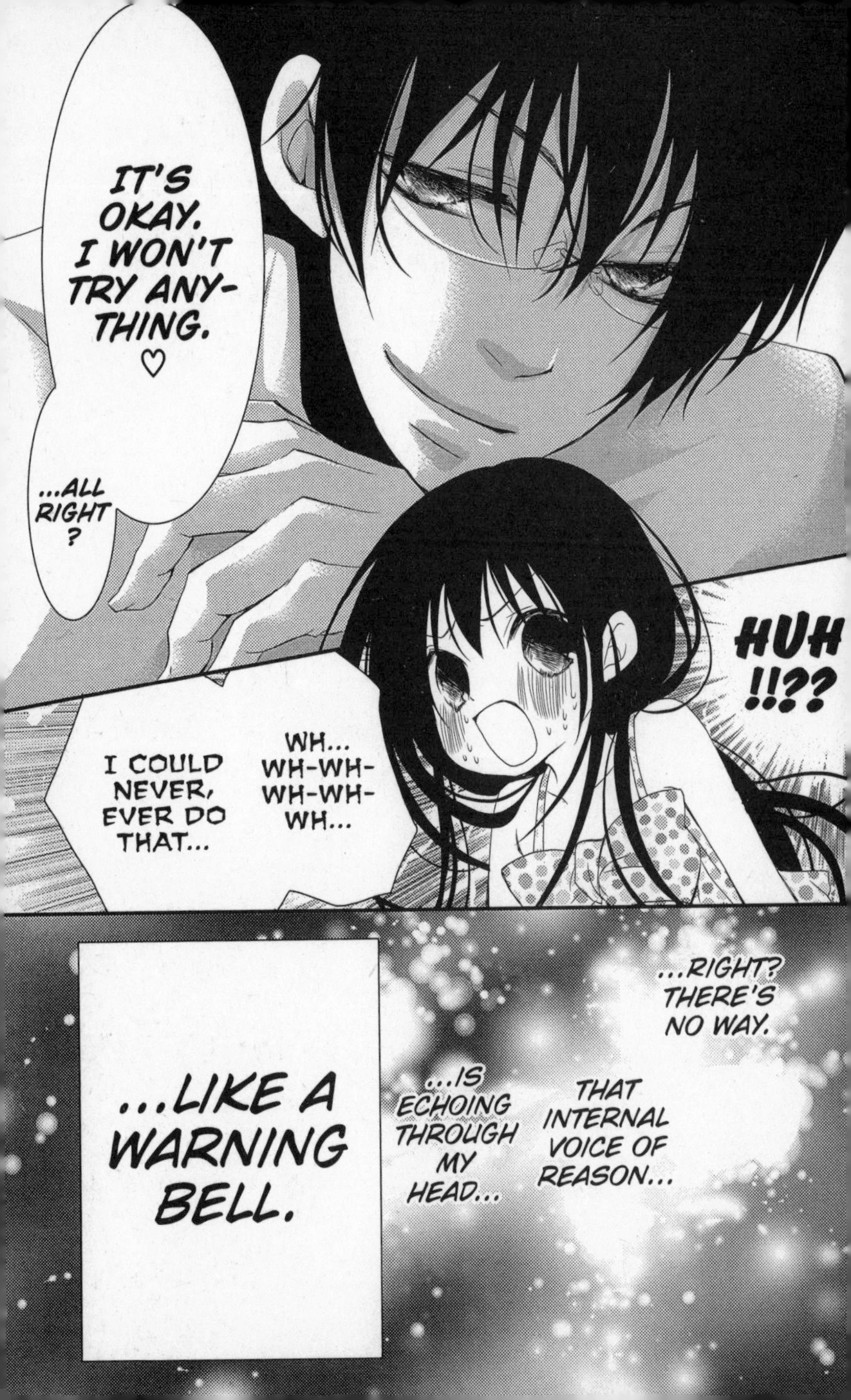
IT'S OKAY. I WON'T TRY ANYTHING. ♡
...ALL RIGHT?
HUH!!??
WH... WH-WH-WH-WH-WH...
I COULD NEVER, EVER DO THAT...
...RIGHT? THERE'S NO WAY.
THAT INTERNAL VOICE OF REASON...
...IS ECHOING THROUGH MY HEAD...
...LIKE A WARNING BELL.

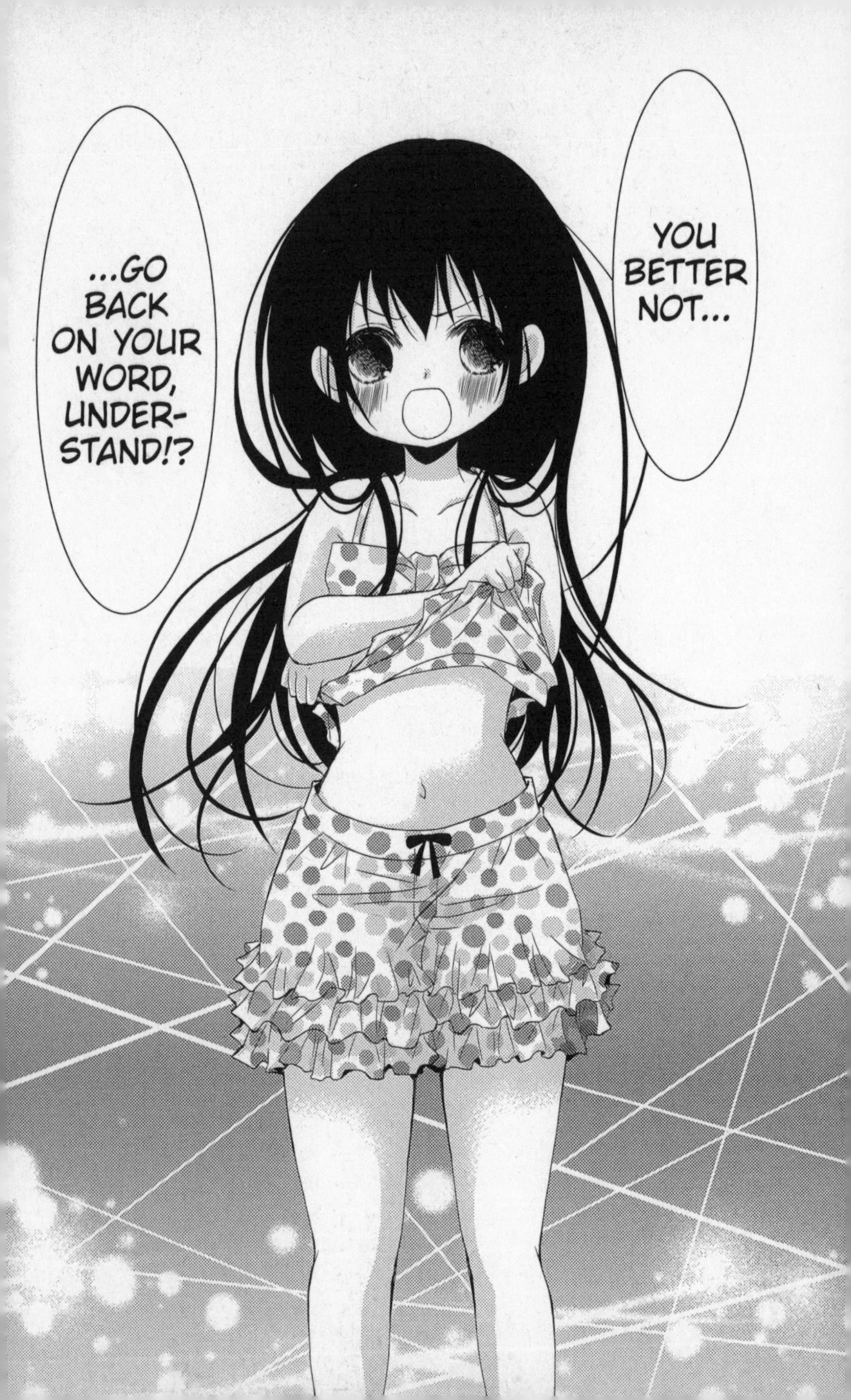
YOU BETTER NOT...
...GO BACK ON YOUR WORD, UNDER-STAND!?

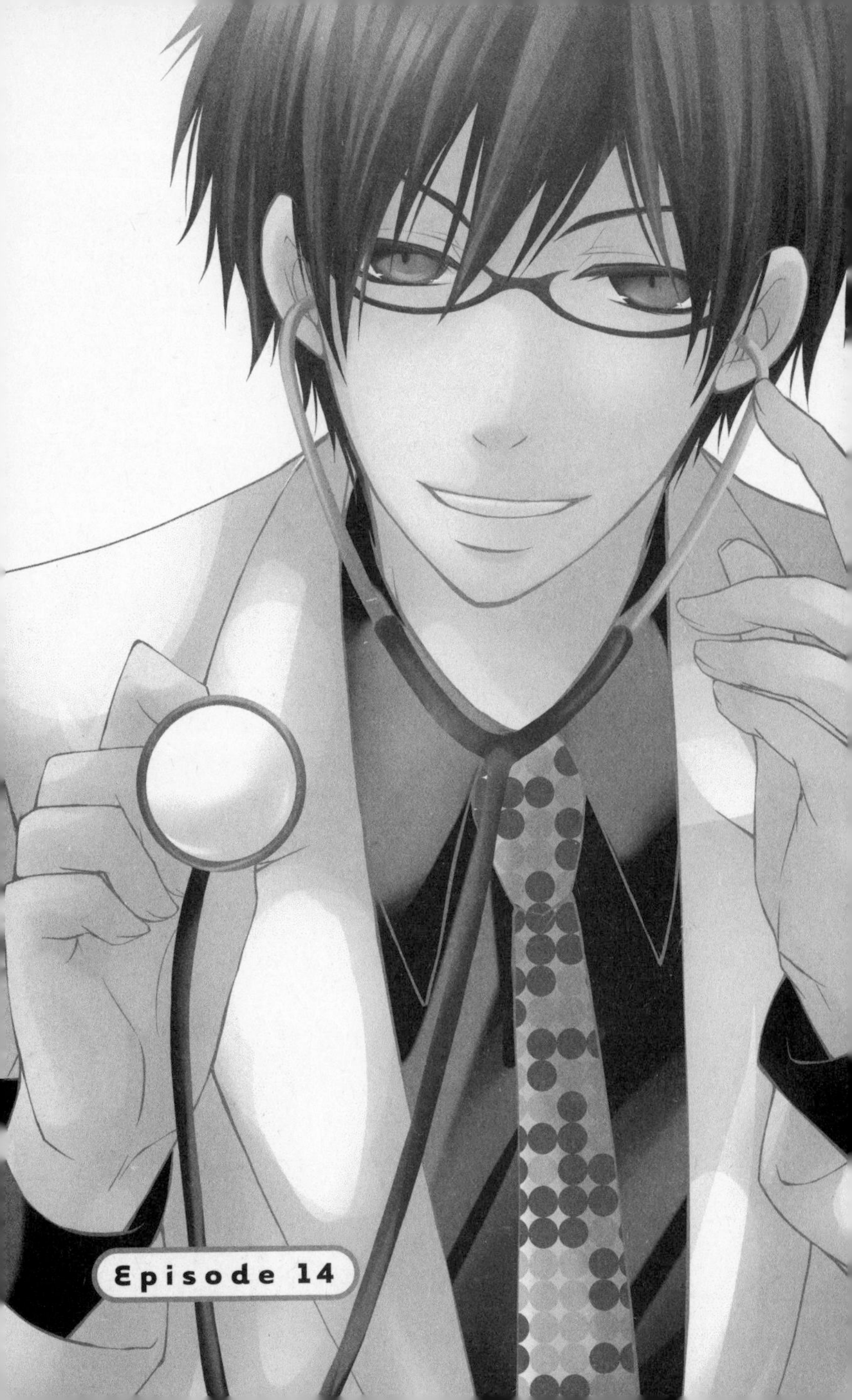
Episode 14

[Ani-Imo]

Big Brother becomes Little Sister;
Little Sister becomes Big Brother.

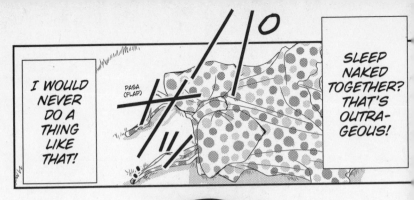

SLEEP NAKED TOGETHER? THAT'S OUTRAGEOUS!

I WOULD NEVER DO A THING LIKE THAT!

PASA (FLAP)

THERE'S NO WAY IN HELL...

AT LEAST, THAT'S WHAT I THOUGHT...

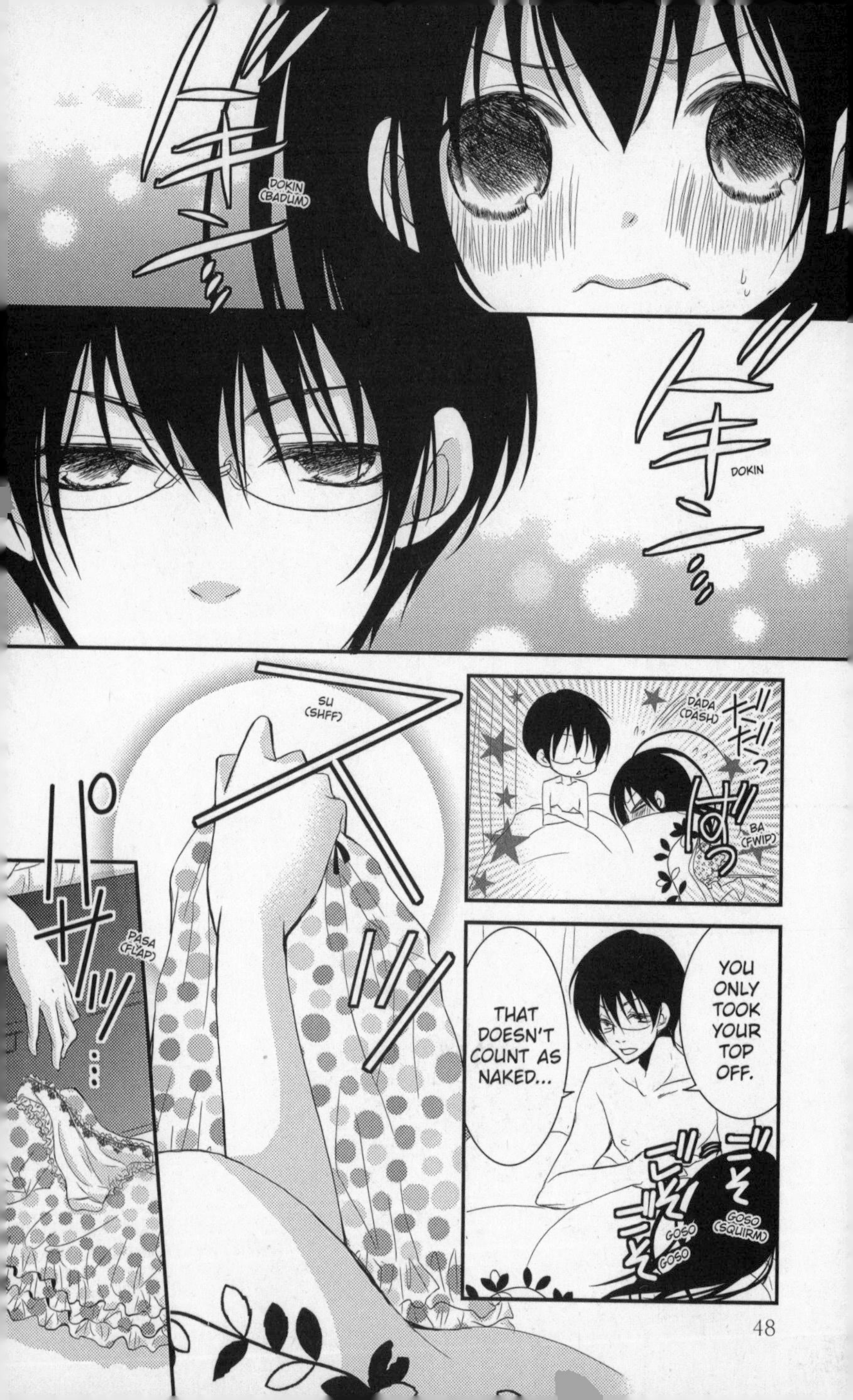
DOKIN (BADUM)
DOKIN
DADA (DASH)
BA (FWIP)
YOU ONLY TOOK YOUR TOP OFF.
THAT DOESN'T COUNT AS NAKED...
GOSO (SQUIRM)
GOSO
GOSO
SU (SHFF)
PASA (FLAP)

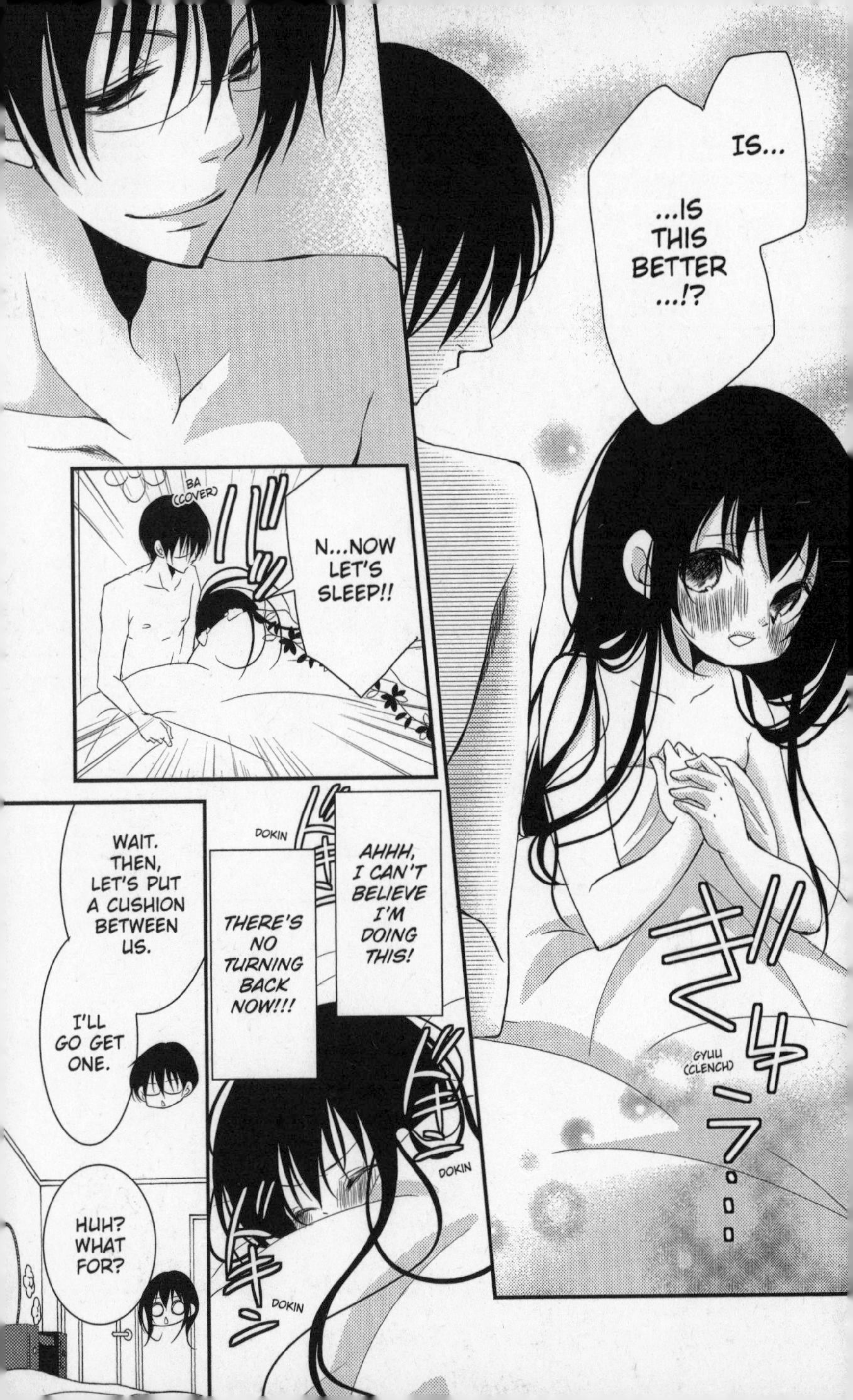
IS...
...IS THIS BETTER ...!?
GYUU (CLENCH)
BA (COVER)
N...NOW LET'S SLEEP!!
DOKIN
AHHH, I CAN'T BELIEVE I'M DOING THIS!
THERE'S NO TURNING BACK NOW!!!
DOKIN
DOKIN
WAIT. THEN, LET'S PUT A CUSHION BETWEEN US.
I'LL GO GET ONE.
HUH? WHAT FOR?

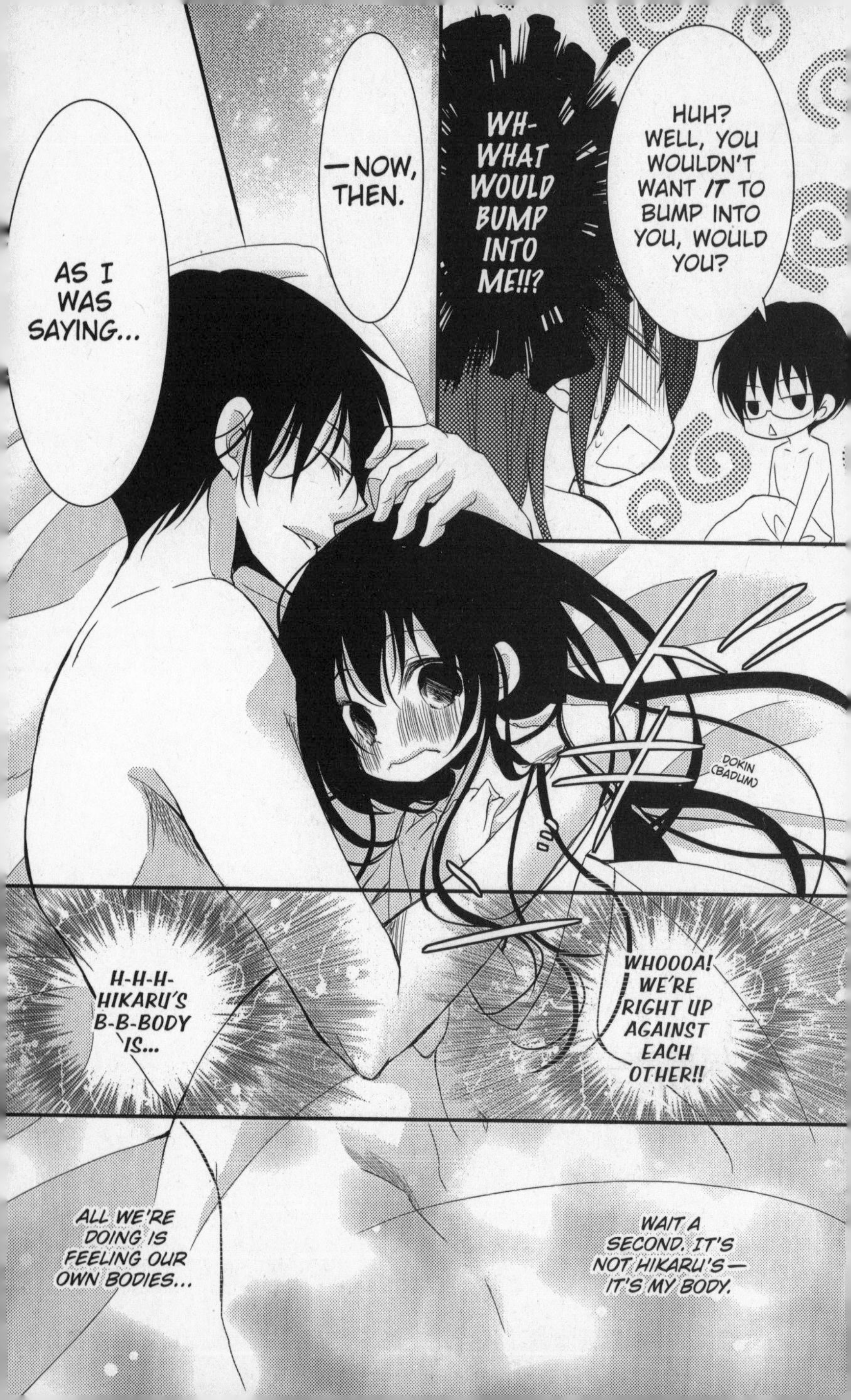
HUH? WELL, YOU WOULDN'T WANT IT TO BUMP INTO YOU, WOULD YOU?
WH-WHAT WOULD BUMP INTO ME!!?
—NOW, THEN.
AS I WAS SAYING...
DOKIN (BADUM)
WHOOOA! WE'RE RIGHT UP AGAINST EACH OTHER!!
H-H-H-HIKARU'S B-B-BODY IS...
WAIT A SECOND. IT'S NOT HIKARU'S—IT'S MY BODY.
ALL WE'RE DOING IS FEELING OUR OWN BODIES...

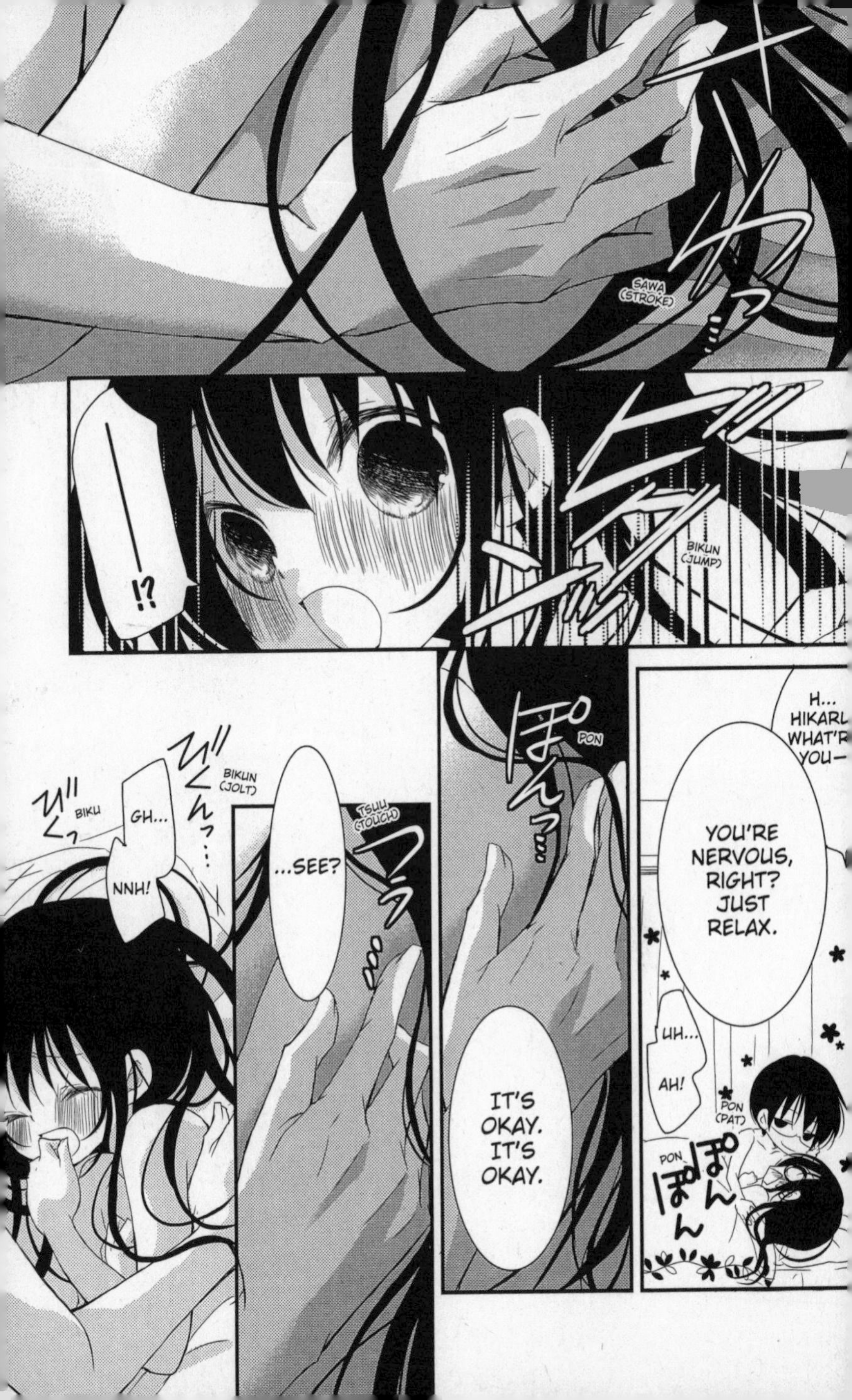
SAWA (STROKE)
BIKUN (JUMP)
—!?
H... HIKARU WHAT'R YOU—
YOU'RE NERVOUS, RIGHT? JUST RELAX.
UH...
AH!
PON (PAT)
PON
PON
IT'S OKAY. IT'S OKAY.
TSUU (TOUCH)
...SEE?
BIKUN (JOLT)
GH...
NNH!
BIKU

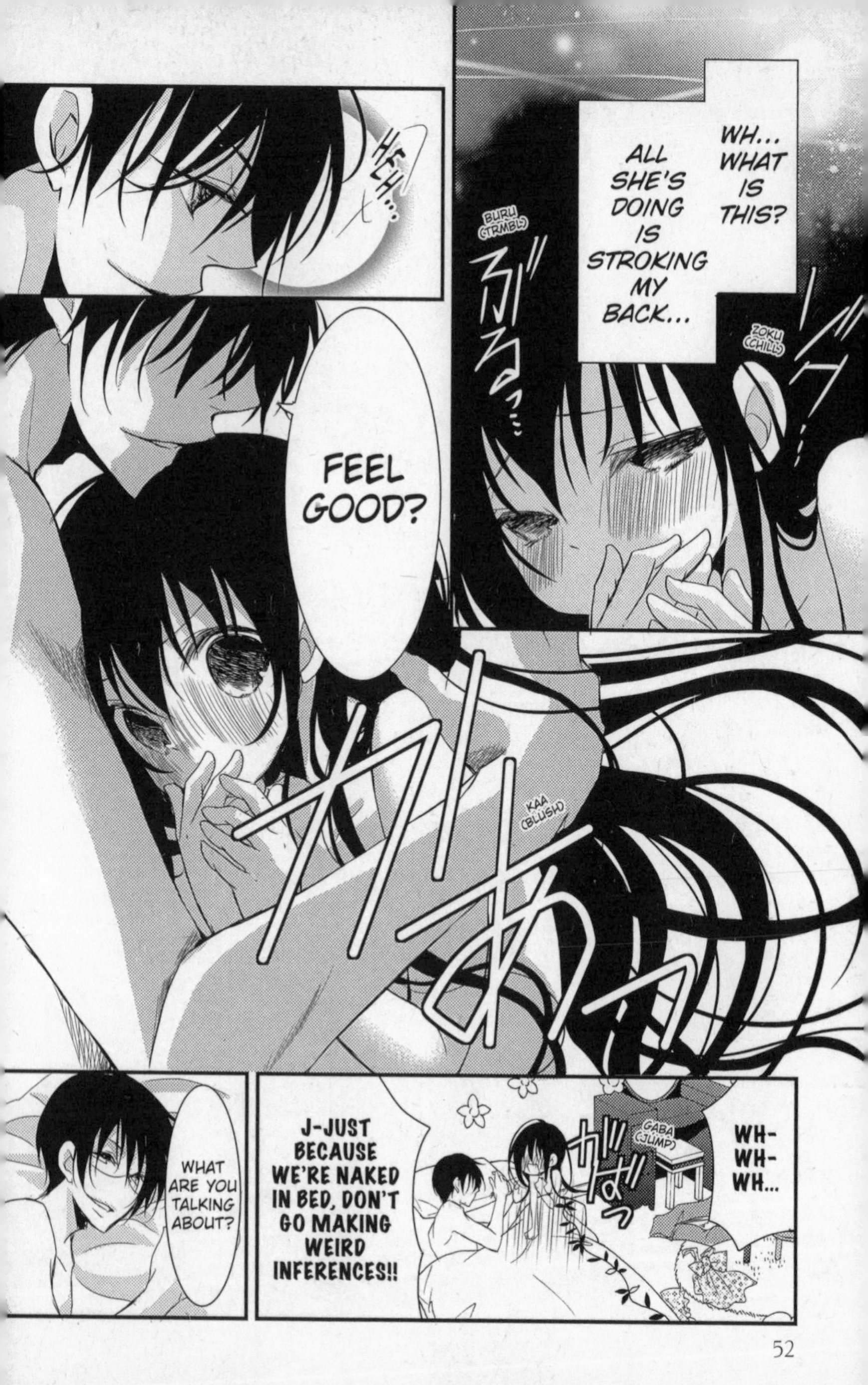
WH... WHAT IS THIS?
ALL SHE'S DOING IS STROKING MY BACK...
ZOKU (CHILL)
BURU (TRMBL)
HEH...
FEEL GOOD?
KAA (BLUSH)
WH-WH-WH...
GABA (JUMP)
J-JUST BECAUSE WE'RE NAKED IN BED, DON'T GO MAKING WEIRD INFERENCES!!
WHAT ARE YOU TALKING ABOUT?

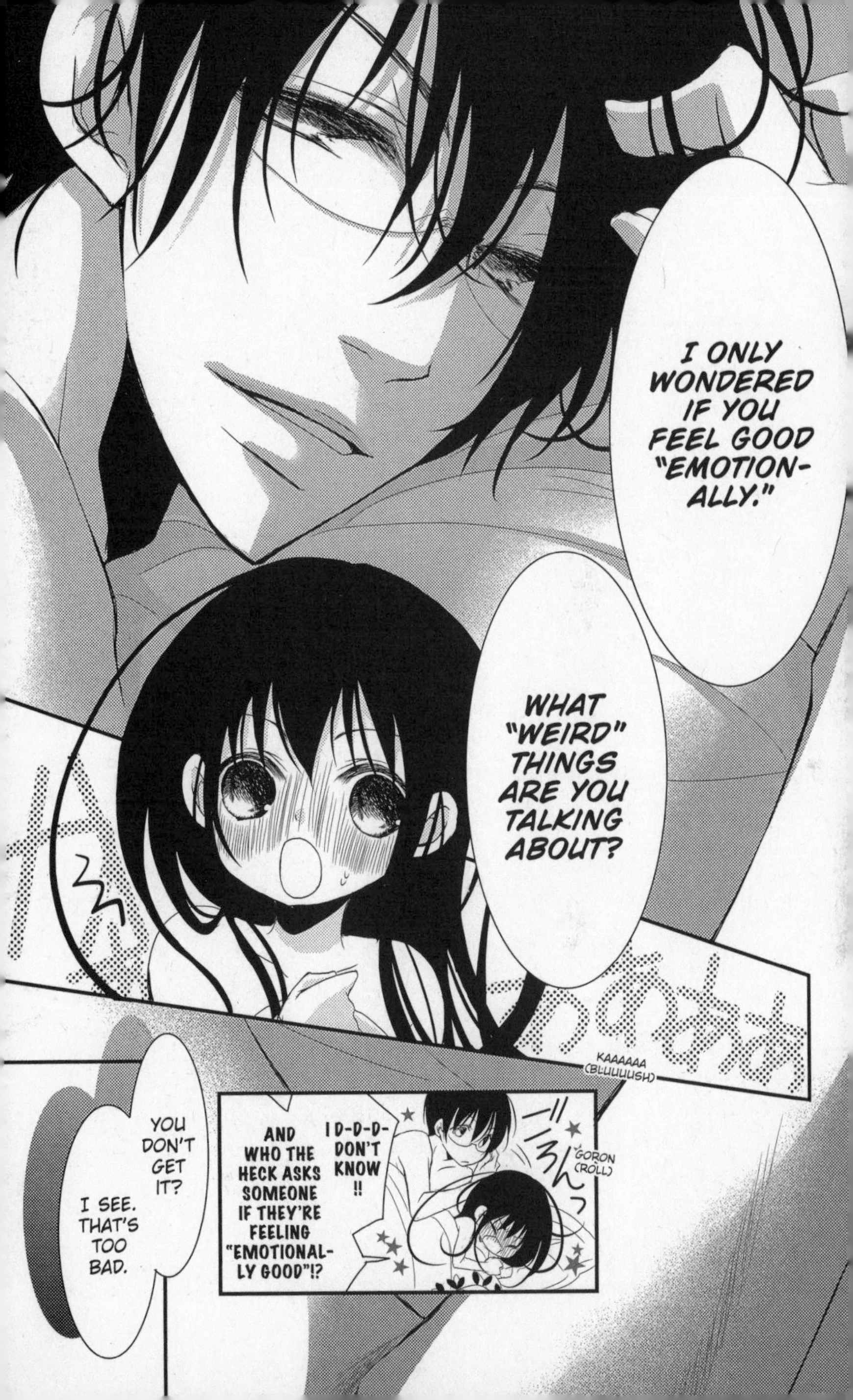
I ONLY WONDERED IF YOU FEEL GOOD "EMOTION-ALLY."
WHAT "WEIRD" THINGS ARE YOU TALKING ABOUT?
KAAAAAA (BLUUUUSH)
GORON (ROLL)
I D-D-D-DON'T KNOW!!
AND WHO THE HECK ASKS SOMEONE IF THEY'RE FEELING "EMOTIONAL-LY GOOD"!?
YOU DON'T GET IT?
I SEE. THAT'S TOO BAD.

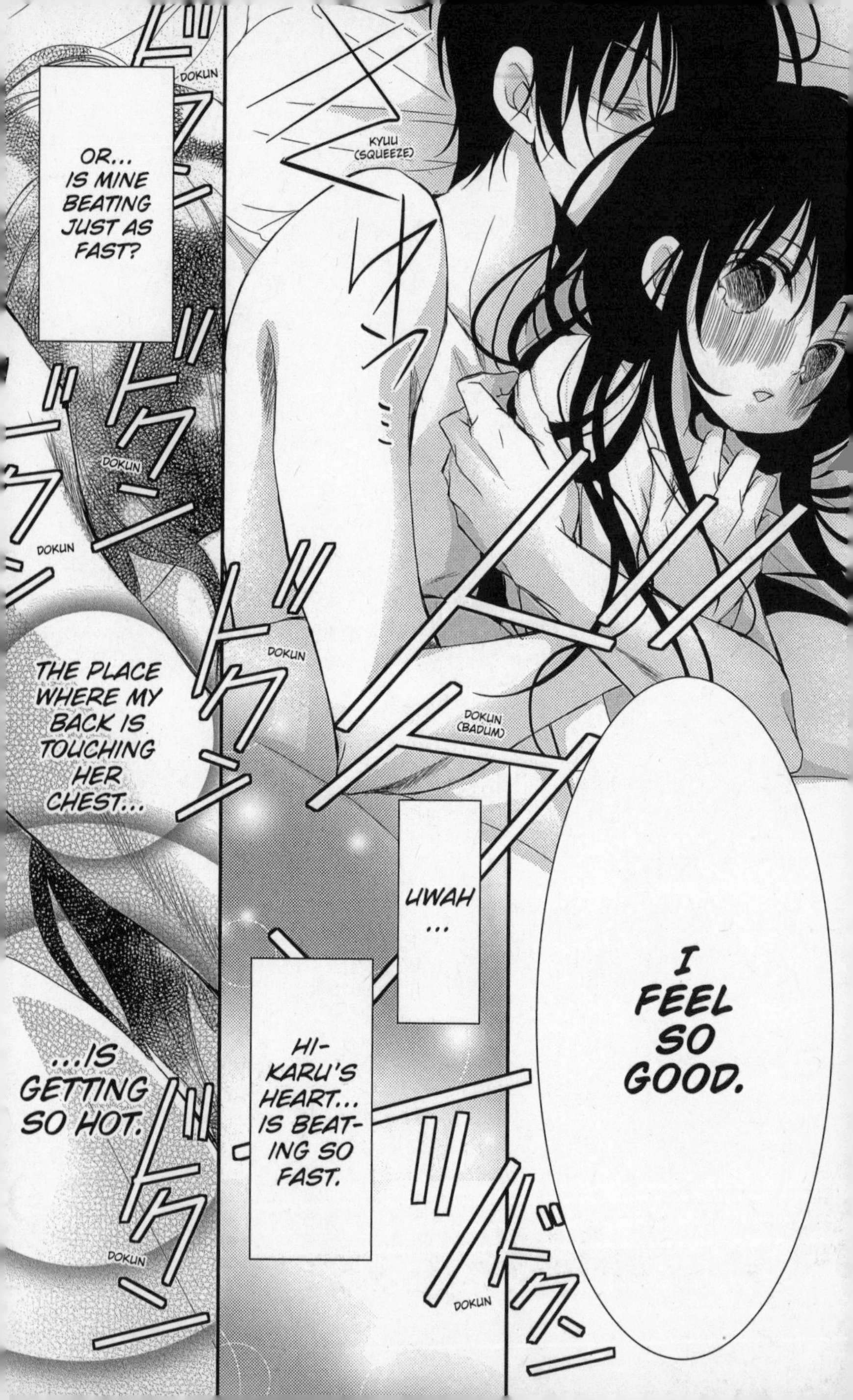
KYUU (SQUEEZE)
DOKUN (BADUM)
I FEEL SO GOOD.
UWAH ...
DOKUN
DOKUN
HI-KARU'S HEART... IS BEATING SO FAST.
DOKUN
OR... IS MINE BEATING JUST AS FAST?
DOKUN
DOKUN
THE PLACE WHERE MY BACK IS TOUCHING HER CHEST...
...IS GETTING SO HOT.
DOKUN

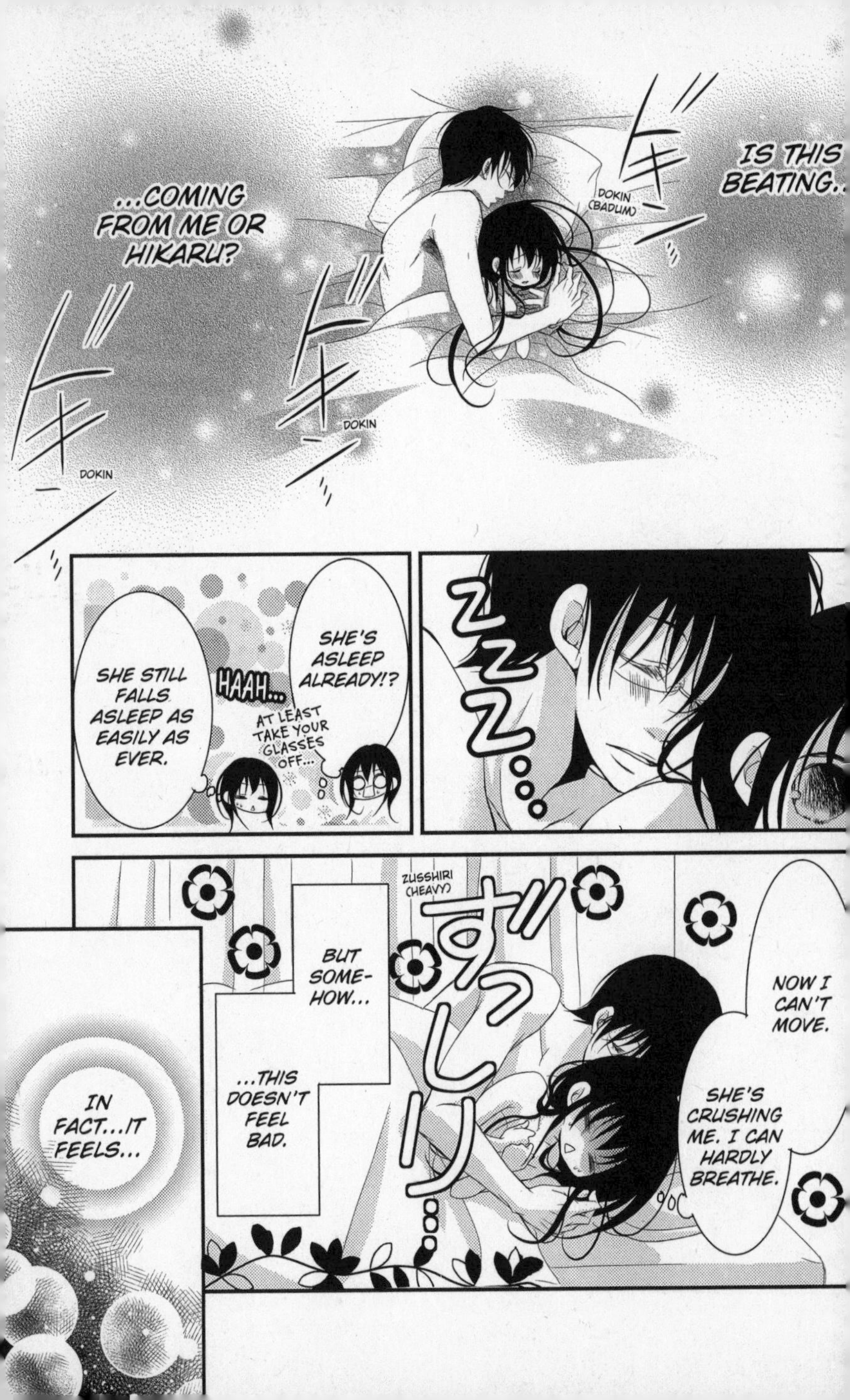
IS THIS BEATING...
DOKIN (BADUM)
DOKIN
...COMING FROM ME OR HIKARU?
DOKIN
ZZZ...
SHE'S ASLEEP ALREADY!?
HAAH...
AT LEAST TAKE YOUR GLASSES OFF...
SHE STILL FALLS ASLEEP AS EASILY AS EVER.
NOW I CAN'T MOVE.
SHE'S CRUSHING ME. I CAN HARDLY BREATHE.
ZUSSHIRI (HEAVY)
BUT SOME-HOW...
...THIS DOESN'T FEEL BAD.
IN FACT...IT FEELS...

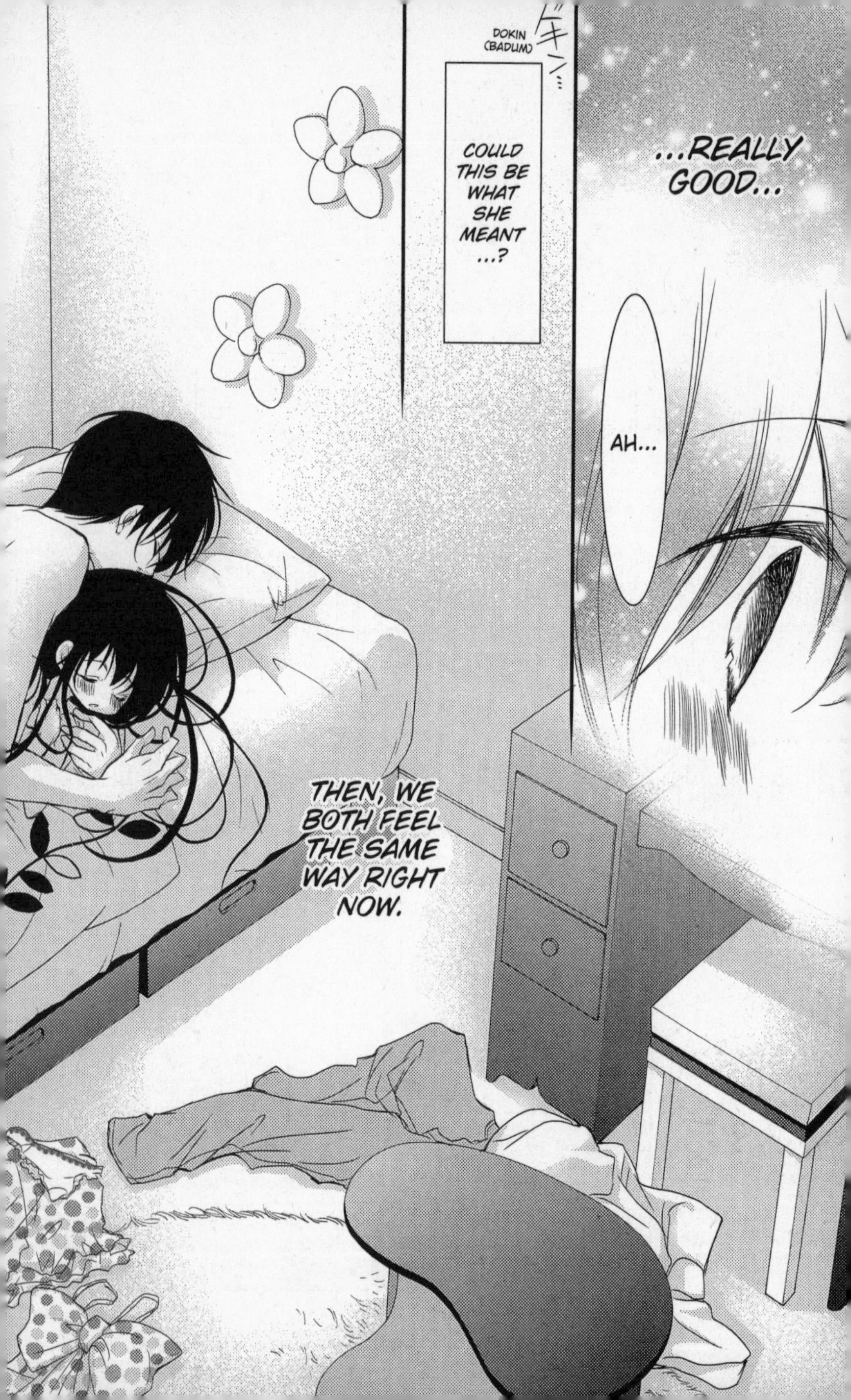
...REALLY GOOD...
AH...
DOKIN (BADUM)
COULD THIS BE WHAT SHE MEANT ...?
THEN, WE BOTH FEEL THE SAME WAY RIGHT NOW.

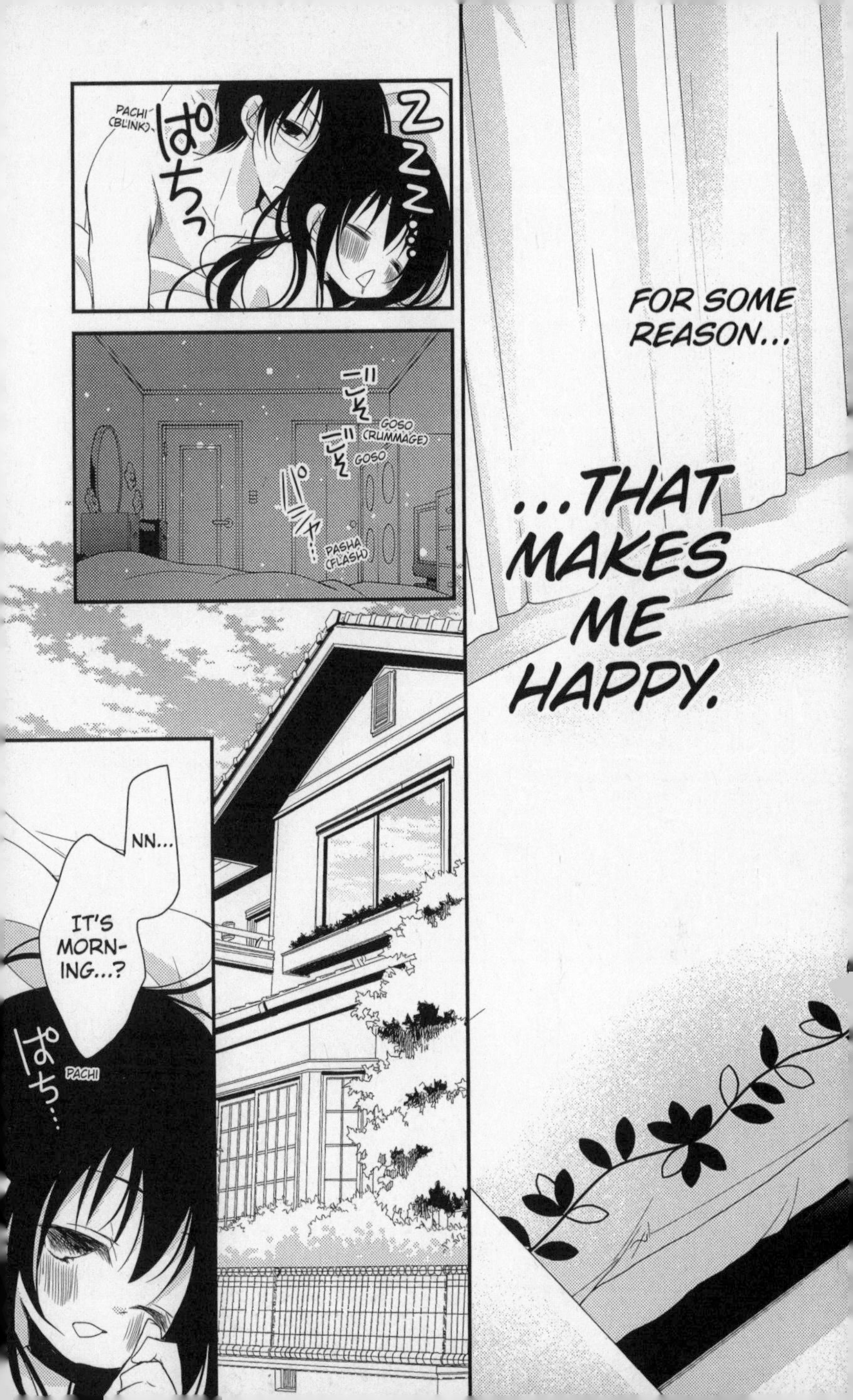
FOR SOME REASON...
...THAT MAKES ME HAPPY.
ぱちっ
PACHI (BLINK)
Z Z Z
ごそ
GOSO (RUMMAGE)
ごそ
GOSO
パシャ…
PASHA (FLASH)
NN...
IT'S MORNING...?
ぱち…
PACHI

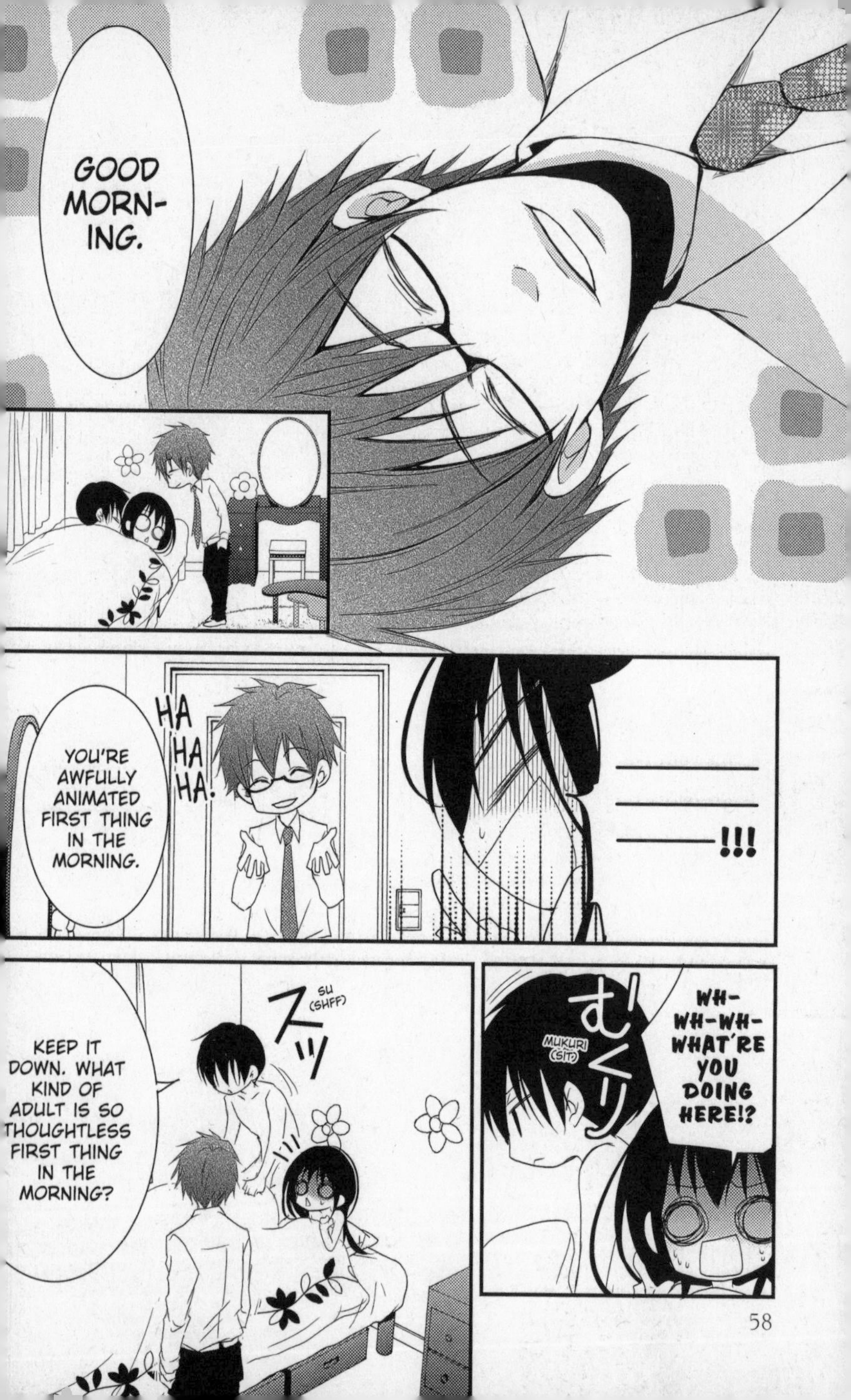
GOOD MORN-ING.
———
———
———!!!
HA HA HA!
YOU'RE AWFULLY ANIMATED FIRST THING IN THE MORNING.
むくり
MUKURI (SIT)
WH-WH-WH-WHAT'RE YOU DOING HERE!?
スッ
SU (SHFF)
KEEP IT DOWN. WHAT KIND OF ADULT IS SO THOUGHTLESS FIRST THING IN THE MORNING?

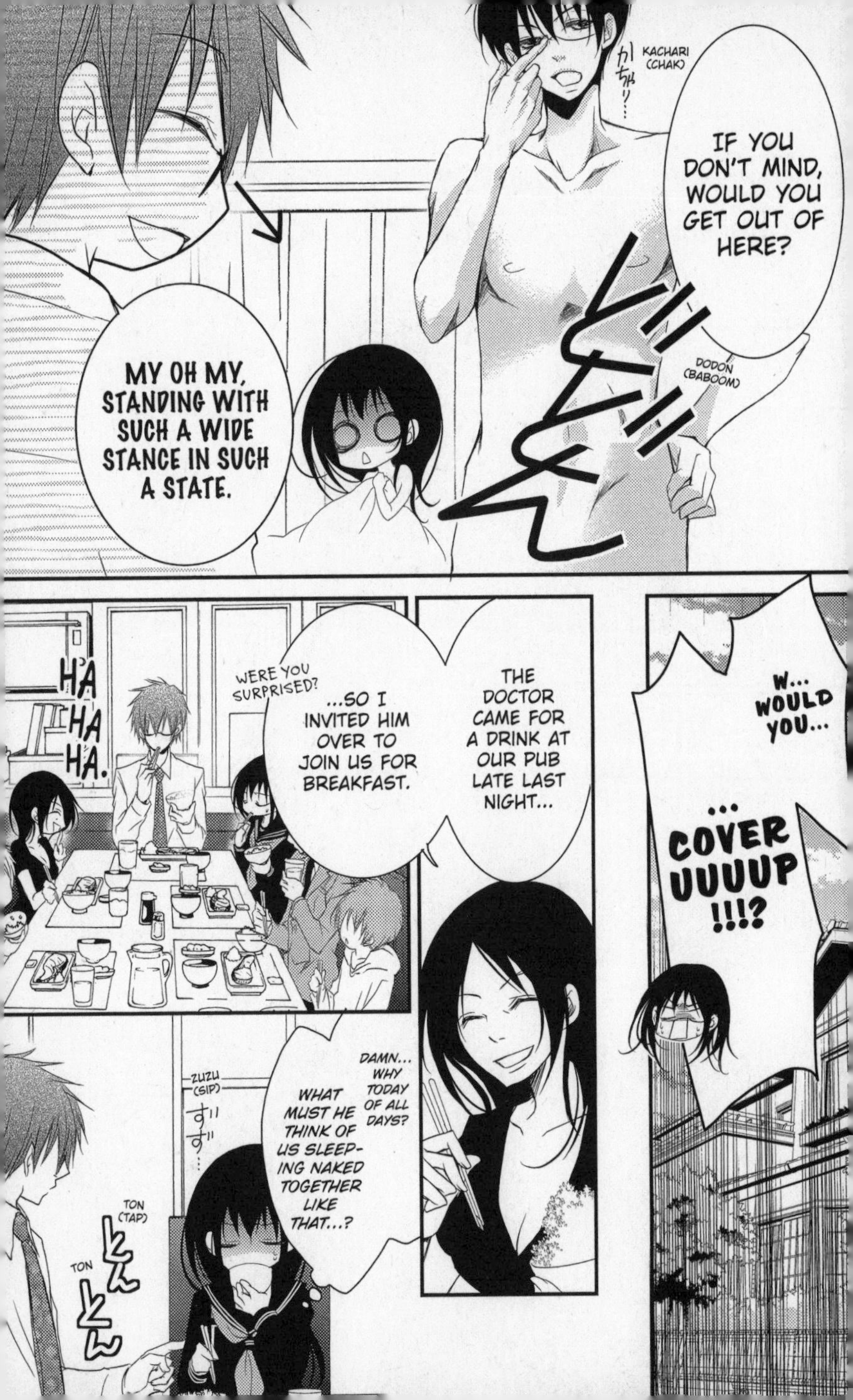

KACHARI (CHAK)
IF YOU DON'T MIND, WOULD YOU GET OUT OF HERE?
DODON (BABOOM)
MY OH MY, STANDING WITH SUCH A WIDE STANCE IN SUCH A STATE.
W... WOULD YOU...
...COVER UUUUP !!!?
THE DOCTOR CAME FOR A DRINK AT OUR PUB LATE LAST NIGHT...
...SO I INVITED HIM OVER TO JOIN US FOR BREAKFAST.
WERE YOU SURPRISED?
HA HA HA.
DAMN... WHY TODAY OF ALL DAYS?
WHAT MUST HE THINK OF US SLEEPING NAKED TOGETHER LIKE THAT...?
ZUZU (SIP)
TON (TAP)
TON

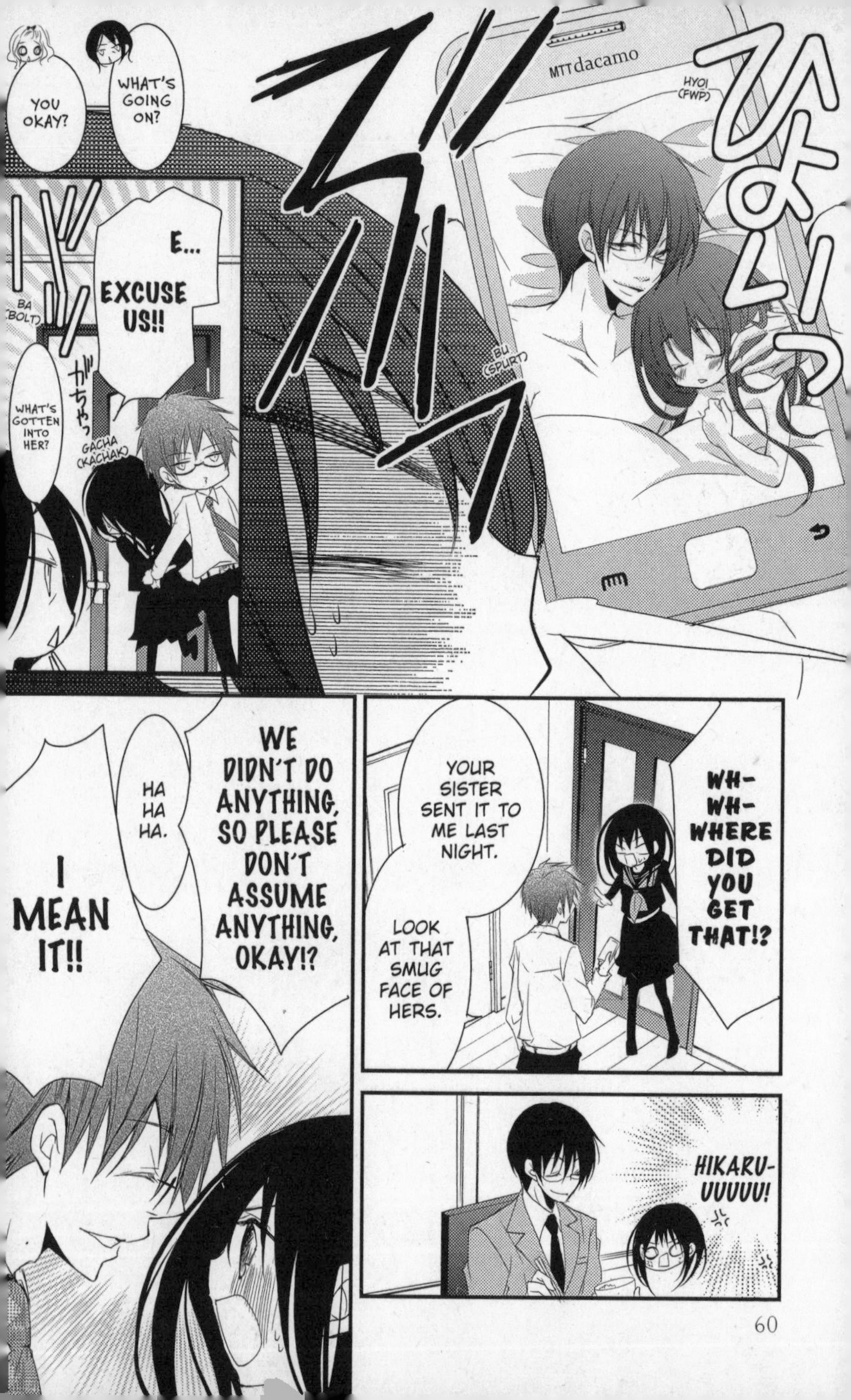
MTTdacamo
ひょいっ
HYOI (FWP)
BU (SPURT)
WHAT'S GOING ON?
YOU OKAY?
E... EXCUSE US!!
BA (BOLT)
がちゃっ
GACHA (KACHAK)
WHAT'S GOTTEN INTO HER?
WH-WH-WHERE DID YOU GET THAT!?
YOUR SISTER SENT IT TO ME LAST NIGHT.
LOOK AT THAT SMUG FACE OF HERS.
HIKARU-UUUUU!
WE DIDN'T DO ANYTHING, SO PLEASE DON'T ASSUME ANYTHING, OKAY!?
HA HA HA.
I MEAN IT!!

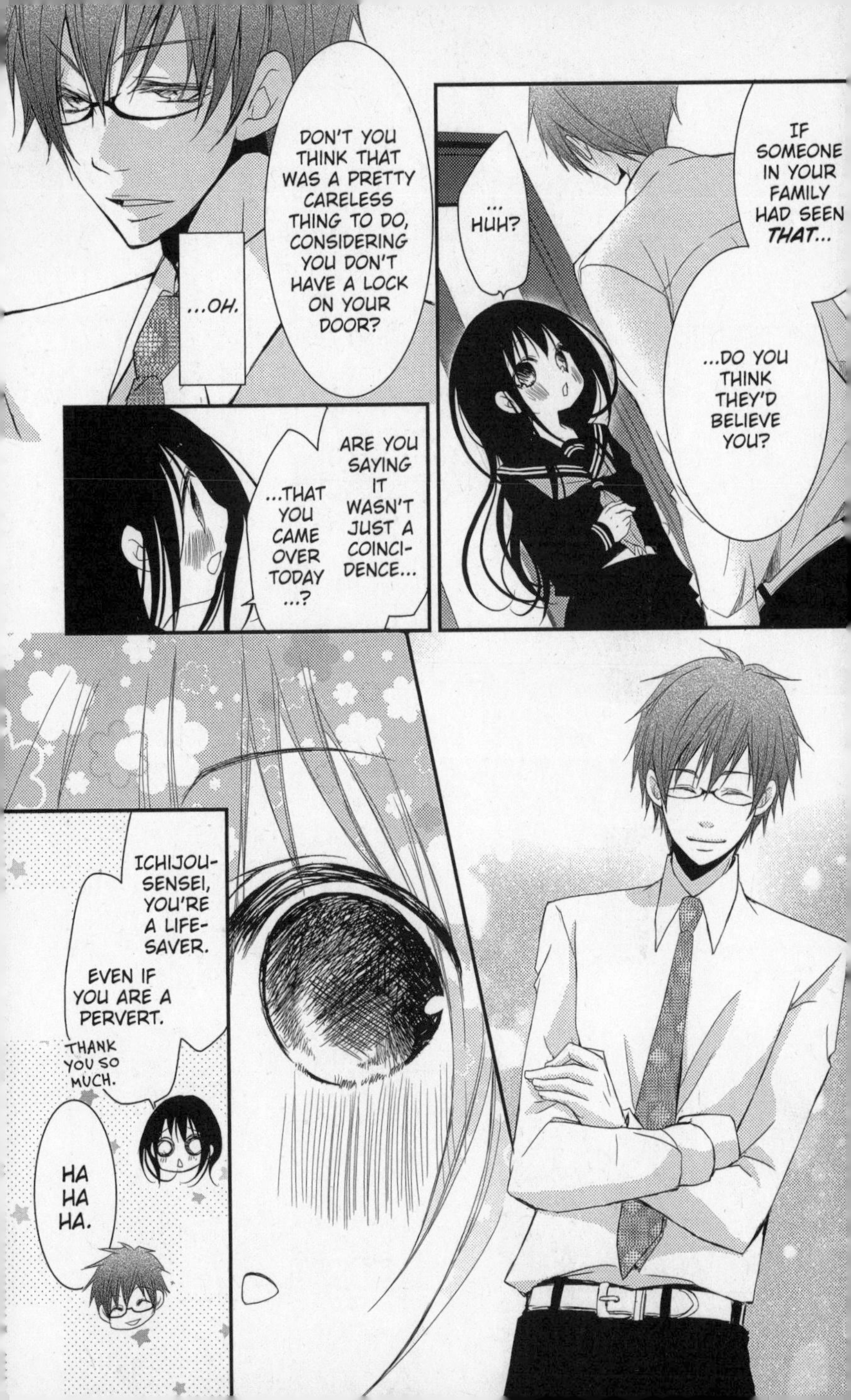
DON'T YOU THINK THAT WAS A PRETTY CARELESS THING TO DO, CONSIDERING YOU DON'T HAVE A LOCK ON YOUR DOOR?
...OH.
IF SOMEONE IN YOUR FAMILY HAD SEEN *THAT*...
...HUH?
...DO YOU THINK THEY'D BELIEVE YOU?
ARE YOU SAYING IT WASN'T JUST A COINCIDENCE...
...THAT YOU CAME OVER TODAY ...?
ICHIJOU-SENSEI, YOU'RE A LIFE-SAVER.
EVEN IF YOU ARE A PERVERT.
THANK YOU SO MUCH.
HA HA HA.

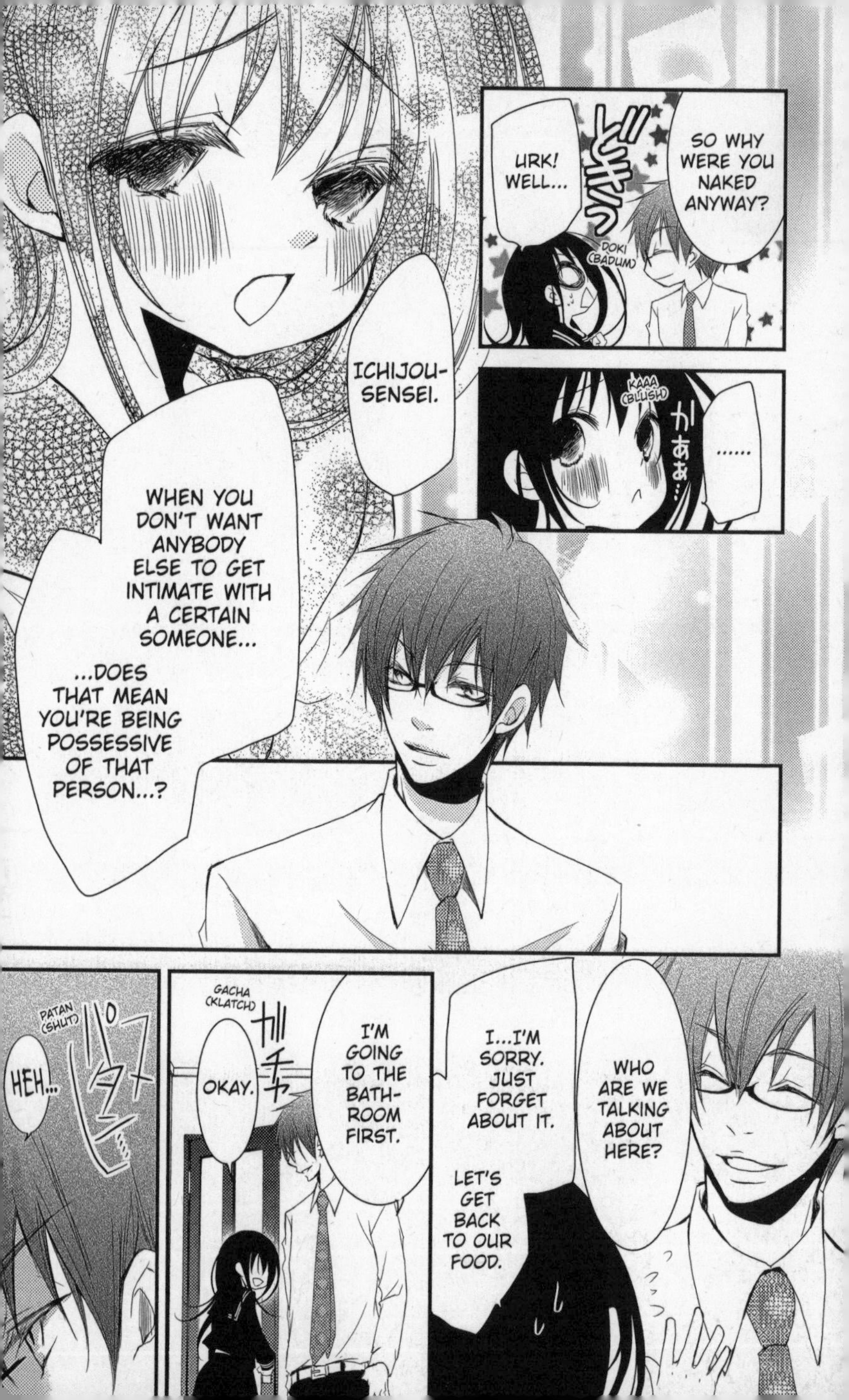
SO WHY WERE YOU NAKED ANYWAY?
URK! WELL...
DOKI (BADUM)
KAAA (BLUSH)
......
ICHIJOU-SENSEI.
WHEN YOU DON'T WANT ANYBODY ELSE TO GET INTIMATE WITH A CERTAIN SOMEONE...
...DOES THAT MEAN YOU'RE BEING POSSESSIVE OF THAT PERSON...?
WHO ARE WE TALKING ABOUT HERE?
I...I'M SORRY. JUST FORGET ABOUT IT.
LET'S GET BACK TO OUR FOOD.
I'M GOING TO THE BATH-ROOM FIRST.
GACHA (KLATCH)
OKAY.
PATAN (SHUT)
HEH...

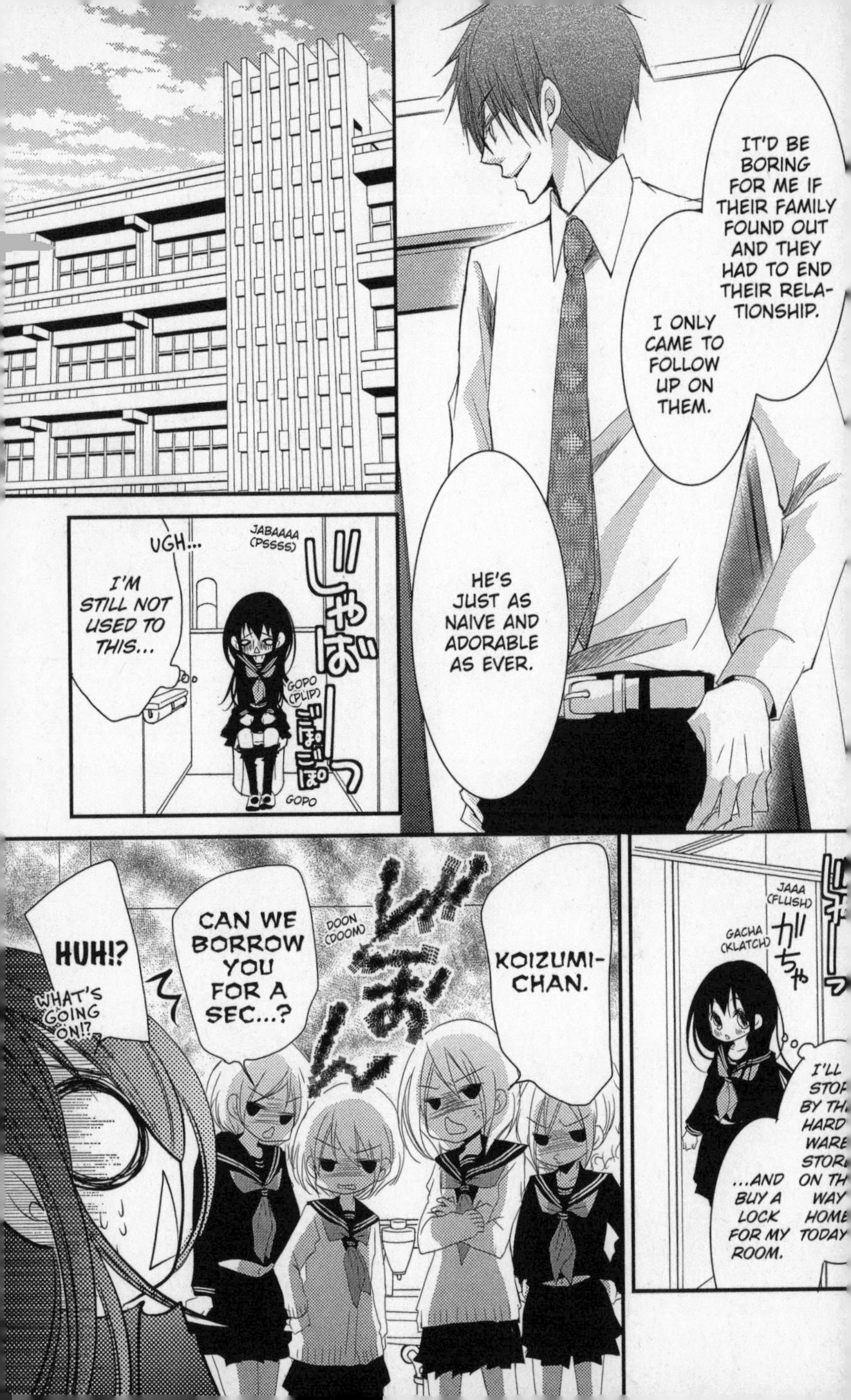
IT'D BE BORING FOR ME IF THEIR FAMILY FOUND OUT AND THEY HAD TO END THEIR RELA-TIONSHIP.
I ONLY CAME TO FOLLOW UP ON THEM.
HE'S JUST AS NAIVE AND ADORABLE AS EVER.
JABAAAA (PSSSS)
UGH...
I'M STILL NOT USED TO THIS...
GOPO (PLIP)
GOPO
JAAA (FLUSH)
GACHA (KLATCH)
I'LL STO BY TH HARD WARE STOR ON TH WAY HOME TODAY
...AND BUY A LOCK FOR MY ROOM.
KOIZUMI-CHAN.
DOON (DOOM)
CAN WE BORROW YOU FOR A SEC...?
HUH!?
WHAT'S GOING ON!?

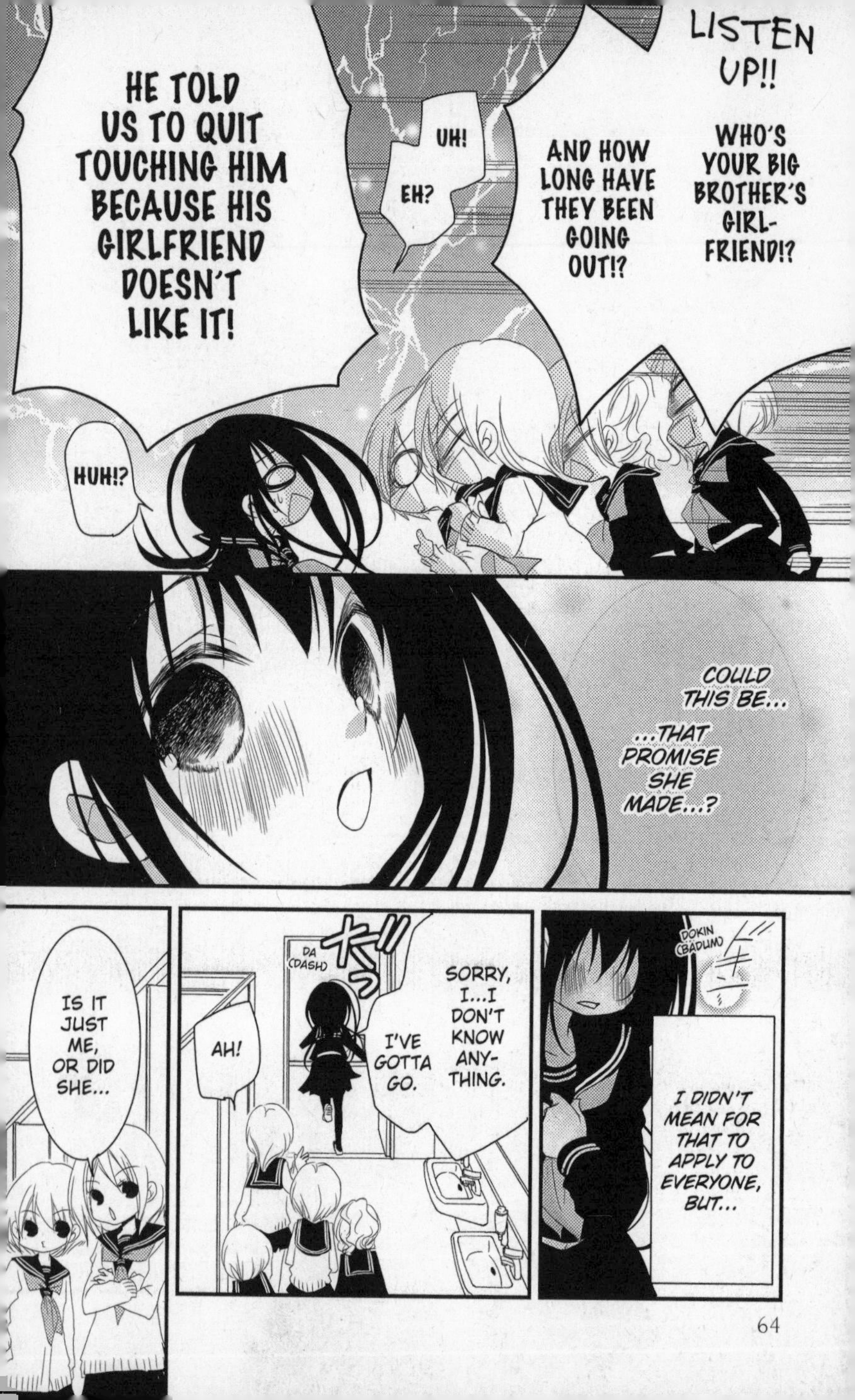
LISTEN UP!!
WHO'S YOUR BIG BROTHER'S GIRL-FRIEND!?
AND HOW LONG HAVE THEY BEEN GOING OUT!?
UH!
EH?
HE TOLD US TO QUIT TOUCHING HIM BECAUSE HIS GIRLFRIEND DOESN'T LIKE IT!
HUH!?
COULD THIS BE...
...THAT PROMISE SHE MADE...?
DOKIN (BADUM)
I DIDN'T MEAN FOR THAT TO APPLY TO EVERYONE, BUT...
DA (DASH)
SORRY, I...I DON'T KNOW ANY-THING.
I'VE GOTTA GO.
AH!
IS IT JUST ME, OR DID SHE...

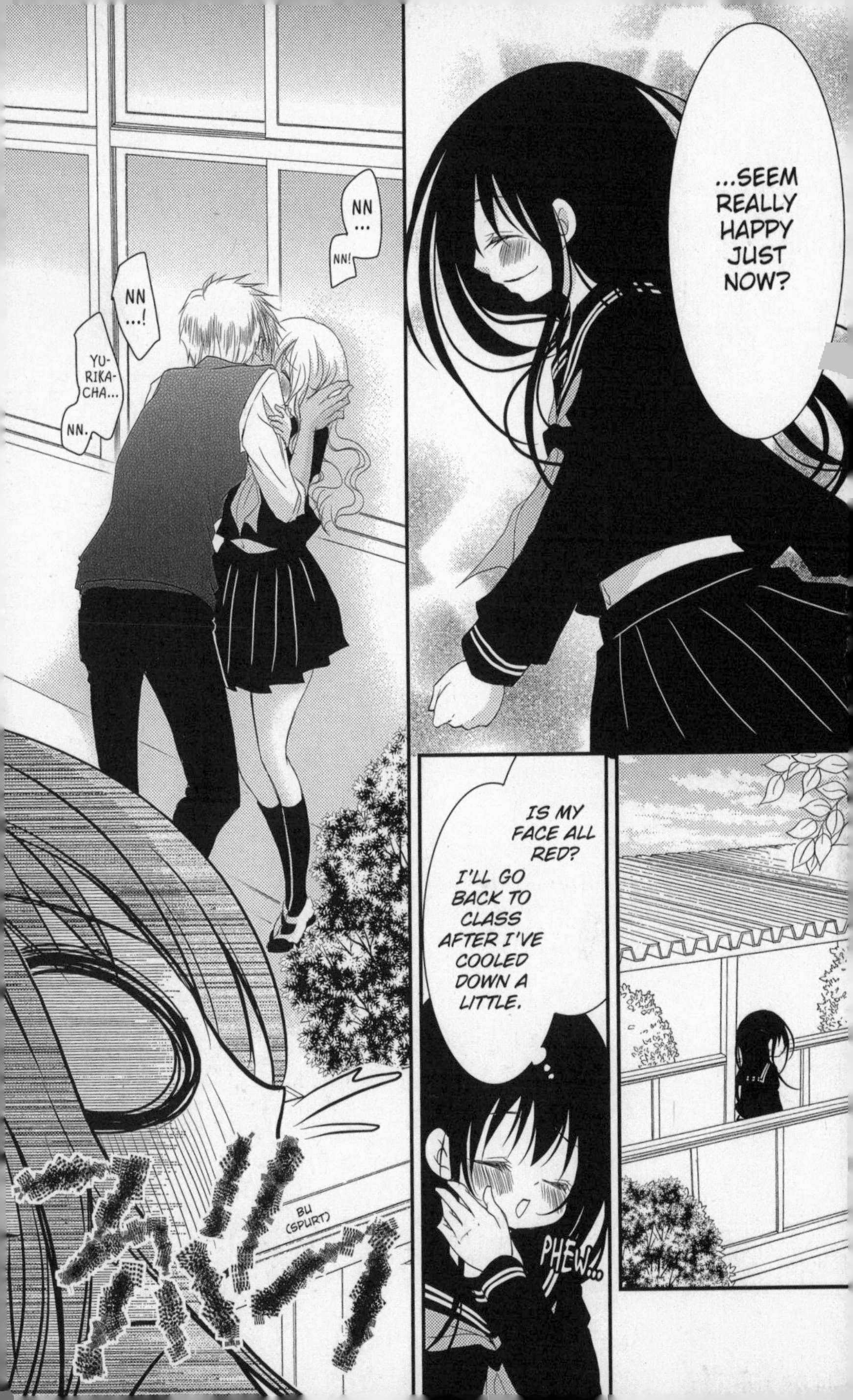
...SEEM REALLY HAPPY JUST NOW?
IS MY FACE ALL RED?
I'LL GO BACK TO CLASS AFTER I'VE COOLED DOWN A LITTLE.
PHEW...
NN... NN!
NN ...!
YU-RIKA-CHA...
NN.
BU (SPURT)

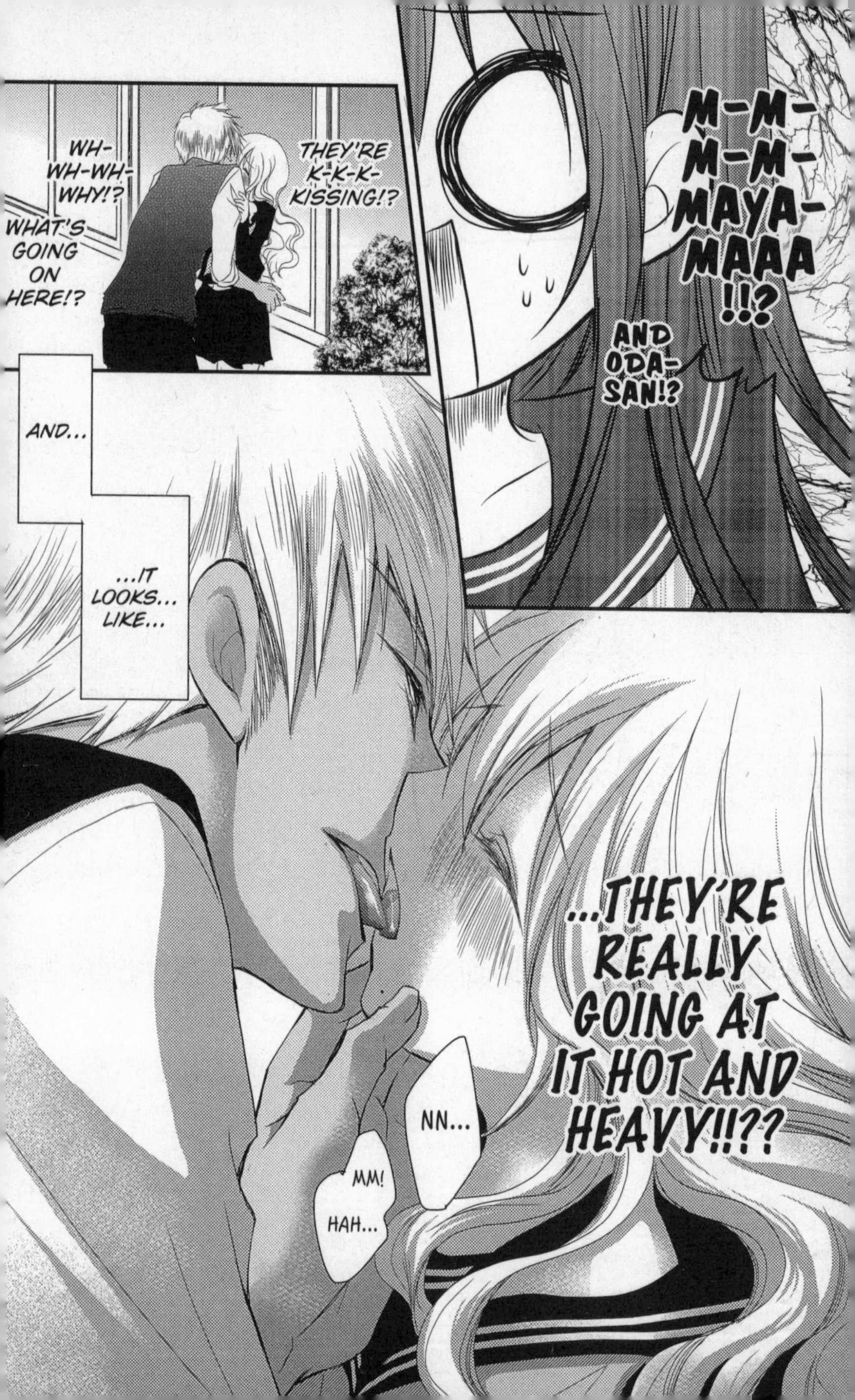

M-M-M-M-MAYA-MAAA!!?
AND ODA-SAN!?
THEY'RE K-K-K-KISSING!?
WH-WH-WH-WHY!?
WHAT'S GOING ON HERE!?
AND...
...IT LOOKS... LIKE...
...THEY'RE REALLY GOING AT IT HOT AND HEAVY!!??
NN...
MM!
HAH...

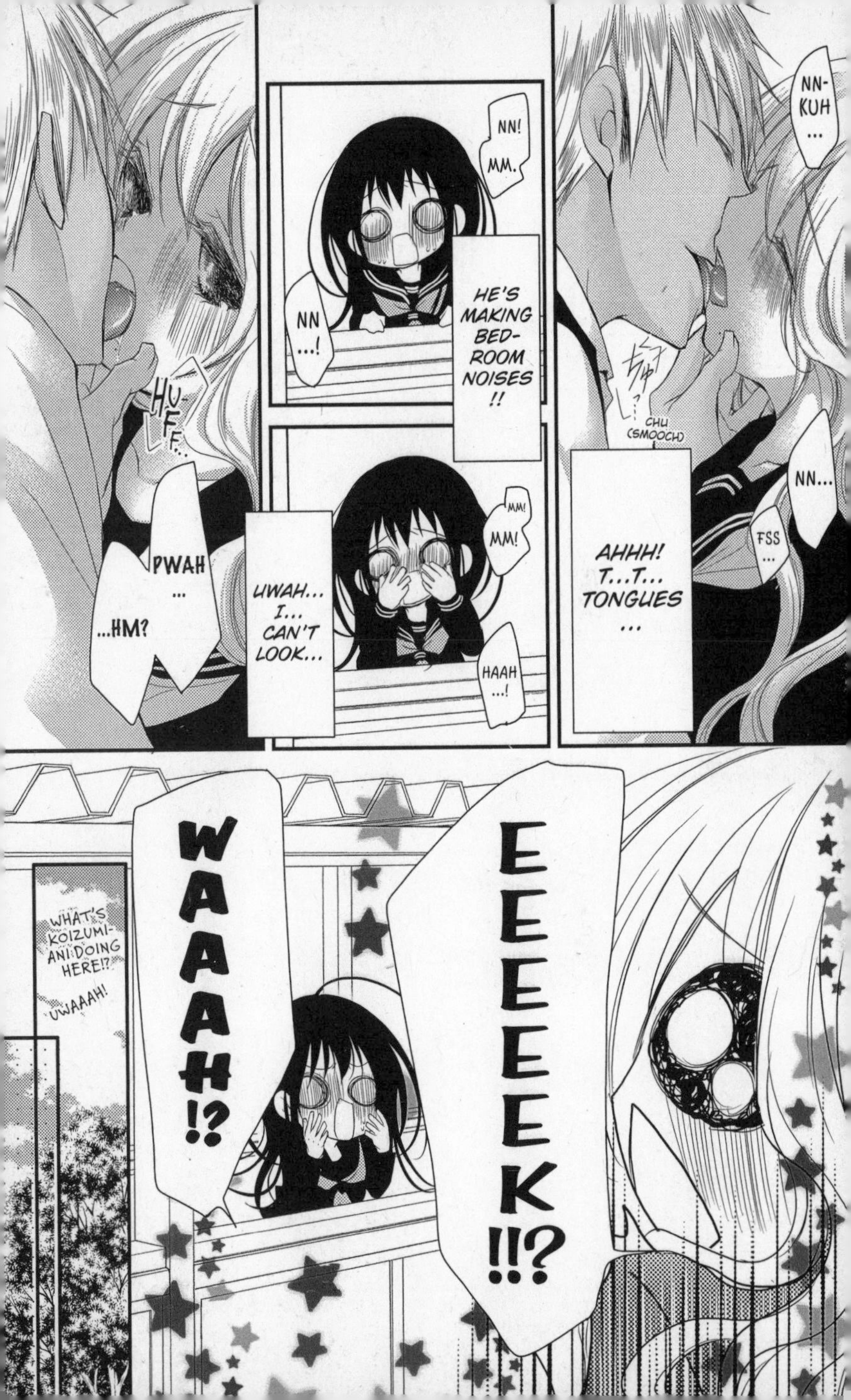

NN-KUH ...
CHU (SMOOCH)
NN...
FSS ...
AHHH! T...T... TONGUES ...
NN! MM.
HE'S MAKING BED-ROOM NOISES !!
NN ...!
MM! MM!
UWAH... I... CAN'T LOOK...
HAAH ...!
HUFF...
PWAH ... ...HM?
EEEEEK !!?
WAAAH !?
WHAT'S KOIZUMI-ANI DOING HERE!!?
UWAAAH!

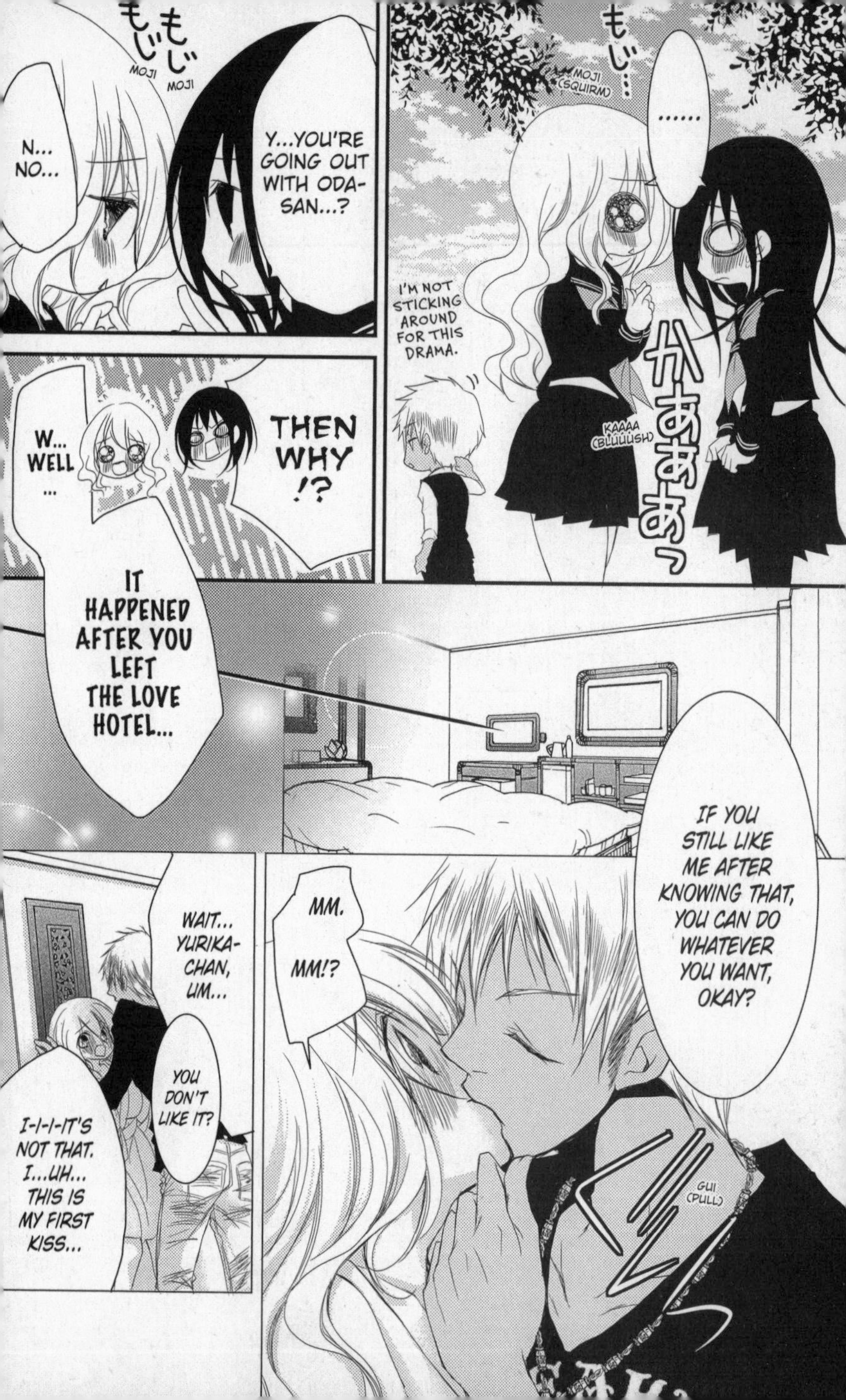

もじ…
MOJI (SQUIRM)
......
I'M NOT STICKING AROUND FOR THIS DRAMA.
かあああっ
KAAAA (BLUUUSH)
もじもじ
MOJI MOJI
Y...YOU'RE GOING OUT WITH ODA-SAN...?
N... NO...
THEN WHY!?
W... WELL ...
IT HAPPENED AFTER YOU LEFT THE LOVE HOTEL...
IF YOU STILL LIKE ME AFTER KNOWING THAT, YOU CAN DO WHATEVER YOU WANT, OKAY?
MM.
MM!?
GUI (PULL)
WAIT... YURIKA-CHAN, UM...
YOU DON'T LIKE IT?
I-I-I-IT'S NOT THAT. I...UH... THIS IS MY FIRST KISS...

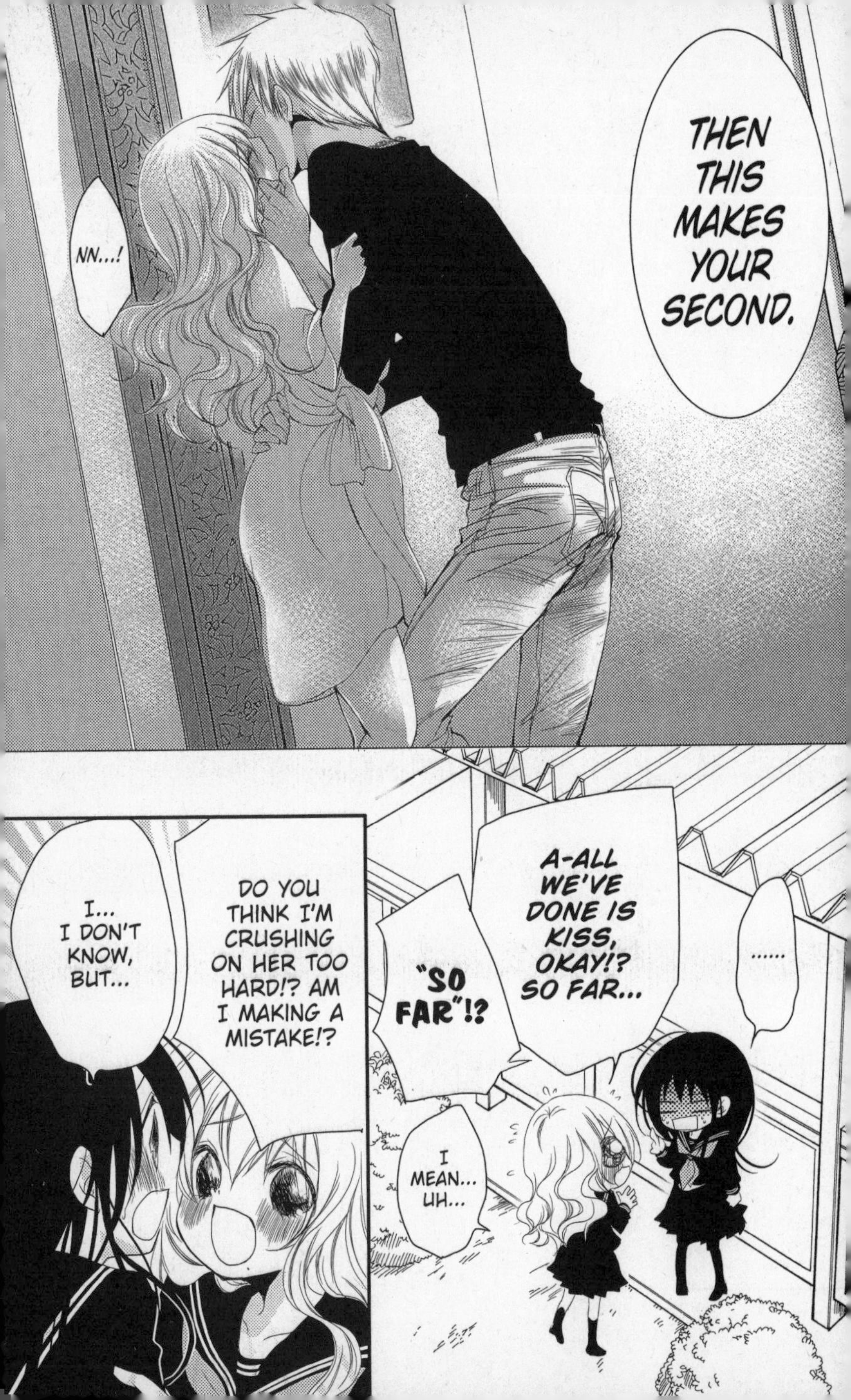
THEN THIS MAKES YOUR SECOND.
NN...!
A-ALL WE'VE DONE IS KISS, OKAY!? SO FAR...
......
"SO FAR"!?
I MEAN... UH...
DO YOU THINK I'M CRUSHING ON HER TOO HARD!? AM I MAKING A MISTAKE!?
I... I DON'T KNOW, BUT...

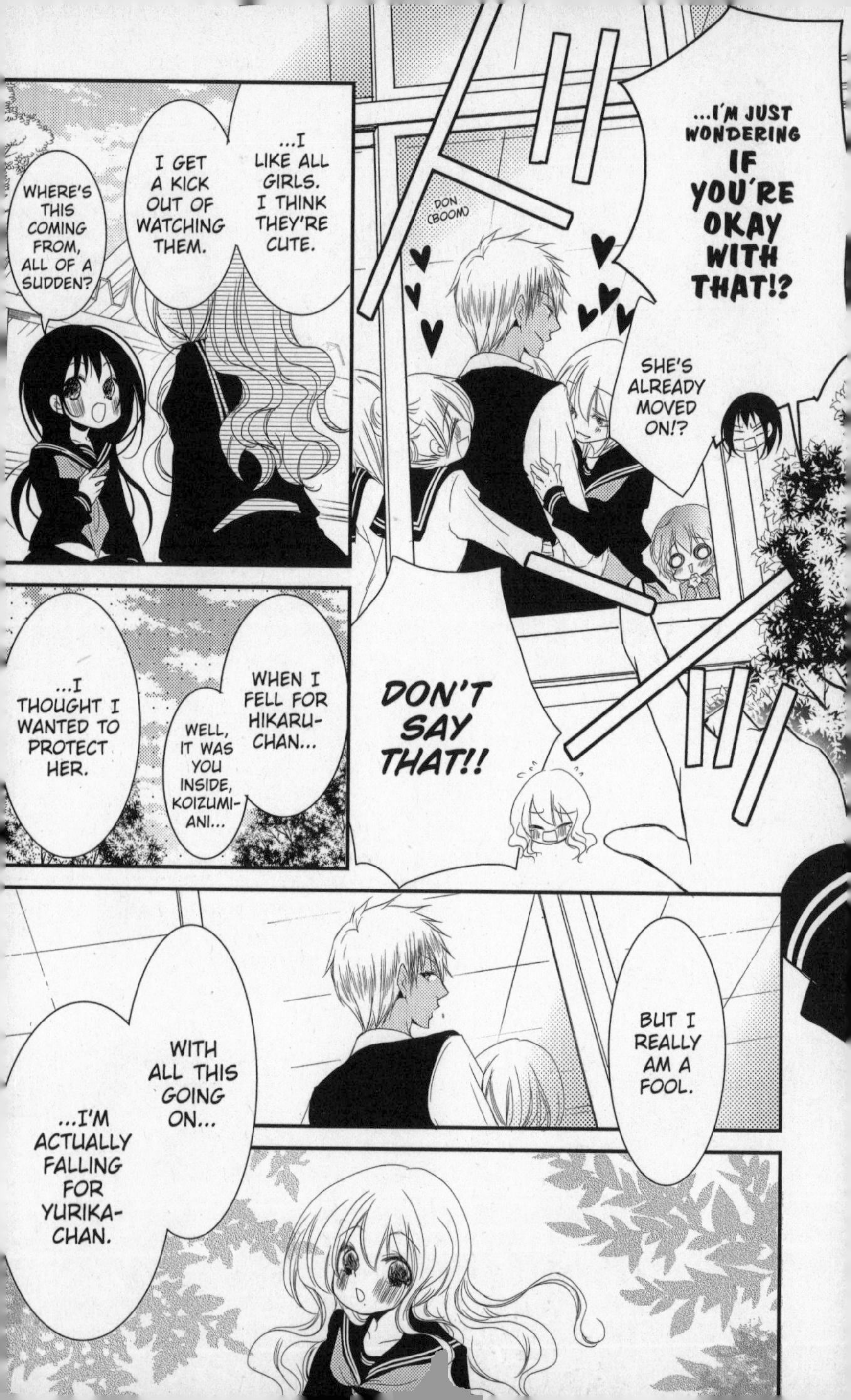
...I'M JUST WONDERING IF YOU'RE OKAY WITH THAT!?
DON (BOOM)
SHE'S ALREADY MOVED ON!?
DON'T SAY THAT!!
...I LIKE ALL GIRLS. I THINK THEY'RE CUTE.
I GET A KICK OUT OF WATCHING THEM.
WHERE'S THIS COMING FROM, ALL OF A SUDDEN?
WHEN I FELL FOR HIKARU-CHAN...
WELL, IT WAS YOU INSIDE, KOIZUMI-ANI...
...I THOUGHT I WANTED TO PROTECT HER.
BUT I REALLY AM A FOOL.
WITH ALL THIS GOING ON...
...I'M ACTUALLY FALLING FOR YURIKA-CHAN.

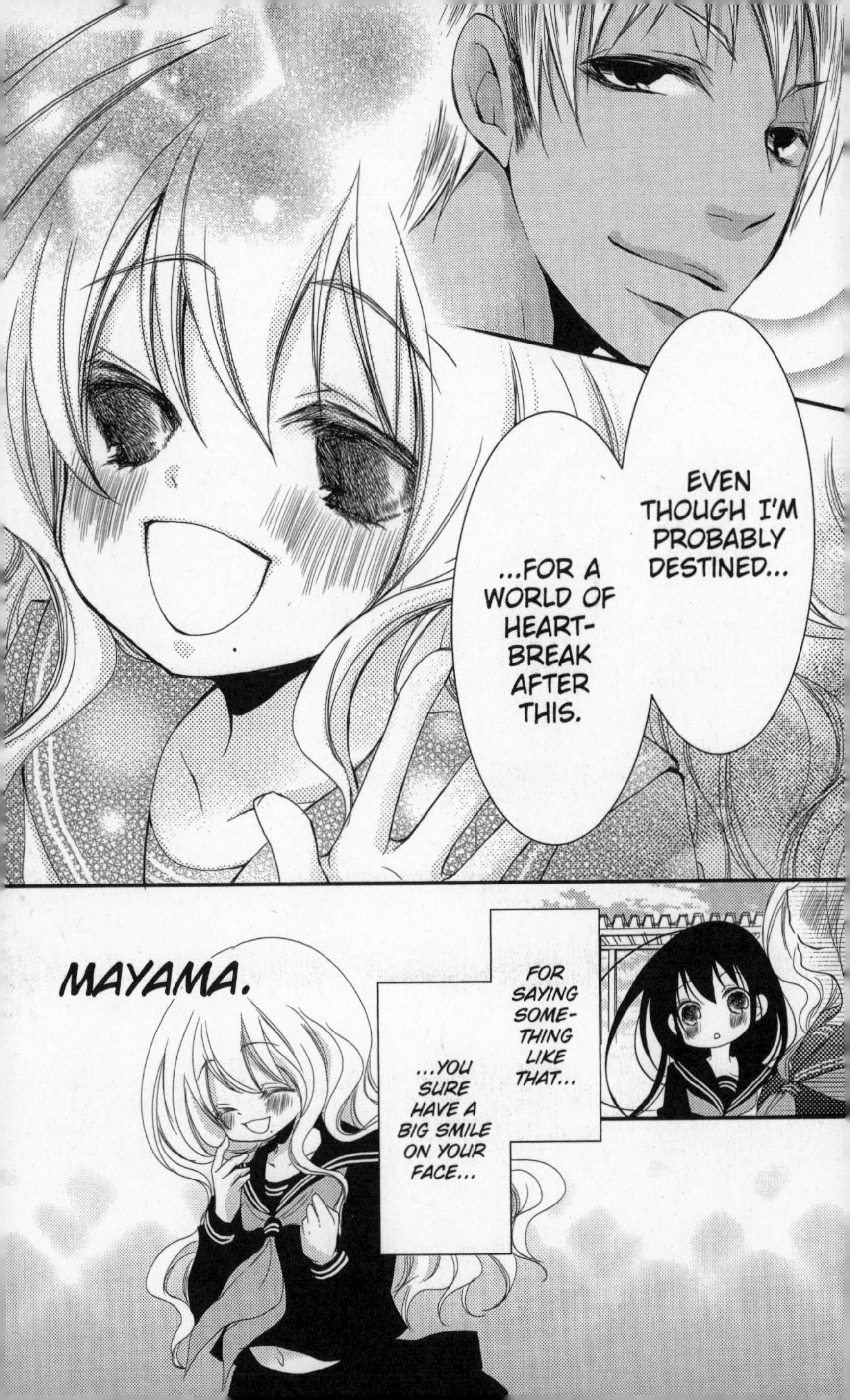
EVEN THOUGH I'M PROBABLY DESTINED...
...FOR A WORLD OF HEART-BREAK AFTER THIS.
FOR SAYING SOME-THING LIKE THAT...
...YOU SURE HAVE A BIG SMILE ON YOUR FACE...
MAYAMA.

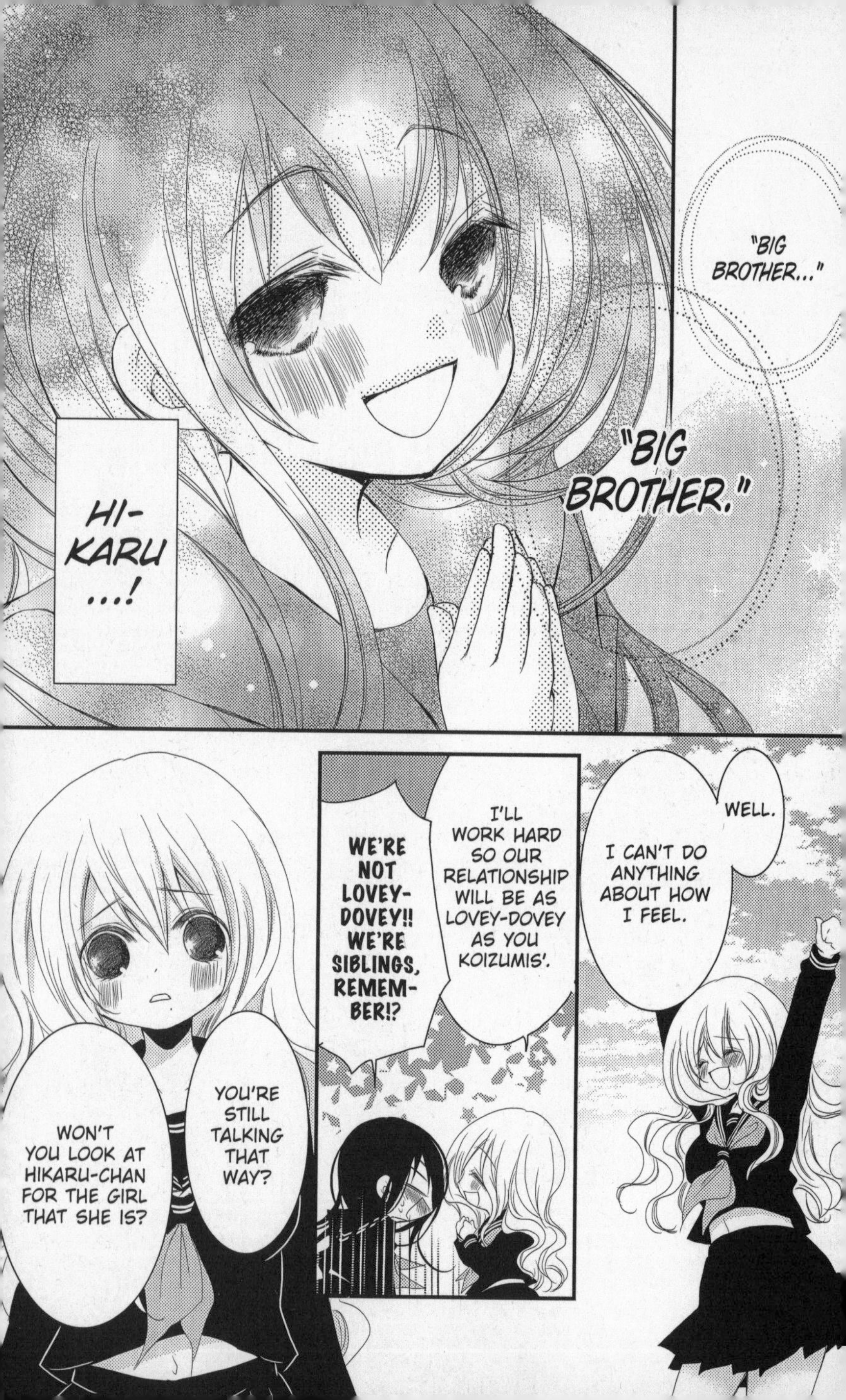
"BIG BROTHER..."
"BIG BROTHER."
HI-KARU...!
WELL.
I CAN'T DO ANYTHING ABOUT HOW I FEEL.
I'LL WORK HARD SO OUR RELATIONSHIP WILL BE AS LOVEY-DOVEY AS YOU KOIZUMIS'.
WE'RE NOT LOVEY-DOVEY!! WE'RE SIBLINGS, REMEMBER!?
YOU'RE STILL TALKING THAT WAY?
WON'T YOU LOOK AT HIKARU-CHAN FOR THE GIRL THAT SHE IS?

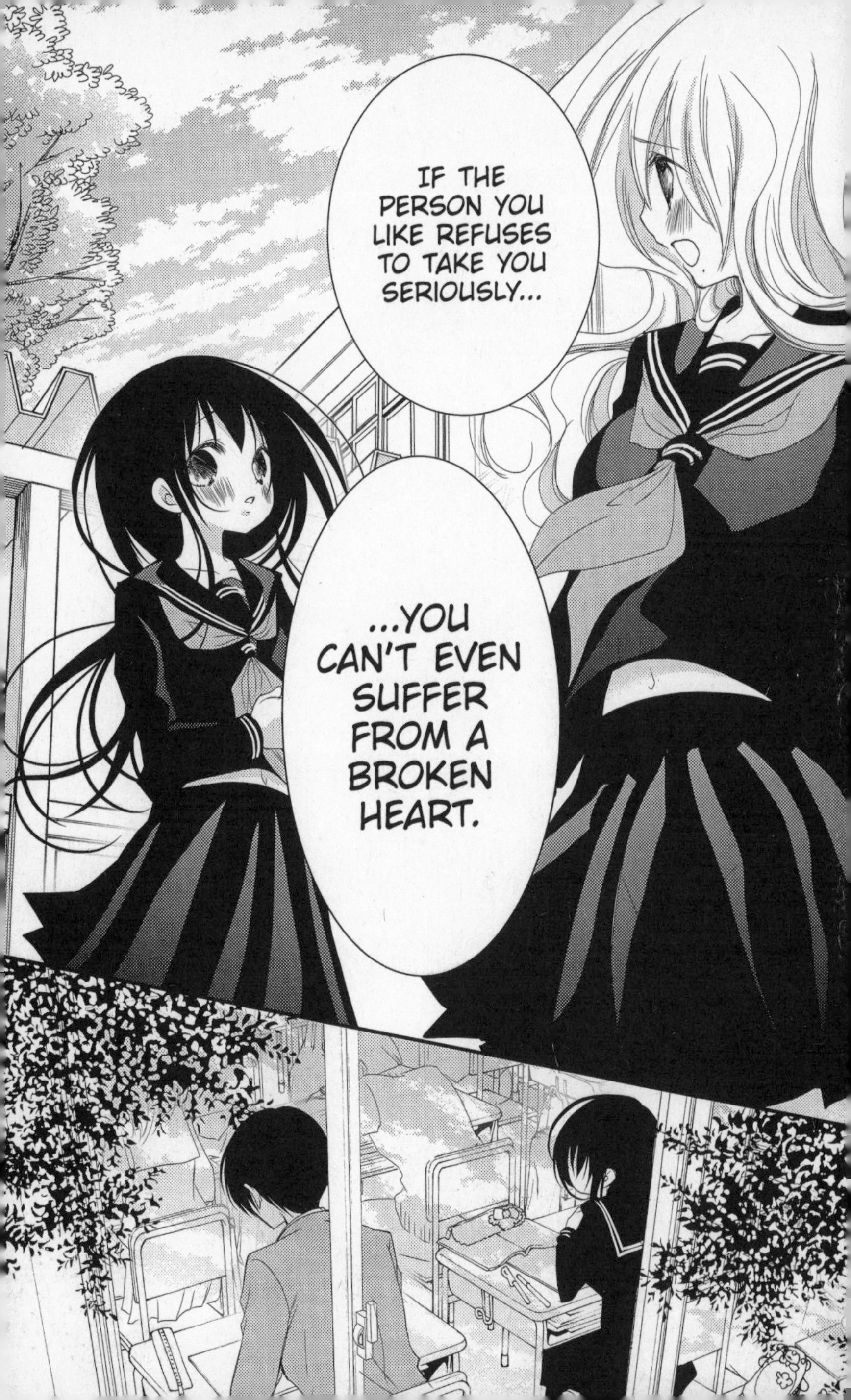
IF THE PERSON YOU LIKE REFUSES TO TAKE YOU SERIOUSLY...
...YOU CAN'T EVEN SUFFER FROM A BROKEN HEART.

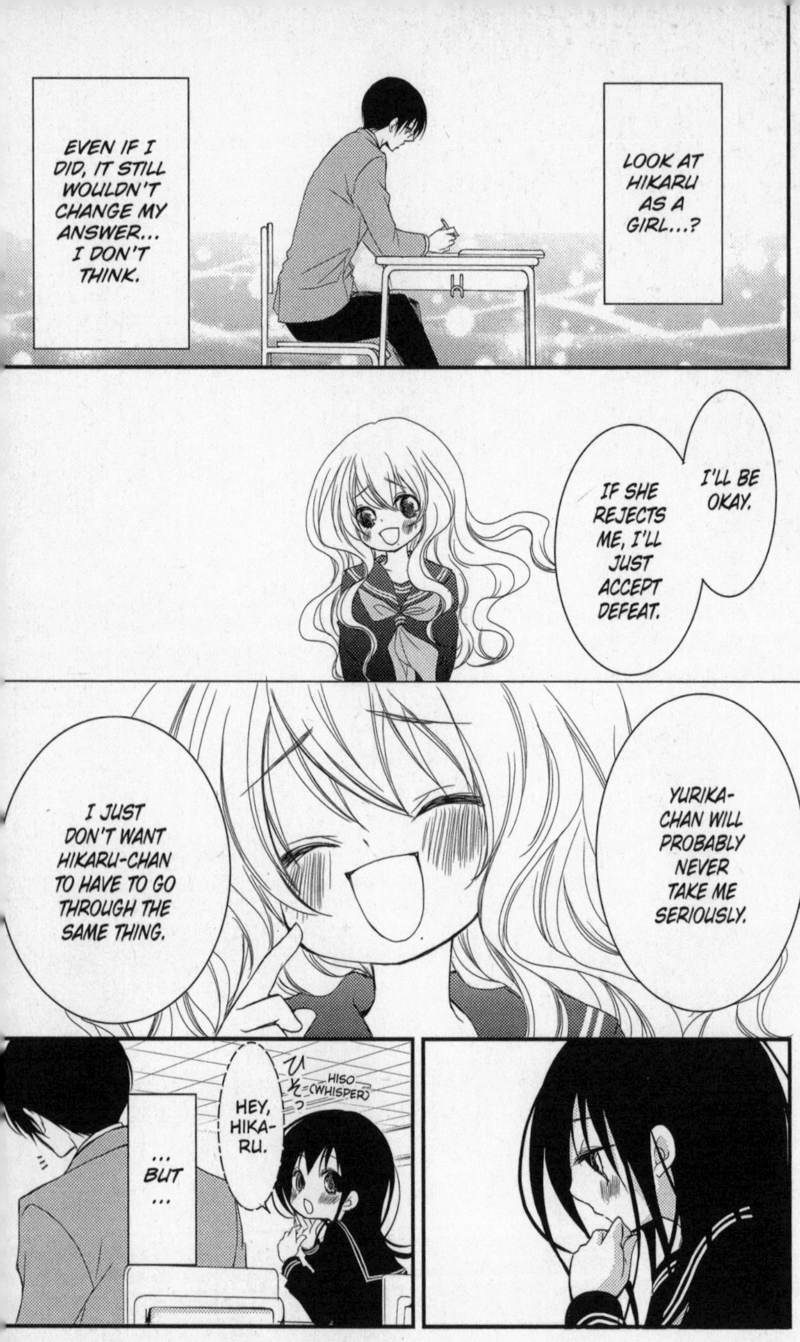
LOOK AT HIKARU AS A GIRL...?
EVEN IF I DID, IT STILL WOULDN'T CHANGE MY ANSWER... I DON'T THINK.
I'LL BE OKAY.
IF SHE REJECTS ME, I'LL JUST ACCEPT DEFEAT.
YURIKA-CHAN WILL PROBABLY NEVER TAKE ME SERIOUSLY.
I JUST DON'T WANT HIKARU-CHAN TO HAVE TO GO THROUGH THE SAME THING.
HISO (WHISPER)
HEY, HIKARU.
... BUT ...

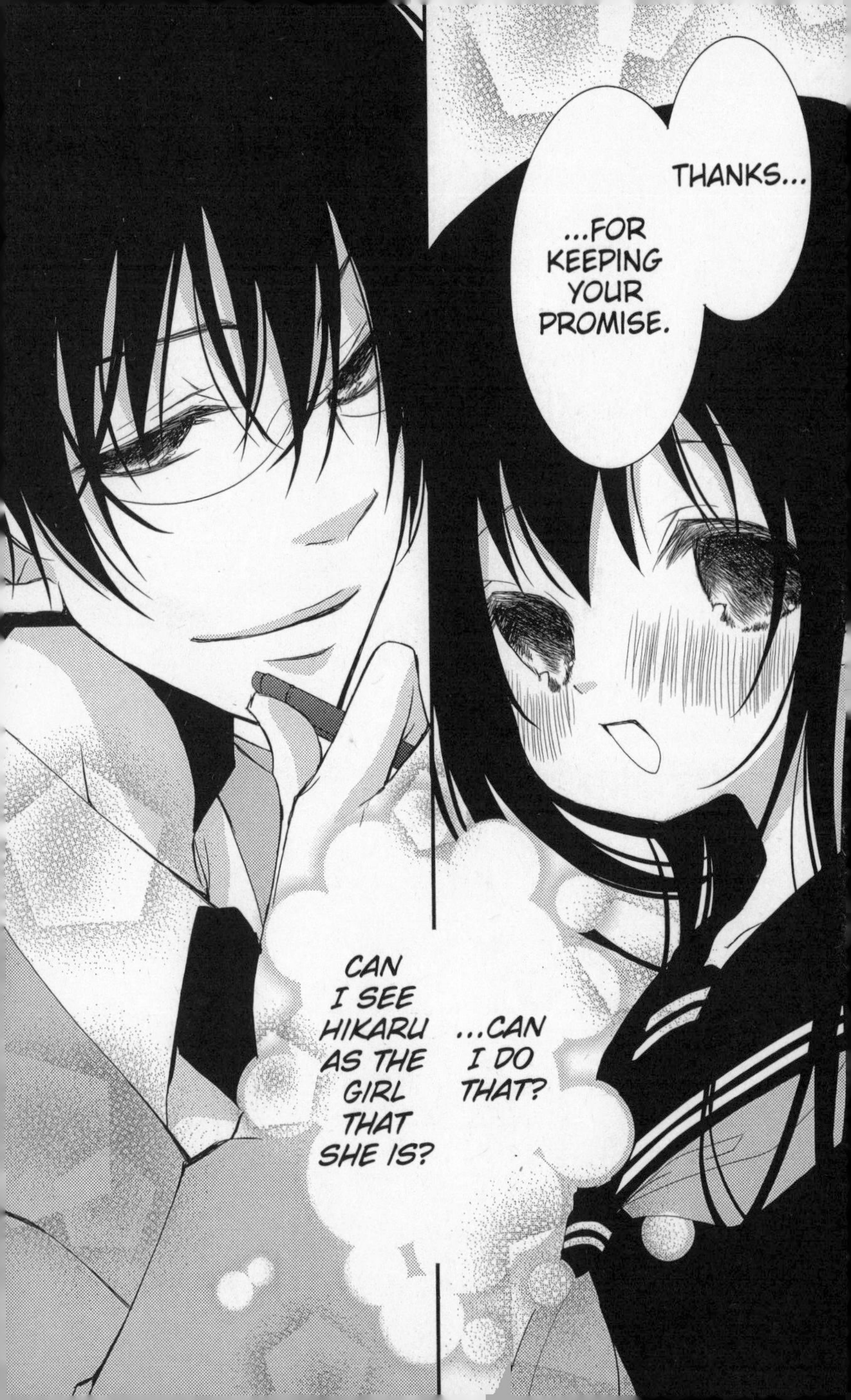
THANKS...
...FOR KEEPING YOUR PROMISE.
...CAN I DO THAT?
CAN I SEE HIKARU AS THE GIRL THAT SHE IS?

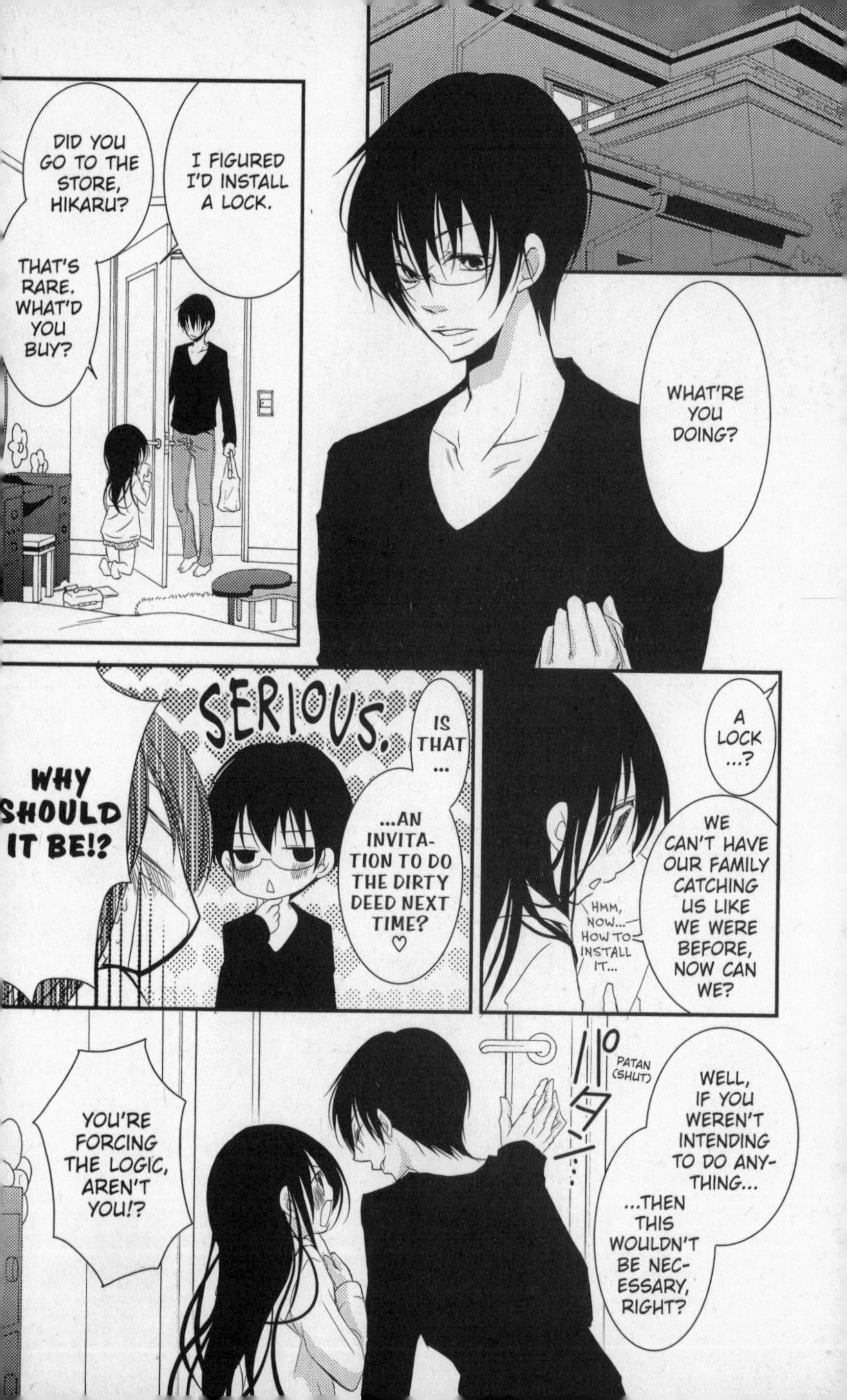
WHAT'RE YOU DOING?
I FIGURED I'D INSTALL A LOCK.
DID YOU GO TO THE STORE, HIKARU?
THAT'S RARE. WHAT'D YOU BUY?
A LOCK ...?
WE CAN'T HAVE OUR FAMILY CATCHING US LIKE WE WERE BEFORE, NOW CAN WE?
HMM, NOW... HOW TO INSTALL IT...
IS THAT ...
...AN INVITATION TO DO THE DIRTY DEED NEXT TIME? ♡
SERIOUS.
WHY SHOULD IT BE!?
PATAN (SHUT)
WELL, IF YOU WEREN'T INTENDING TO DO ANYTHING...
...THEN THIS WOULDN'T BE NECESSARY, RIGHT?
YOU'RE FORCING THE LOGIC, AREN'T YOU!?

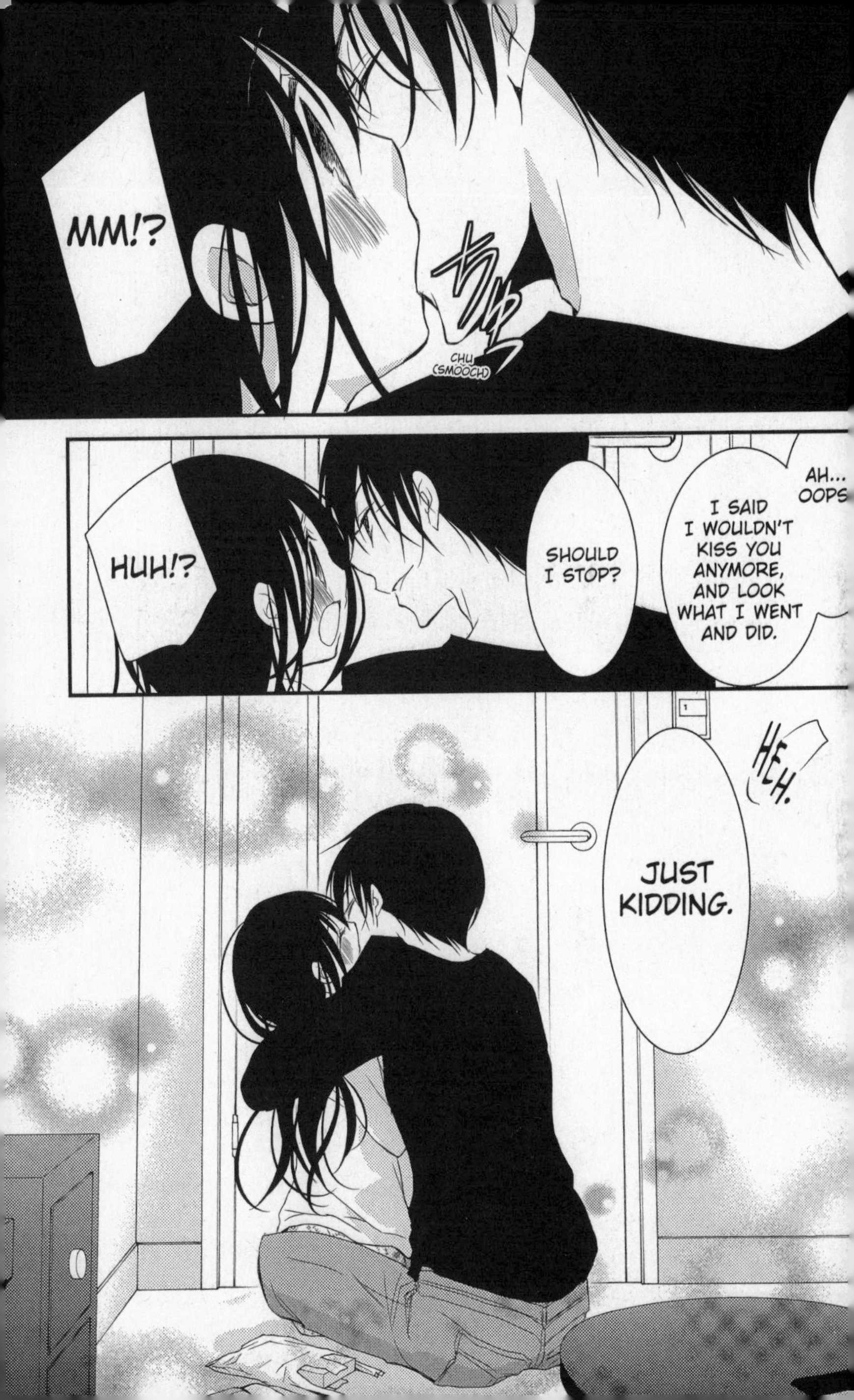
MM!?
CHU (SMOOCH)
AH... OOPS
I SAID I WOULDN'T KISS YOU ANYMORE, AND LOOK WHAT I WENT AND DID.
SHOULD I STOP?
HUH!?
HEH.
JUST KIDDING.

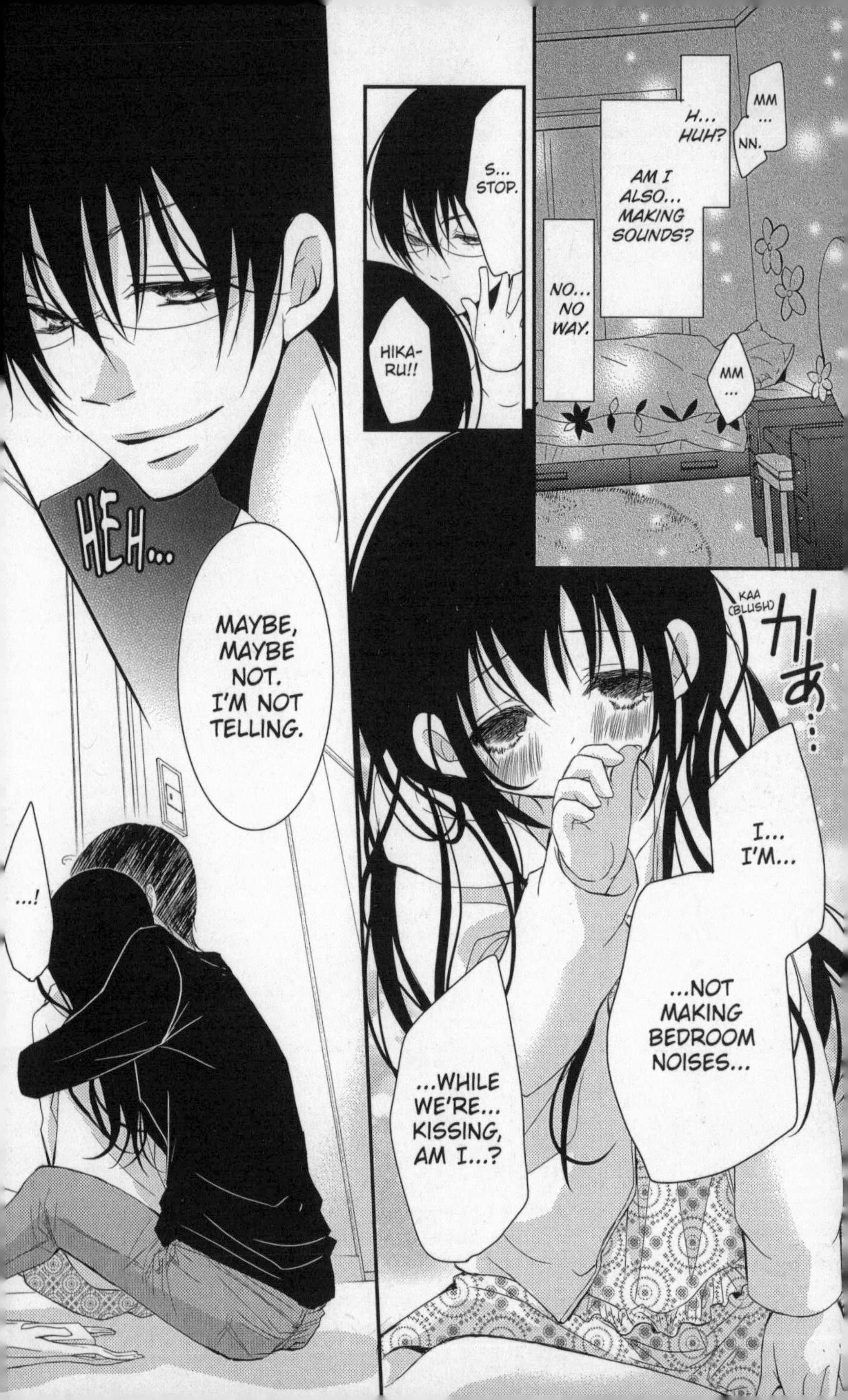
MM... NN.
H... HUH?
AM I ALSO... MAKING SOUNDS?
NO... NO WAY.
MM...
S... STOP.
HIKA-RU!!
KAA (BLUSH)
I... I'M...
...NOT MAKING BEDROOM NOISES...
...WHILE WE'RE... KISSING, AM I...?
HEH...
MAYBE, MAYBE NOT. I'M NOT TELLING.
...!

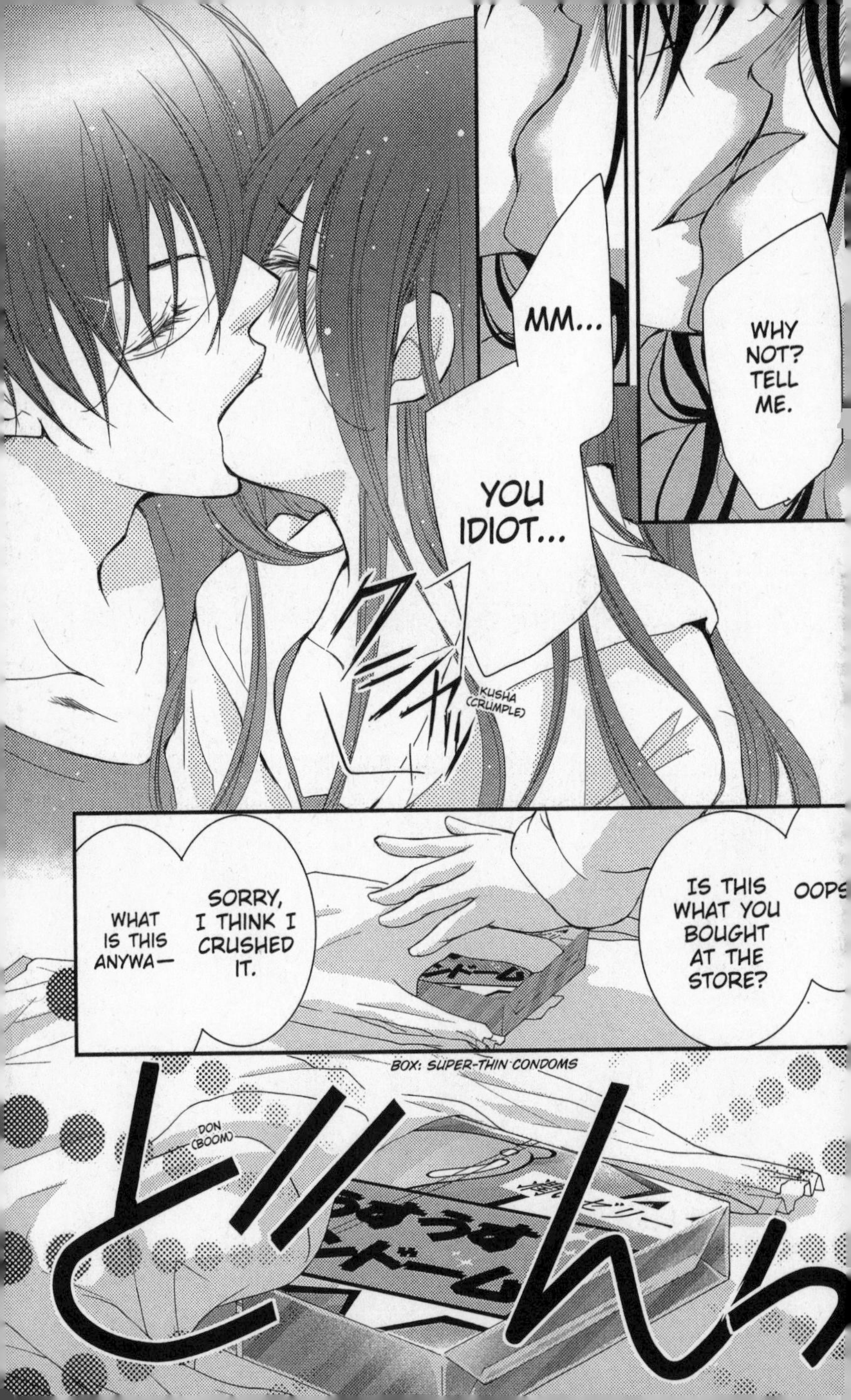
WHY NOT? TELL ME.
MM...
YOU IDIOT...
KUSHA (CRUMPLE)
OOPS
IS THIS WHAT YOU BOUGHT AT THE STORE?
SORRY, I THINK I CRUSHED IT.
WHAT IS THIS ANYWA—
BOX: SUPER-THIN CONDOMS
DON (BOOM)

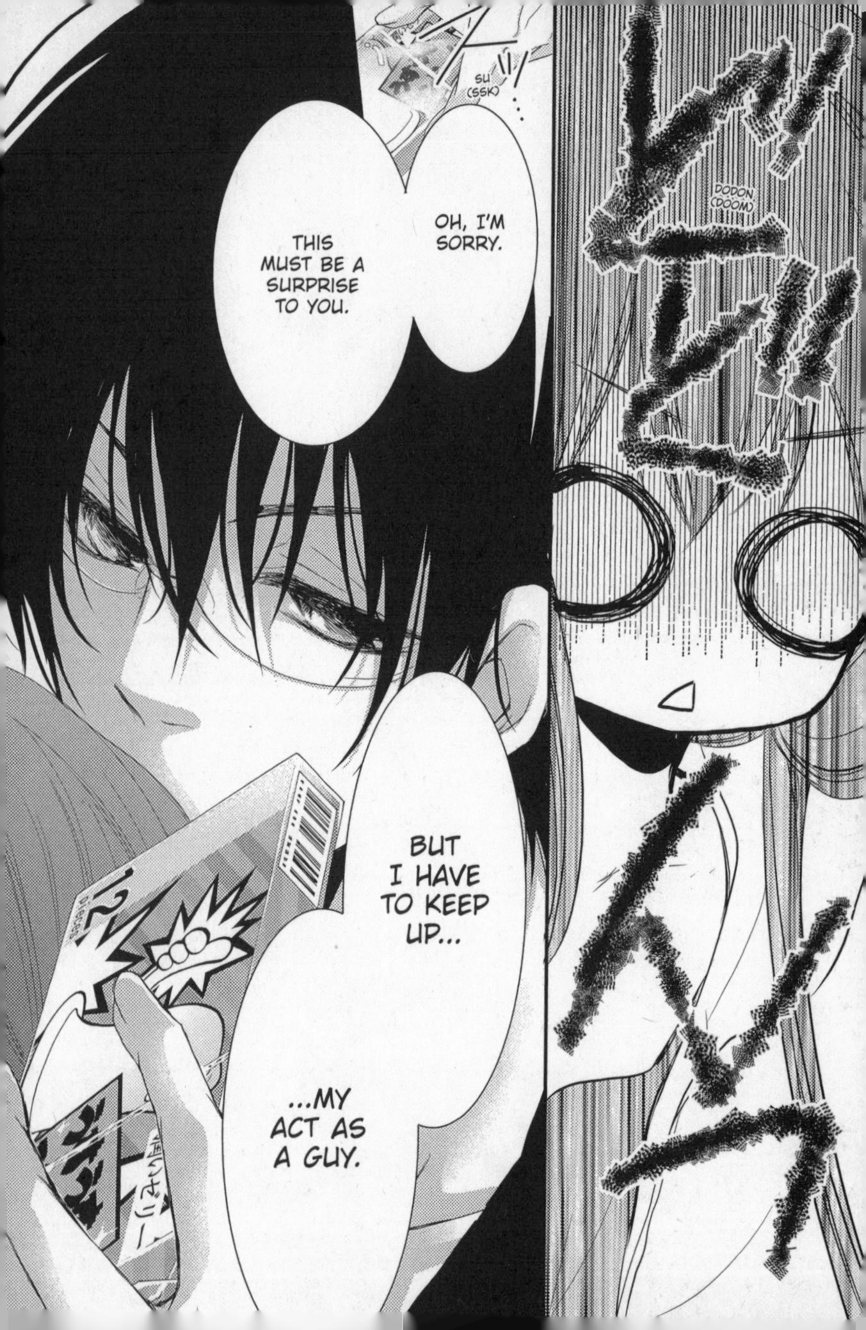
DODON
(DOOM)
SU
(SSK)
OH, I'M SORRY.
THIS MUST BE A SURPRISE TO YOU.
BUT I HAVE TO KEEP UP...
...MY ACT AS A GUY.

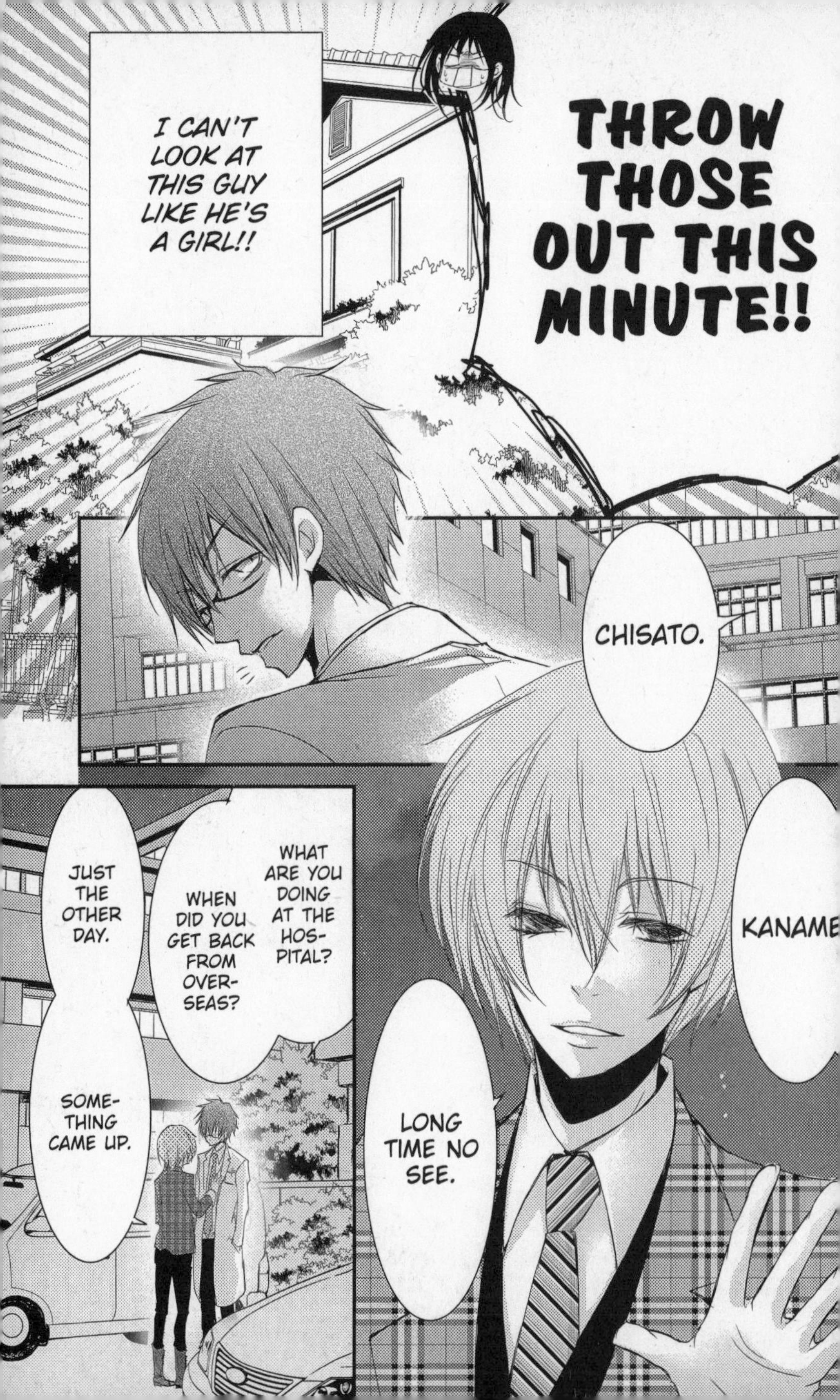
THROW THOSE OUT THIS MINUTE!!
I CAN'T LOOK AT THIS GUY LIKE HE'S A GIRL!!
CHISATO.
KANAME
LONG TIME NO SEE.
WHAT ARE YOU DOING AT THE HOS-PITAL?
WHEN DID YOU GET BACK FROM OVER-SEAS?
JUST THE OTHER DAY.
SOME-THING CAME UP.

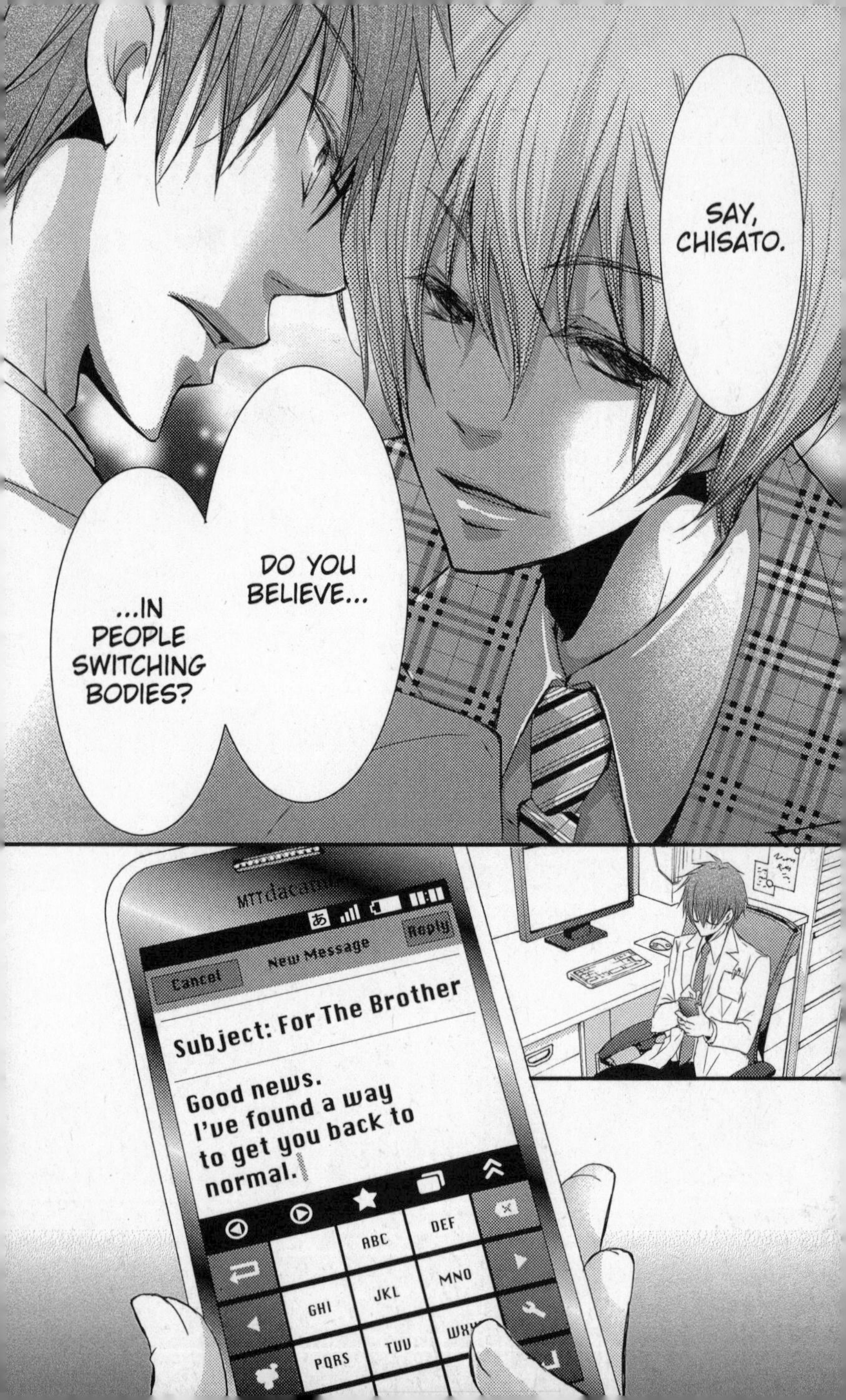
SAY, CHISATO.
DO YOU BELIEVE...
...IN PEOPLE SWITCHING BODIES?
Reply
New Message
Cancel
Subject: For The Brother
Good news. I've found a way to get you back to normal.
ABC
DEF
GHI
JKL
MNO
PQRS
TUV

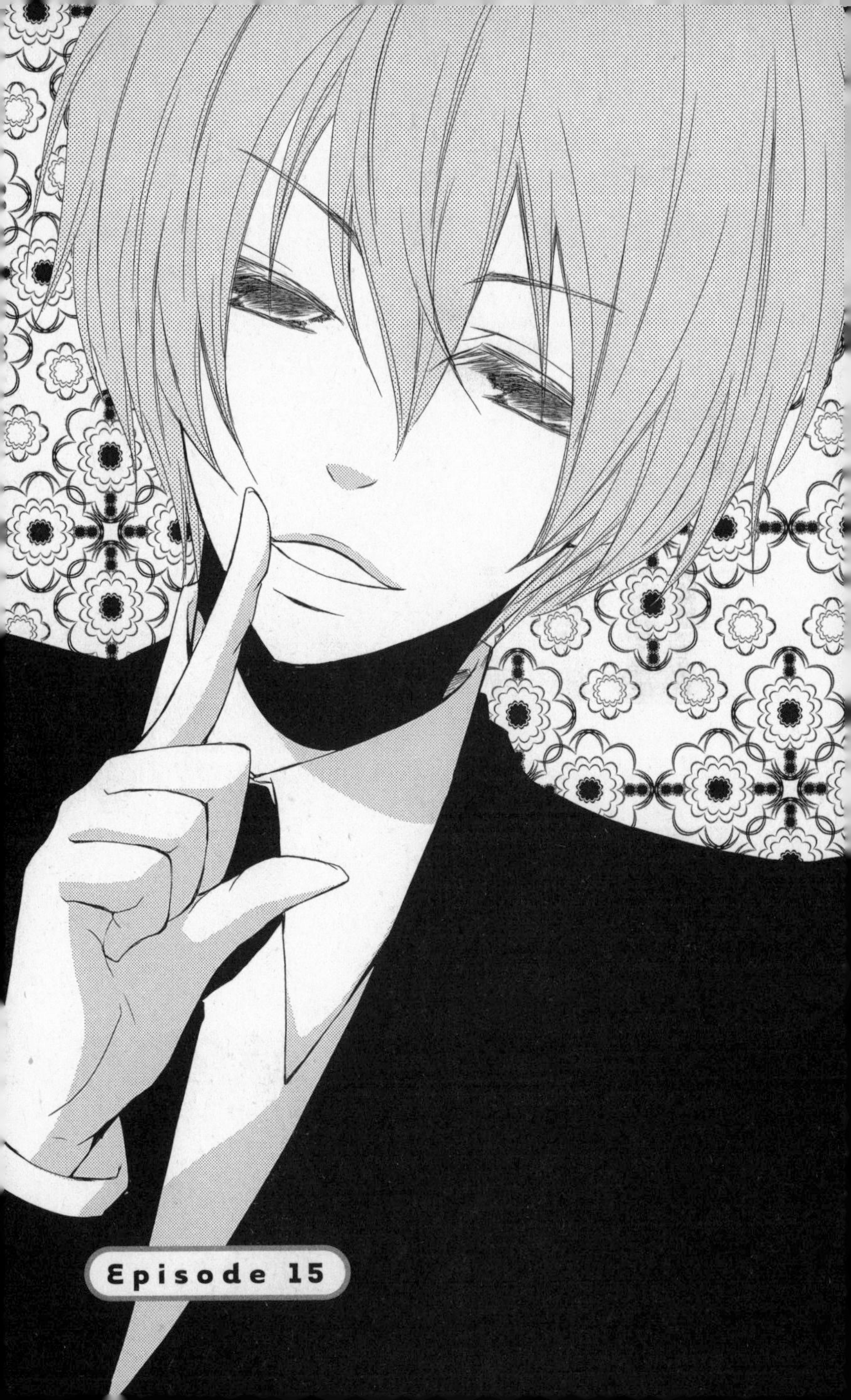
Episode 15

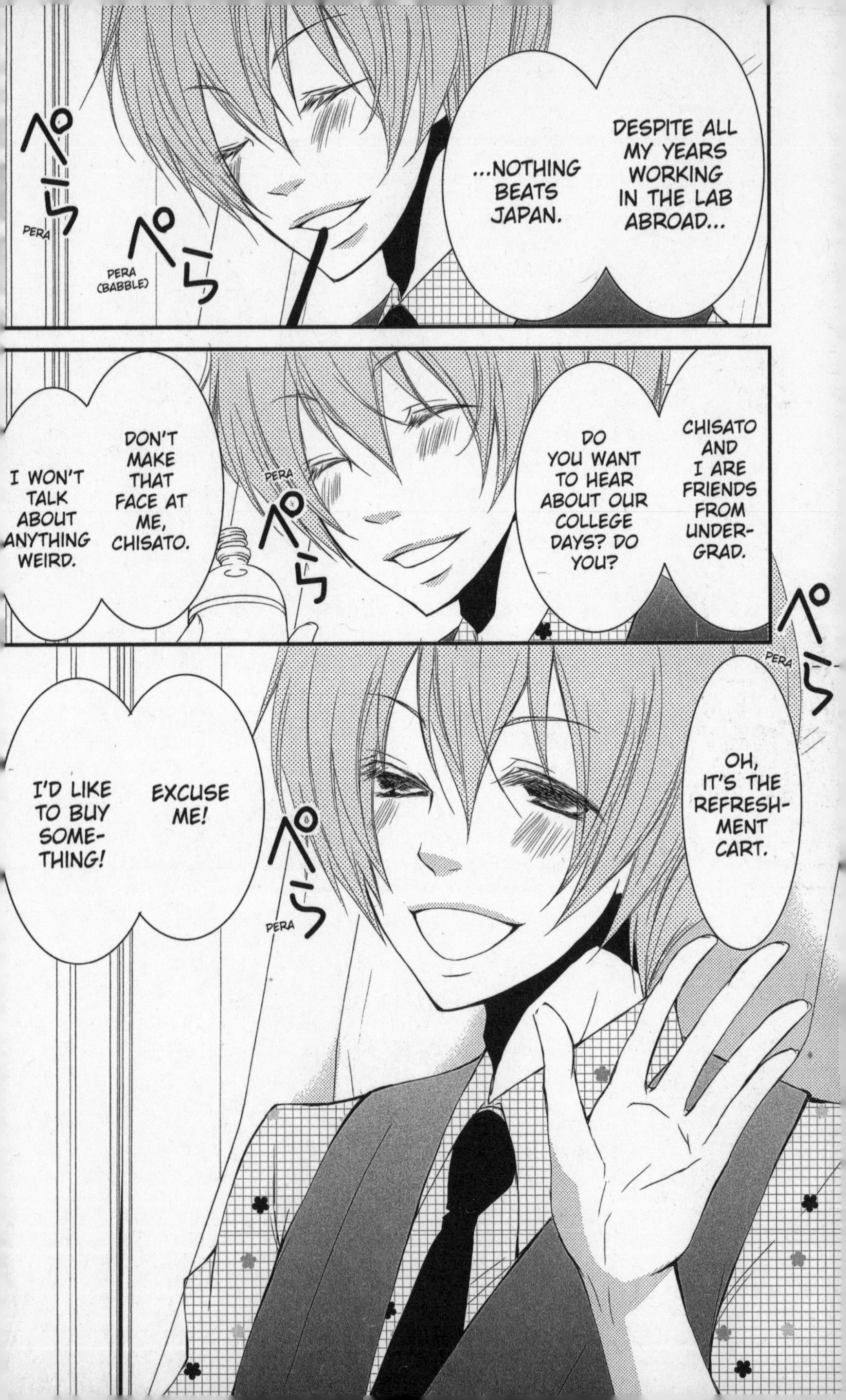
DESPITE ALL MY YEARS WORKING IN THE LAB ABROAD...
...NOTHING BEATS JAPAN.
ぺら
PERA (BABBLE)
ぺら
PERA
CHISATO AND I ARE FRIENDS FROM UNDER-GRAD.
DO YOU WANT TO HEAR ABOUT OUR COLLEGE DAYS? DO YOU?
ぺら
PERA
DON'T MAKE THAT FACE AT ME, CHISATO.
I WON'T TALK ABOUT ANYTHING WEIRD.
ぺら
PERA
OH, IT'S THE REFRESH-MENT CART.
ぺら
PERA
EXCUSE ME!
I'D LIKE TO BUY SOME-THING!

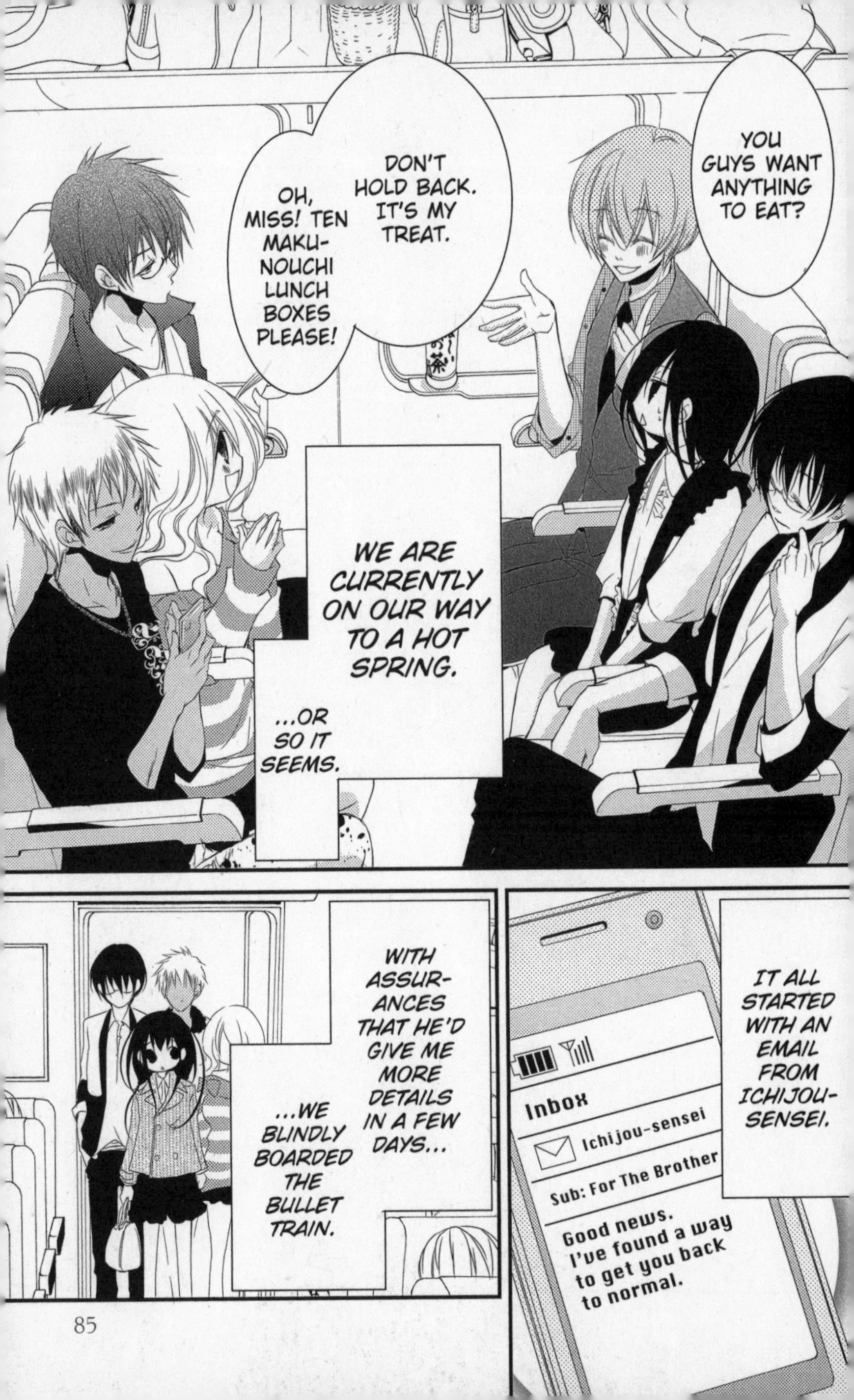
YOU GUYS WANT ANYTHING TO EAT?
DON'T HOLD BACK. IT'S MY TREAT.
OH, MISS! TEN MAKU-NOUCHI LUNCH BOXES PLEASE!
WE ARE CURRENTLY ON OUR WAY TO A HOT SPRING.
...OR SO IT SEEMS.
IT ALL STARTED WITH AN EMAIL FROM ICHIJOU-SENSEI.
Inbox
Ichijou-sensei
Sub: For The Brother
Good news. I've found a way to get you back to normal.
WITH ASSUR-ANCES THAT HE'D GIVE ME MORE DETAILS IN A FEW DAYS...
...WE BLINDLY BOARDED THE BULLET TRAIN.

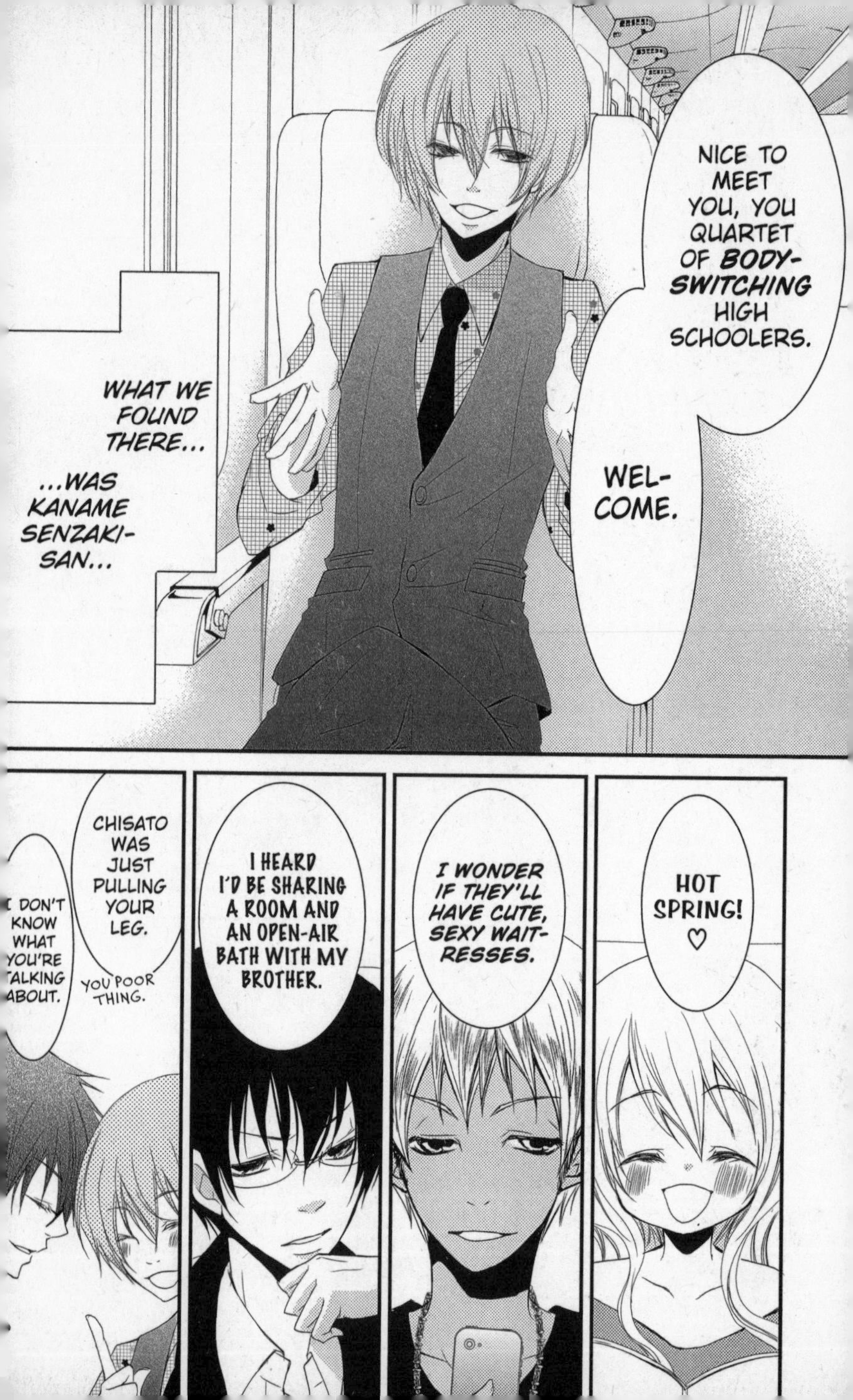
NICE TO MEET YOU, YOU QUARTET OF **BODY-SWITCHING** HIGH SCHOOLERS.
WEL-COME.
WHAT WE FOUND THERE...
...WAS KANAME SENZAKI-SAN...
HOT SPRING! ♡
I WONDER IF THEY'LL HAVE CUTE, SEXY WAIT-RESSES.
I HEARD I'D BE SHARING A ROOM AND AN OPEN-AIR BATH WITH MY BROTHER.
CHISATO WAS JUST PULLING YOUR LEG.
YOU POOR THING.
I DON'T KNOW WHAT YOU'RE TALKING ABOUT.

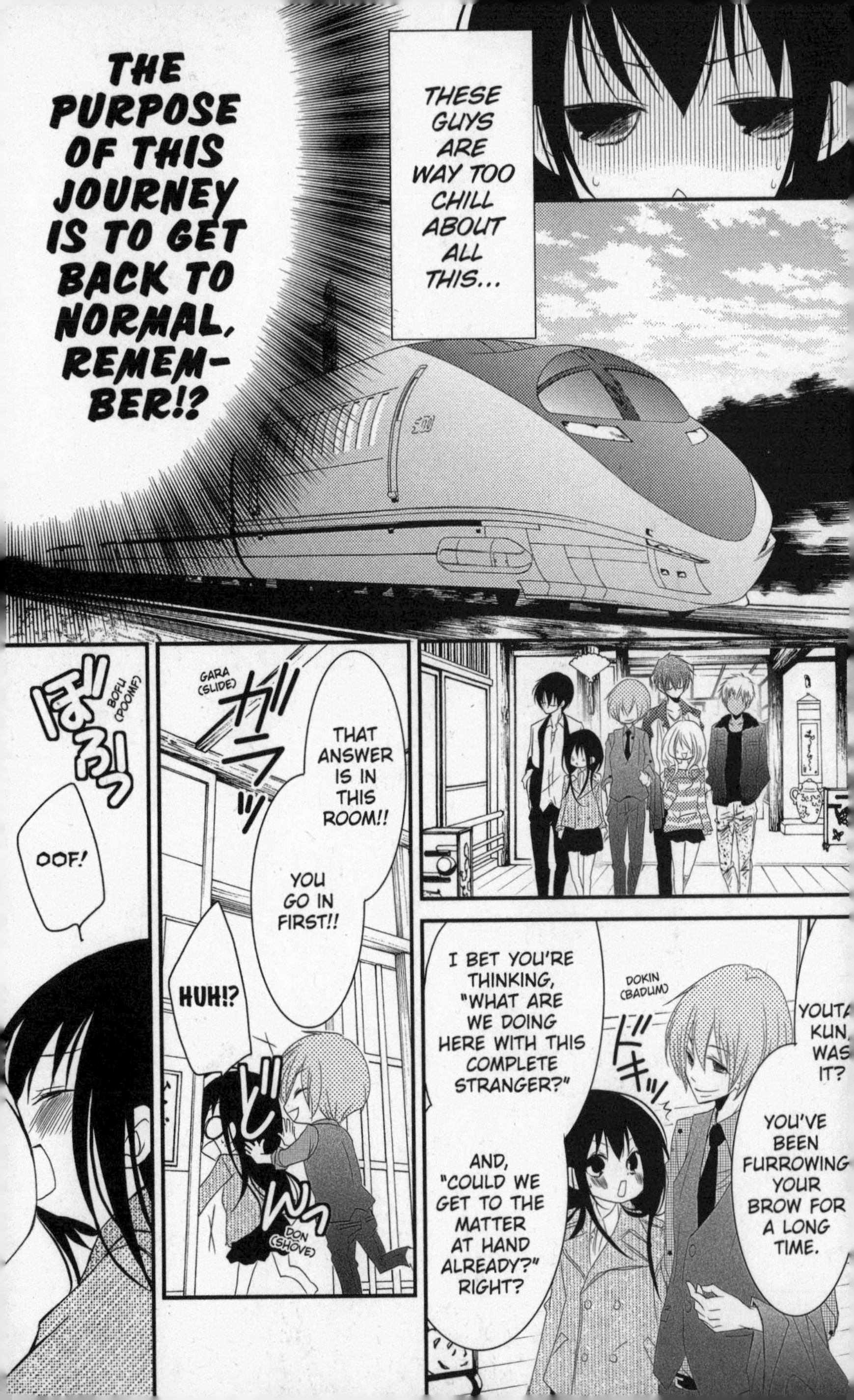

THESE GUYS ARE WAY TOO CHILL ABOUT ALL THIS...
THE PURPOSE OF THIS JOURNEY IS TO GET BACK TO NORMAL, REMEMBER!?
YOUTA-KUN, WAS IT?
YOU'VE BEEN FURROWING YOUR BROW FOR A LONG TIME.
DOKIN (BADUM)
I BET YOU'RE THINKING, "WHAT ARE WE DOING HERE WITH THIS COMPLETE STRANGER?"
AND, "COULD WE GET TO THE MATTER AT HAND ALREADY?" RIGHT?
GARA (SLIDE)
THAT ANSWER IS IN THIS ROOM!!
YOU GO IN FIRST!!
HUH!?
DON (SHOVE)
BOFU (POOMF)
OOF!

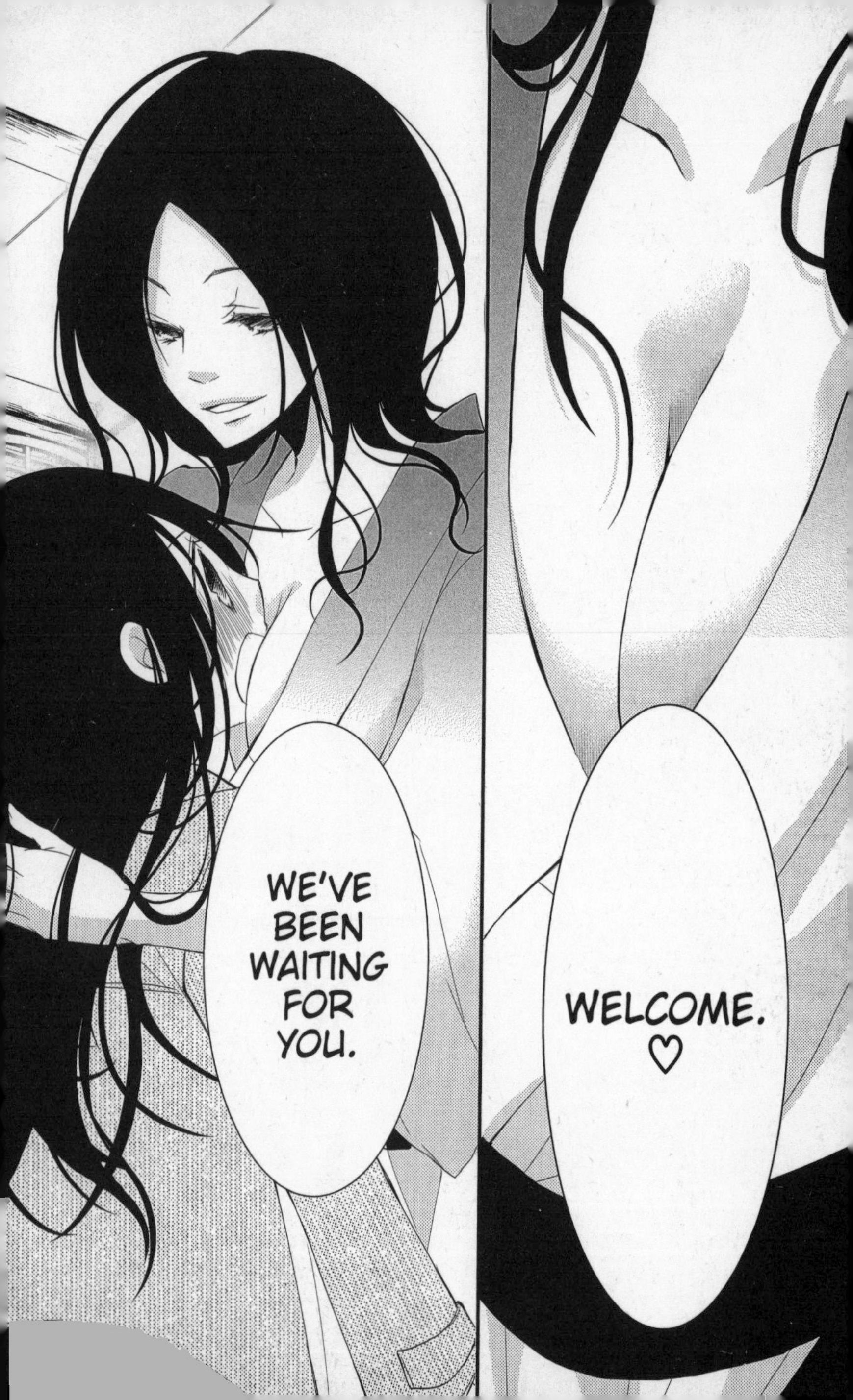
WELCOME. ♡
WE'VE BEEN WAITING FOR YOU.

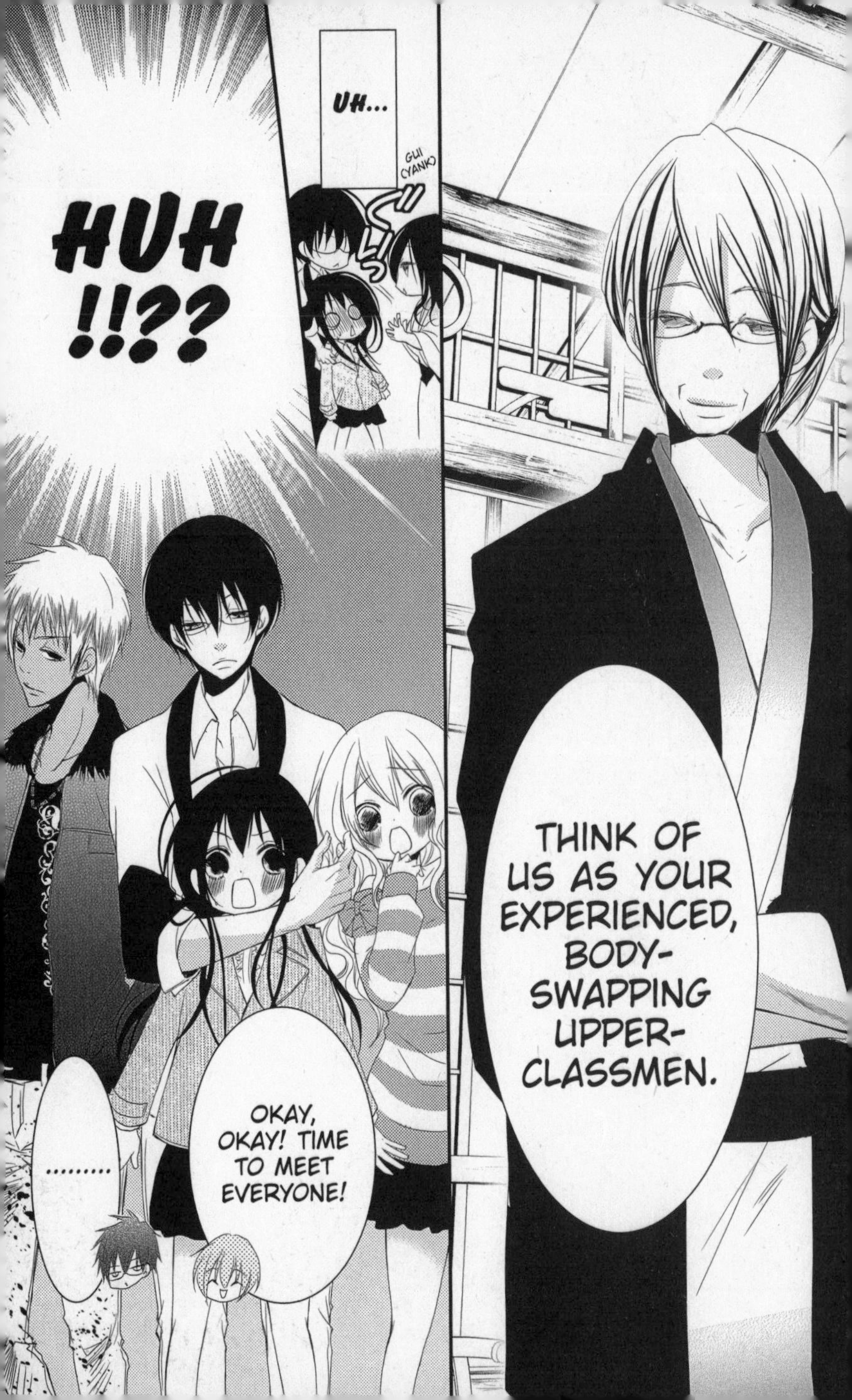
THINK OF US AS YOUR EXPERIENCED, BODY-SWAPPING UPPER-CLASSMEN.
UH...
GUI (YANK)
HUH !!??
OKAY, OKAY! TIME TO MEET EVERYONE!
....

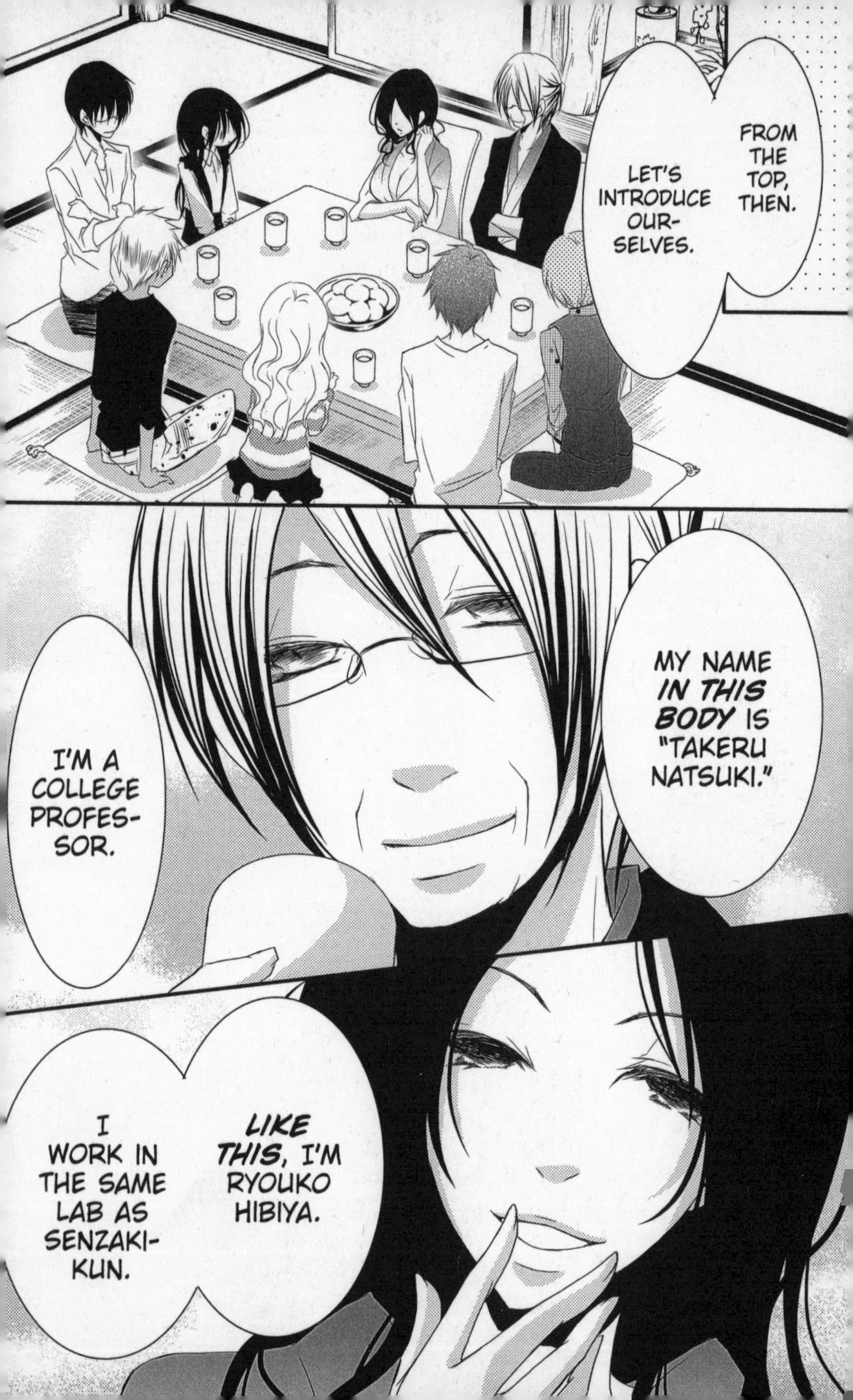
FROM THE TOP, THEN.
LET'S INTRODUCE OUR-SELVES.
MY NAME *IN THIS BODY* IS "TAKERU NATSUKI."
I'M A COLLEGE PROFES-SOR.
LIKE THIS, I'M RYOUKO HIBIYA.
I WORK IN THE SAME LAB AS SENZAKI-KUN.

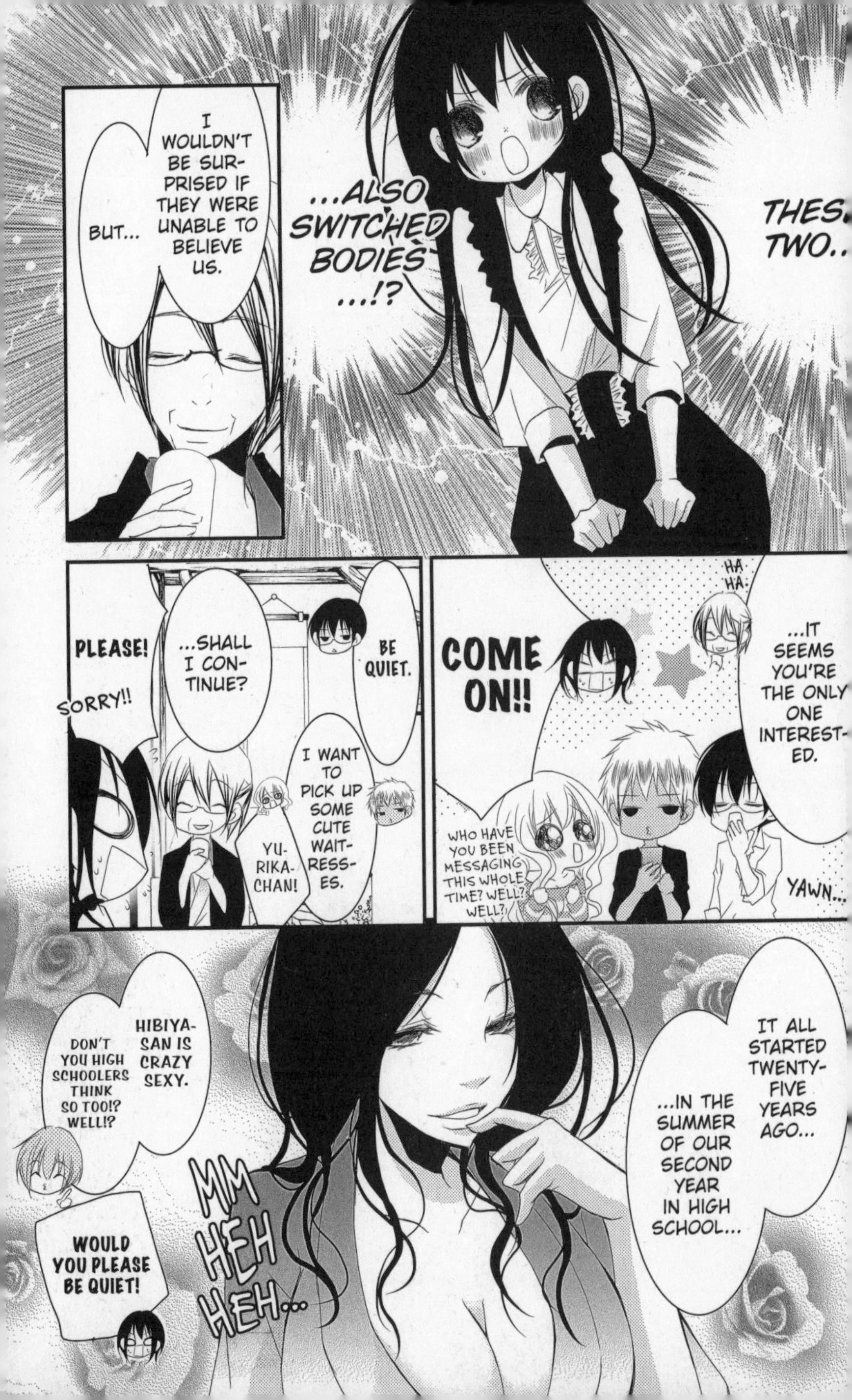
THES. TWO...
...ALSO SWITCHED BODIES ...!?
I WOULDN'T BE SURPRISED IF THEY WERE UNABLE TO BELIEVE US.
BUT...
HA HA.
...IT SEEMS YOU'RE THE ONLY ONE INTERESTED.
COME ON!!
YAWN...
WHO HAVE YOU BEEN MESSAGING THIS WHOLE TIME? WELL? WELL?
BE QUIET.
...SHALL I CONTINUE?
PLEASE!
SORRY!!
I WANT TO PICK UP SOME CUTE WAITRESSES.
YURIKA-CHAN!
IT ALL STARTED TWENTY-FIVE YEARS AGO...
...IN THE SUMMER OF OUR SECOND YEAR IN HIGH SCHOOL...
MM HEH HEH...
HIBIYA-SAN IS CRAZY SEXY.
DON'T YOU HIGH SCHOOLERS THINK SO TOO!? WELL!?
WOULD YOU PLEASE BE QUIET!

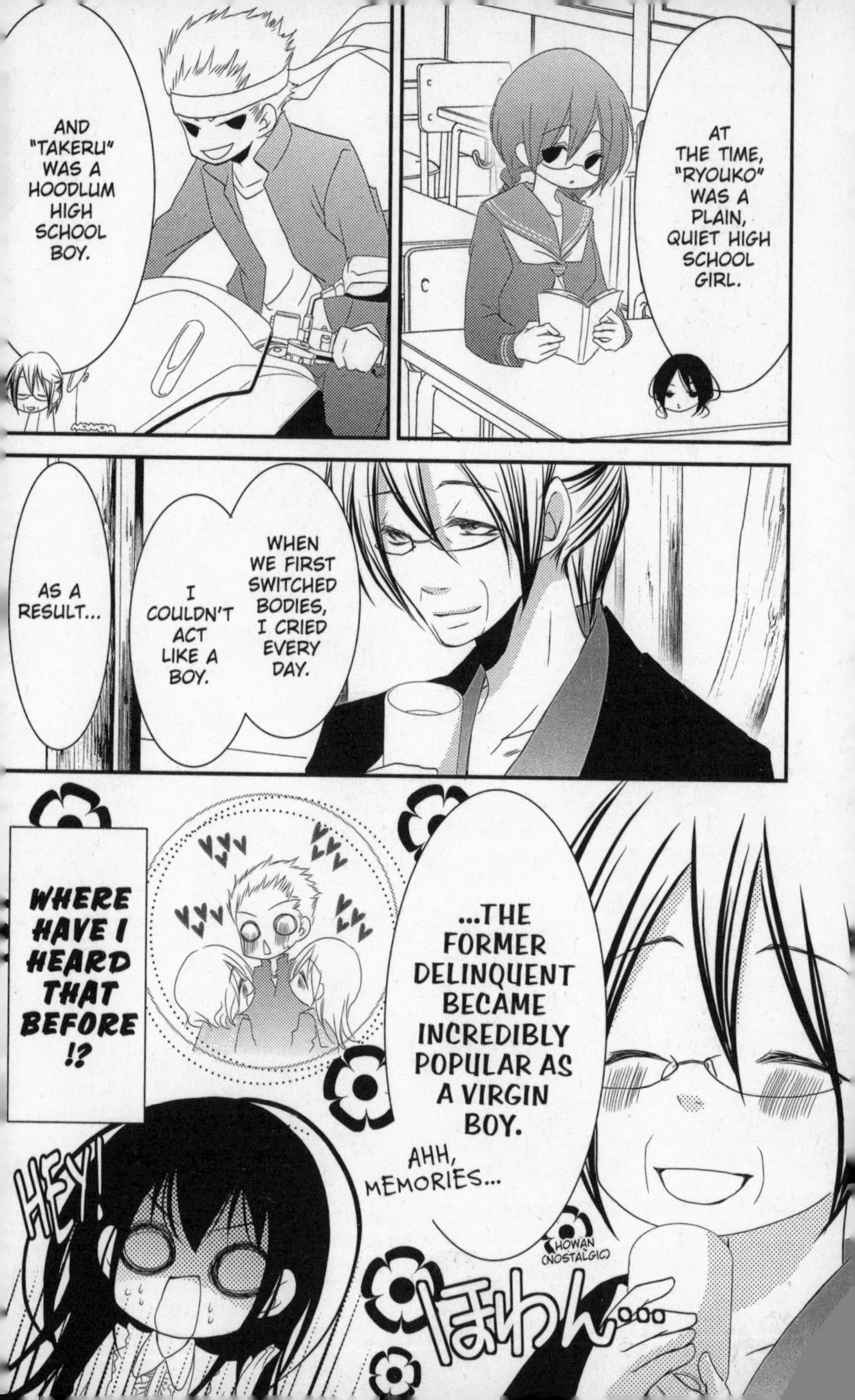
AT THE TIME, "RYOUKO" WAS A PLAIN, QUIET HIGH SCHOOL GIRL.
AND "TAKERU" WAS A HOODLUM HIGH SCHOOL BOY.
WHEN WE FIRST SWITCHED BODIES, I CRIED EVERY DAY.
I COULDN'T ACT LIKE A BOY.
AS A RESULT...
...THE FORMER DELINQUENT BECAME INCREDIBLY POPULAR AS A VIRGIN BOY.
AHH, MEMORIES...
HOWAN (NOSTALGIC)
ほわん…
WHERE HAVE I HEARD THAT BEFORE !?
HEY!

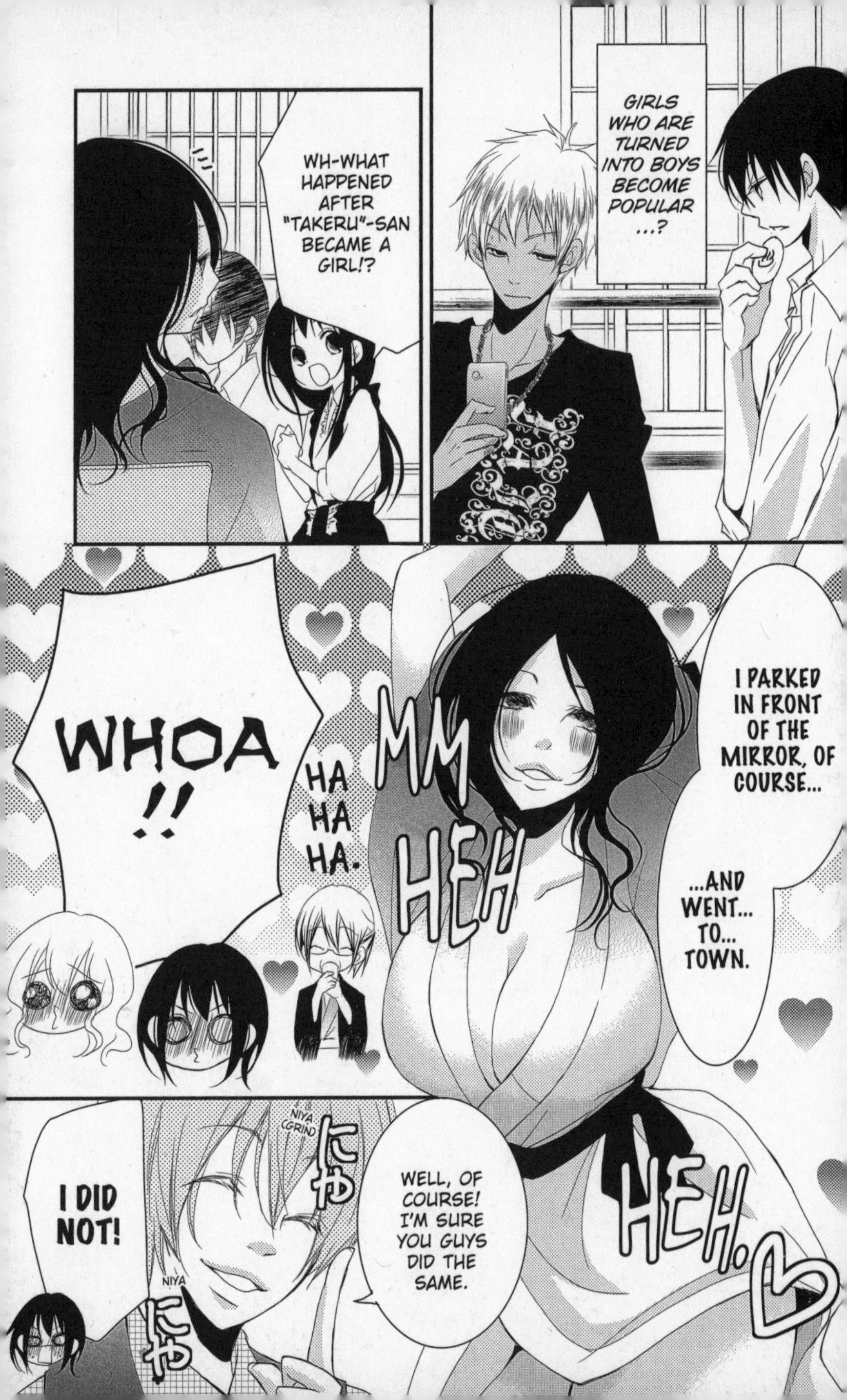
GIRLS WHO ARE TURNED INTO BOYS BECOME POPULAR ...?
WH-WHAT HAPPENED AFTER "TAKERU"-SAN BECAME A GIRL!?
I PARKED IN FRONT OF THE MIRROR, OF COURSE...
...AND WENT... TO... TOWN.
MM HEH
HA HA HA.
WHOA !!
HEH.
NIYA (GRIN)
にゆ
WELL, OF COURSE! I'M SURE YOU GUYS DID THE SAME.
I DID NOT!
NIYA
にゆ

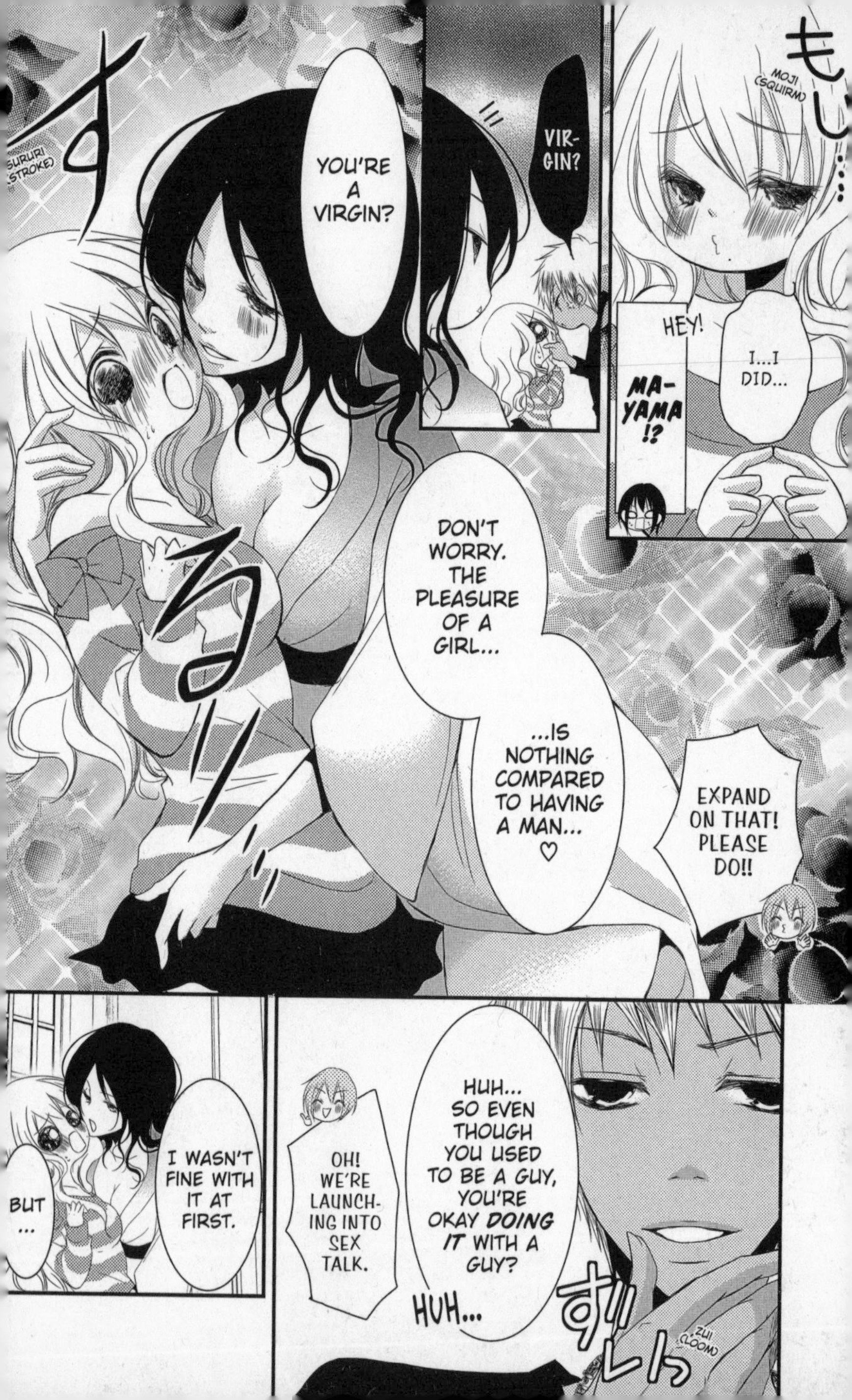
MOJI (SQUIRM)
I...I DID...
HEY!
MA-YAMA!?
VIR-GIN?
SURURI (STROKE)
YOU'RE A VIRGIN?
DON'T WORRY. THE PLEASURE OF A GIRL...
...IS NOTHING COMPARED TO HAVING A MAN... ♡
EXPAND ON THAT! PLEASE DO!!
HUH... SO EVEN THOUGH YOU USED TO BE A GUY, YOU'RE OKAY *DOING IT* WITH A GUY?
OH! WE'RE LAUNCH-ING INTO SEX TALK.
HUH...
ZUI (LOOM)
I WASN'T FINE WITH IT AT FIRST.
BUT ...

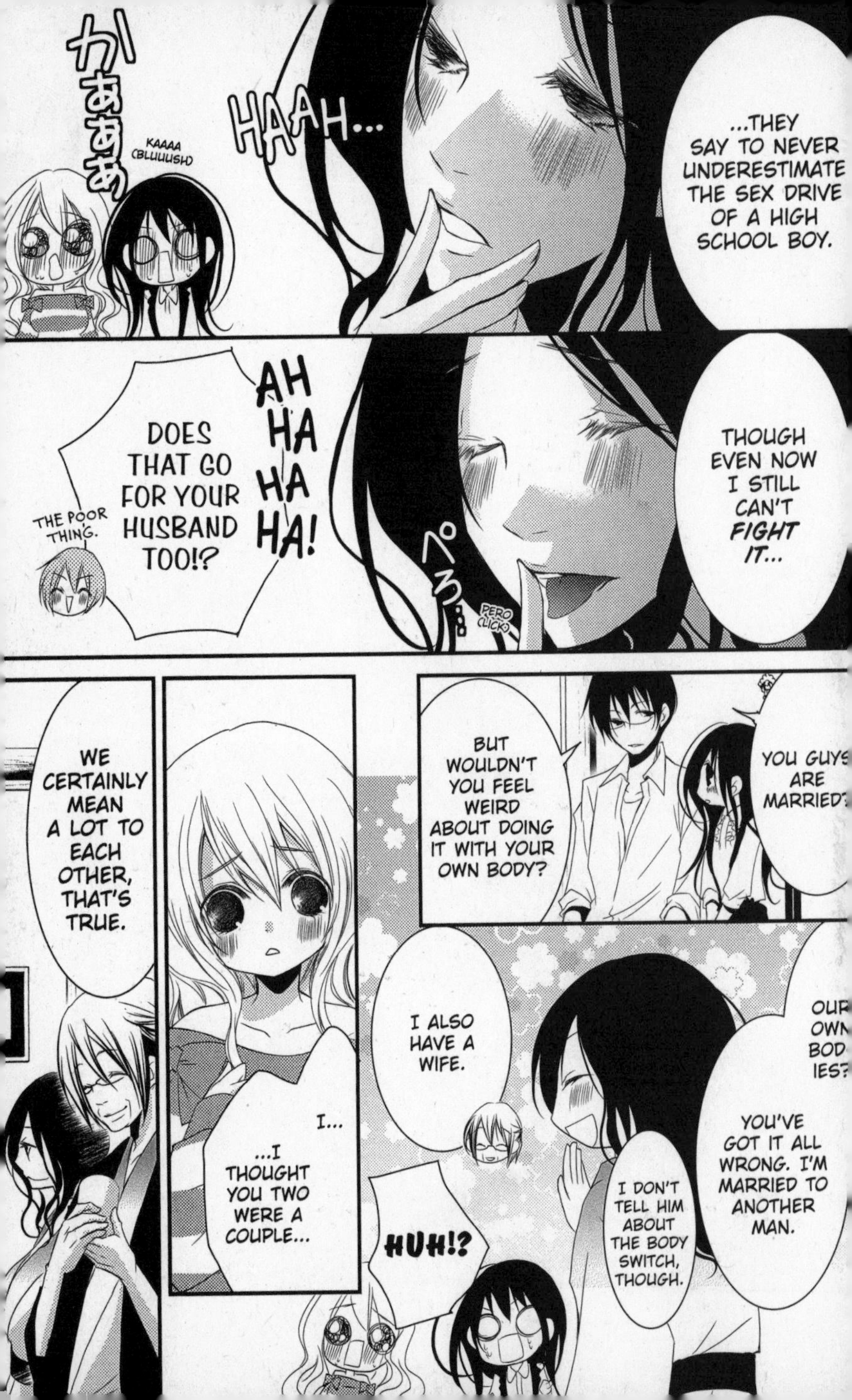
...THEY SAY TO NEVER UNDERESTIMATE THE SEX DRIVE OF A HIGH SCHOOL BOY.
HAAAH...
かあああ
KAAAA (BLUUUSH)
THOUGH EVEN NOW I STILL CAN'T *FIGHT IT*...
ぺろ
PERO (LICK)
AH HA HA HA!
DOES THAT GO FOR YOUR HUSBAND TOO!?
THE POOR THING.
YOU GUYS ARE MARRIED?
BUT WOULDN'T YOU FEEL WEIRD ABOUT DOING IT WITH YOUR OWN BODY?
OUR OWN BODIES?
YOU'VE GOT IT ALL WRONG. I'M MARRIED TO ANOTHER MAN.
I DON'T TELL HIM ABOUT THE BODY SWITCH, THOUGH.
I ALSO HAVE A WIFE.
HUH!?
I...
...I THOUGHT YOU TWO WERE A COUPLE...
WE CERTAINLY MEAN A LOT TO EACH OTHER, THAT'S TRUE.

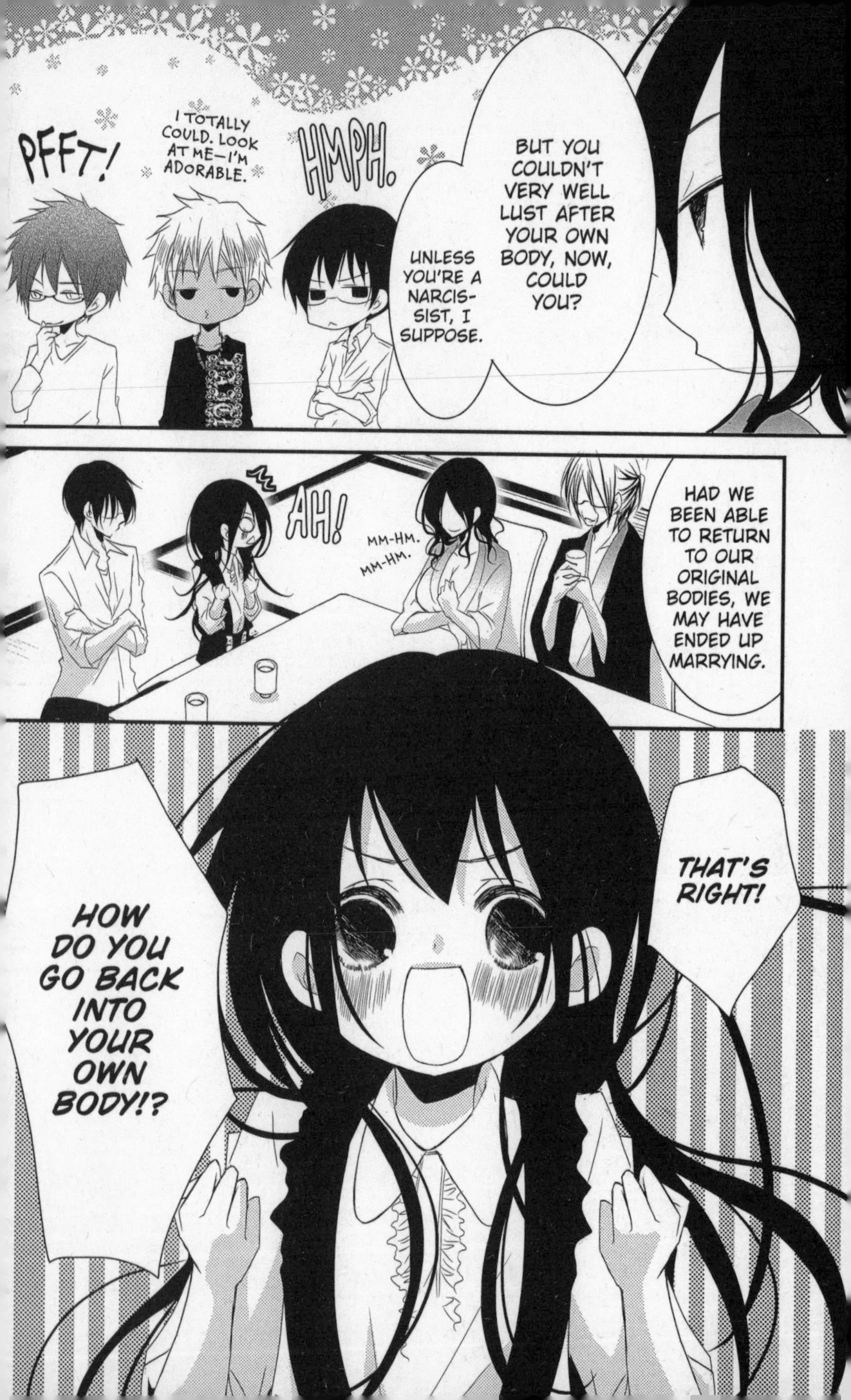
BUT YOU COULDN'T VERY WELL LUST AFTER YOUR OWN BODY, NOW, COULD YOU?
UNLESS YOU'RE A NARCISSIST, I SUPPOSE.
HMPH.
I TOTALLY COULD. LOOK AT ME—I'M ADORABLE.
PFFT!
HAD WE BEEN ABLE TO RETURN TO OUR ORIGINAL BODIES, WE MAY HAVE ENDED UP MARRYING.
MM-HM. MM-HM.
AH!
THAT'S RIGHT!
HOW DO YOU GO BACK INTO YOUR OWN BODY!?

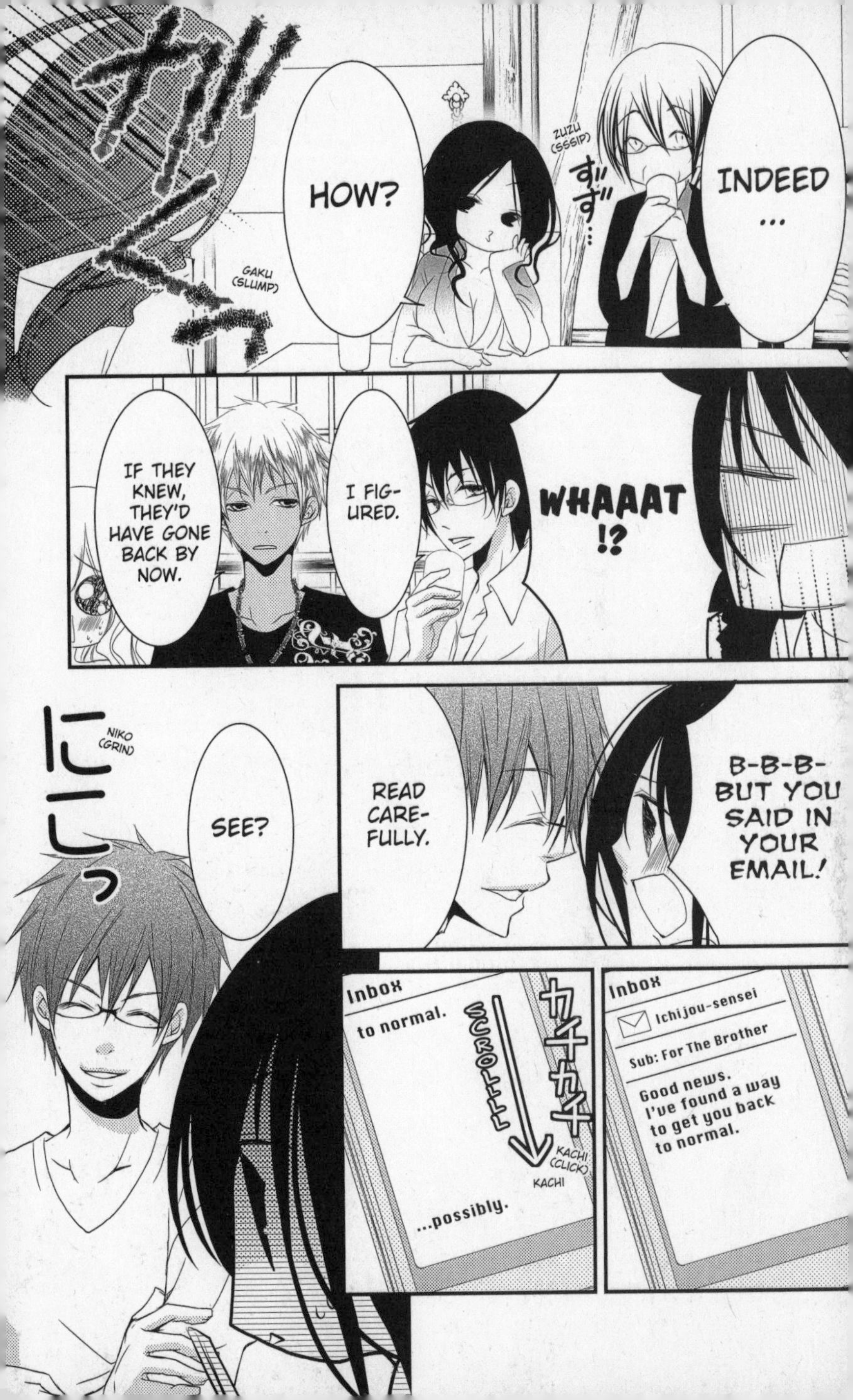
INDEED ...
ZUZU (SSSIP)
HOW?
GAKU (SLUMP)
WHAAAT !?
I FIG- URED.
IF THEY KNEW, THEY'D HAVE GONE BACK BY NOW.
B-B-B- BUT YOU SAID IN YOUR EMAIL!
READ CARE- FULLY.
Inbox
Ichijou-sensei
Sub: For The Brother
Good news. I've found a way to get you back to normal.
KACHI (CLICK)
KACHI
SCROLLLL
Inbox
to normal.
...possibly.
NIKO (GRIN)
SEE?

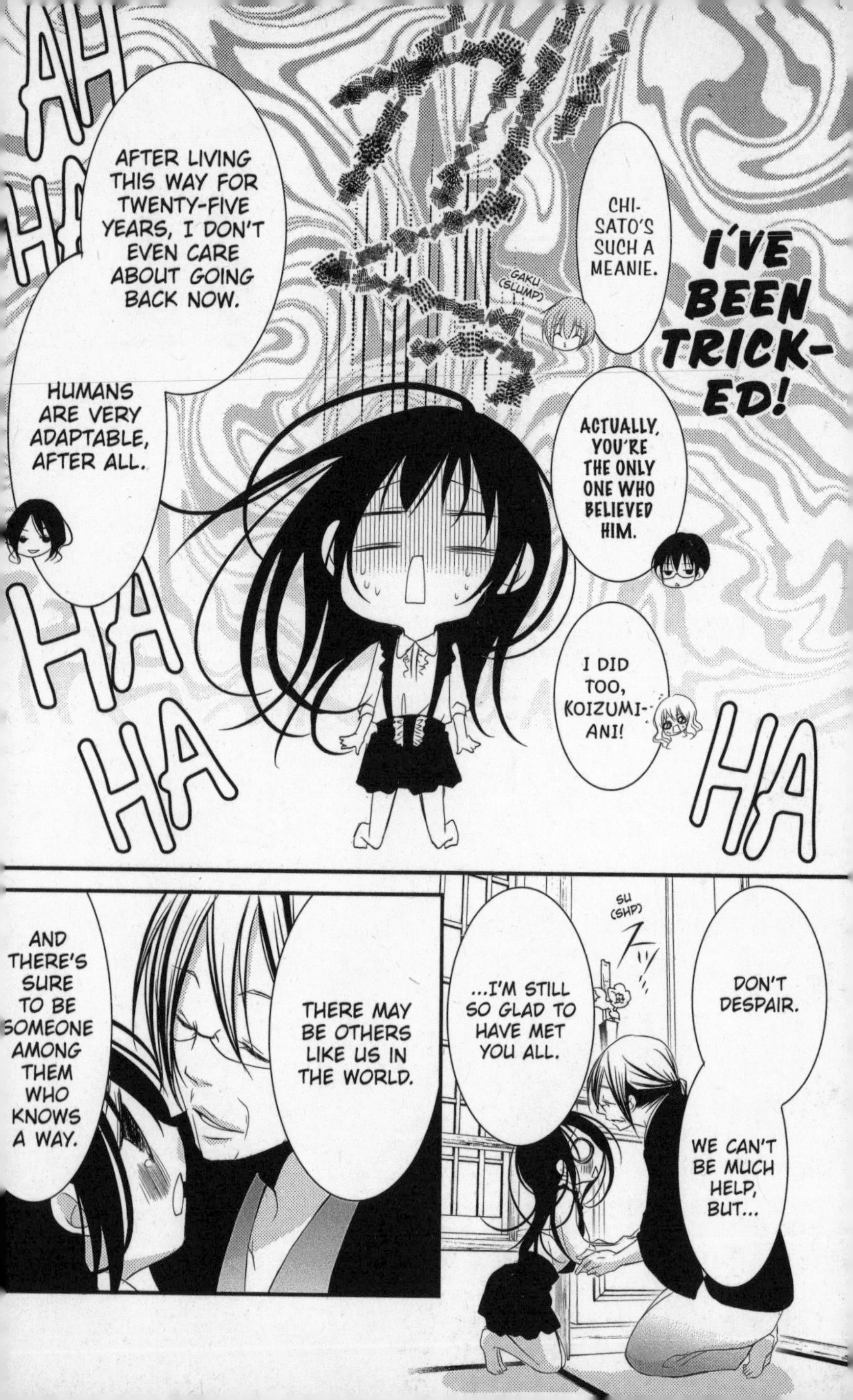

I'VE BEEN TRICK-ED!
CHI-SATO'S SUCH A MEANIE.
GAKU (SLUMP)
ACTUALLY, YOU'RE THE ONLY ONE WHO BELIEVED HIM.
I DID TOO, KOIZUMI-ANI!
HA
AH HA
AFTER LIVING THIS WAY FOR TWENTY-FIVE YEARS, I DON'T EVEN CARE ABOUT GOING BACK NOW.
HUMANS ARE VERY ADAPTABLE, AFTER ALL.
HA HA HA
DON'T DESPAIR.
WE CAN'T BE MUCH HELP, BUT...
SU (SHP)
...I'M STILL SO GLAD TO HAVE MET YOU ALL.
THERE MAY BE OTHERS LIKE US IN THE WORLD.
AND THERE'S SURE TO BE SOMEONE AMONG THEM WHO KNOWS A WAY.

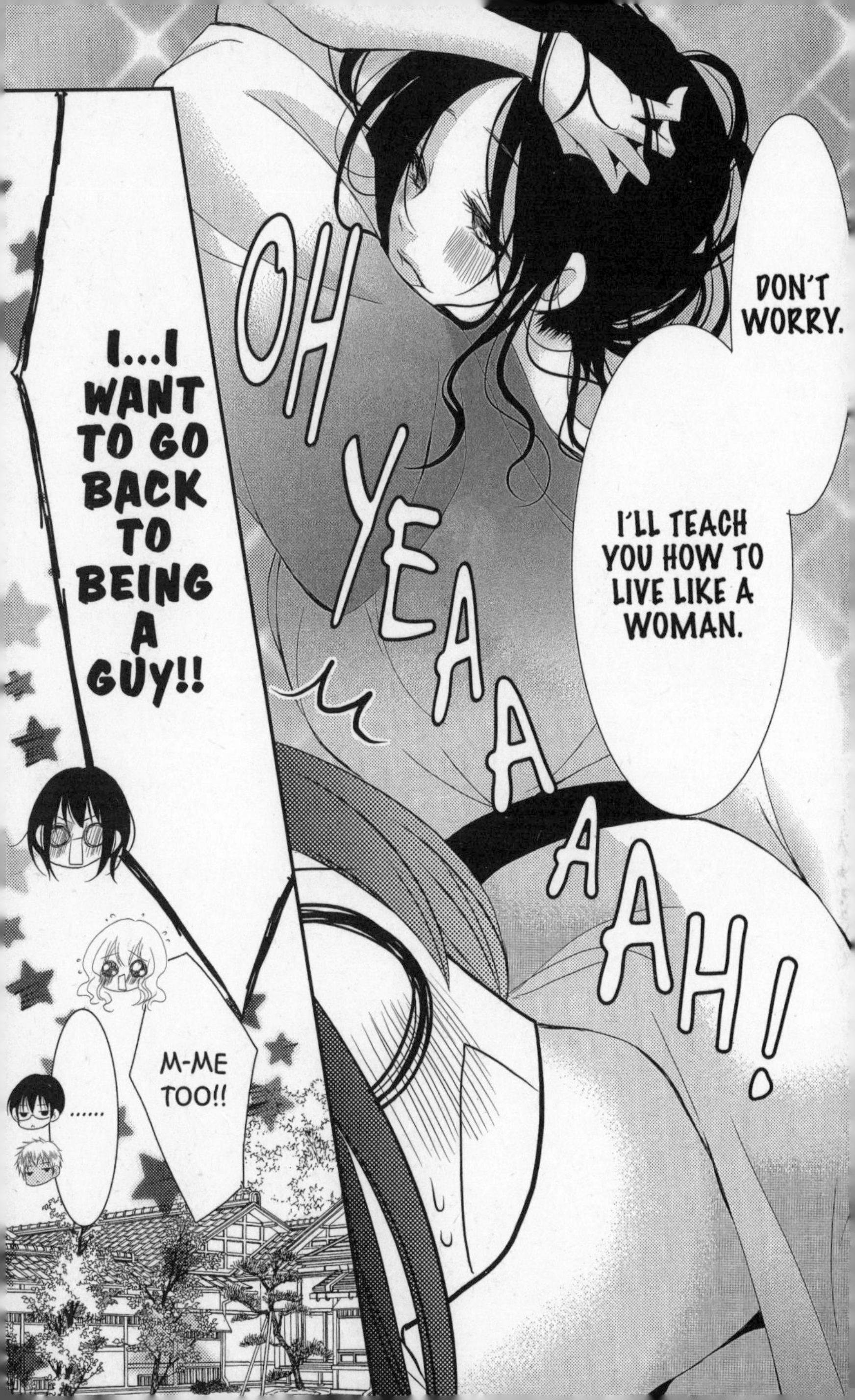
DON'T WORRY.
I'LL TEACH YOU HOW TO LIVE LIKE A WOMAN.
OH YEAAAAAH!
I...I WANT TO GO BACK TO BEING A GUY!!
M-ME TOO!!
......

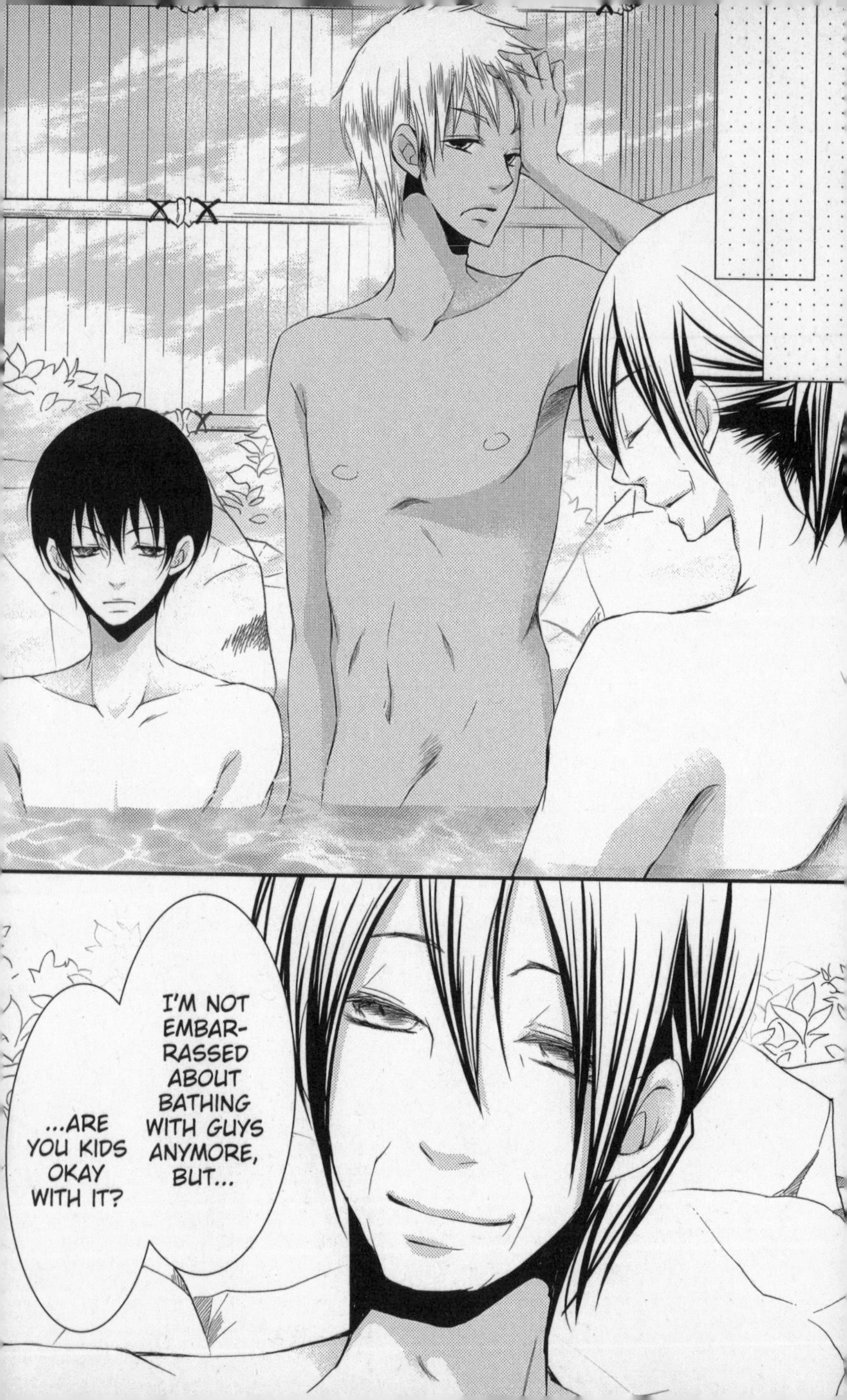
I'M NOT EMBAR-RASSED ABOUT BATHING WITH GUYS ANYMORE, BUT...
...ARE YOU KIDS OKAY WITH IT?

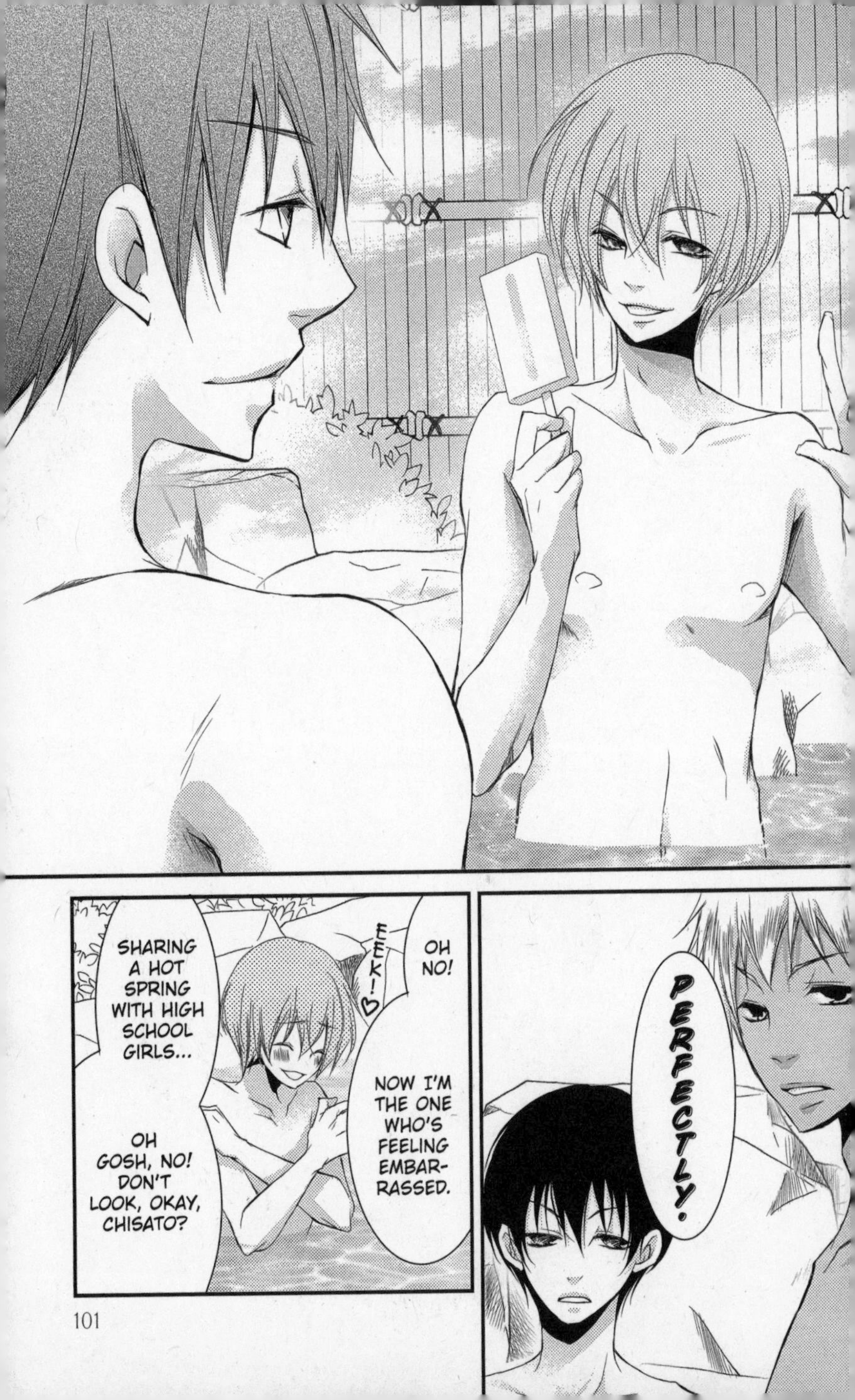
PERFECTLY.
OH NO! NOW I'M THE ONE WHO'S FEELING EMBARRASSED.
EEK! ♡
SHARING A HOT SPRING WITH HIGH SCHOOL GIRLS... OH GOSH, NO! DON'T LOOK, OKAY, CHISATO?

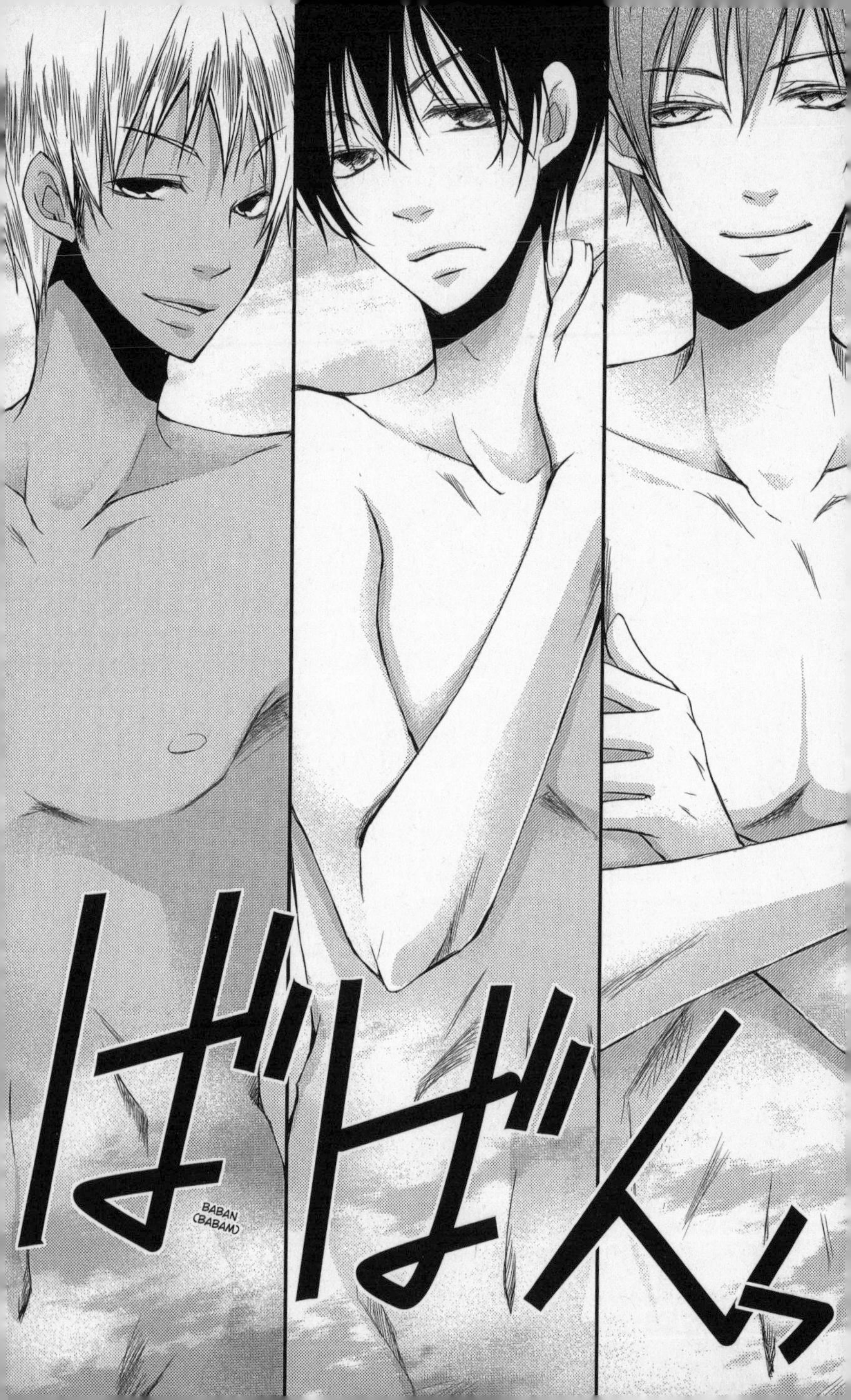
ばばん
BABAN
(BABAM)

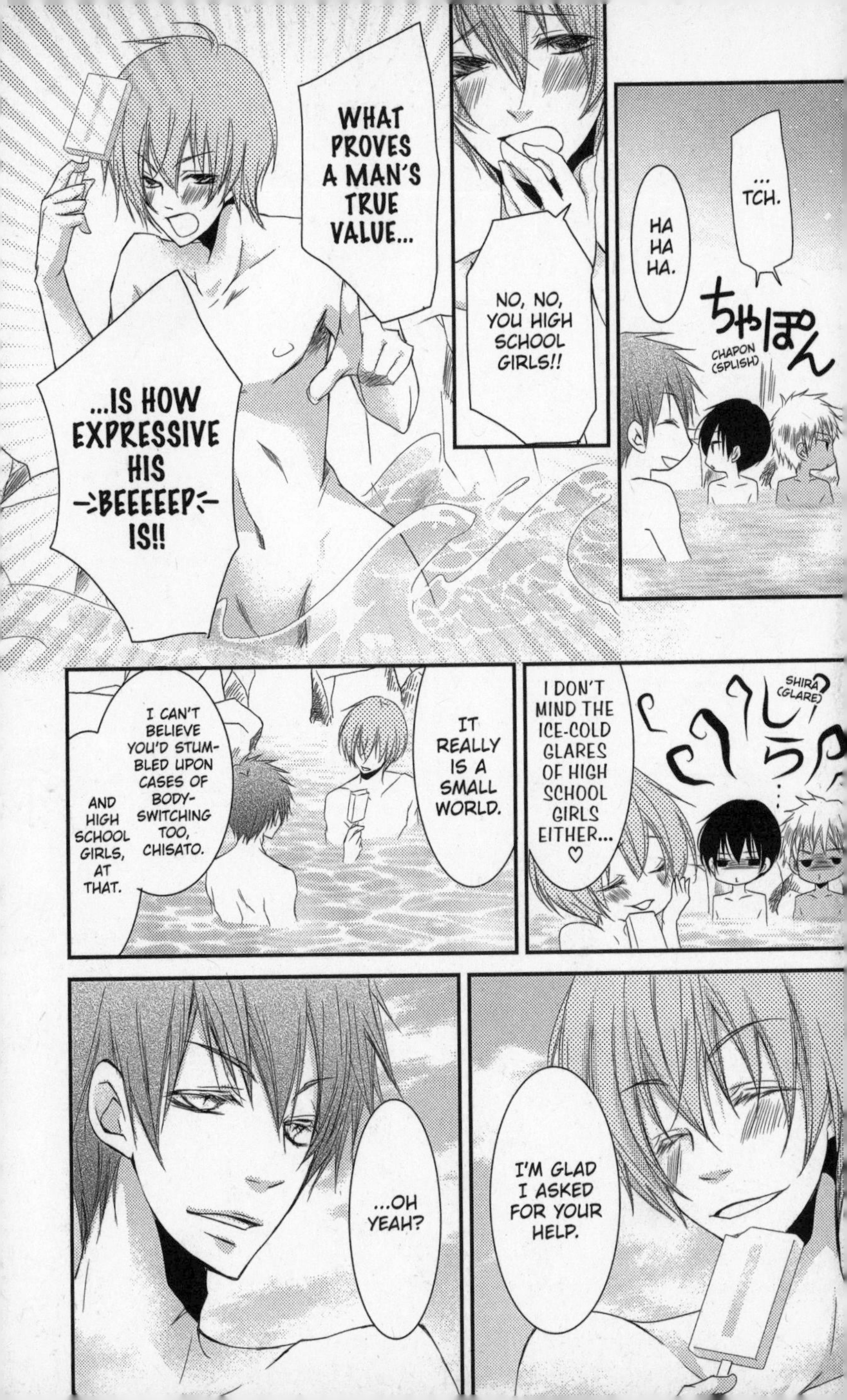
WHAT PROVES A MAN'S TRUE VALUE...
...IS HOW EXPRESSIVE HIS -BEEEEEP- IS!!
NO, NO, YOU HIGH SCHOOL GIRLS!!
...TCH.
HA HA HA.
ちゃぽん
CHAPON (SPLISH)
しら
SHIRA (GLARE)
I DON'T MIND THE ICE-COLD GLARES OF HIGH SCHOOL GIRLS EITHER...♡
IT REALLY IS A SMALL WORLD.
I CAN'T BELIEVE YOU'D STUMBLED UPON CASES OF BODY-SWITCHING TOO, CHISATO.
AND HIGH SCHOOL GIRLS, AT THAT.
I'M GLAD I ASKED FOR YOUR HELP.
...OH YEAH?

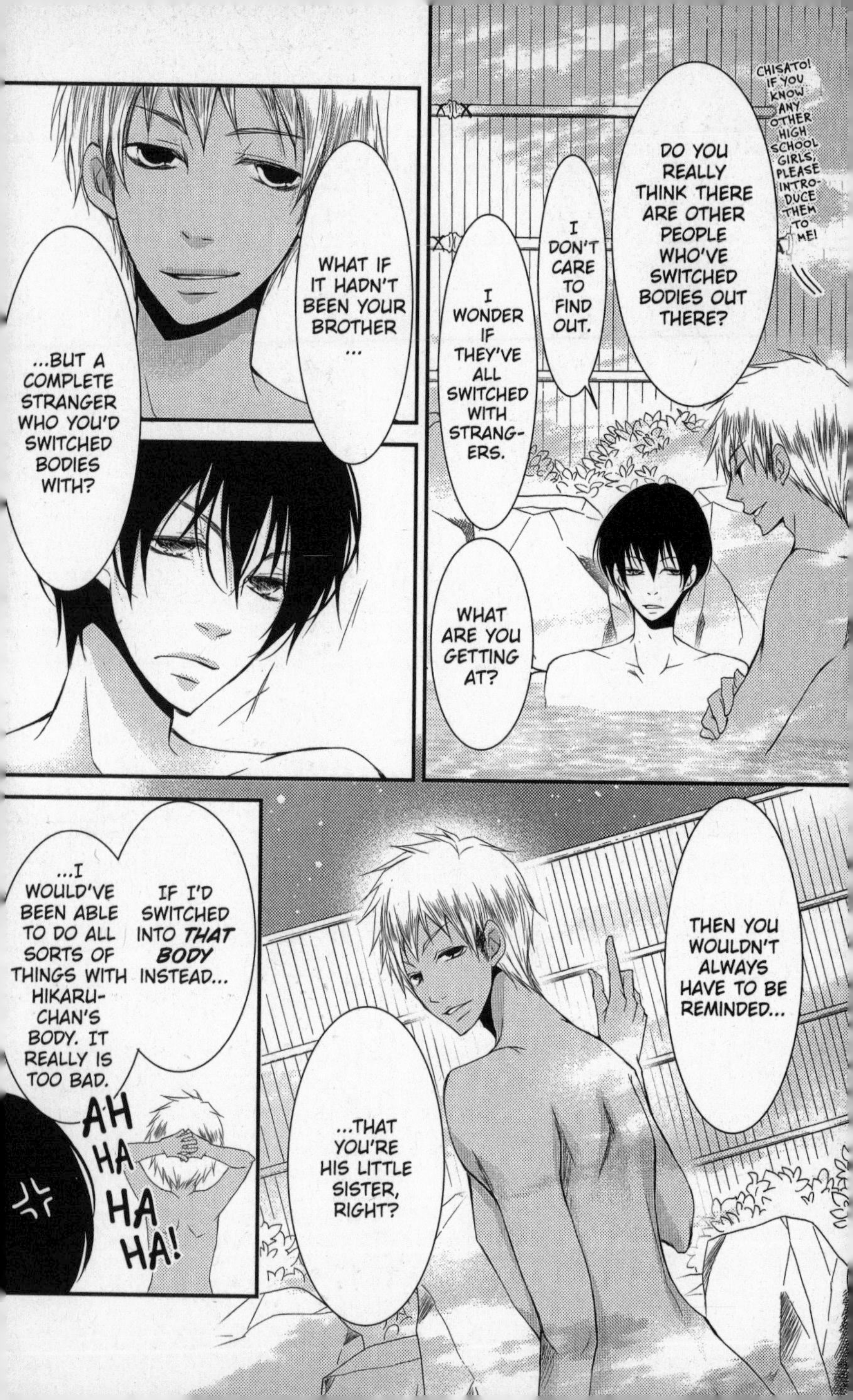
CHISATO! IF YOU KNOW ANY OTHER HIGH SCHOOL GIRLS, PLEASE INTRODUCE THEM TO ME!
DO YOU REALLY THINK THERE ARE OTHER PEOPLE WHO'VE SWITCHED BODIES OUT THERE?
I DON'T CARE TO FIND OUT.
I WONDER IF THEY'VE ALL SWITCHED WITH STRANGERS.
WHAT ARE YOU GETTING AT?
WHAT IF IT HADN'T BEEN YOUR BROTHER...
...BUT A COMPLETE STRANGER WHO YOU'D SWITCHED BODIES WITH?
THEN YOU WOULDN'T ALWAYS HAVE TO BE REMINDED...
...THAT YOU'RE HIS LITTLE SISTER, RIGHT?
IF I'D SWITCHED INTO *THAT BODY* INSTEAD...
...I WOULD'VE BEEN ABLE TO DO ALL SORTS OF THINGS WITH HIKARU-CHAN'S BODY. IT REALLY IS TOO BAD.
AH HA HA HA!

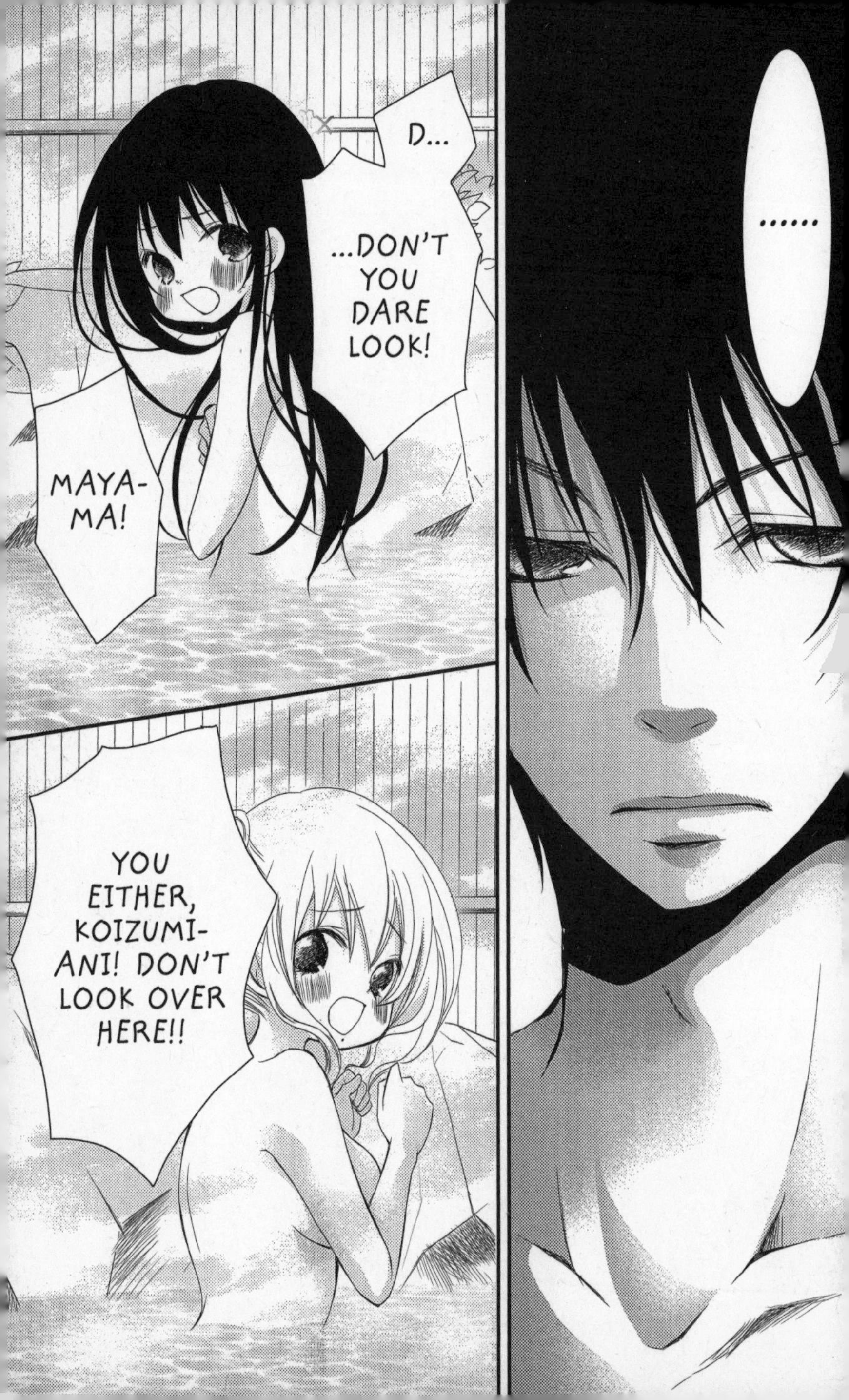
......
D...
...DON'T YOU DARE LOOK!
MAYA-MA!
YOU EITHER, KOIZUMI-ANI! DON'T LOOK OVER HERE!!

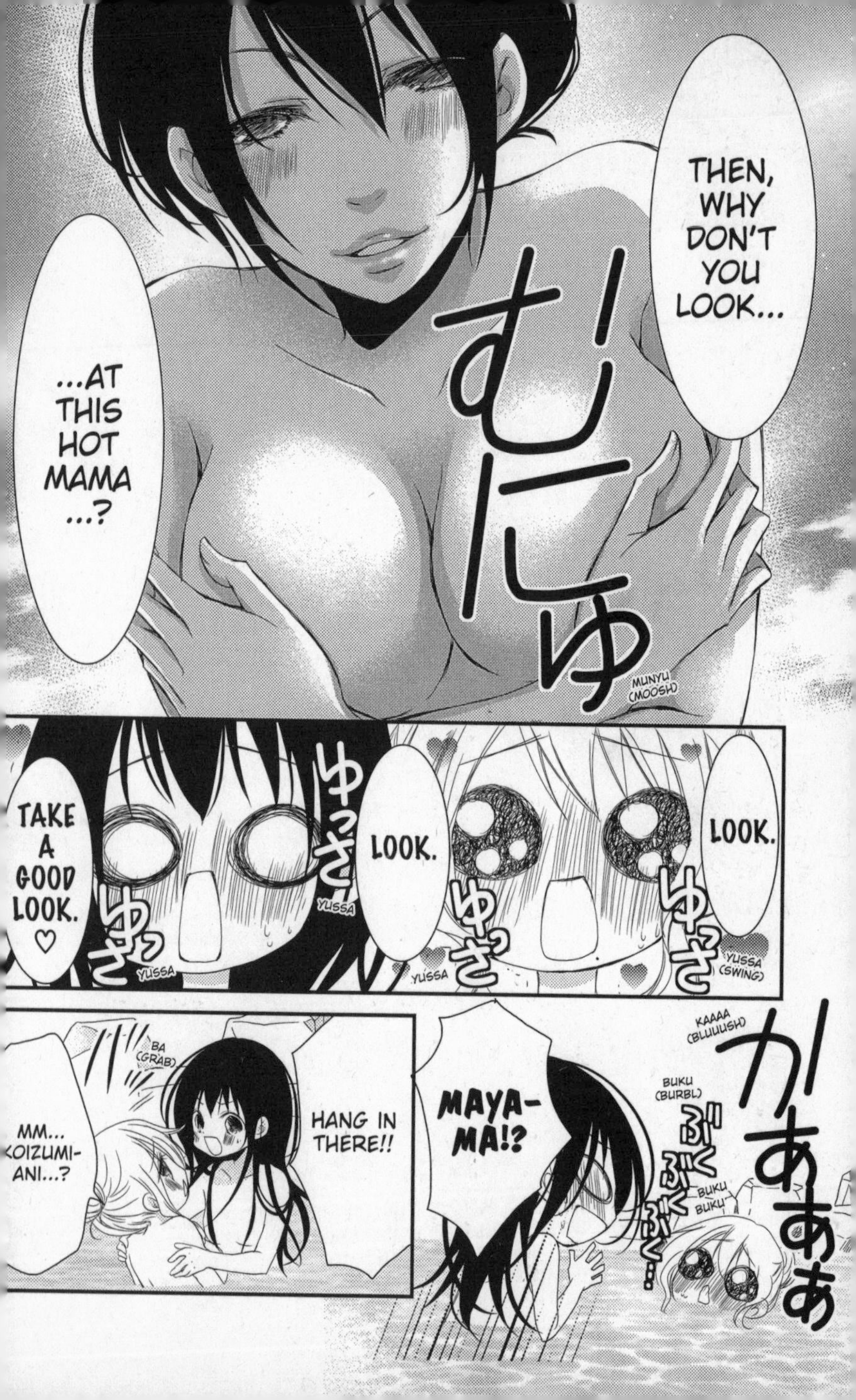
THEN, WHY DON'T YOU LOOK...
...AT THIS HOT MAMA...?
むにゅ
MUNYU (MOOSH)
ゆっさ
YUSSA (SWING)
LOOK.
ゆっさ
YUSSA
LOOK.
ゆっさ
YUSSA
ゆっさ
YUSSA
TAKE A GOOD LOOK. ♡
かあああ
KAAAA (BLUUUSH)
BUKU (BURBL)
ぶくぶくぶく…
BUKU BUKU
MAYA-MA!?
BA (GRAB)
HANG IN THERE!!
MM... KOIZUMI-ANI...?

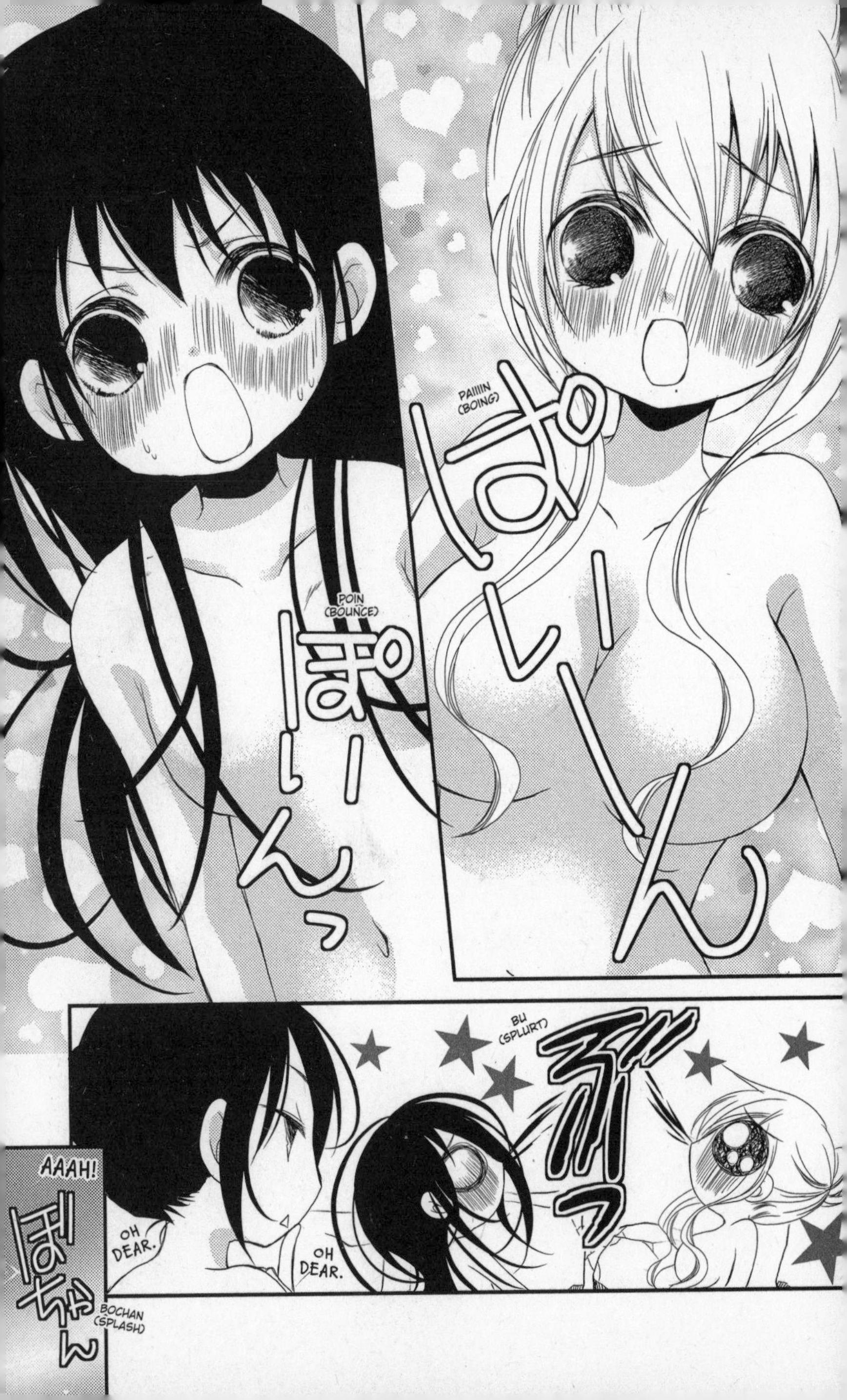
PAIIIIN (BOING)
ぱいーん
POIN (BOUNCE)
ぽいーんっ
BU (SPLURT)
ぶっ
OH DEAR.
OH DEAR.
AAAH!
ぼちゃん
BOCHAN (SPLASH)

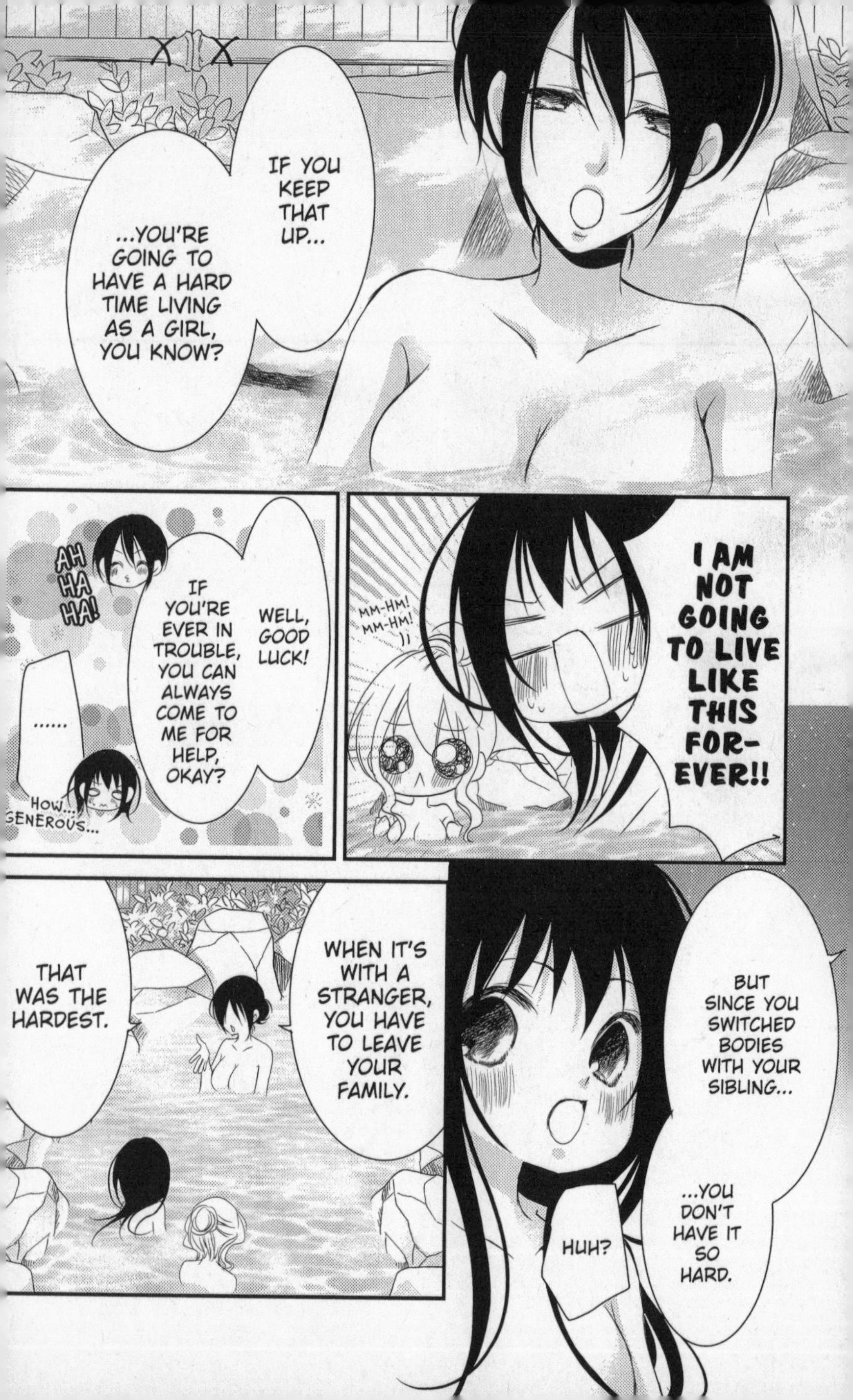
IF YOU KEEP THAT UP...
...YOU'RE GOING TO HAVE A HARD TIME LIVING AS A GIRL, YOU KNOW?
I AM NOT GOING TO LIVE LIKE THIS FOR-EVER!!
MM-HM! MM-HM!
WELL, GOOD LUCK!
IF YOU'RE EVER IN TROUBLE, YOU CAN ALWAYS COME TO ME FOR HELP, OKAY?
AH HA HA!
......
HOW... GENEROUS...
BUT SINCE YOU SWITCHED BODIES WITH YOUR SIBLING...
...YOU DON'T HAVE IT SO HARD.
HUH?
WHEN IT'S WITH A STRANGER, YOU HAVE TO LEAVE YOUR FAMILY.
THAT WAS THE HARDEST.

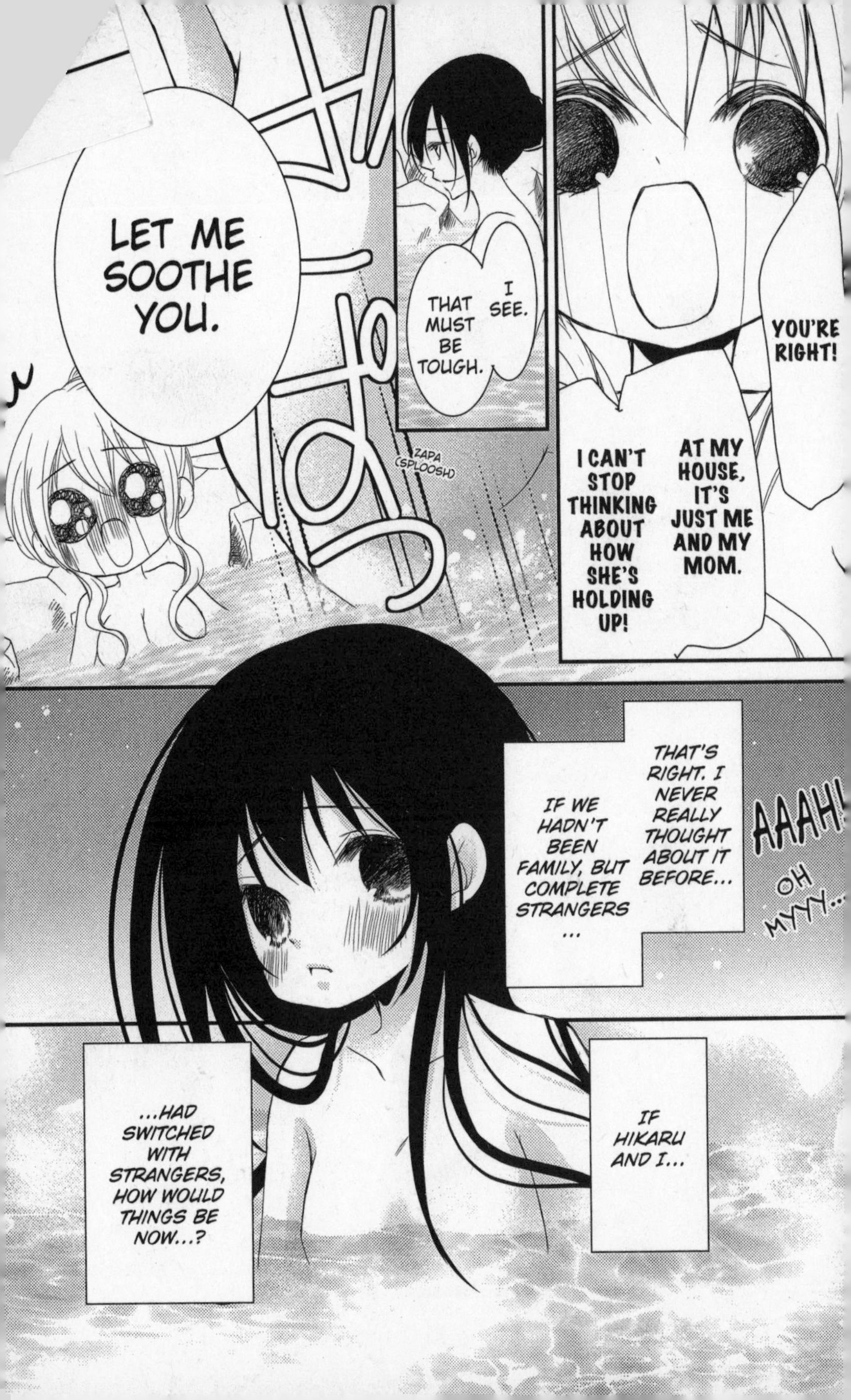
YOU'RE RIGHT!
AT MY HOUSE, IT'S JUST ME AND MY MOM.
I CAN'T STOP THINKING ABOUT HOW SHE'S HOLDING UP!
I SEE.
THAT MUST BE TOUGH.
LET ME SOOTHE YOU.
ZAPA (SPLOOSH)
AAAH!
OH MYYY...
THAT'S RIGHT. I NEVER REALLY THOUGHT ABOUT IT BEFORE...
IF WE HADN'T BEEN FAMILY, BUT COMPLETE STRANGERS...
IF HIKARU AND I...
...HAD SWITCHED WITH STRANGERS, HOW WOULD THINGS BE NOW...?

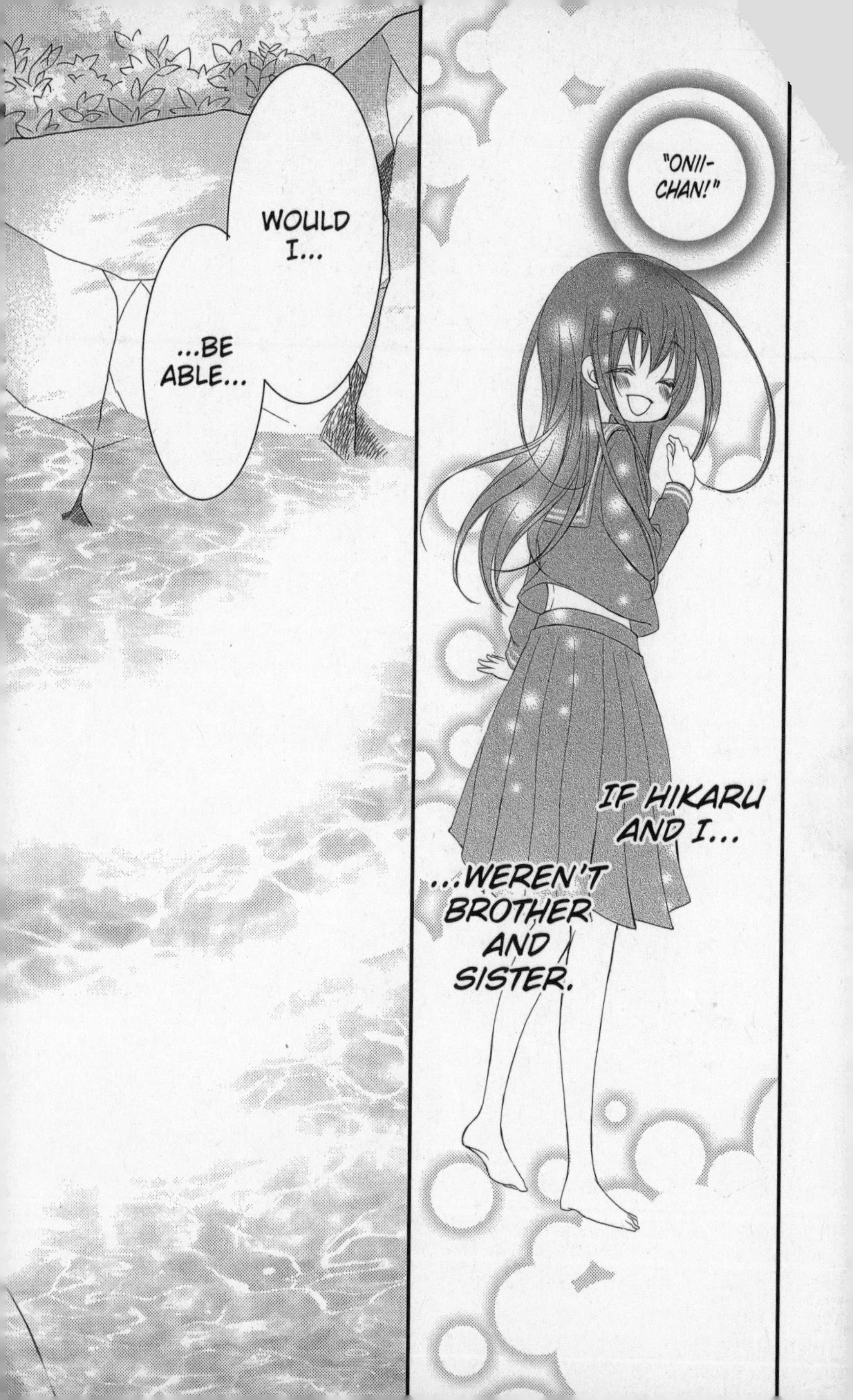
"ONII-CHAN!"
IF HIKARU AND I...
...WEREN'T BROTHER AND SISTER.
WOULD I...
...BE ABLE...

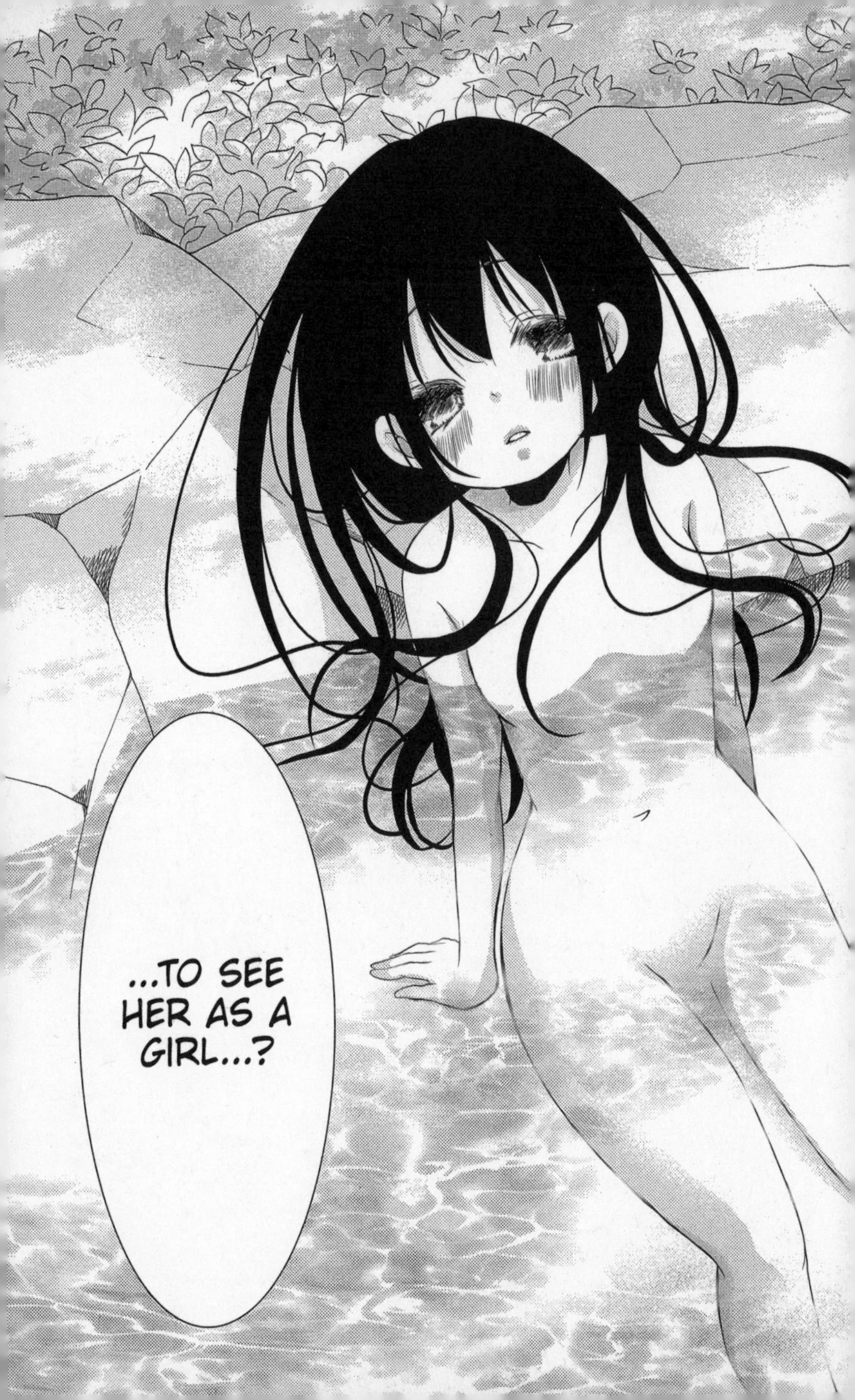
...TO SEE HER AS A GIRL...?

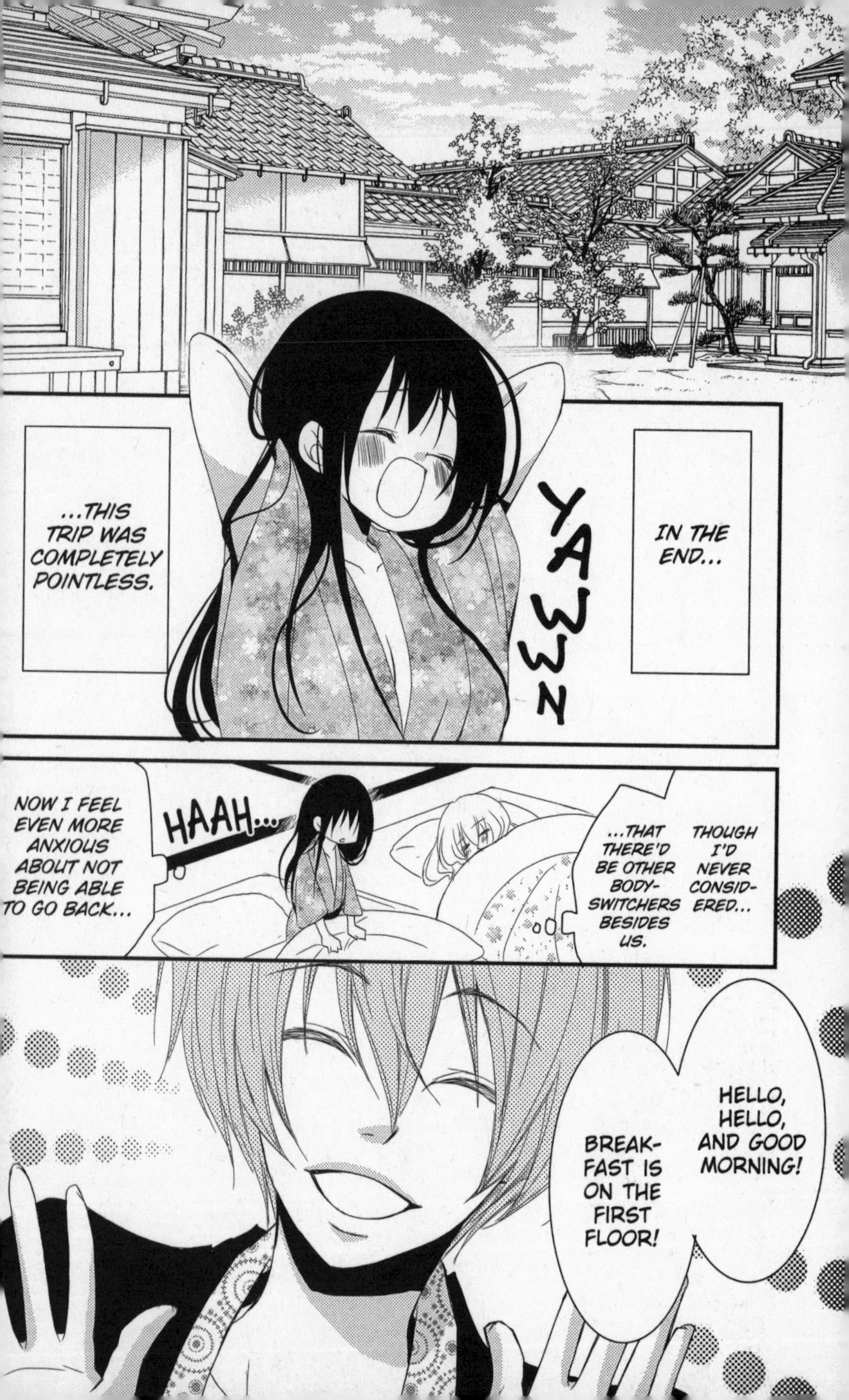
IN THE END...
YAWN
...THIS TRIP WAS COMPLETELY POINTLESS.
THOUGH I'D NEVER CONSIDERED...
...THAT THERE'D BE OTHER BODY-SWITCHERS BESIDES US.
HAAH...
NOW I FEEL EVEN MORE ANXIOUS ABOUT NOT BEING ABLE TO GO BACK...
HELLO, HELLO, AND GOOD MORNING!
BREAKFAST IS ON THE FIRST FLOOR!

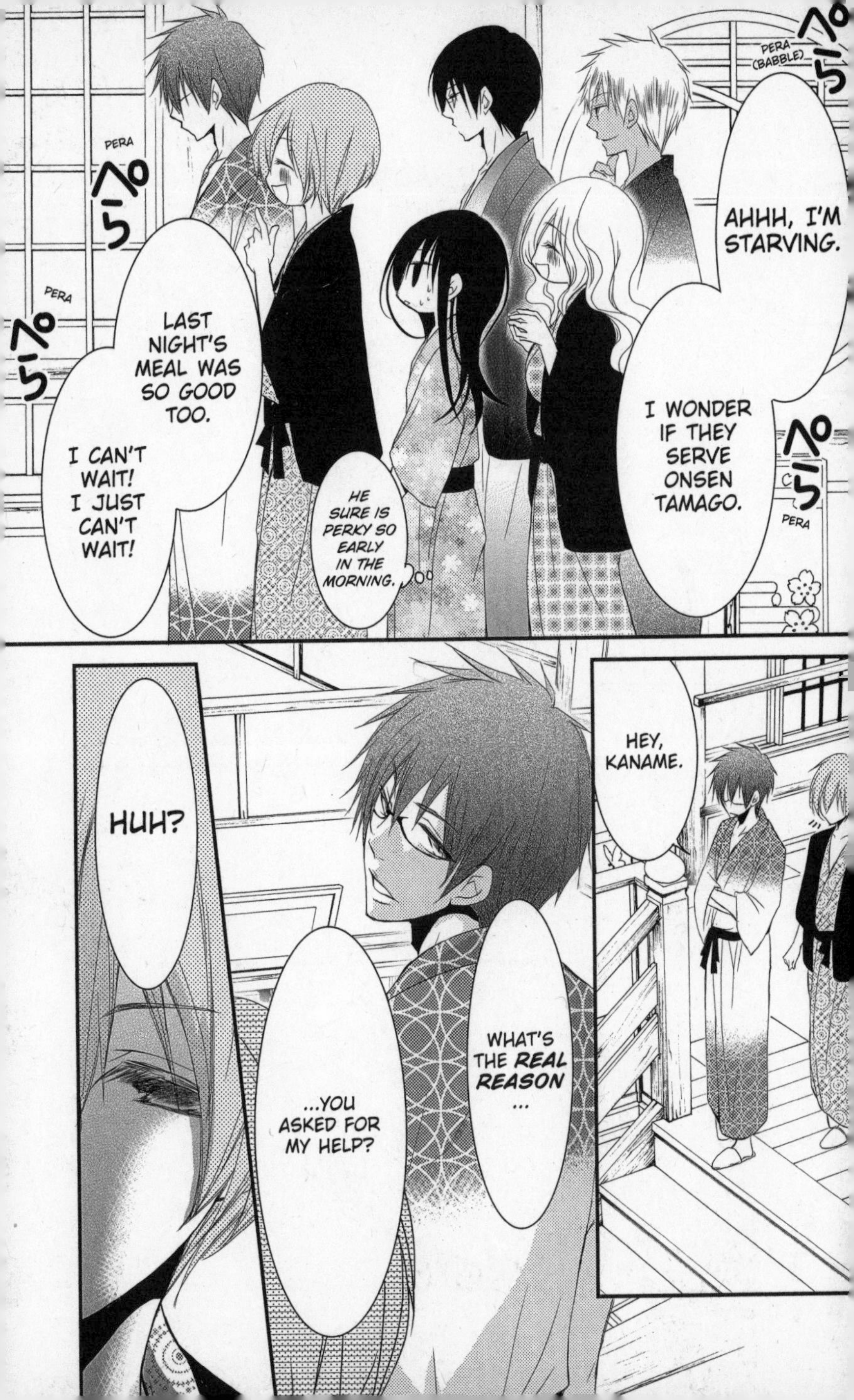
PERA (BABBLE)
AHHH, I'M STARVING.
I WONDER IF THEY SERVE ONSEN TAMAGO.
PERA
HE SURE IS PERKY SO EARLY IN THE MORNING.
PERA
LAST NIGHT'S MEAL WAS SO GOOD TOO.
I CAN'T WAIT! I JUST CAN'T WAIT!
PERA
HEY, KANAME.
WHAT'S THE *REAL REASON* ...
...YOU ASKED FOR MY HELP?
HUH?

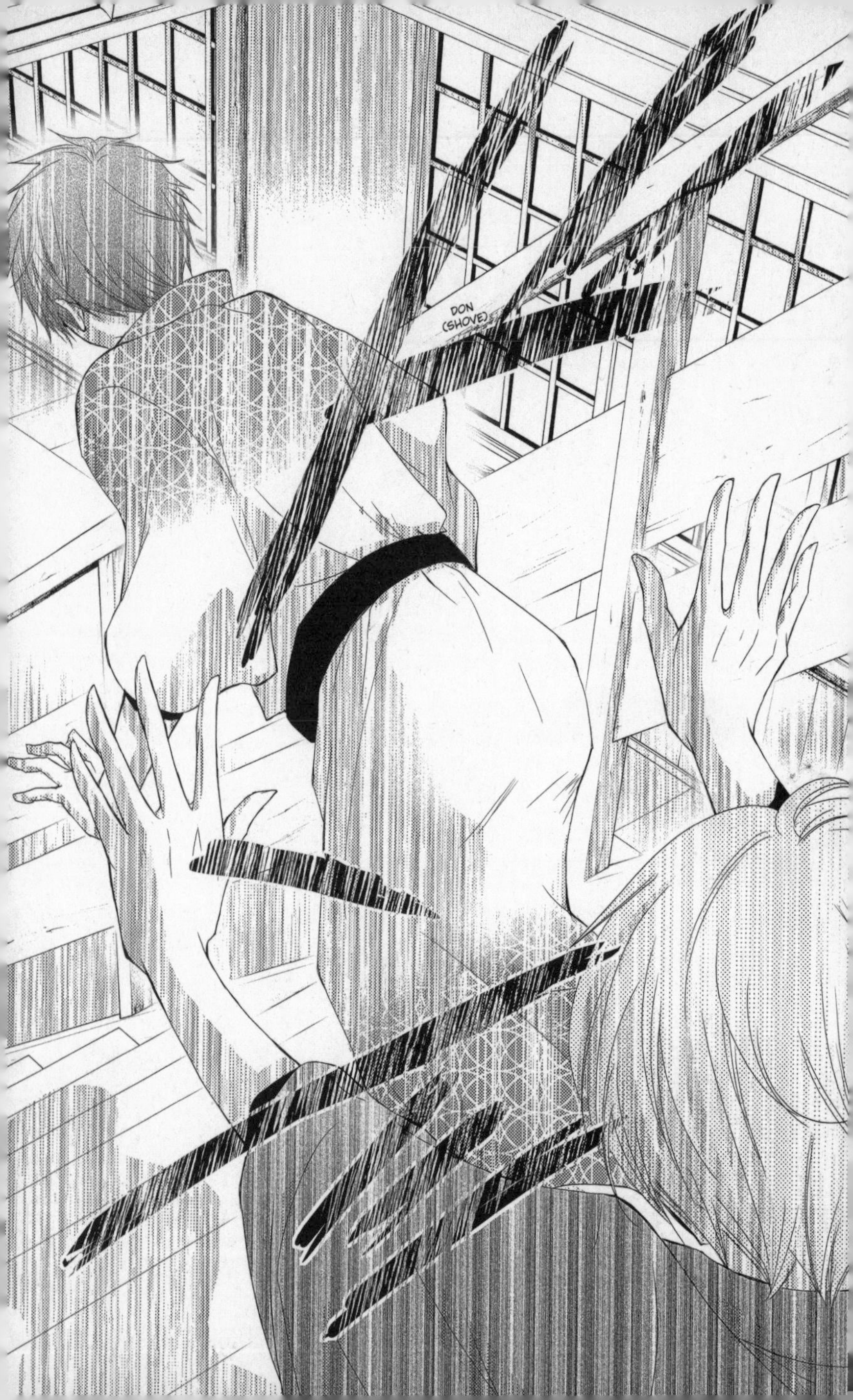
DON
(SHOVE)

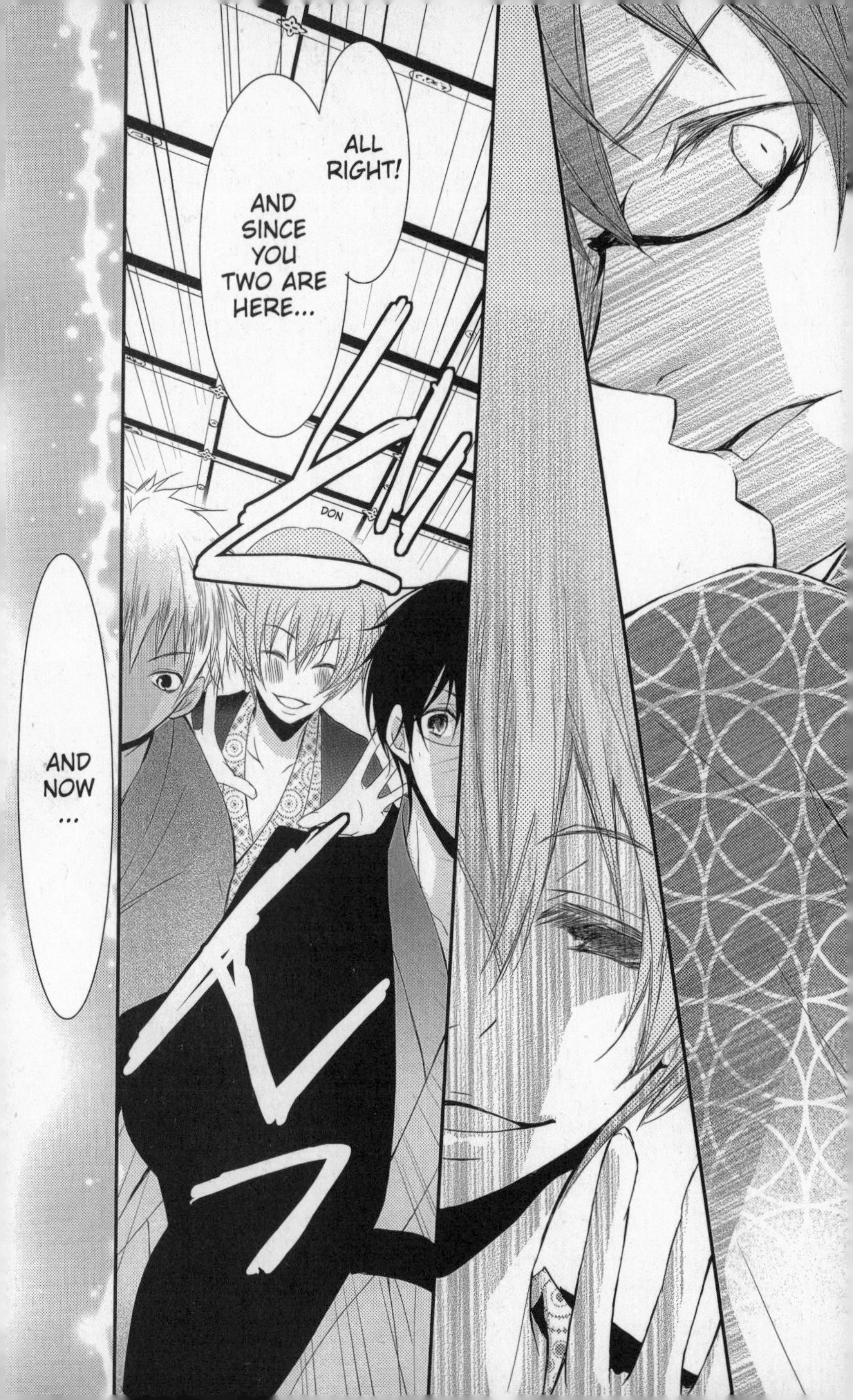
ALL RIGHT!
AND SINCE YOU TWO ARE HERE...
DON
AND NOW...

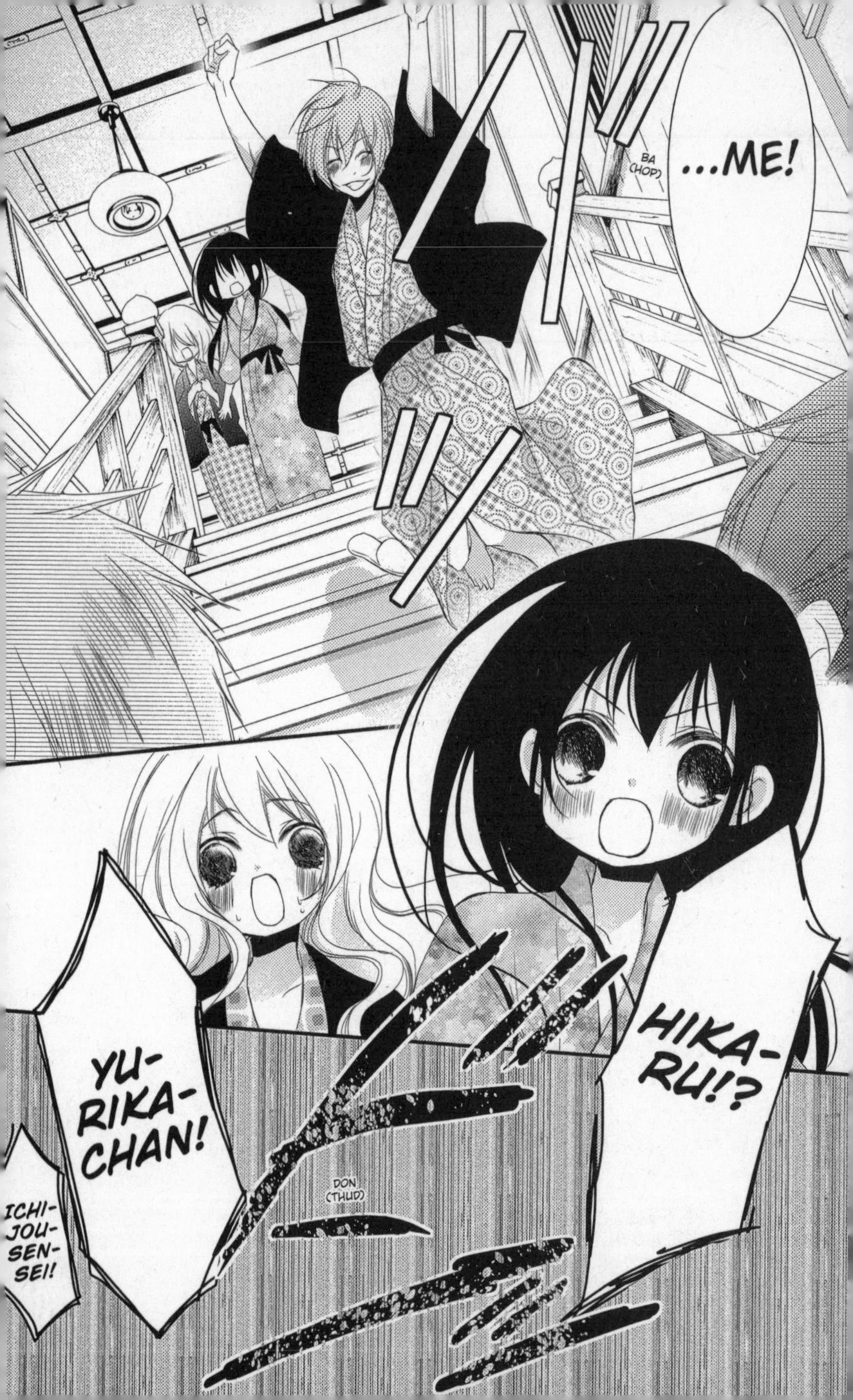
...ME!
BA (HOP)
HIKA-RU!?
DON (THUD)
YU-RIKA-CHAN!
ICHI-JOU-SEN-SEI!

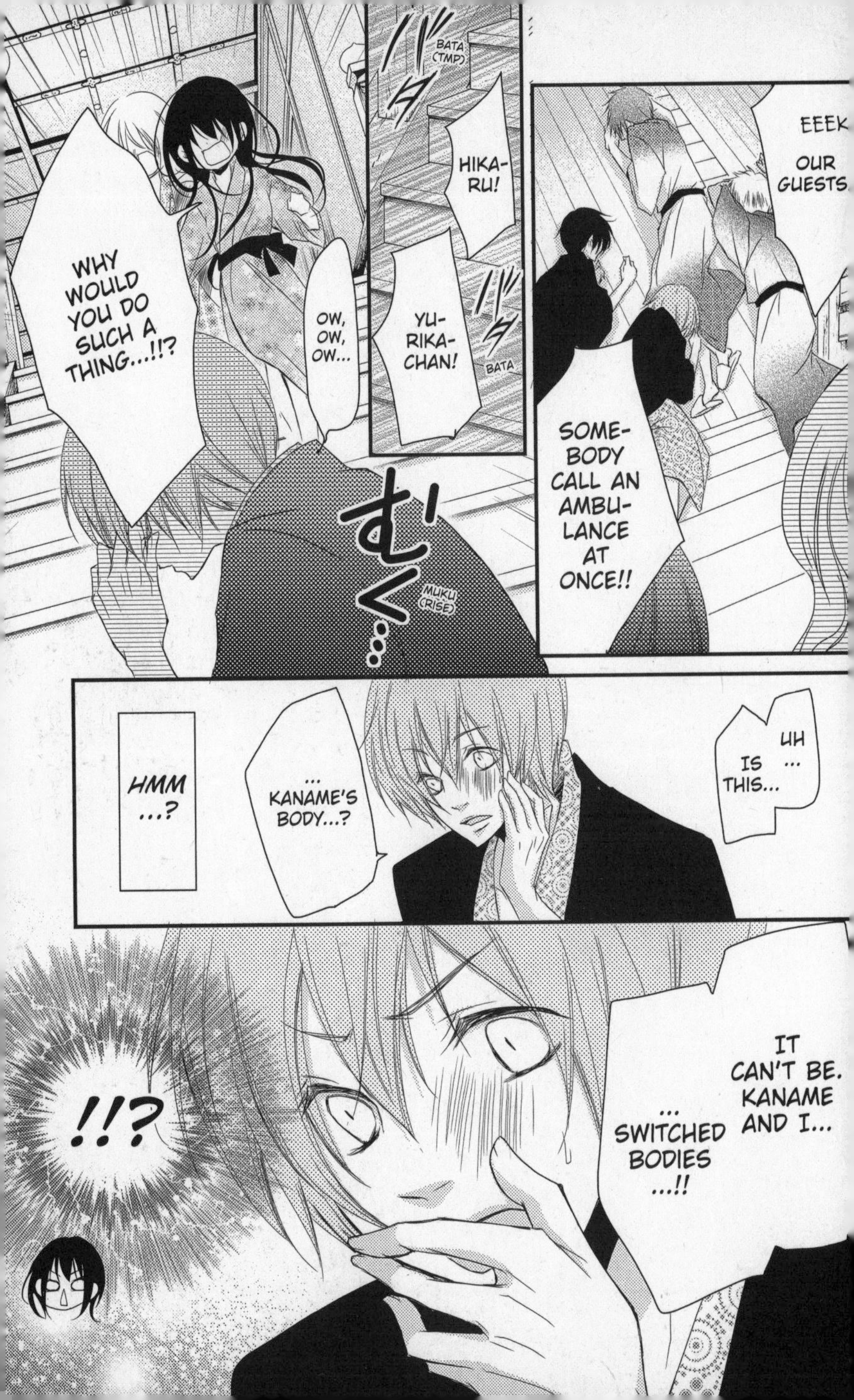
EEEK
OUR GUESTS.
SOMEBODY CALL AN AMBULANCE AT ONCE!!
バタ
BATA (TMP)
HIKA-RU!
YU-RIKA-CHAN!
バタ
BATA
WHY WOULD YOU DO SUCH A THING...!!?
OW, OW, OW...
むく...
MUKU (RISE)
UH ... IS THIS...
... KANAME'S BODY...?
HMM ...?
IT CAN'T BE. KANAME AND I...
... SWITCHED BODIES ...!!
!!?

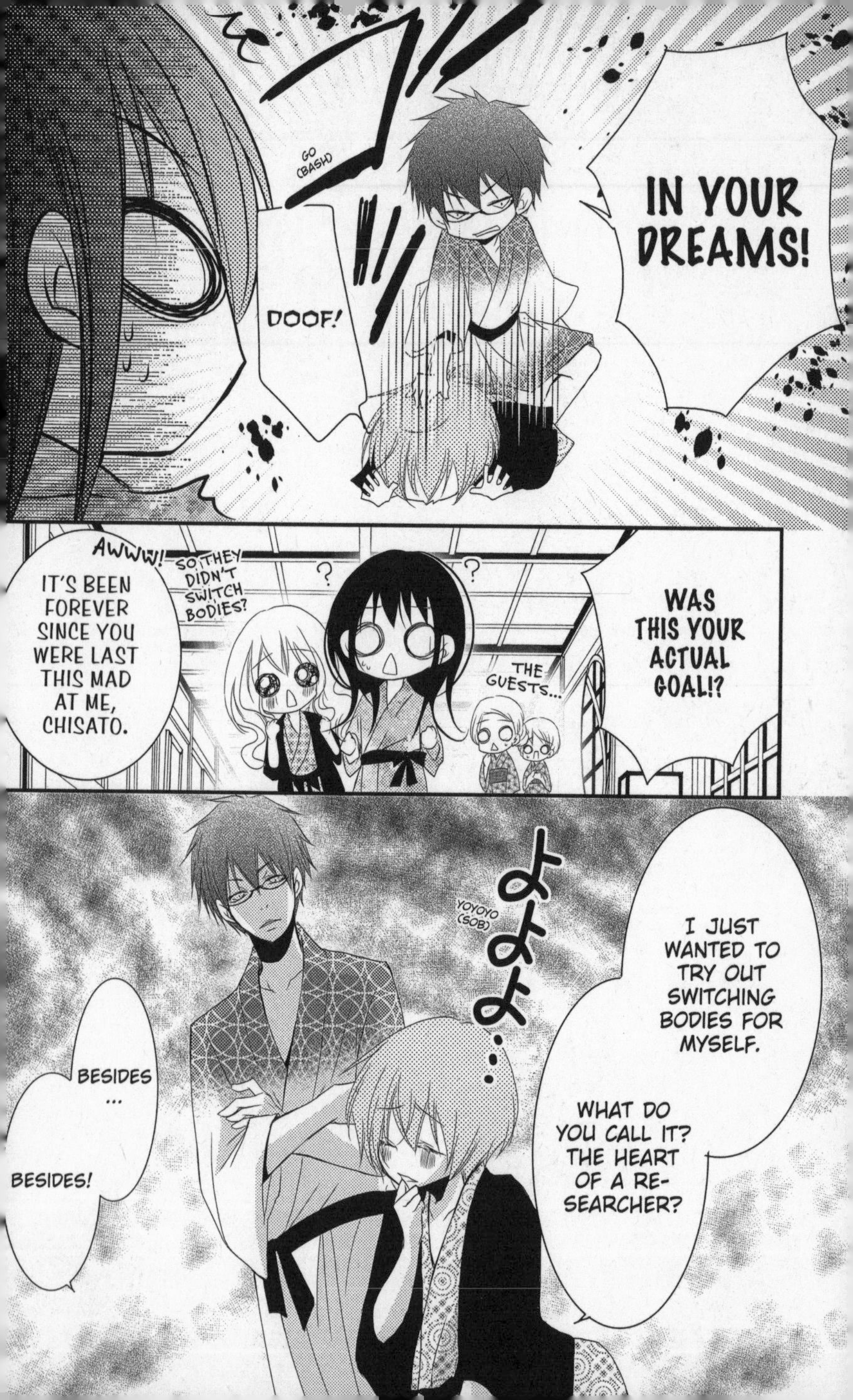
IN YOUR DREAMS!
GO (BASH)
DOOF!
WAS THIS YOUR ACTUAL GOAL!?
THE GUESTS...
SO THEY DIDN'T SWITCH BODIES?
AWWW!
IT'S BEEN FOREVER SINCE YOU WERE LAST THIS MAD AT ME, CHISATO.
I JUST WANTED TO TRY OUT SWITCHING BODIES FOR MYSELF.
よよよ…
YOYOYO (SOB)
WHAT DO YOU CALL IT? THE HEART OF A RE-SEARCHER?
BESIDES ...
BESIDES!

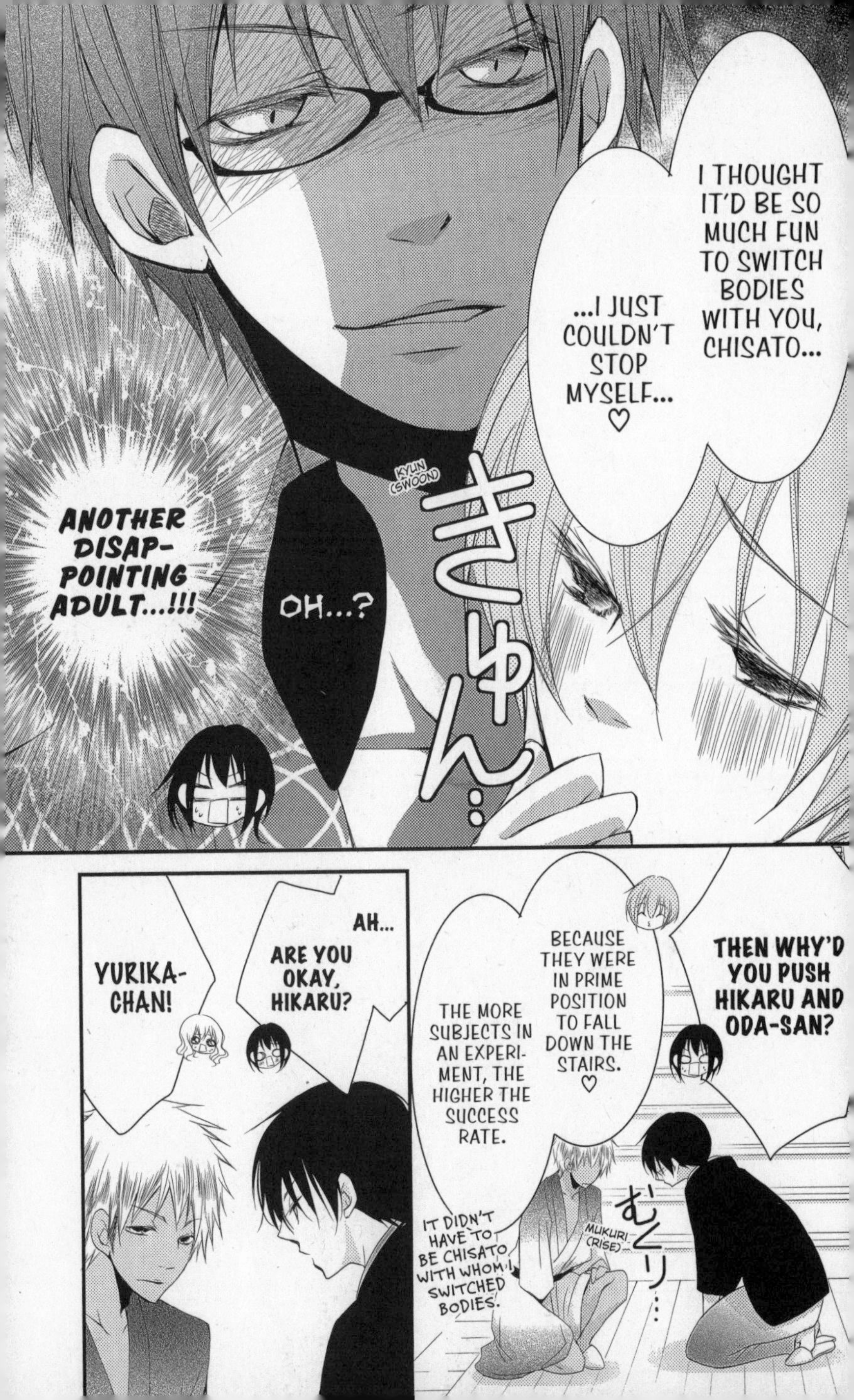
I THOUGHT IT'D BE SO MUCH FUN TO SWITCH BODIES WITH YOU, CHISATO...
...I JUST COULDN'T STOP MYSELF... ♡
きゅん
KYUN (SWOON)
OH...?
ANOTHER DISAP-POINTING ADULT...!!!
THEN WHY'D YOU PUSH HIKARU AND ODA-SAN?
BECAUSE THEY WERE IN PRIME POSITION TO FALL DOWN THE STAIRS. ♡
THE MORE SUBJECTS IN AN EXPERI-MENT, THE HIGHER THE SUCCESS RATE.
IT DIDN'T HAVE TO BE CHISATO WITH WHOM I SWITCHED BODIES.
むくり…
MUKURI (RISE)
AH...
ARE YOU OKAY, HIKARU?
YURIKA-CHAN!

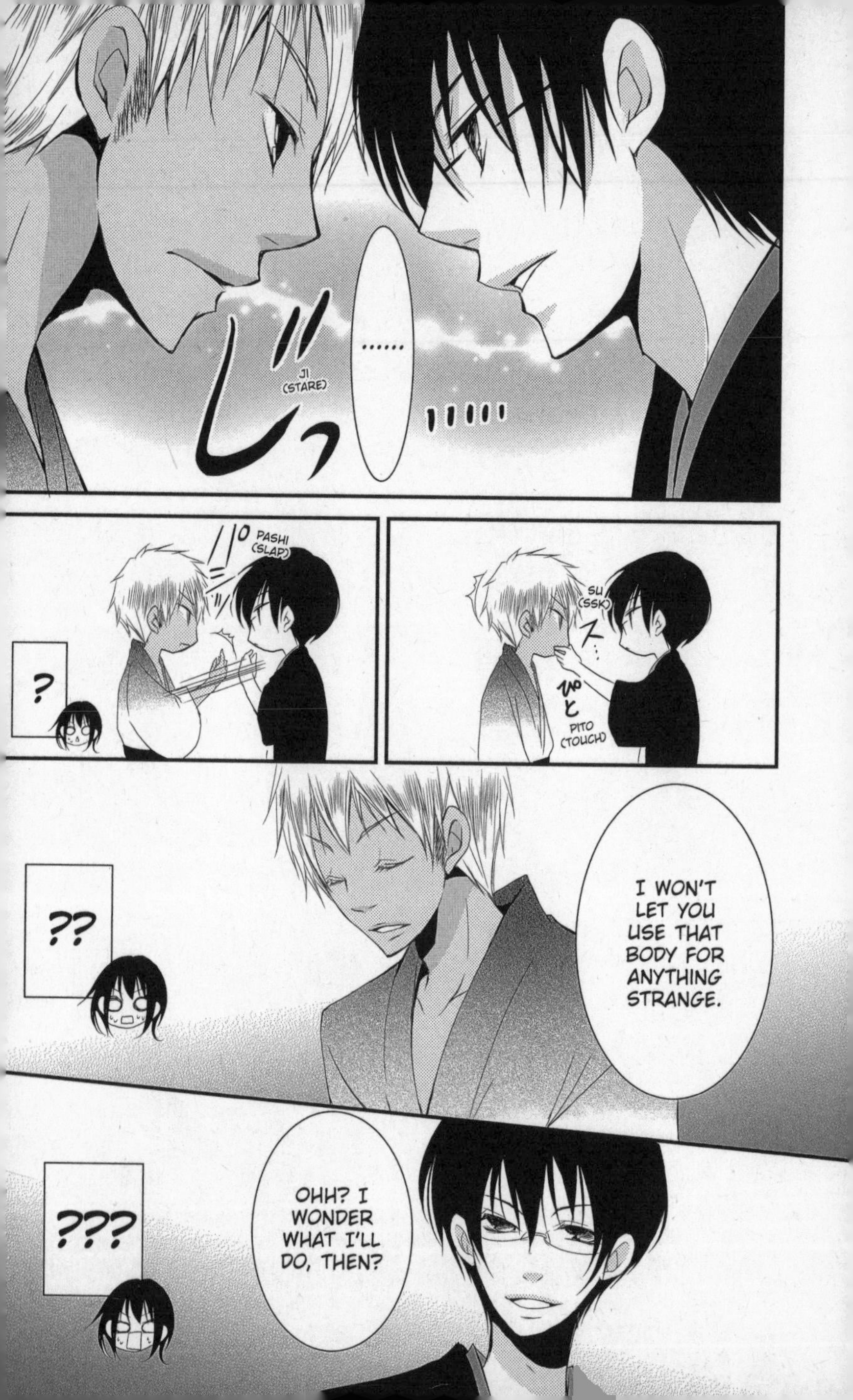
......
じっ
JI (STARE)
ス…
SU (SSK)
ぴと
PITO (TOUCH)
PASHI (SLAP)
?
I WON'T LET YOU USE THAT BODY FOR ANYTHING STRANGE.
??
OHH? I WONDER WHAT I'LL DO, THEN?
???

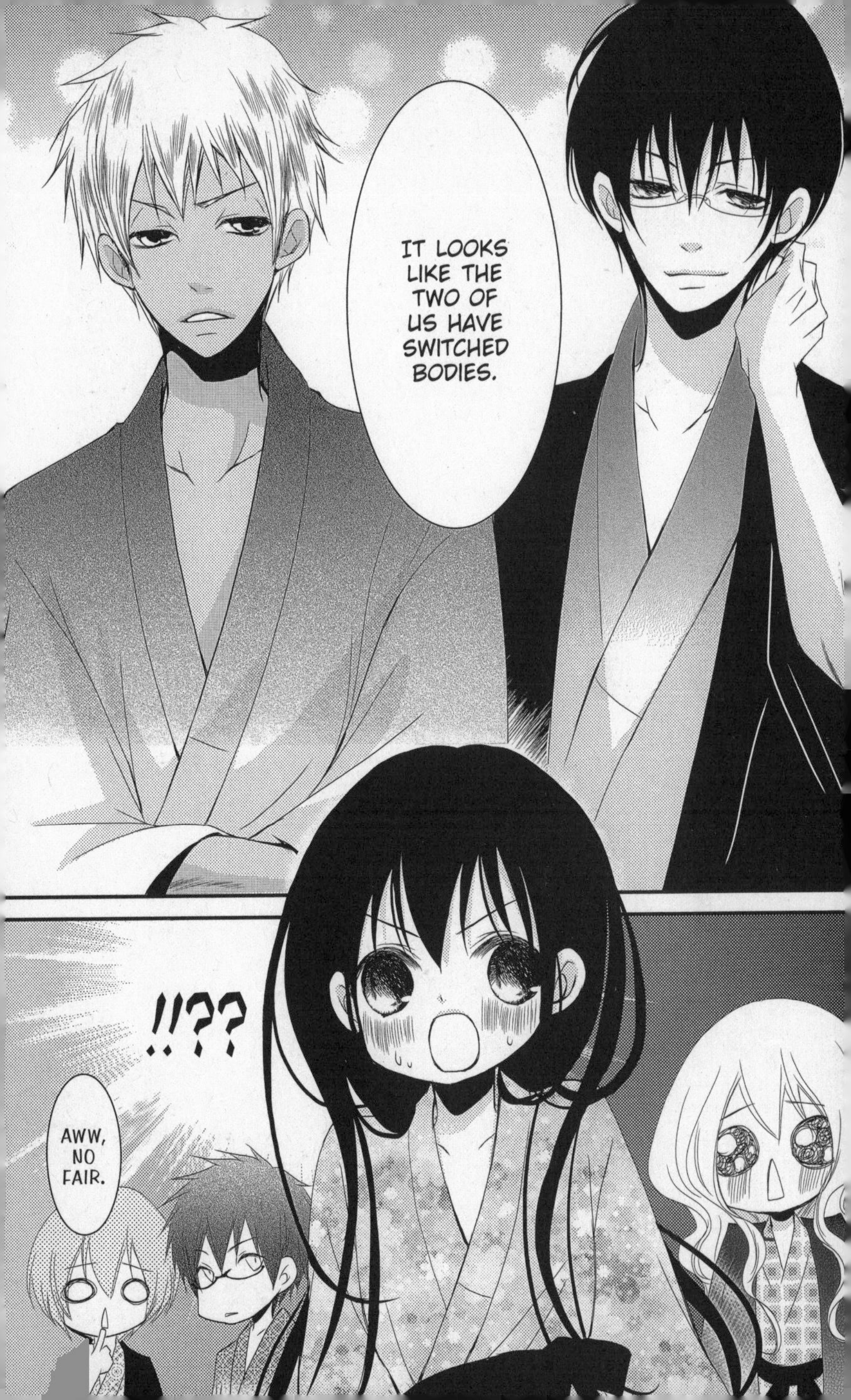
IT LOOKS LIKE THE TWO OF US HAVE SWITCHED BODIES.
!!??
AWW, NO FAIR.

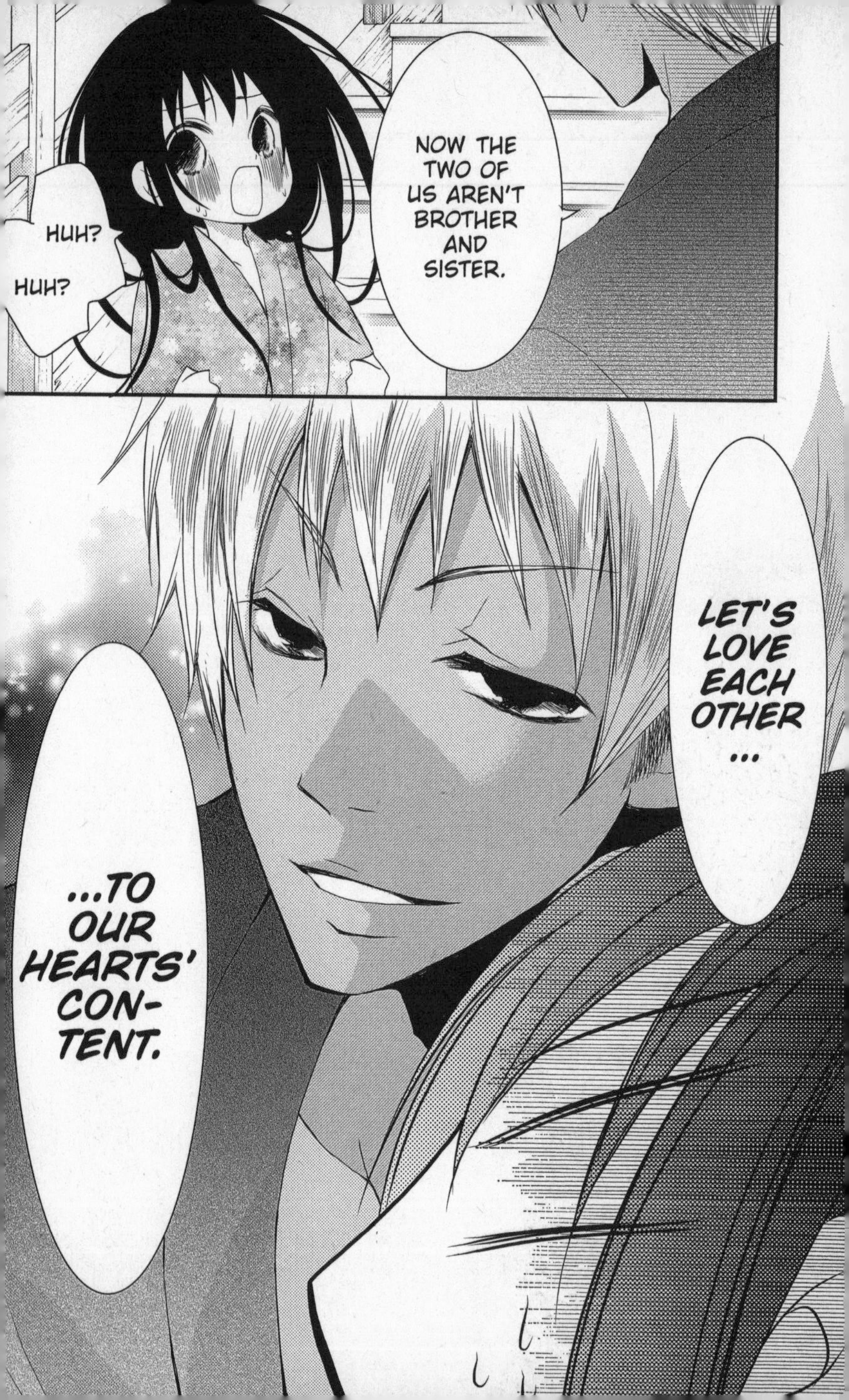
NOW THE TWO OF US AREN'T BROTHER AND SISTER.
HUH?
HUH?
LET'S LOVE EACH OTHER ...
...TO OUR HEARTS' CON-TENT.

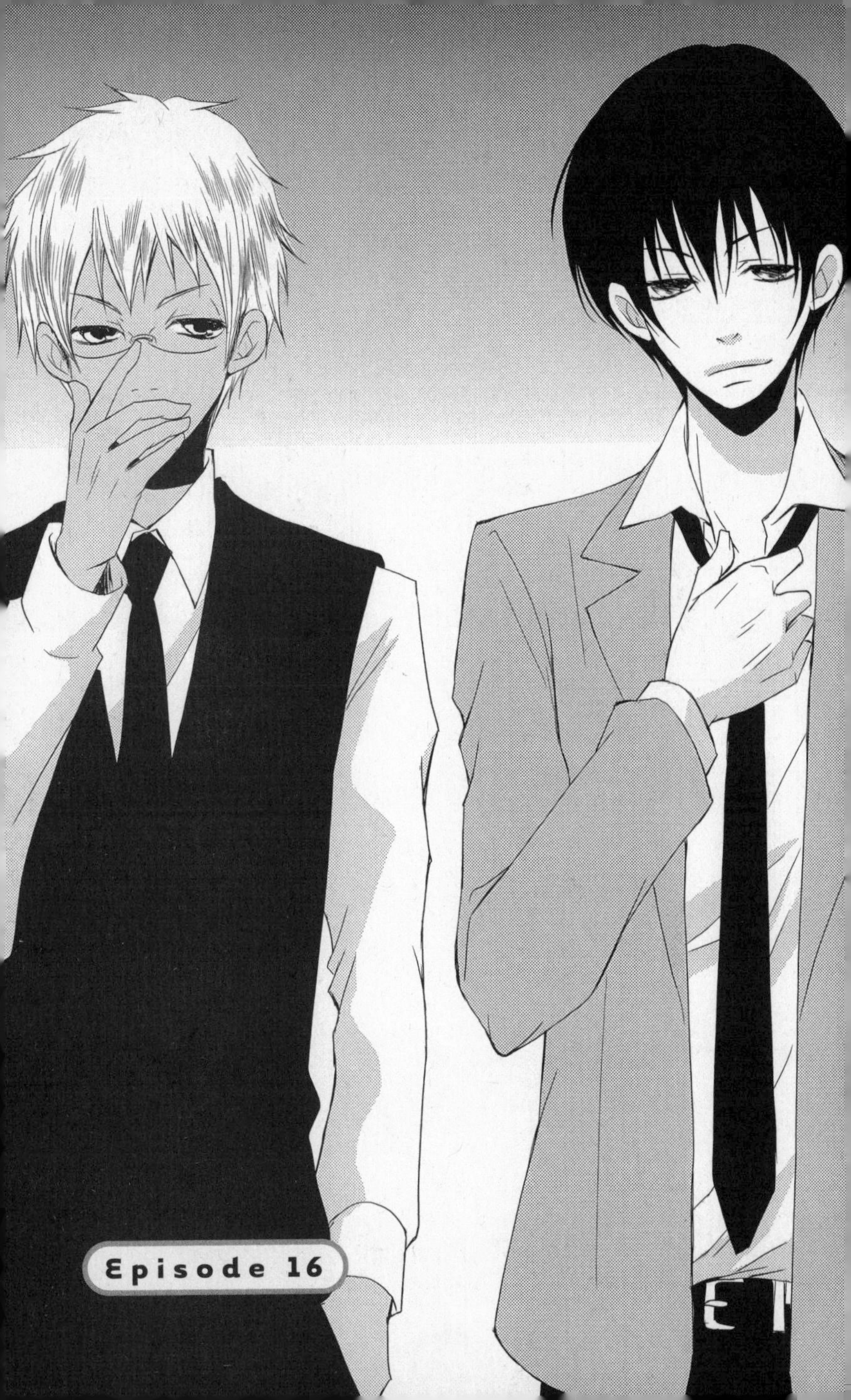
Episode 16

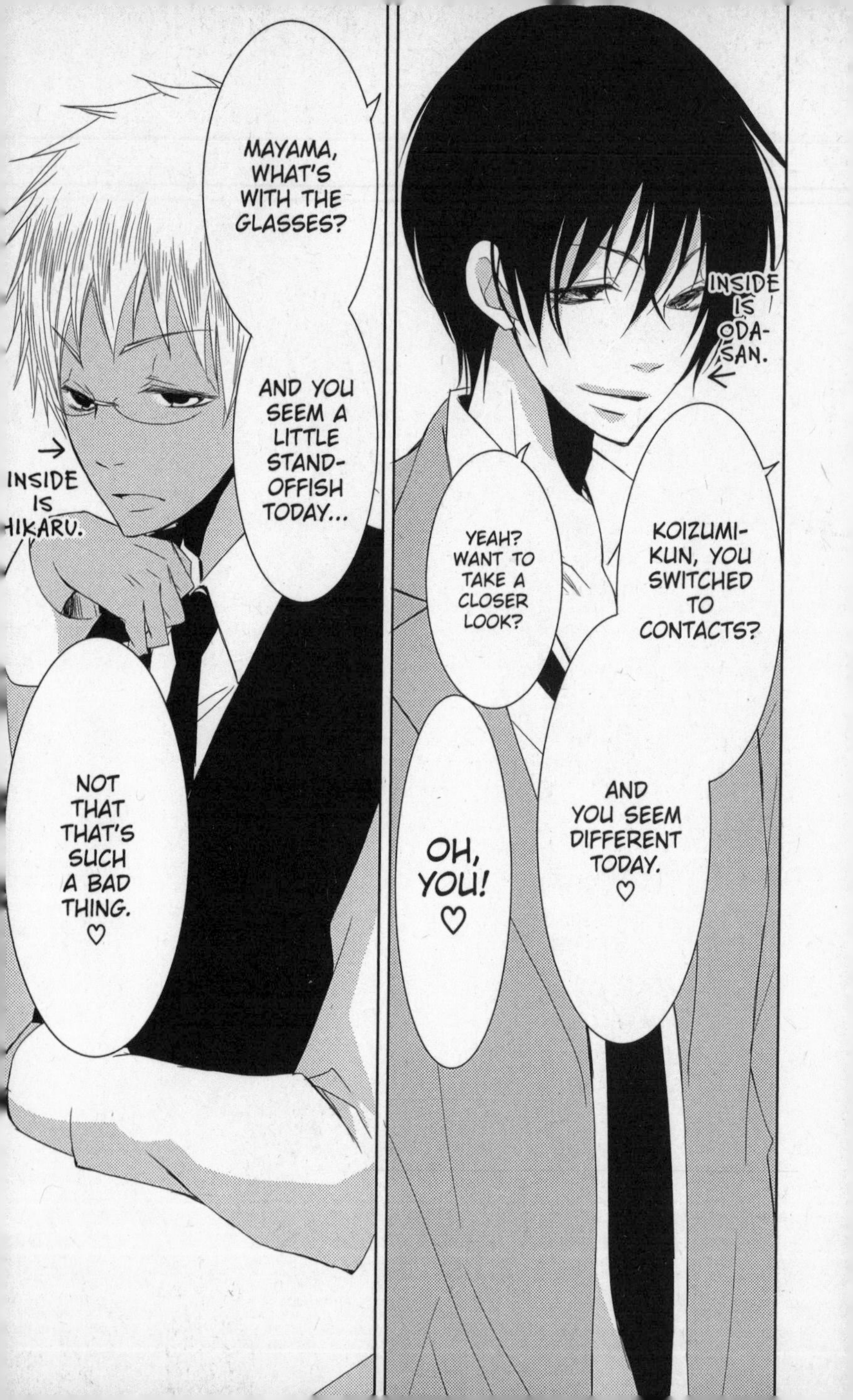
INSIDE IS ODA-SAN.
KOIZUMI-KUN, YOU SWITCHED TO CONTACTS?
YEAH? WANT TO TAKE A CLOSER LOOK?
AND YOU SEEM DIFFERENT TODAY. ♡
OH, YOU! ♡
MAYAMA, WHAT'S WITH THE GLASSES?
AND YOU SEEM A LITTLE STAND-OFFISH TODAY...
INSIDE IS HIKARU.
NOT THAT THAT'S SUCH A BAD THING. ♡

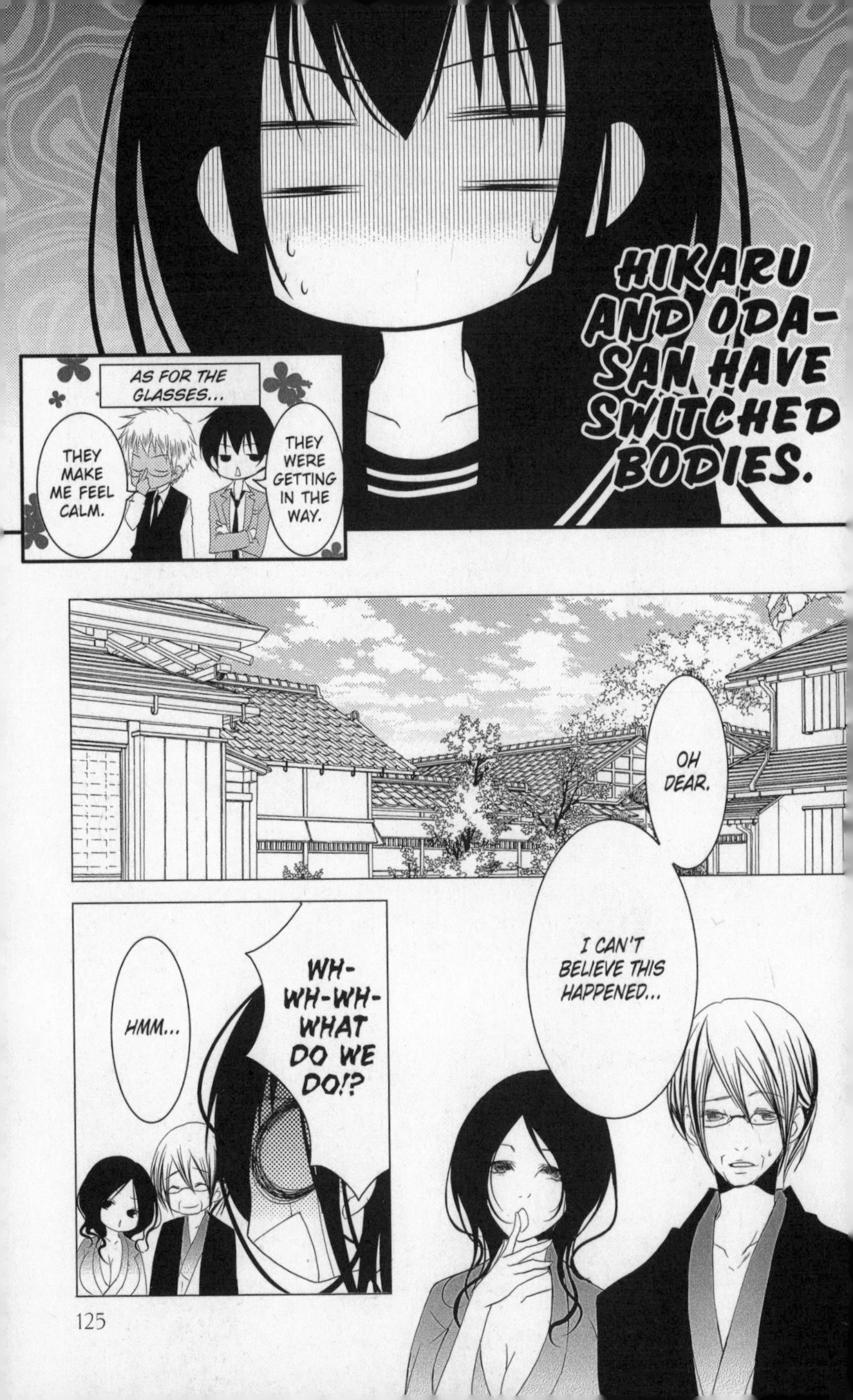
HIKARU AND ODA-SAN HAVE SWITCHED BODIES.
AS FOR THE GLASSES...
THEY WERE GETTING IN THE WAY.
THEY MAKE ME FEEL CALM.
OH DEAR.
I CAN'T BELIEVE THIS HAPPENED...
WH-WH-WH-WHAT DO WE DO!?
HMM...

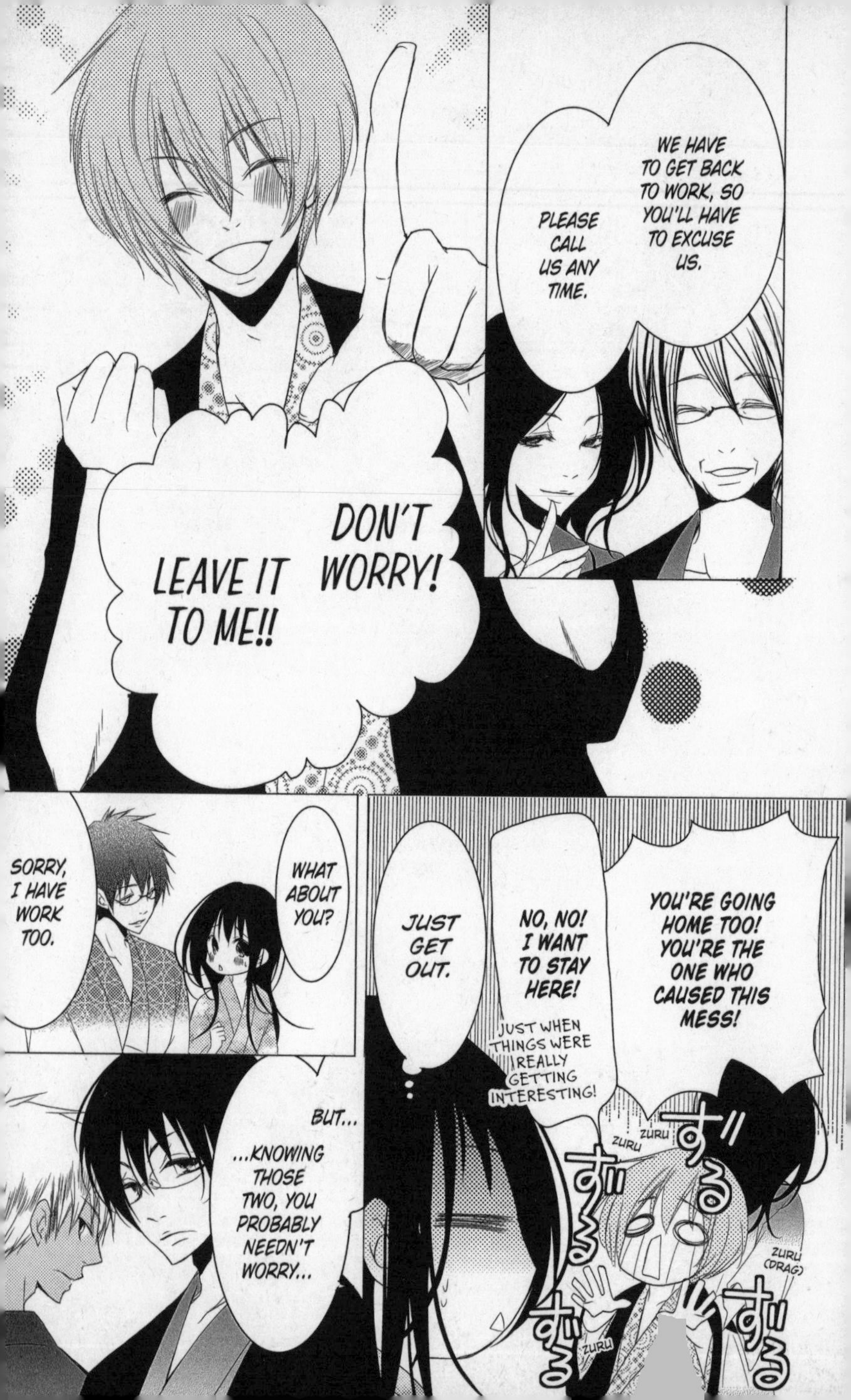
WE HAVE TO GET BACK TO WORK, SO YOU'LL HAVE TO EXCUSE US.
PLEASE CALL US ANY TIME.
DON'T WORRY!
LEAVE IT TO ME!!
YOU'RE GOING HOME TOO! YOU'RE THE ONE WHO CAUSED THIS MESS!
NO, NO! I WANT TO STAY HERE!
JUST GET OUT.
JUST WHEN THINGS WERE REALLY GETTING INTERESTING!
ずる
ZURU
ZURU
ずる
ZURU (DRAG)
ずる
ZURU
ずる
WHAT ABOUT YOU?
SORRY, I HAVE WORK TOO.
BUT...
...KNOWING THOSE TWO, YOU PROBABLY NEEDN'T WORRY...

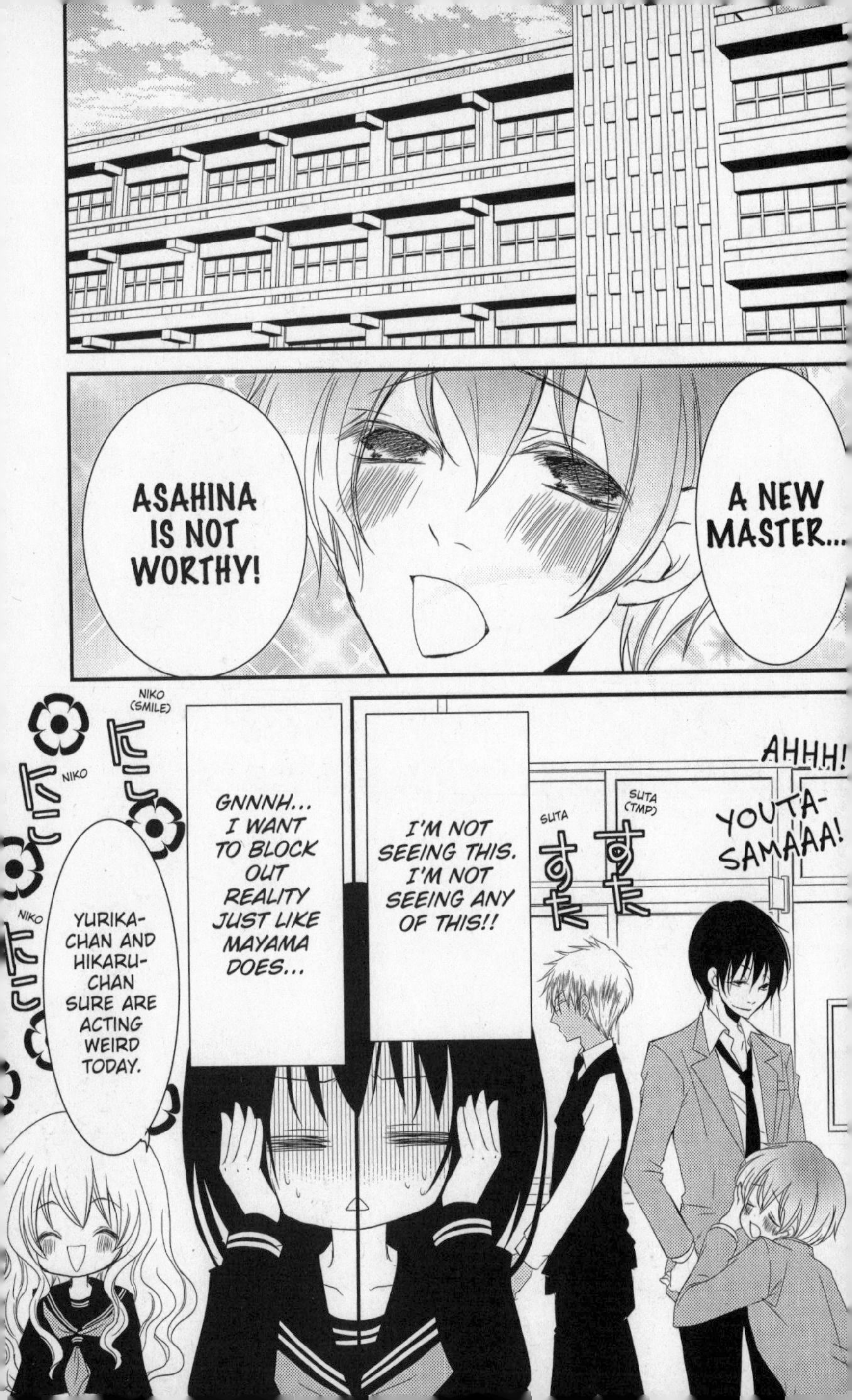
A NEW MASTER...
ASAHINA IS NOT WORTHY!
AHHH! YOUTA-SAMAAA!
SUTA (TMP)
すた
SUTA
すた
I'M NOT SEEING THIS. I'M NOT SEEING ANY OF THIS!!
GNNNH... I WANT TO BLOCK OUT REALITY JUST LIKE MAYAMA DOES...
NIKO (SMILE)
にこ
NIKO
にこ
NIKO
YURIKA-CHAN AND HIKARU-CHAN SURE ARE ACTING WEIRD TODAY.

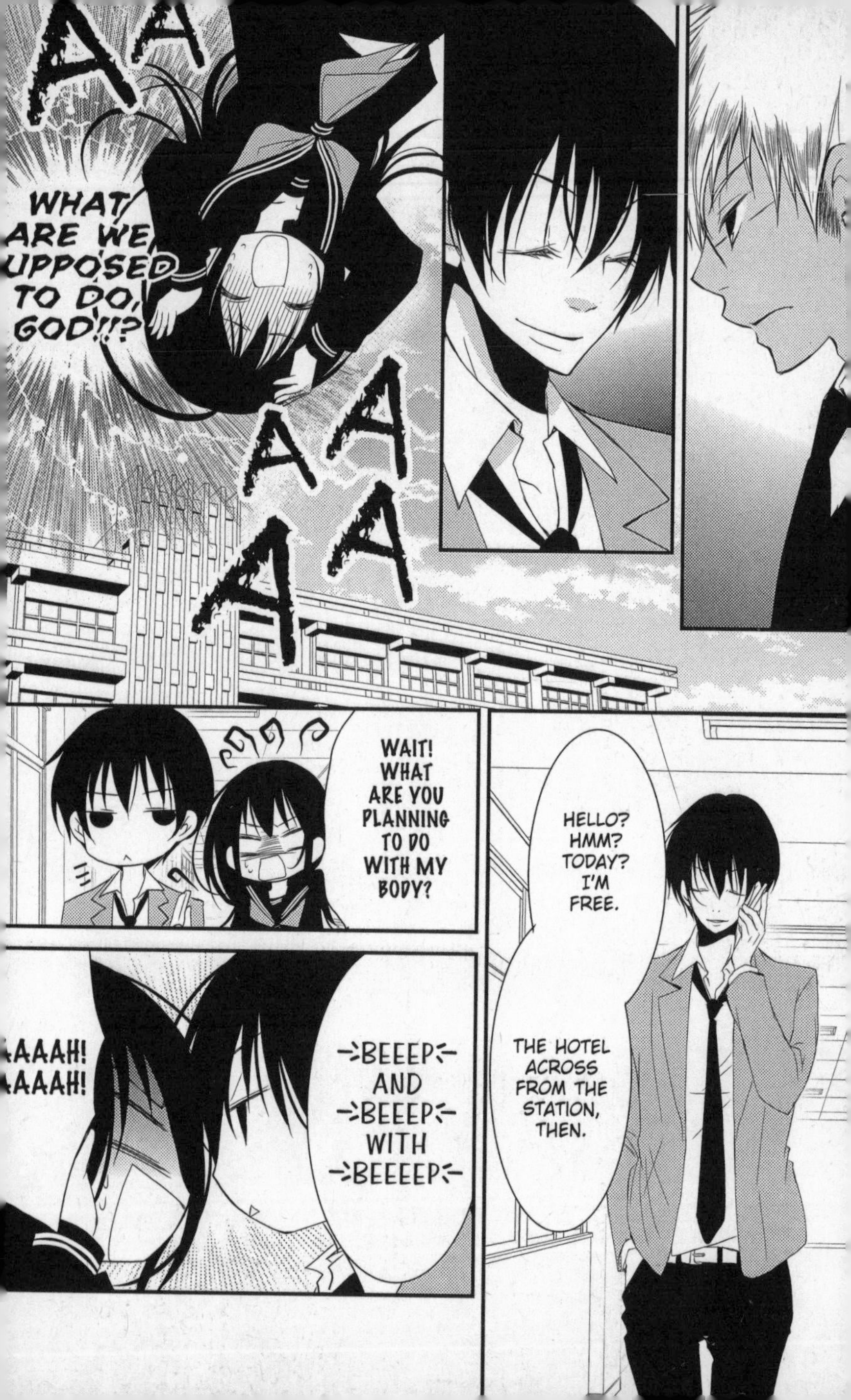
AA
WHAT ARE WE UPPOSED TO DO, GOD!!?
AAAA
HELLO? HMM? TODAY? I'M FREE.
THE HOTEL ACROSS FROM THE STATION, THEN.
WAIT! WHAT ARE YOU PLANNING TO DO WITH MY BODY?
AAAH! AAAH!
-BEEEP- AND -BEEEP- WITH -BEEEEP-

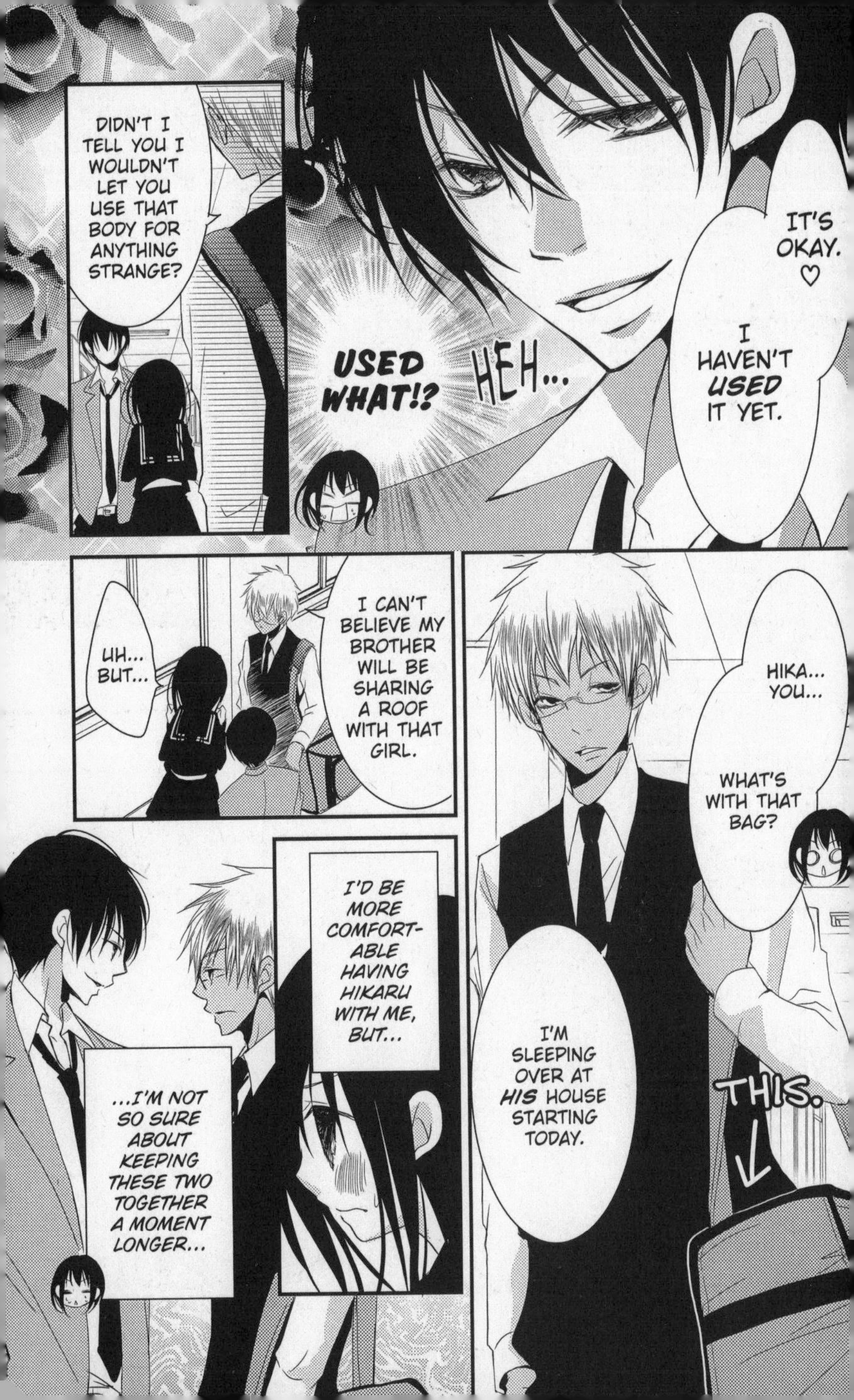
IT'S OKAY. ♡
I HAVEN'T *USED* IT YET.
HEH...
USED WHAT!?
DIDN'T I TELL YOU I WOULDN'T LET YOU USE THAT BODY FOR ANYTHING STRANGE?
HIKA... YOU...
WHAT'S WITH THAT BAG?
THIS.
I'M SLEEPING OVER AT *HIS* HOUSE STARTING TODAY.
I CAN'T BELIEVE MY BROTHER WILL BE SHARING A ROOF WITH THAT GIRL.
UH... BUT...
I'D BE MORE COMFORTABLE HAVING HIKARU WITH ME, BUT...
...I'M NOT SO SURE ABOUT KEEPING THESE TWO TOGETHER A MOMENT LONGER...

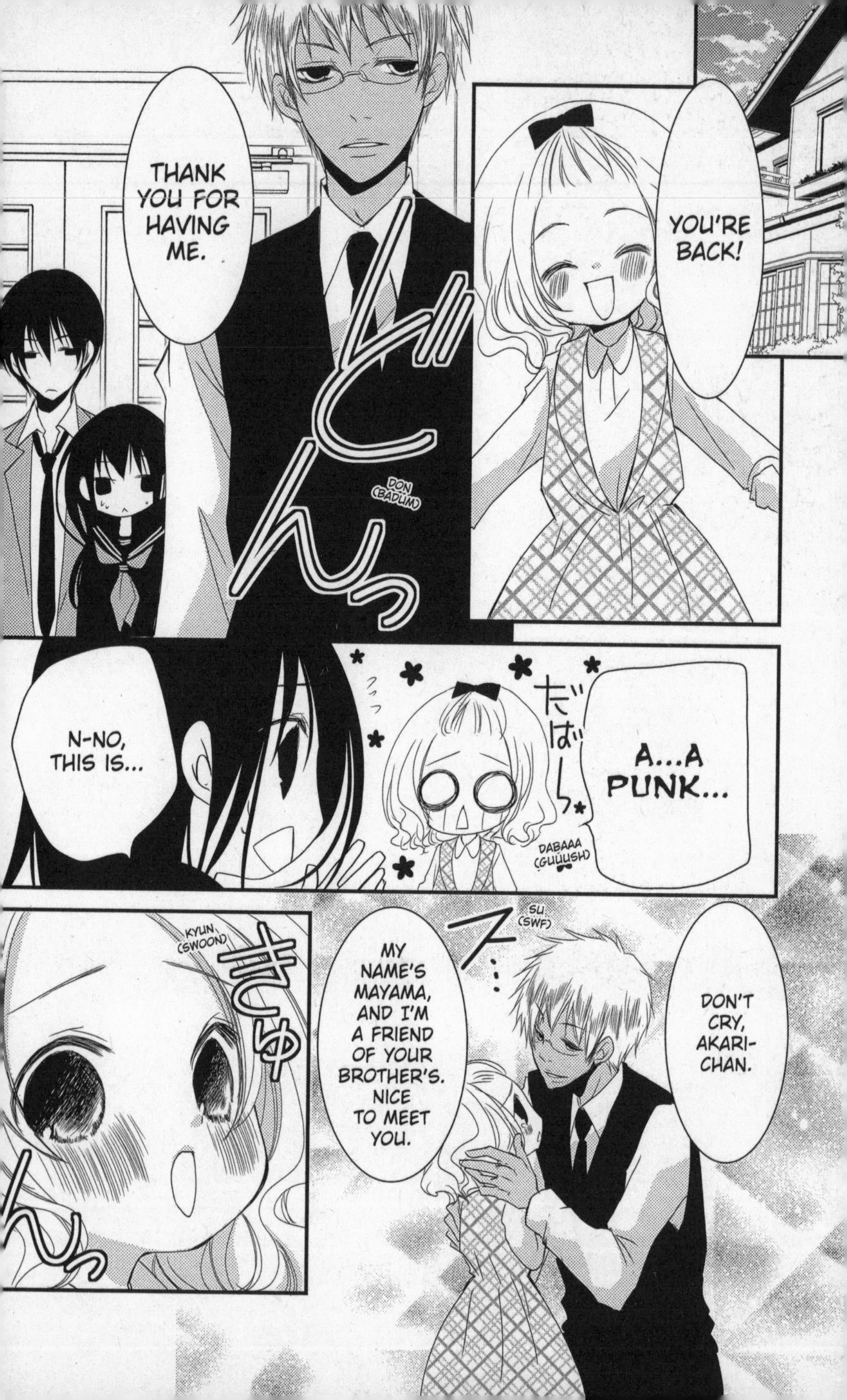
YOU'RE BACK!
THANK YOU FOR HAVING ME.
DON (BADUM)
A...A PUNK...
DABAAA (GUUUSH)
N-NO, THIS IS...
DON'T CRY, AKARI-CHAN.
SU (SWF)
MY NAME'S MAYAMA, AND I'M A FRIEND OF YOUR BROTHER'S. NICE TO MEET YOU.
KYUN (SWOON)

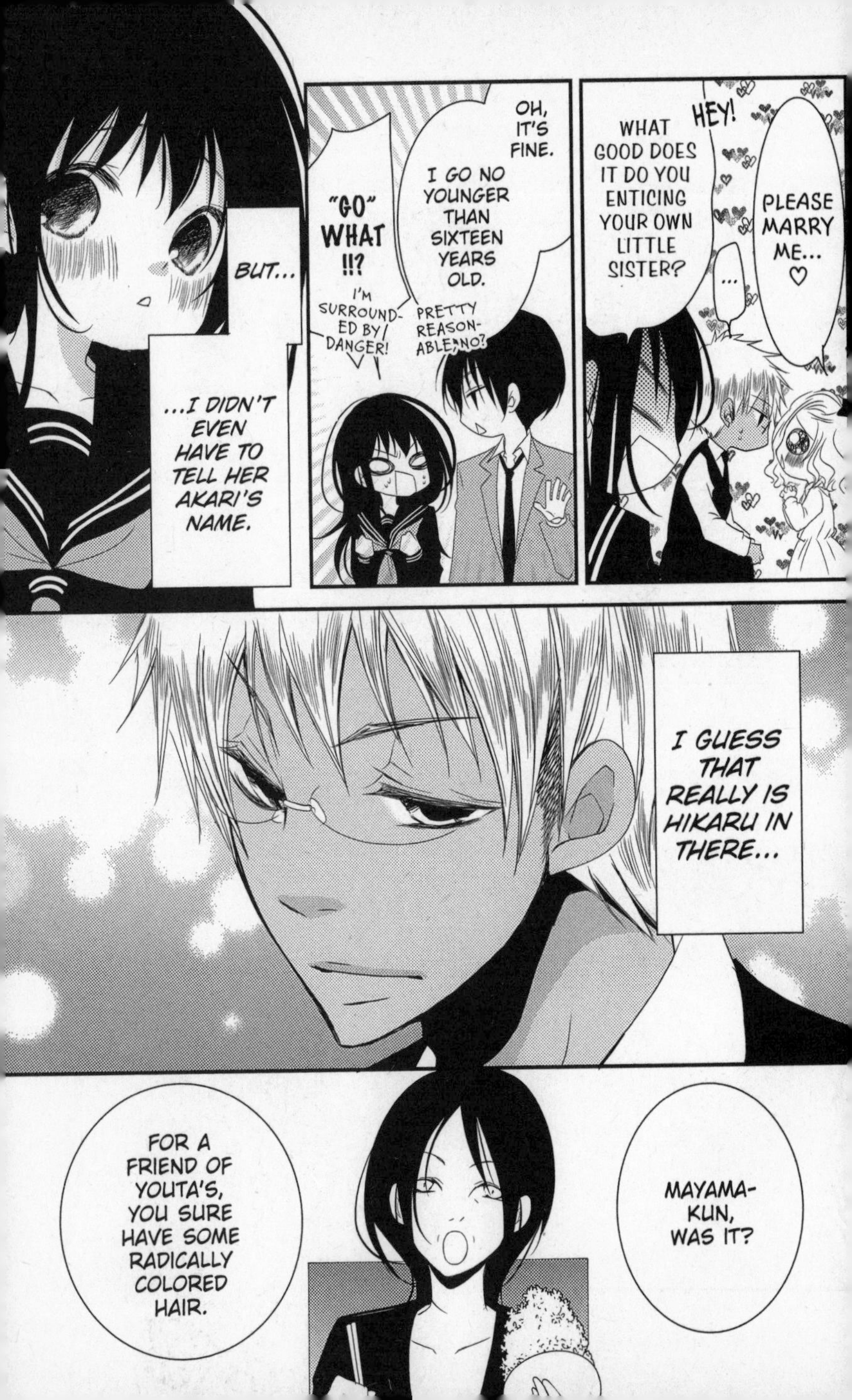
PLEASE MARRY ME... ♡
HEY!
WHAT GOOD DOES IT DO YOU ENTICING YOUR OWN LITTLE SISTER?
...
OH, IT'S FINE.
I GO NO YOUNGER THAN SIXTEEN YEARS OLD.
"GO" WHAT!!?
PRETTY REASONABLE, NO?
I'M SURROUNDED BY DANGER!
BUT...
...I DIDN'T EVEN HAVE TO TELL HER AKARI'S NAME.
I GUESS THAT REALLY IS HIKARU IN THERE...
MAYAMA-KUN, WAS IT?
FOR A FRIEND OF YOUTA'S, YOU SURE HAVE SOME RADICALLY COLORED HAIR.

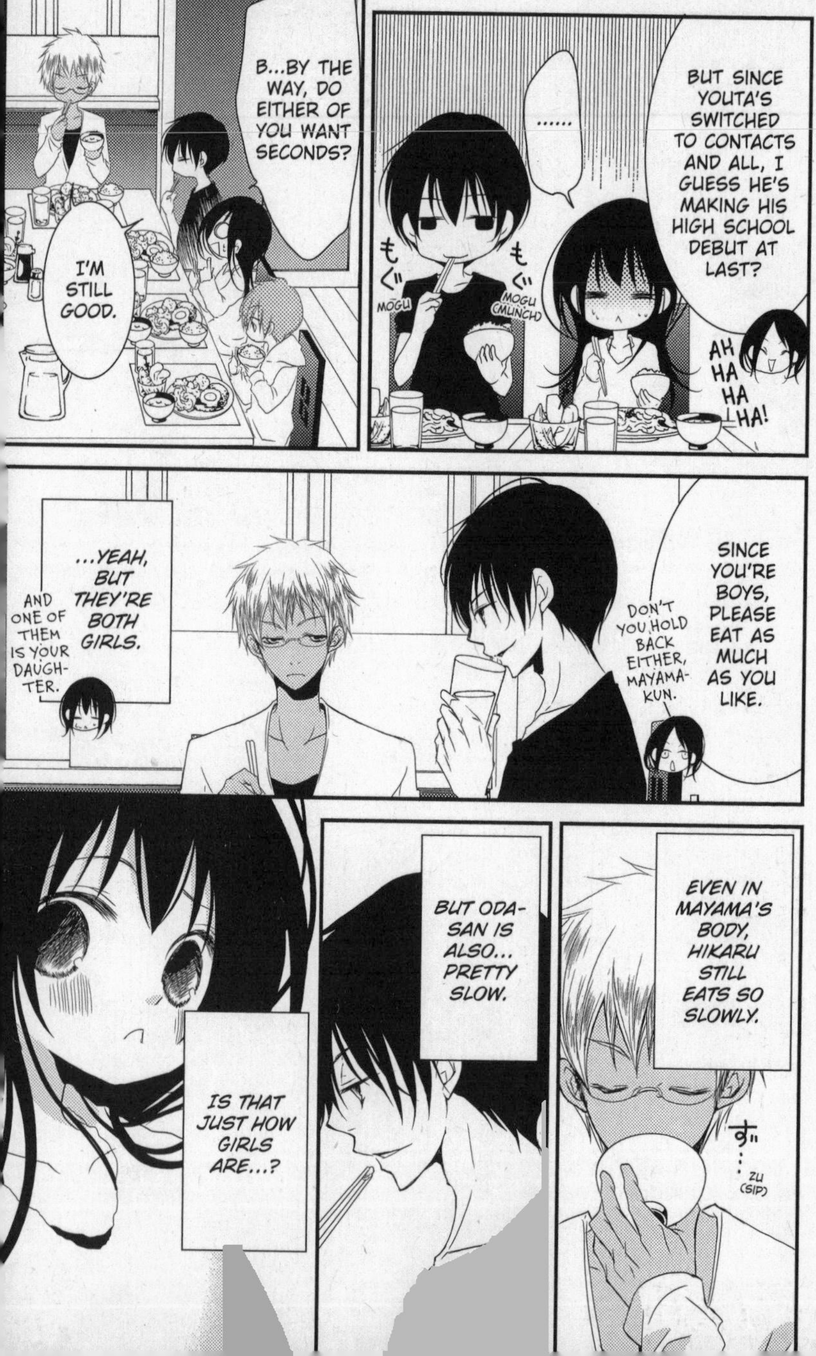
BUT SINCE YOUTA'S SWITCHED TO CONTACTS AND ALL, I GUESS HE'S MAKING HIS HIGH SCHOOL DEBUT AT LAST?
AH HA HA HA!
......
もぐ MOGU (MUNCH)
もぐ MOGU
B...BY THE WAY, DO EITHER OF YOU WANT SECONDS?
I'M STILL GOOD.
SINCE YOU'RE BOYS, PLEASE EAT AS MUCH AS YOU LIKE.
DON'T YOU HOLD BACK EITHER, MAYAMA-KUN.
...YEAH, BUT THEY'RE BOTH GIRLS.
AND ONE OF THEM IS YOUR DAUGHTER.
EVEN IN MAYAMA'S BODY, HIKARU STILL EATS SO SLOWLY.
ず… ZU (SIP)
BUT ODA-SAN IS ALSO... PRETTY SLOW.
IS THAT JUST HOW GIRLS ARE...?

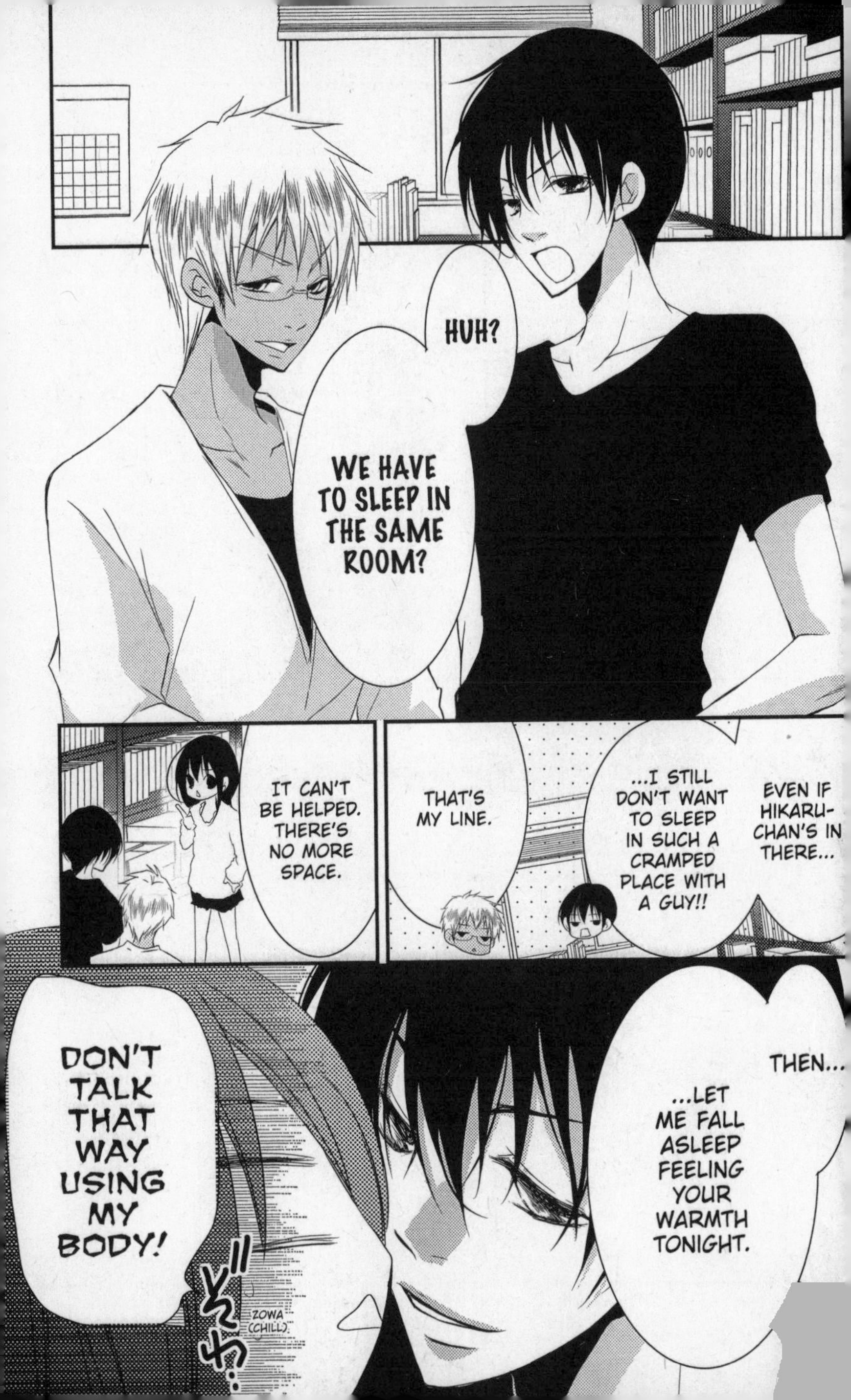
HUH?
WE HAVE TO SLEEP IN THE SAME ROOM?
EVEN IF HIKARU-CHAN'S IN THERE...
...I STILL DON'T WANT TO SLEEP IN SUCH A CRAMPED PLACE WITH A GUY!!
THAT'S MY LINE.
IT CAN'T BE HELPED. THERE'S NO MORE SPACE.
THEN...
...LET ME FALL ASLEEP FEELING YOUR WARMTH TONIGHT.
DON'T TALK THAT WAY USING MY BODY!
ZOWA (CHILL)

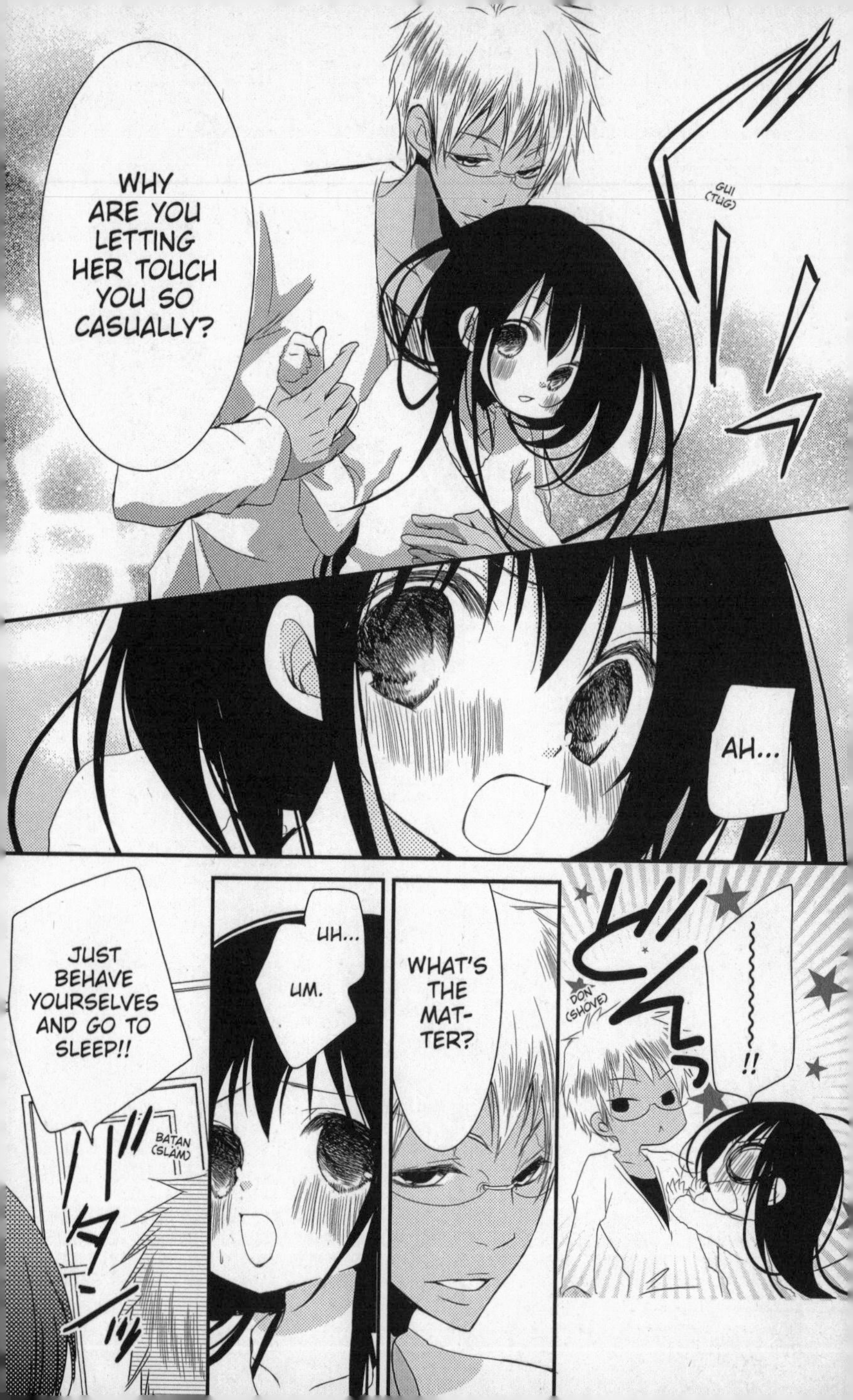
GUI (TUG)
WHY ARE YOU LETTING HER TOUCH YOU SO CASUALLY?
AH...
~~~~~~!!
DON (SHOVE)
WHAT'S THE MAT-TER?
UH...
UM.
JUST BEHAVE YOURSELVES AND GO TO SLEEP!!
BATAN (SLAM)
~~~~~~

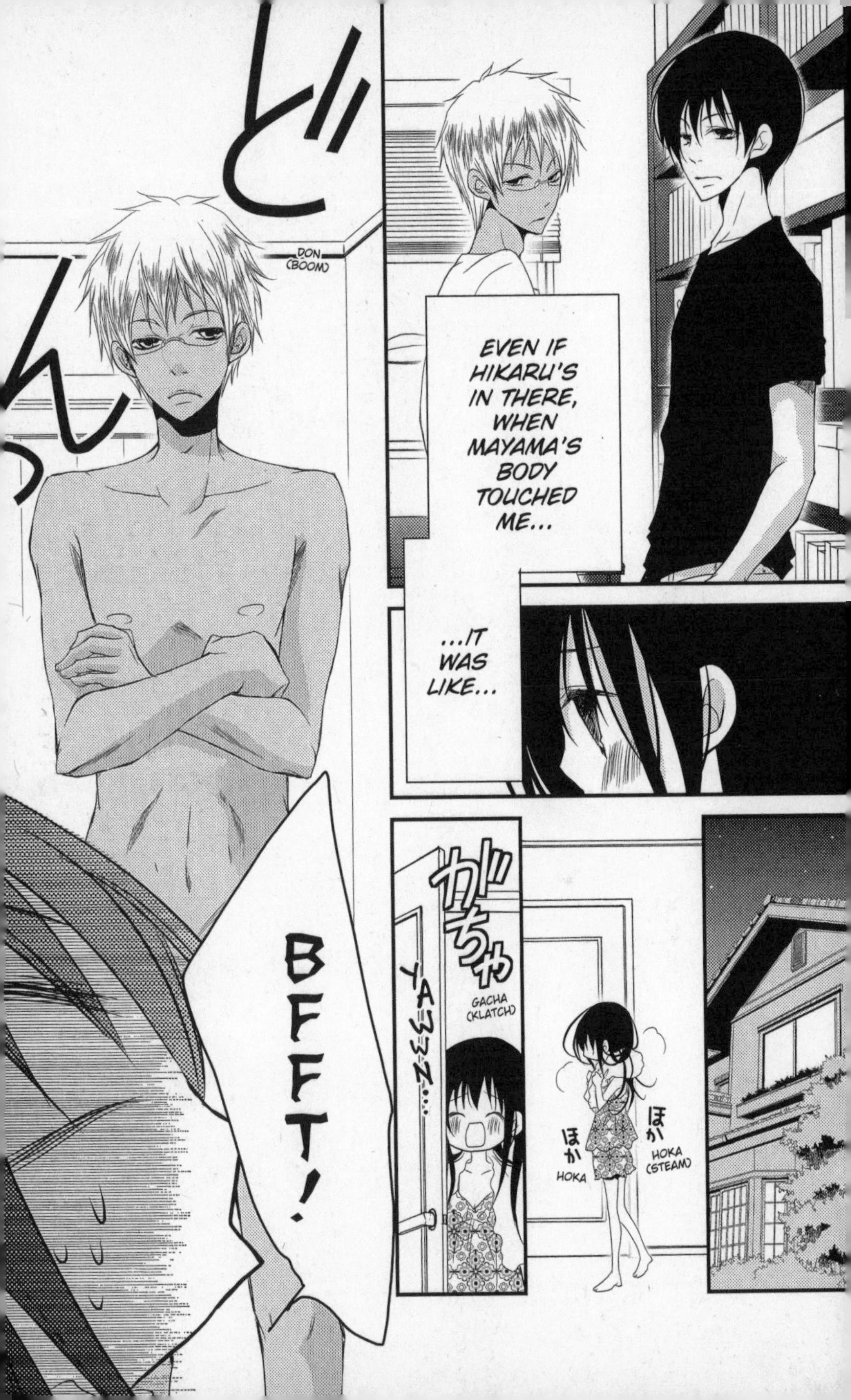

EVEN IF HIKARU'S IN THERE, WHEN MAYAMA'S BODY TOUCHED ME...
...IT WAS LIKE...
ほか
HOKA (STEAM)
ほか
HOKA
がちゃ
GACHA (KLATCH)
YAWWN...
どん
DON (BOOM)
BFFT!

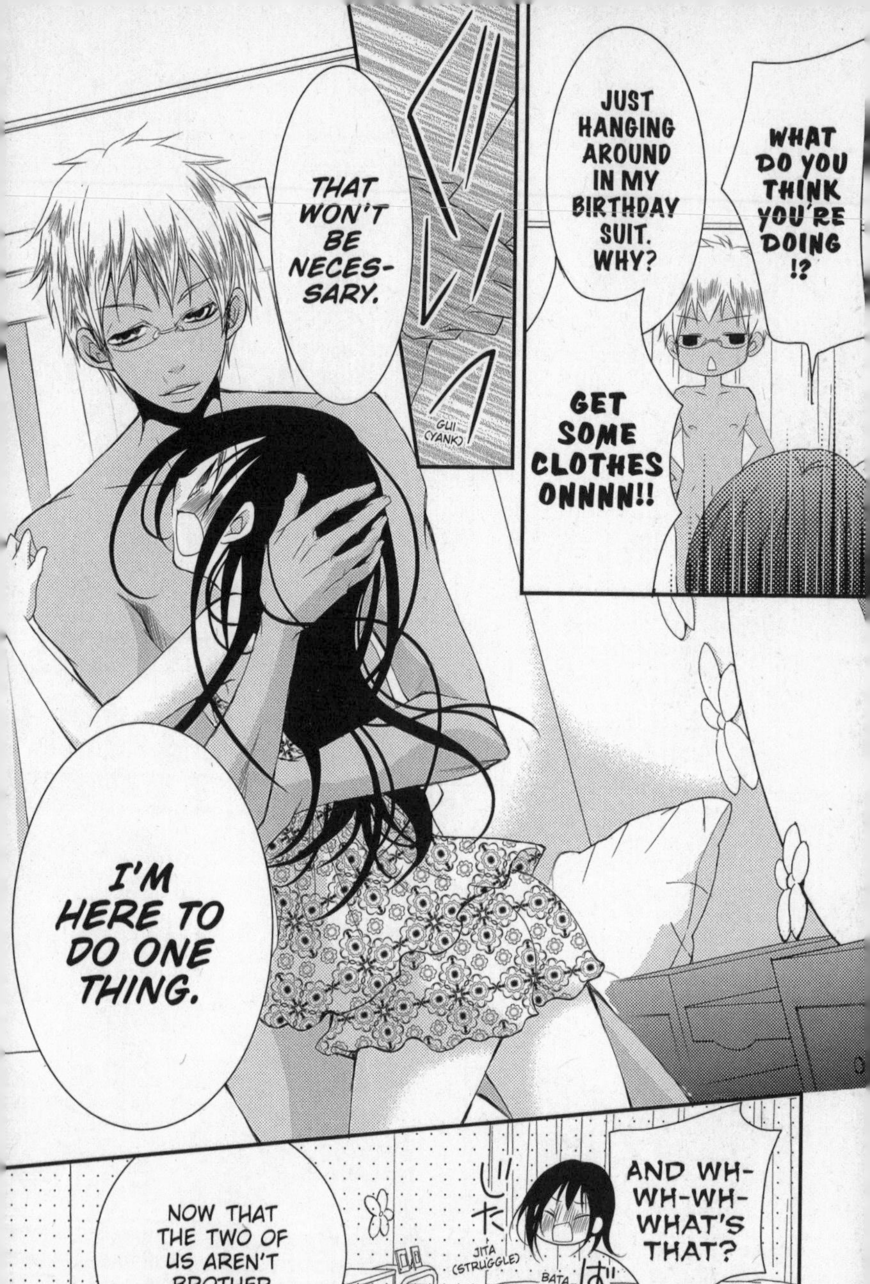
WHAT DO YOU THINK YOU'RE DOING!?
JUST HANGING AROUND IN MY BIRTHDAY SUIT. WHY?
GET SOME CLOTHES ONNNN!!
THAT WON'T BE NECES-SARY.
GUI (YANK)
I'M HERE TO DO ONE THING.
AND WH-WH-WH-WHAT'S THAT?
JITA (STRUGGLE)
BATA (FLAIL)
NOW THAT THE TWO OF US AREN'T BROTHER AND SISTER...

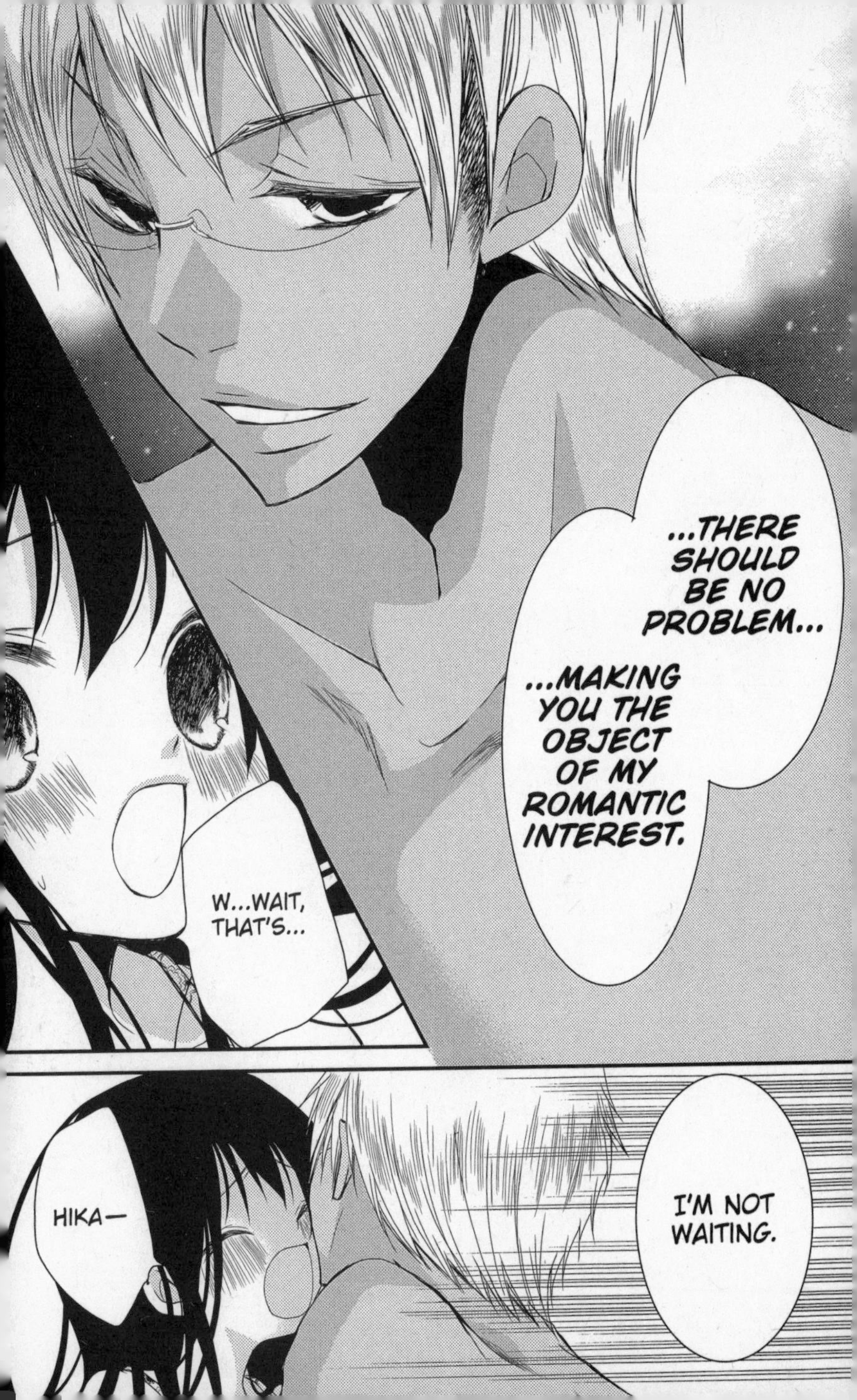
...THERE SHOULD BE NO PROBLEM...
...MAKING YOU THE OBJECT OF MY ROMANTIC INTEREST.
W...WAIT, THAT'S...
I'M NOT WAITING.
HIKA—

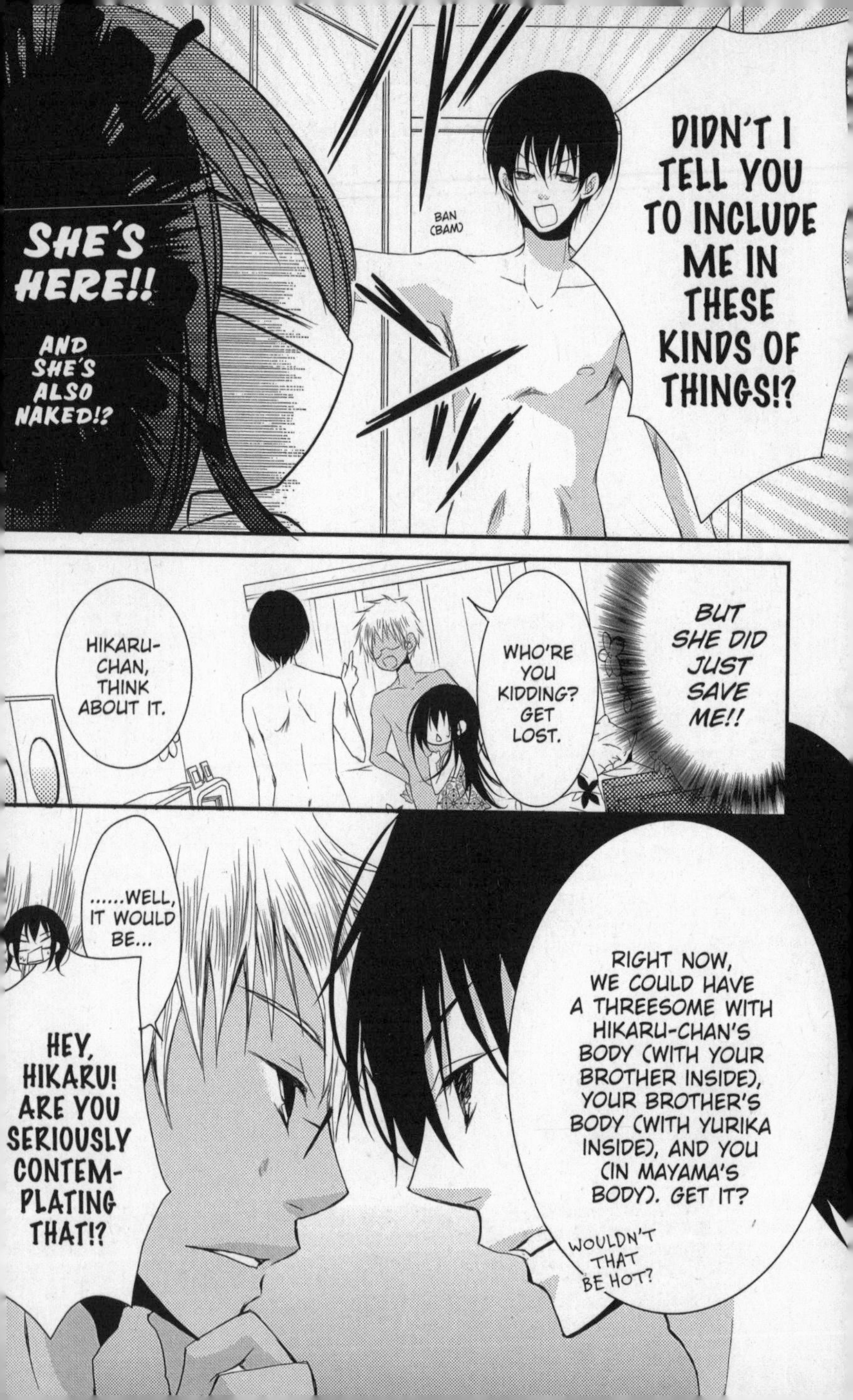
DIDN'T I TELL YOU TO INCLUDE ME IN THESE KINDS OF THINGS!?
BAN (BAM)
SHE'S HERE!!
AND SHE'S ALSO NAKED!?
BUT SHE DID JUST SAVE ME!!
WHO'RE YOU KIDDING? GET LOST.
HIKARU-CHAN, THINK ABOUT IT.
RIGHT NOW, WE COULD HAVE A THREESOME WITH HIKARU-CHAN'S BODY (WITH YOUR BROTHER INSIDE), YOUR BROTHER'S BODY (WITH YURIKA INSIDE), AND YOU (IN MAYAMA'S BODY). GET IT?
WOULDN'T THAT BE HOT?
......WELL, IT WOULD BE...
HEY, HIKARU! ARE YOU SERIOUSLY CONTEM-PLATING THAT!?

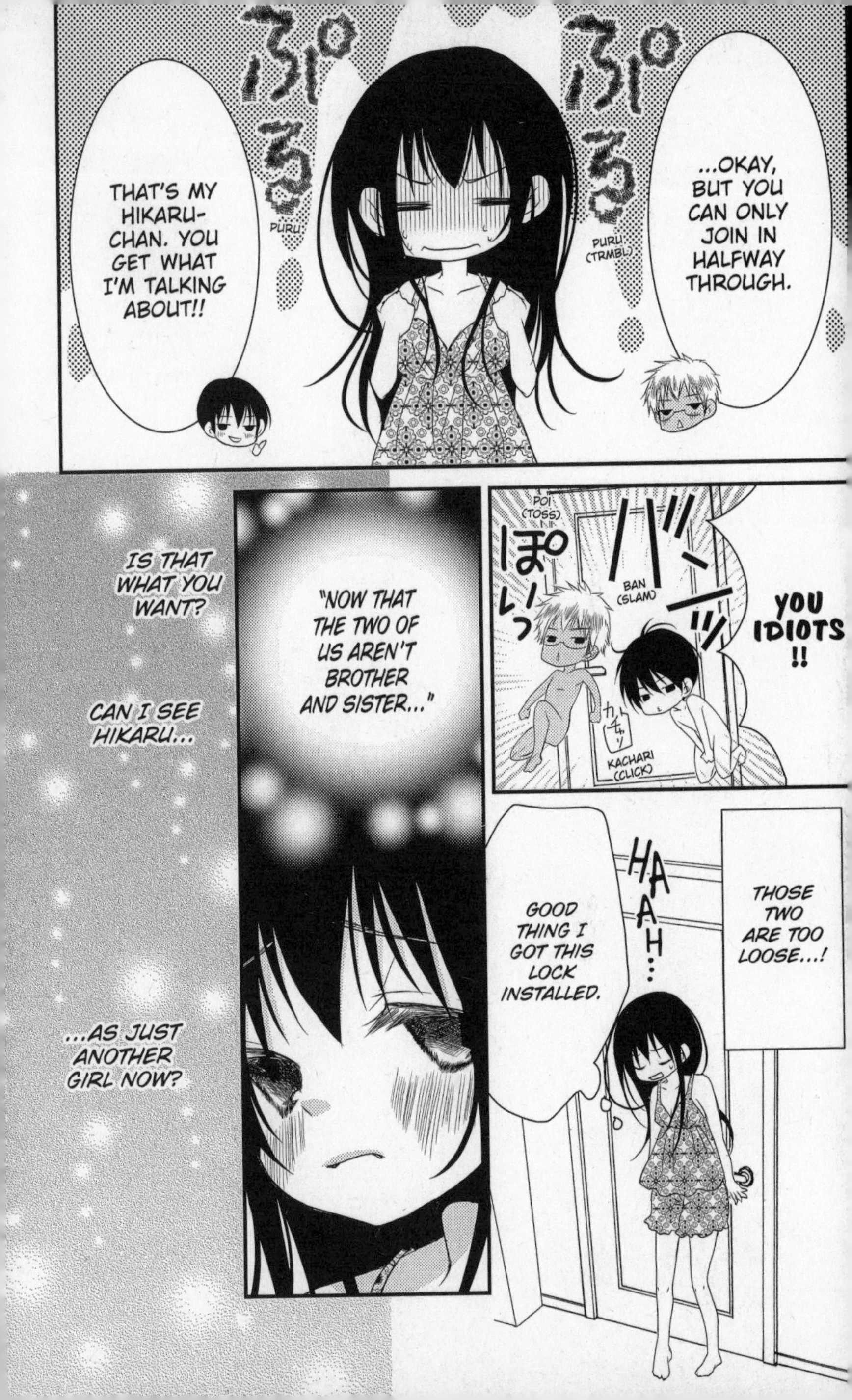
ぷる
PURU (TRMBL)
...OKAY, BUT YOU CAN ONLY JOIN IN HALFWAY THROUGH.
ぷる
PURU
THAT'S MY HIKARU-CHAN. YOU GET WHAT I'M TALKING ABOUT!!
YOU IDIOTS!!
バンッ
BAN (SLAM)
ぽいっ
POI (TOSS)
カチャリ
KACHARI (CLICK)
THOSE TWO ARE TOO LOOSE...!
HAAAH...
GOOD THING I GOT THIS LOCK INSTALLED.
"NOW THAT THE TWO OF US AREN'T BROTHER AND SISTER..."
IS THAT WHAT YOU WANT?
CAN I SEE HIKARU...
...AS JUST ANOTHER GIRL NOW?

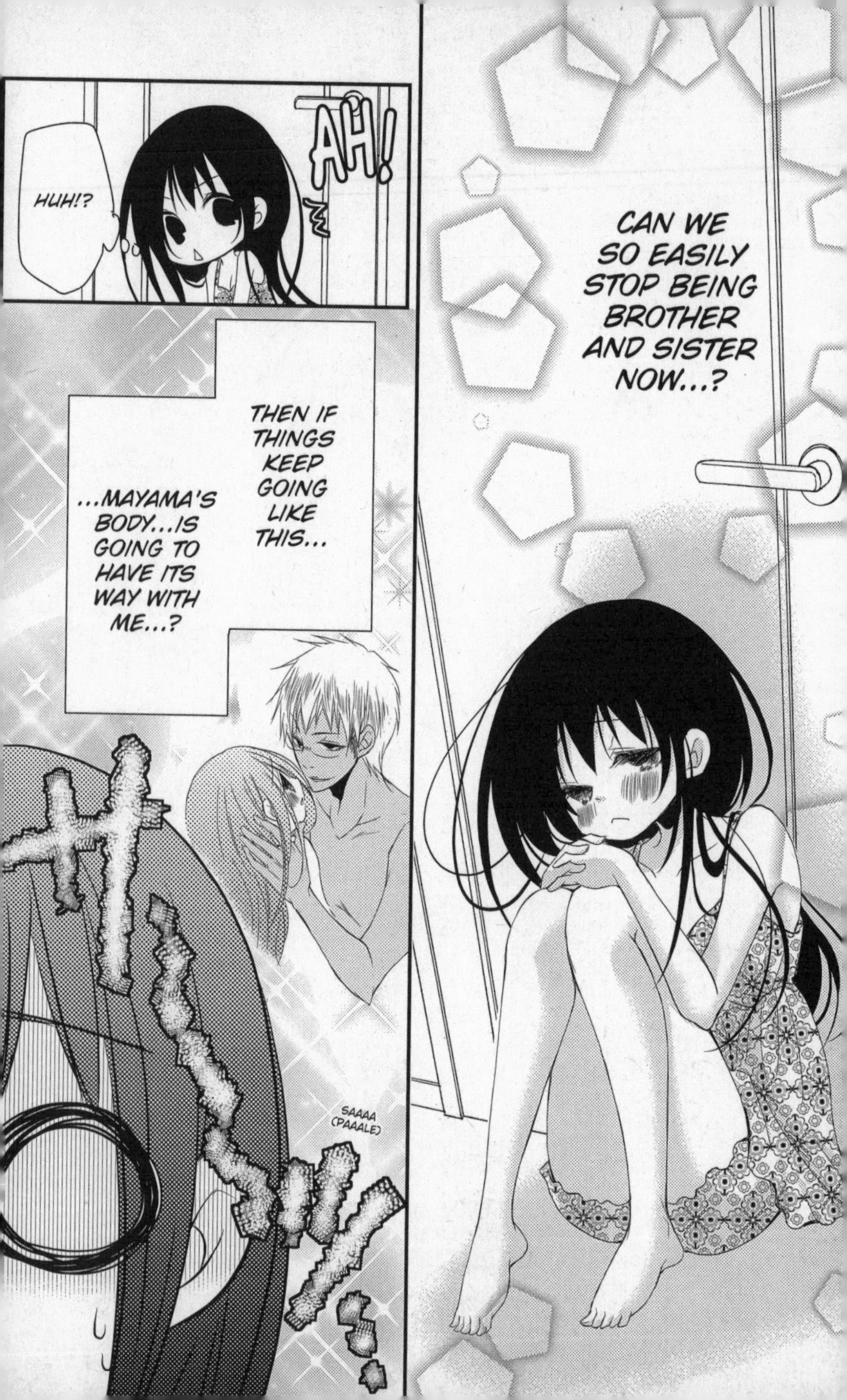
CAN WE SO EASILY STOP BEING BROTHER AND SISTER NOW...?
AH!
HUH!?
THEN IF THINGS KEEP GOING LIKE THIS...
...MAYAMA'S BODY...IS GOING TO HAVE ITS WAY WITH ME...?
SAAAA (PAAALE)

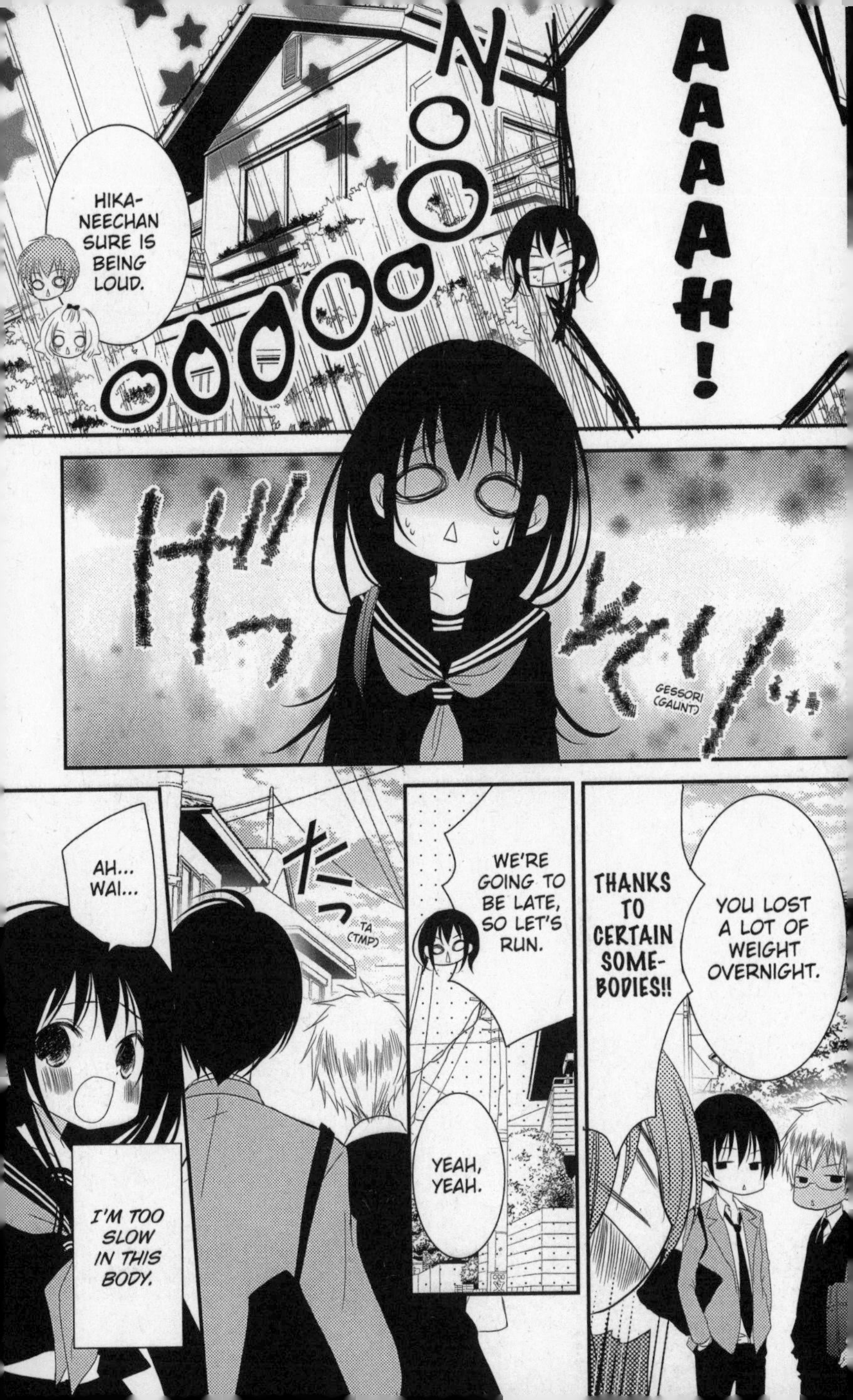
AAAAH!
NOOOOOOO
HIKA-NEECHAN SURE IS BEING LOUD.
GESSORI (GAUNT)
YOU LOST A LOT OF WEIGHT OVERNIGHT.
THANKS TO CERTAIN SOME-BODIES!!
WE'RE GOING TO BE LATE, SO LET'S RUN.
YEAH, YEAH.
TA (TMP)
AH... WAI...
I'M TOO SLOW IN THIS BODY.

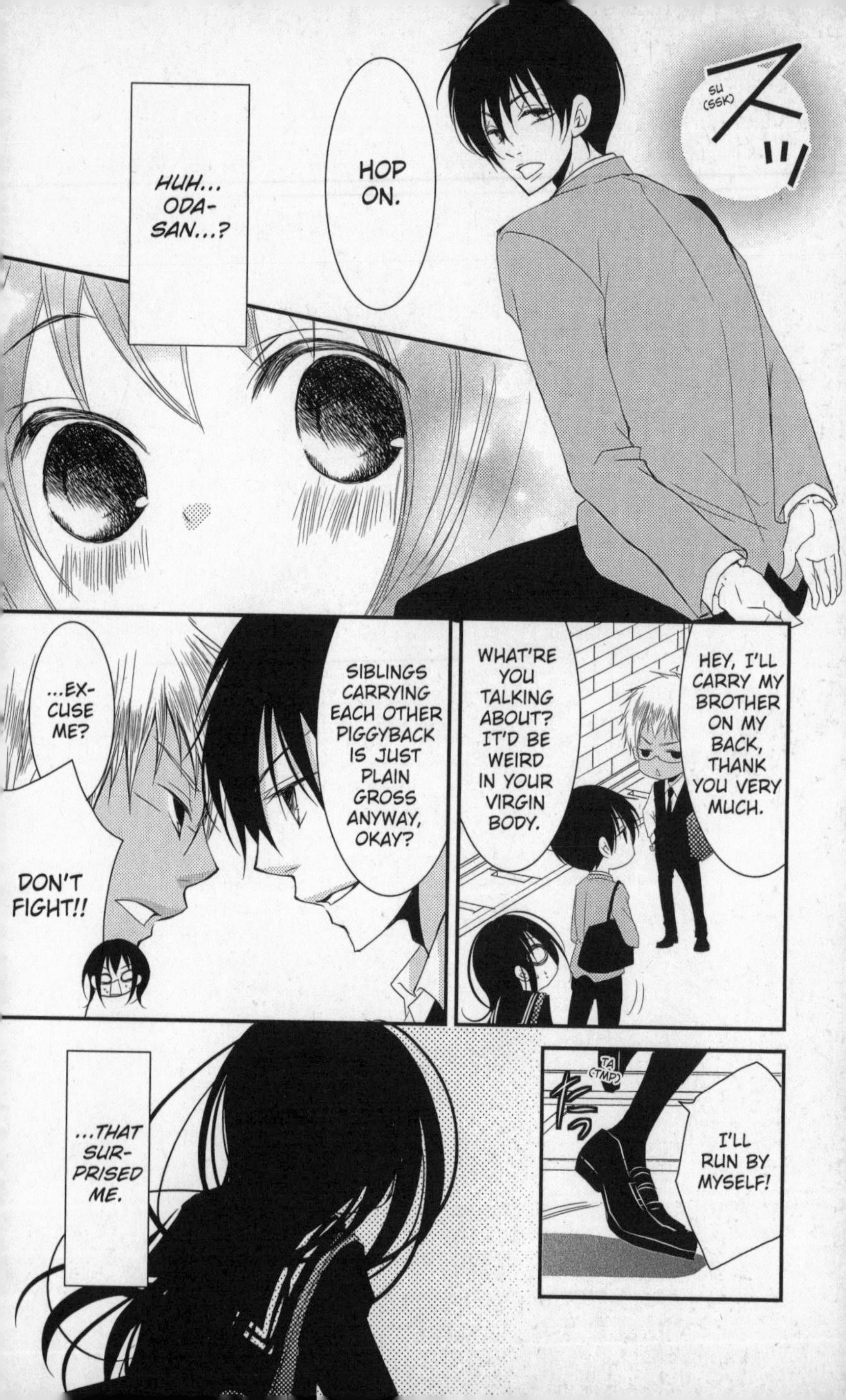
SU (SSK)
HOP ON.
HUH... ODA-SAN...?
HEY, I'LL CARRY MY BROTHER ON MY BACK, THANK YOU VERY MUCH.
WHAT'RE YOU TALKING ABOUT? IT'D BE WEIRD IN YOUR VIRGIN BODY.
SIBLINGS CARRYING EACH OTHER PIGGYBACK IS JUST PLAIN GROSS ANYWAY, OKAY?
...EX-CUSE ME?
DON'T FIGHT!!
TA (TMP)
I'LL RUN BY MYSELF!
...THAT SUR-PRISED ME.

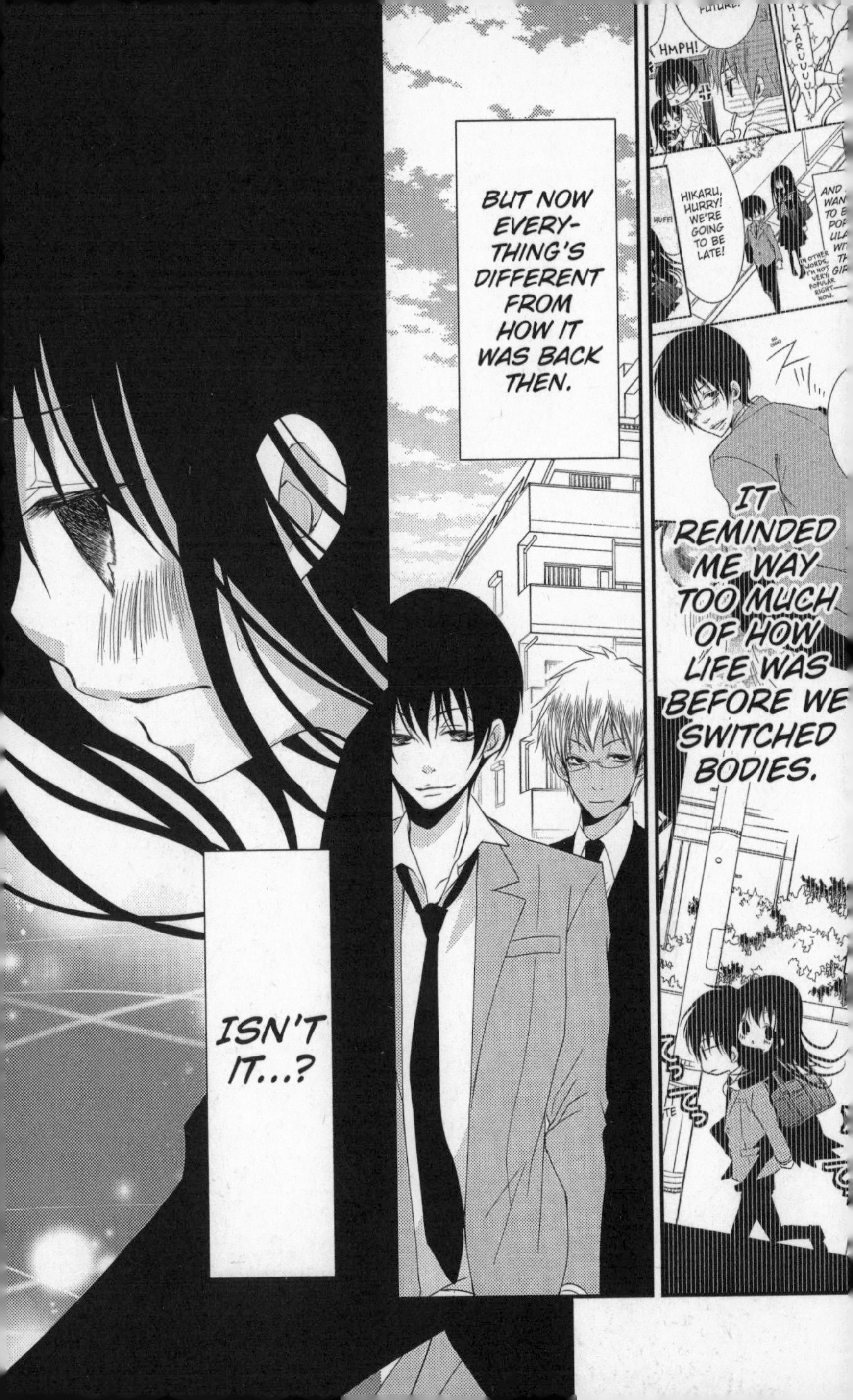
HIKARUUUUU!
HMPH!
IN OTHER WORDS, I'M NOT VERY POPULAR RIGHT NOW.
HIKARU, HURRY! WE'RE GOING TO BE LATE!
HUFF!
IT REMINDED ME WAY TOO MUCH OF HOW LIFE WAS BEFORE WE SWITCHED BODIES.
BUT NOW EVERYTHING'S DIFFERENT FROM HOW IT WAS BACK THEN.
ISN'T IT...?

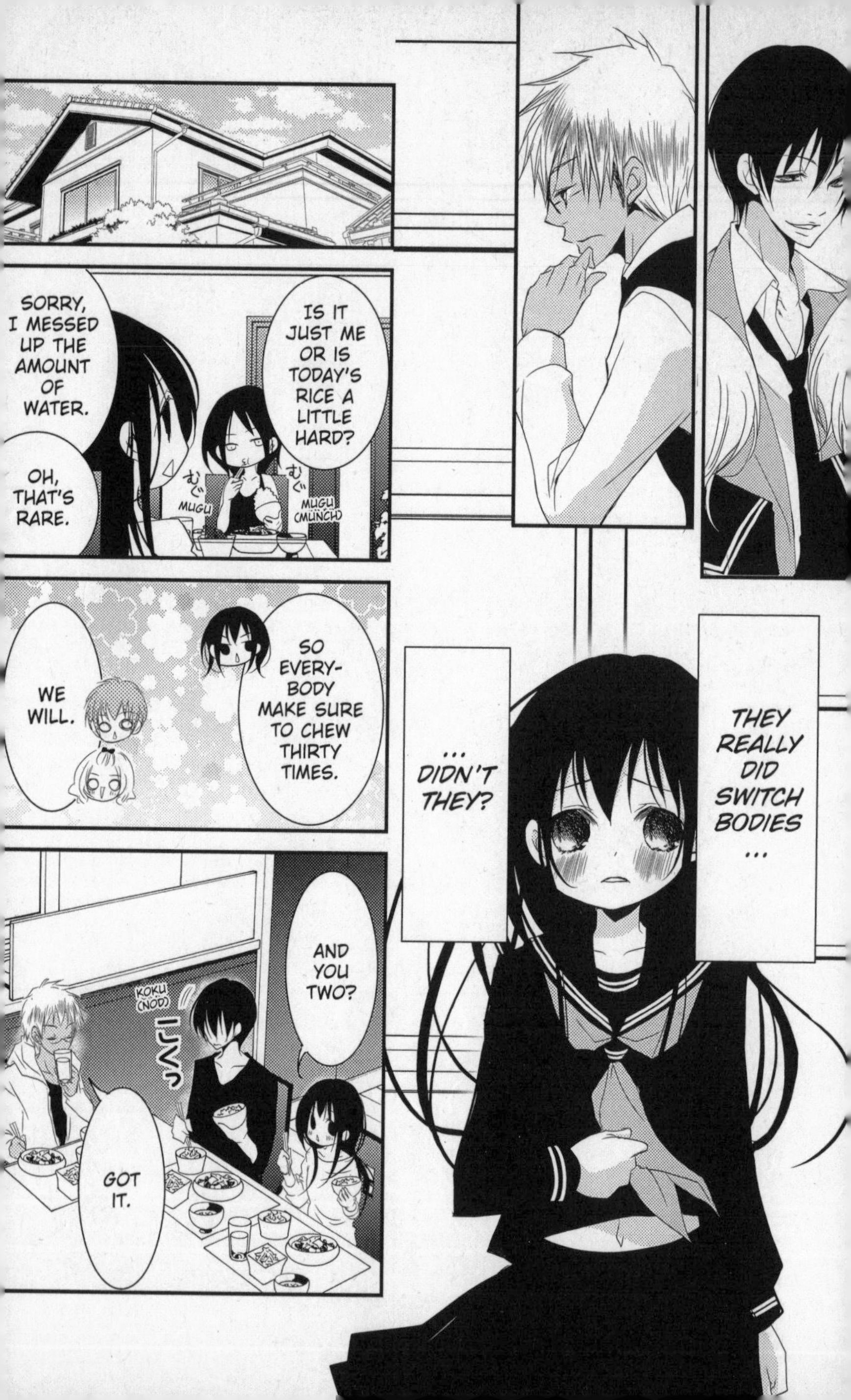
THEY REALLY DID SWITCH BODIES...
...DIDN'T THEY?
IS IT JUST ME OR IS TODAY'S RICE A LITTLE HARD?
むぐ MUGU (MUNCH)
むぐ MUGU
SORRY, I MESSED UP THE AMOUNT OF WATER.
OH, THAT'S RARE.
SO EVERYBODY MAKE SURE TO CHEW THIRTY TIMES.
WE WILL.
AND YOU TWO?
こくっ KOKU (NOD)
GOT IT.

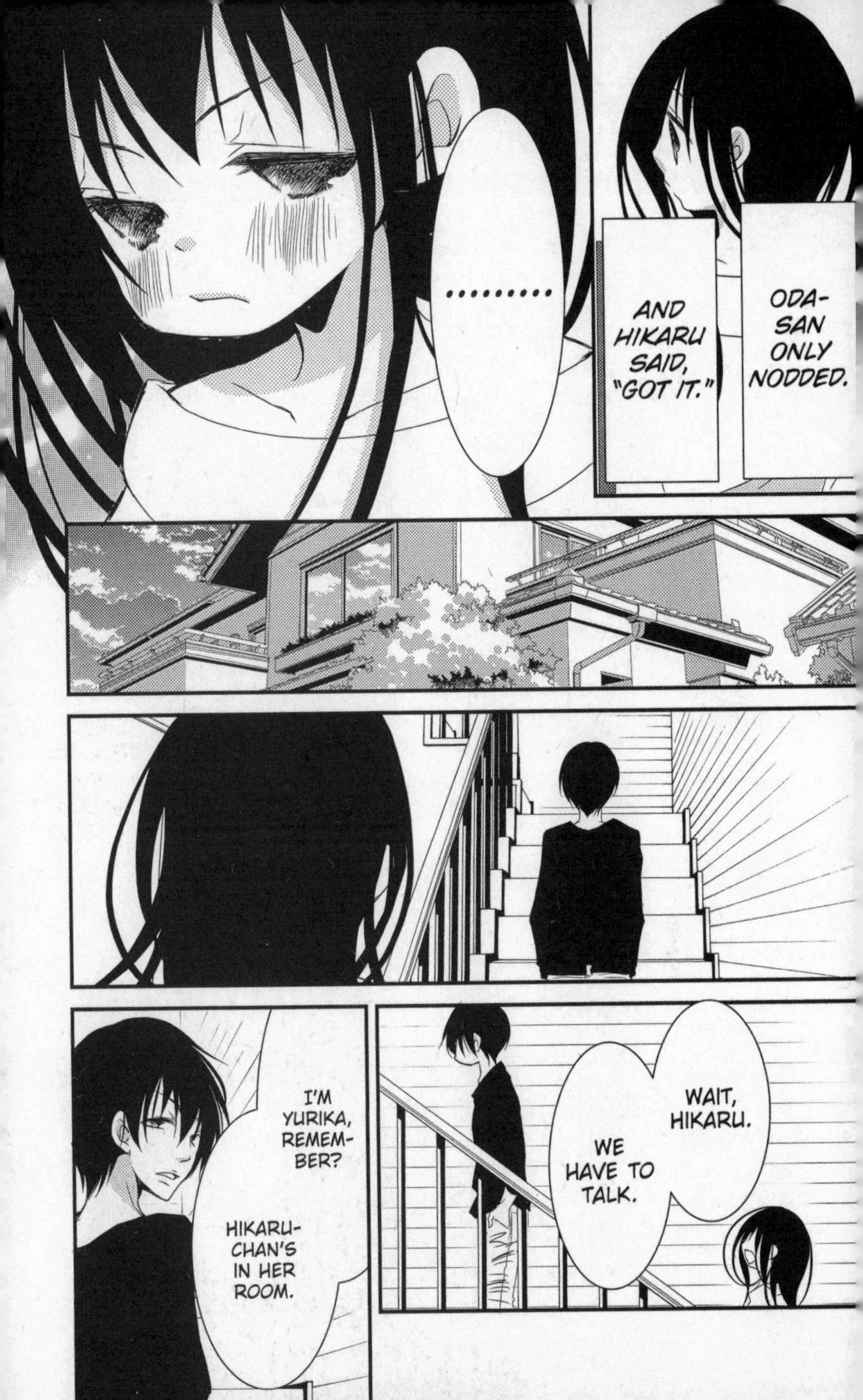
ODA-SAN ONLY NODDED.
AND HIKARU SAID, "GOT IT."
....
WAIT, HIKARU.
WE HAVE TO TALK.
I'M YURIKA, REMEMBER?
HIKARU-CHAN'S IN HER ROOM.

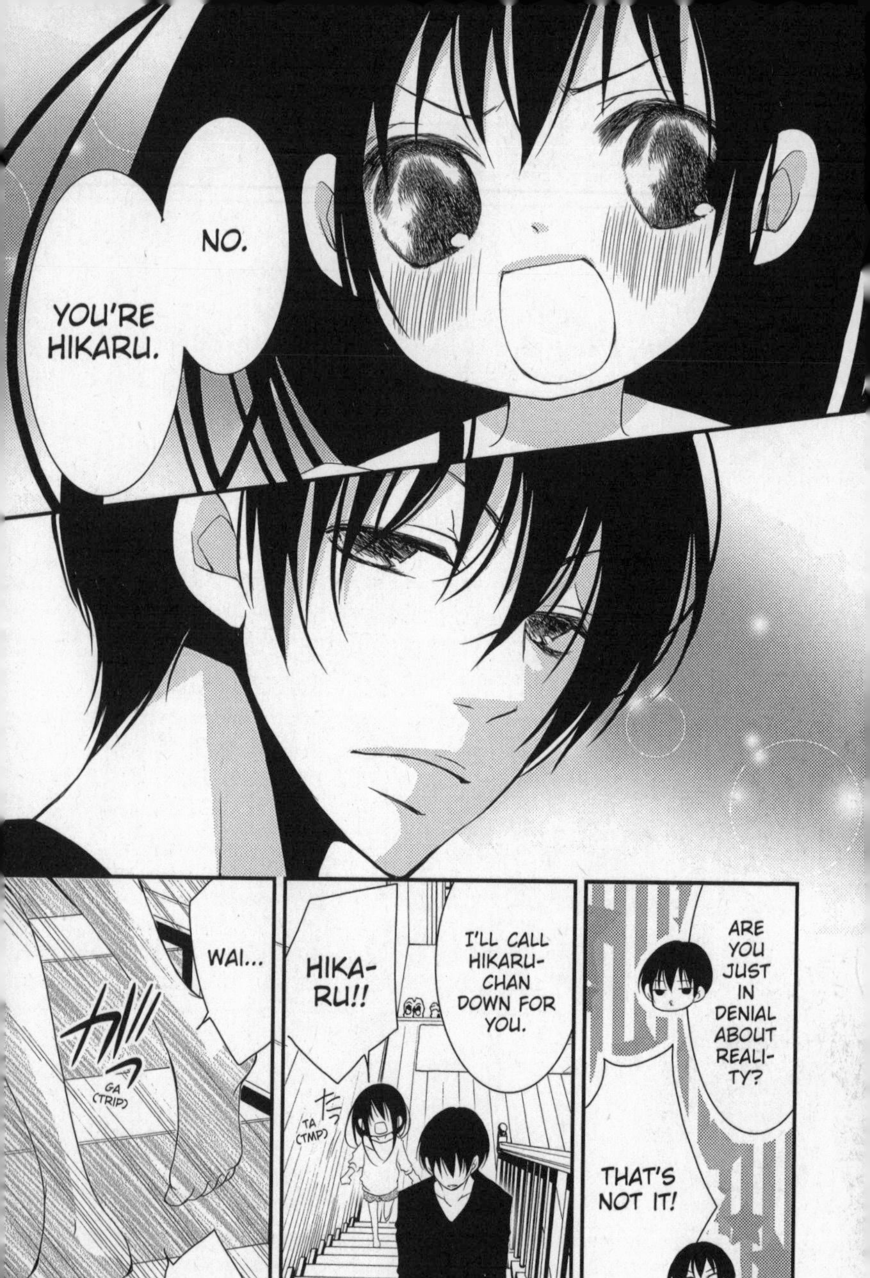
NO.
YOU'RE HIKARU.
ARE YOU JUST IN DENIAL ABOUT REALITY?
THAT'S NOT IT!
I'LL CALL HIKARU-CHAN DOWN FOR YOU.
HIKA-RU!!
TA (TMP)
WAI...
GA (TRIP)
AH!

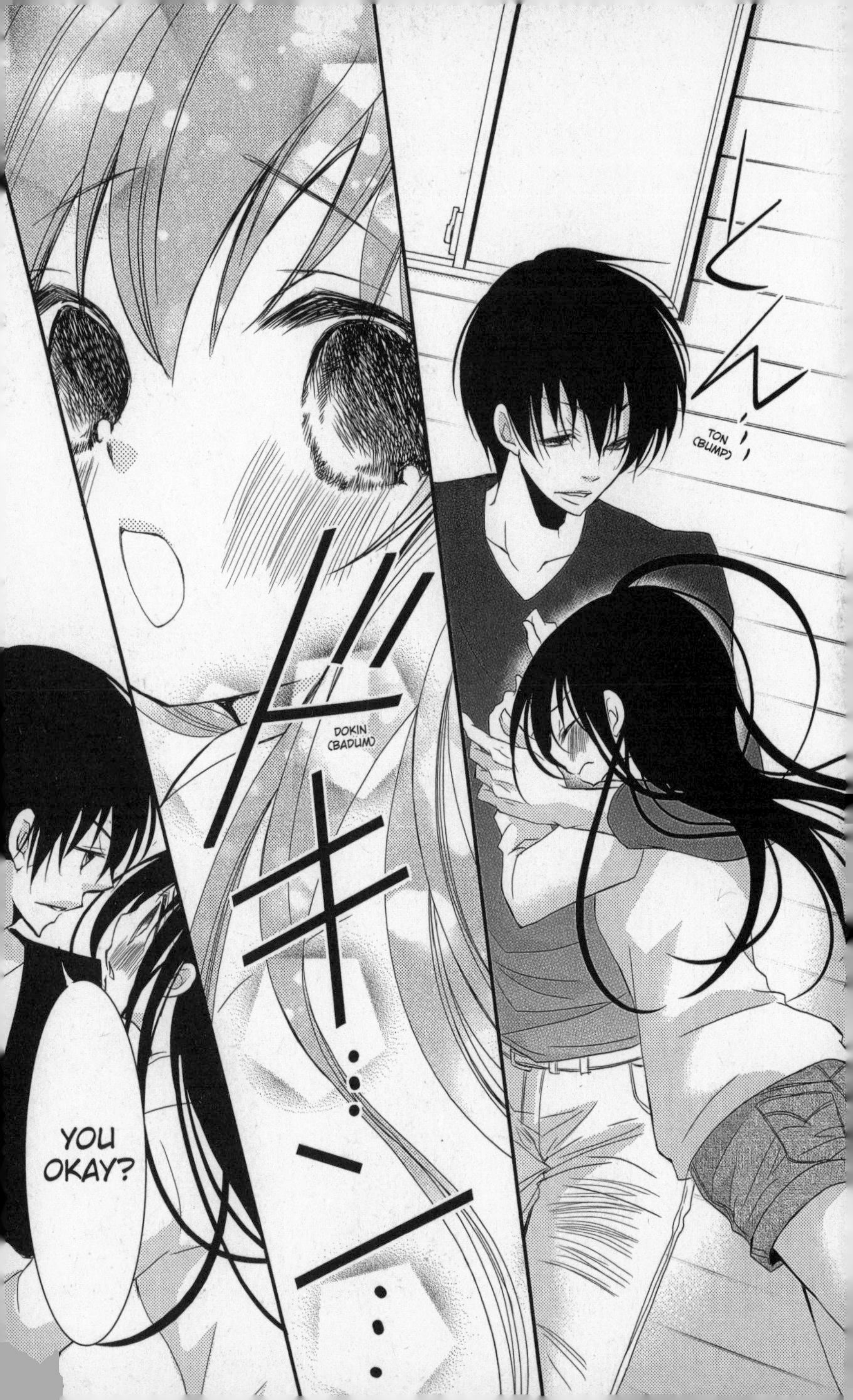
TON (BUMP)
DOKIN (BADUM)
YOU OKAY?

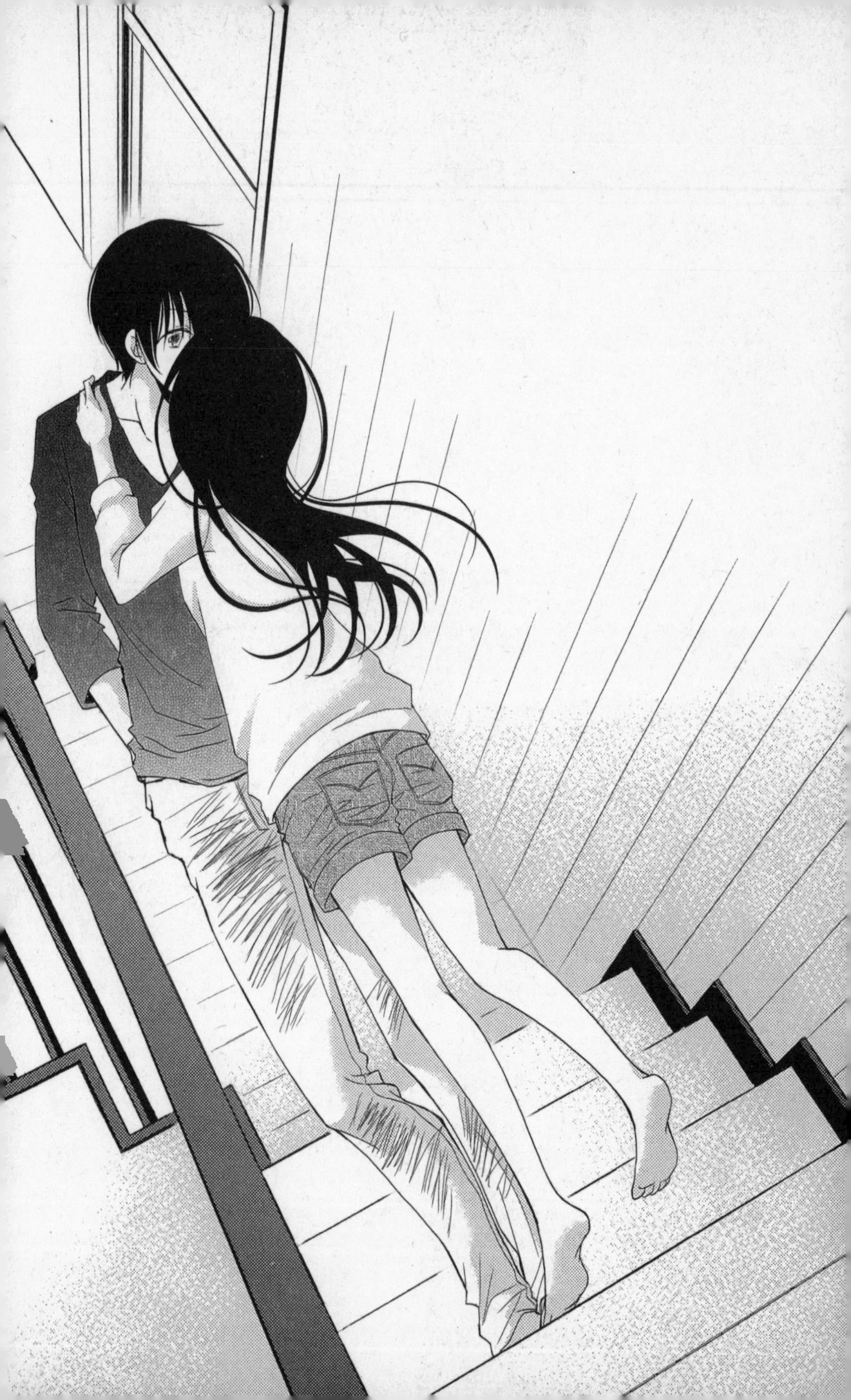

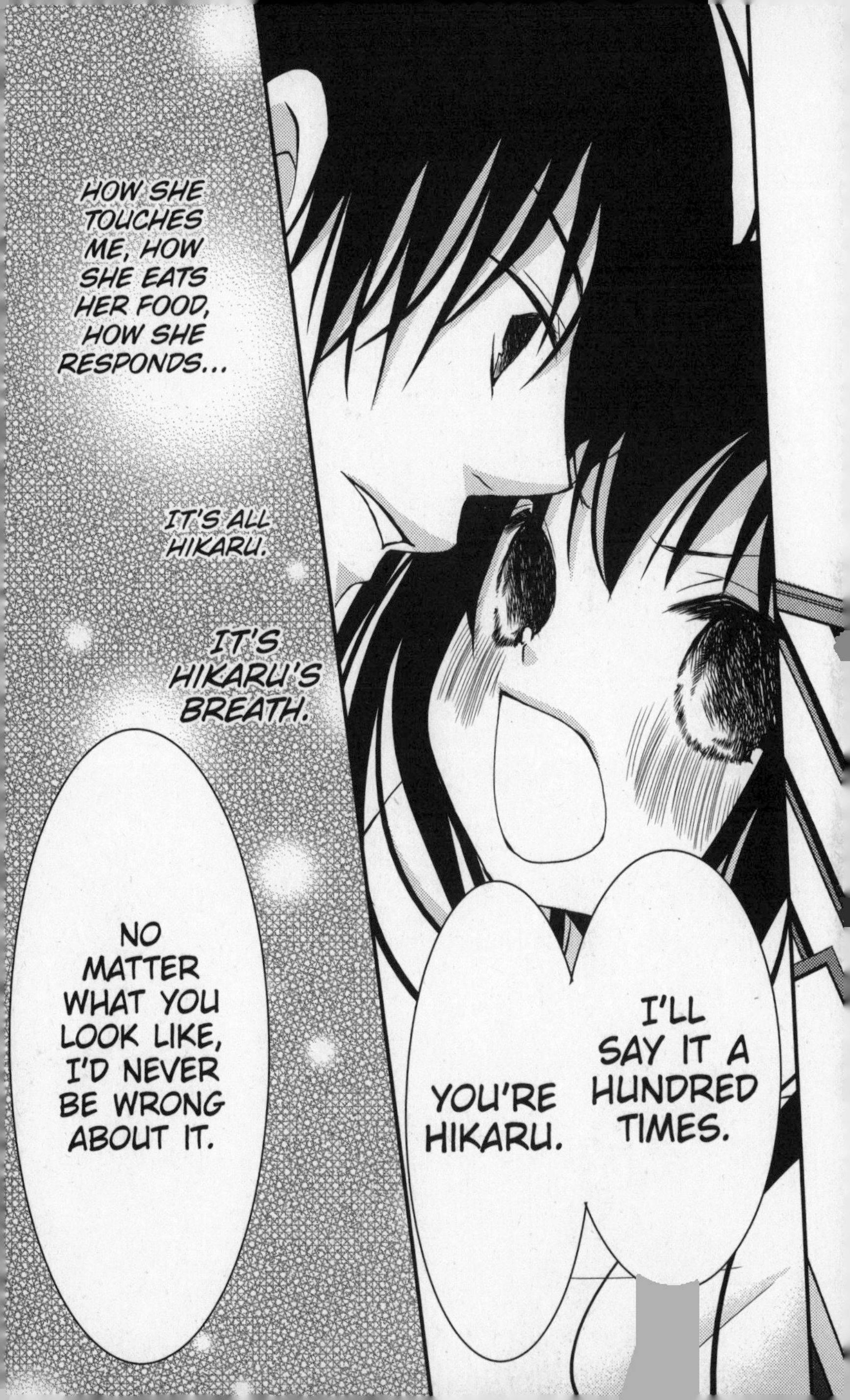
HOW SHE TOUCHES ME, HOW SHE EATS HER FOOD, HOW SHE RESPONDS...
IT'S ALL HIKARU.
IT'S HIKARU'S BREATH.
NO MATTER WHAT YOU LOOK LIKE, I'D NEVER BE WRONG ABOUT IT.
I'LL SAY IT A HUNDRED TIMES.
YOU'RE HIKARU.

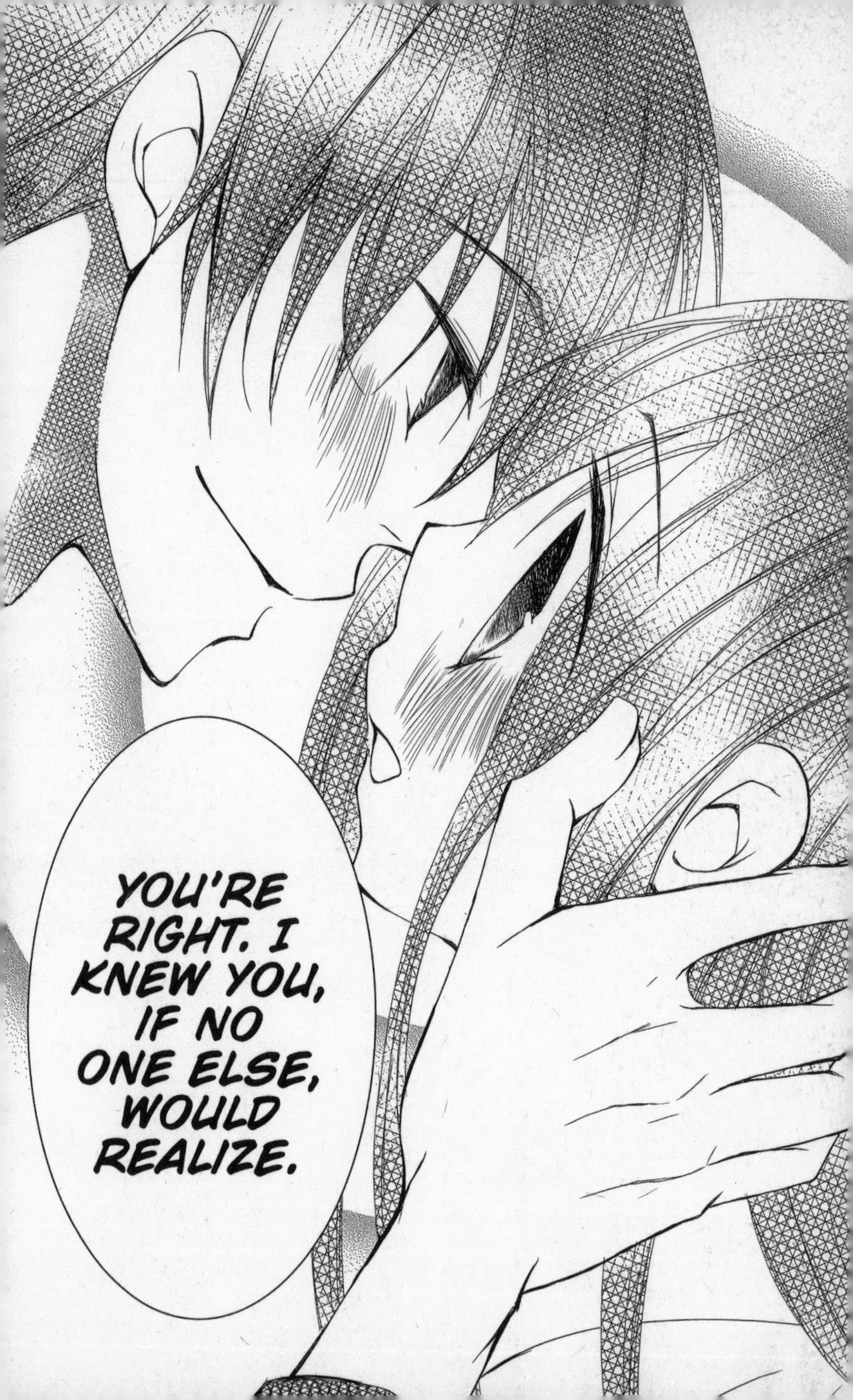
YOU'RE RIGHT. I KNEW YOU, IF NO ONE ELSE, WOULD REALIZE.

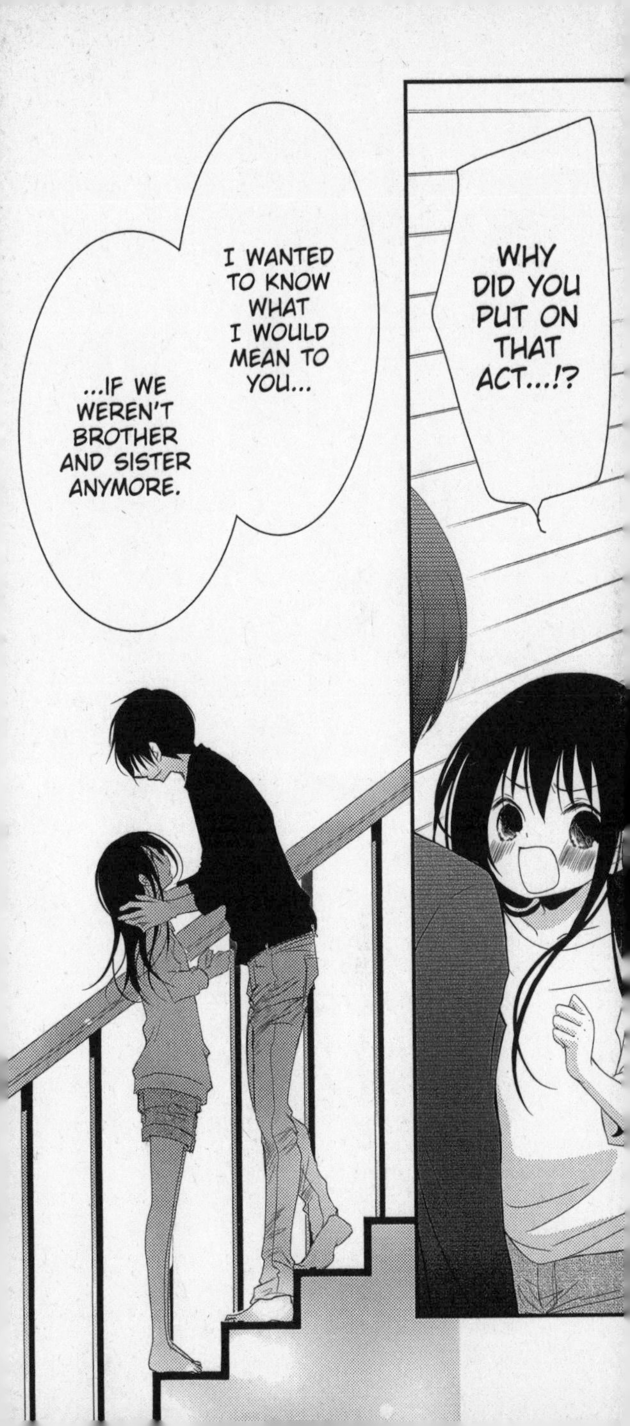
WHY DID YOU PUT ON THAT ACT...!?
I WANTED TO KNOW WHAT I WOULD MEAN TO YOU...
...IF WE WEREN'T BROTHER AND SISTER ANYMORE.

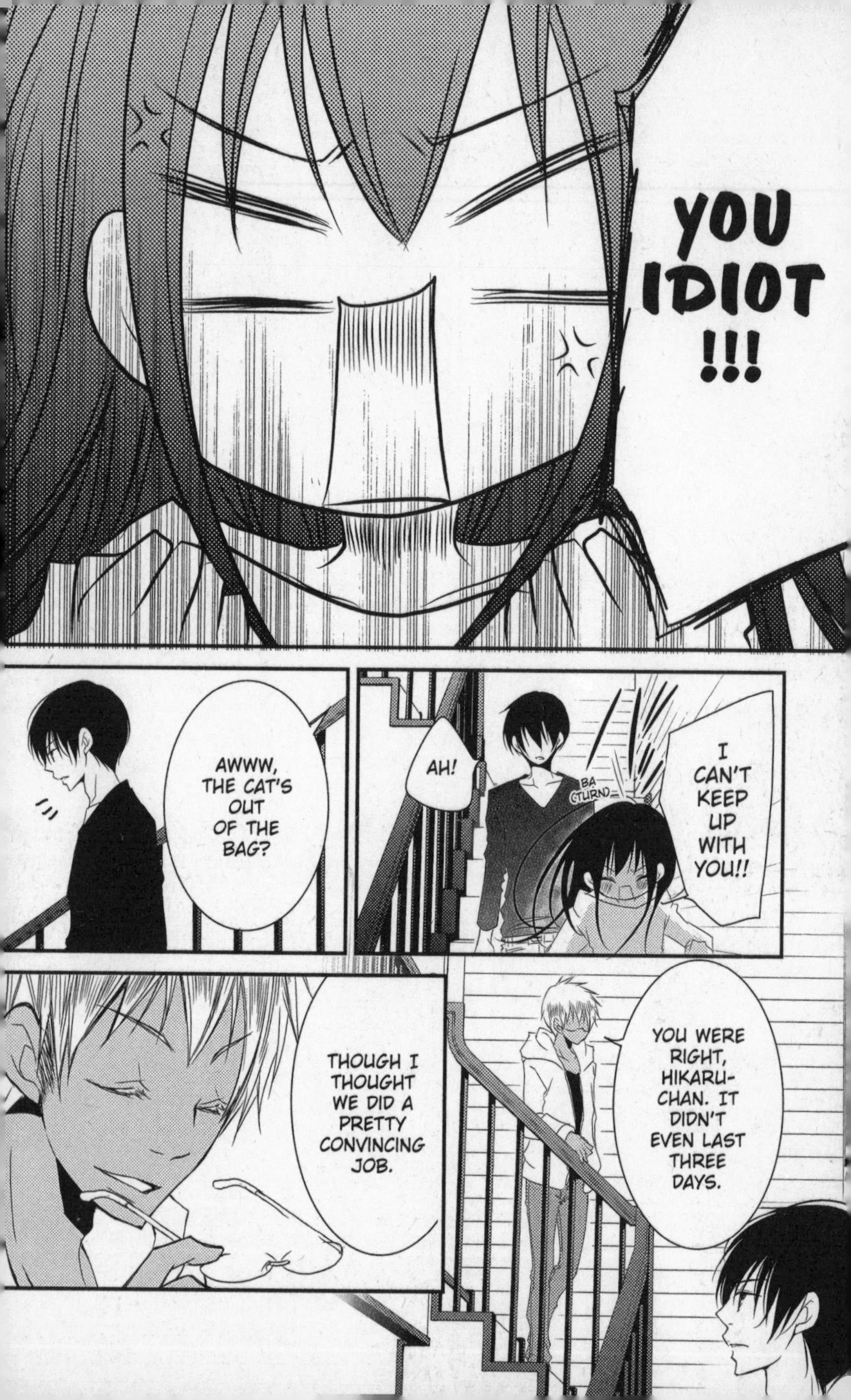
YOU IDIOT !!!
I CAN'T KEEP UP WITH YOU!!
BA TURN
AH!
AWWW, THE CAT'S OUT OF THE BAG?
YOU WERE RIGHT, HIKARU-CHAN. IT DIDN'T EVEN LAST THREE DAYS.
THOUGH I THOUGHT WE DID A PRETTY CONVINCING JOB.

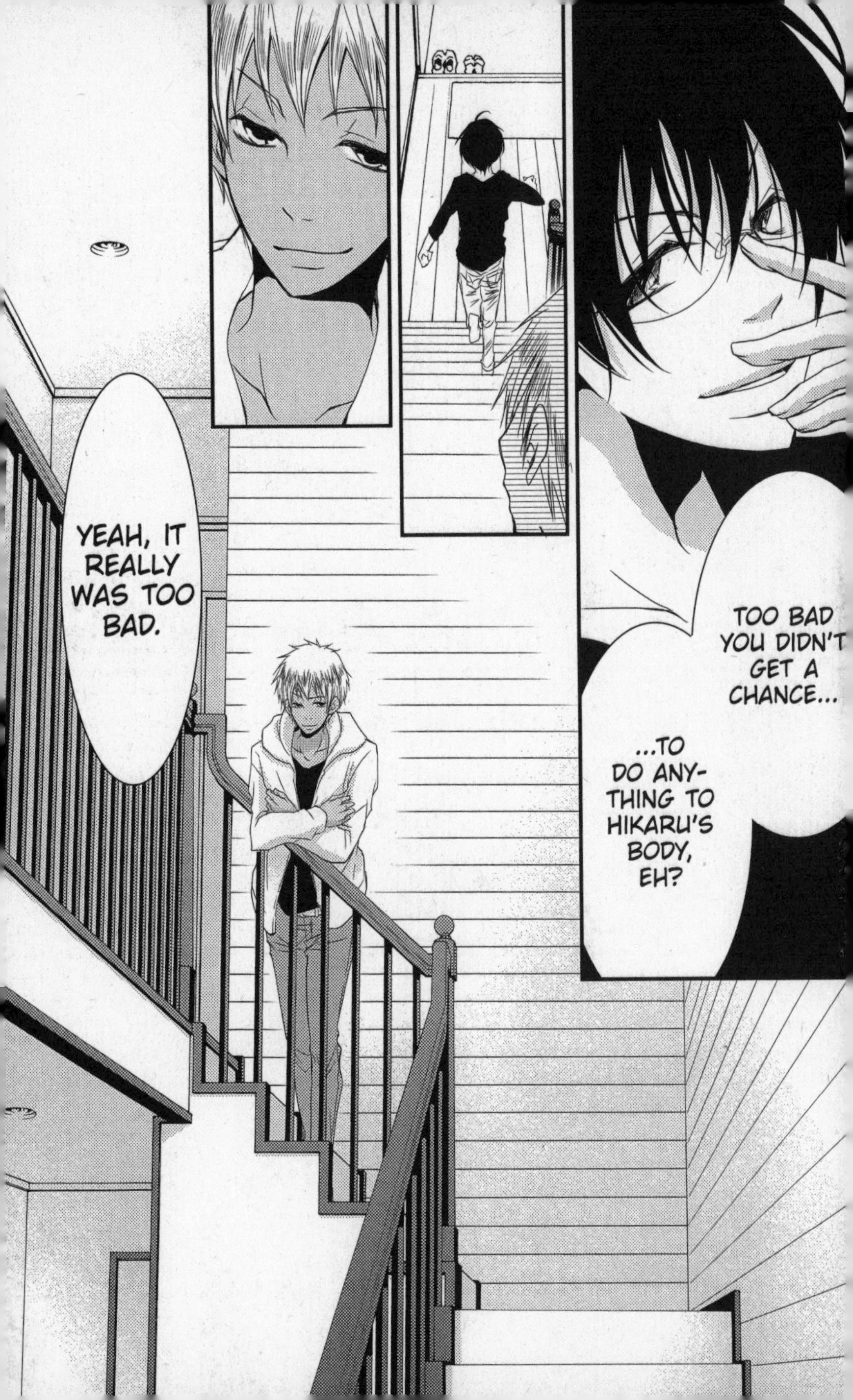
TOO BAD YOU DIDN'T GET A CHANCE...
...TO DO ANY-THING TO HIKARU'S BODY, EH?
YEAH, IT REALLY WAS TOO BAD.

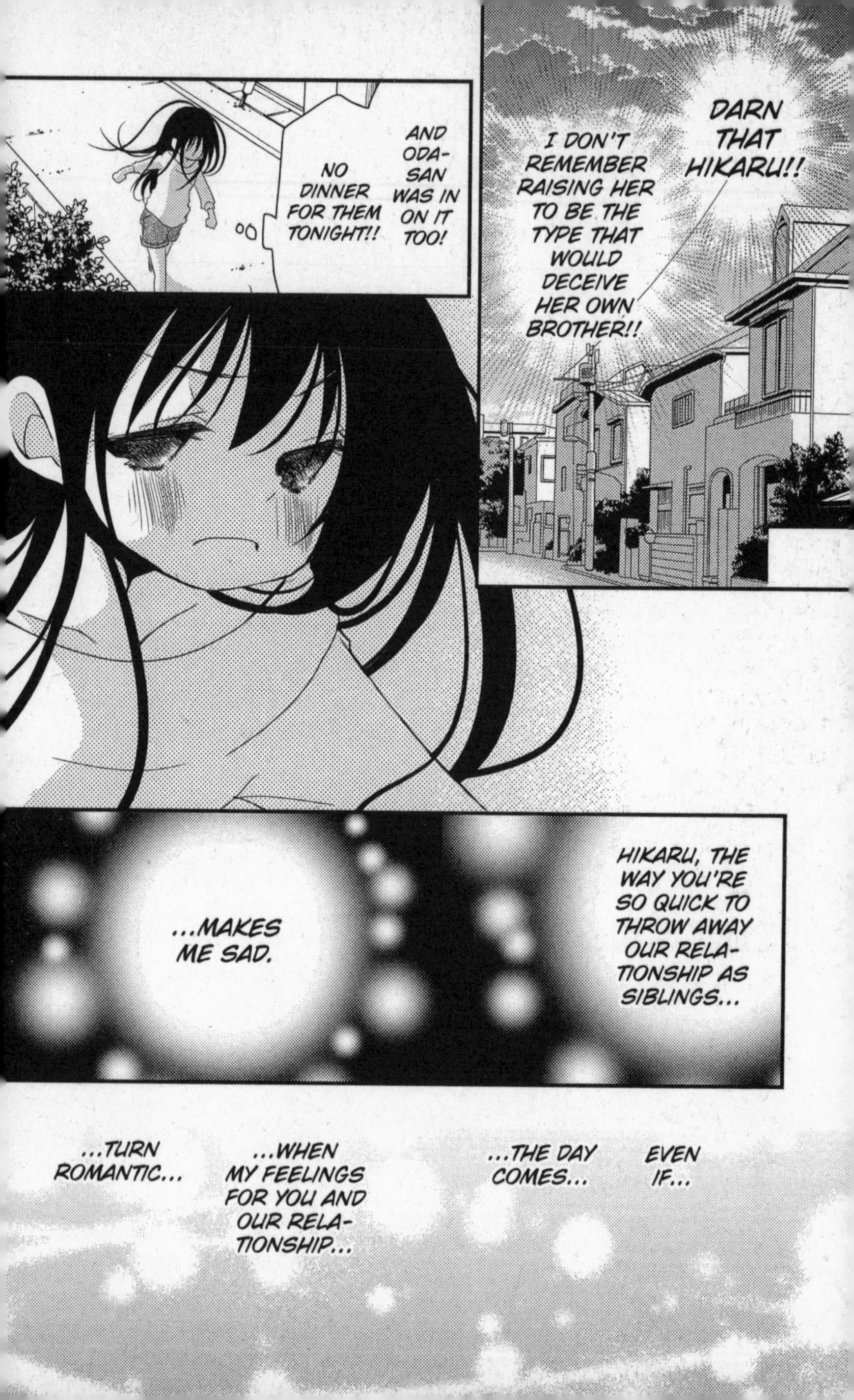
DARN THAT HIKARU!!
I DON'T REMEMBER RAISING HER TO BE THE TYPE THAT WOULD DECEIVE HER OWN BROTHER!!
AND ODA-SAN WAS IN ON IT TOO!
NO DINNER FOR THEM TONIGHT!!
HIKARU, THE WAY YOU'RE SO QUICK TO THROW AWAY OUR RELA-TIONSHIP AS SIBLINGS...
...MAKES ME SAD.
EVEN IF...
...THE DAY COMES...
...WHEN MY FEELINGS FOR YOU AND OUR RELA-TIONSHIP...
...TURN ROMANTIC...

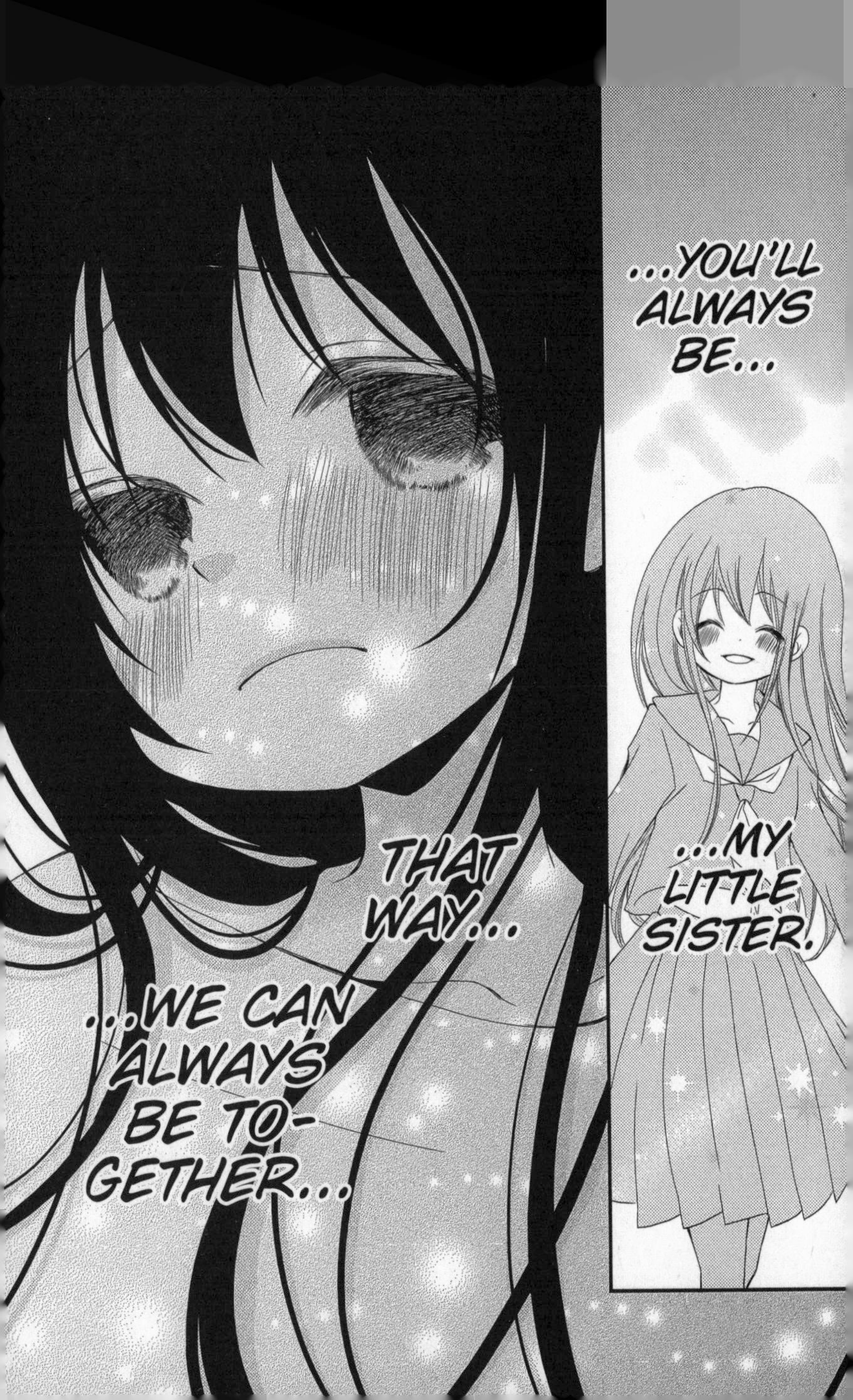
...YOU'LL ALWAYS BE...
...MY LITTLE SISTER.
THAT WAY...
...WE CAN ALWAYS BE TO-GETHER...

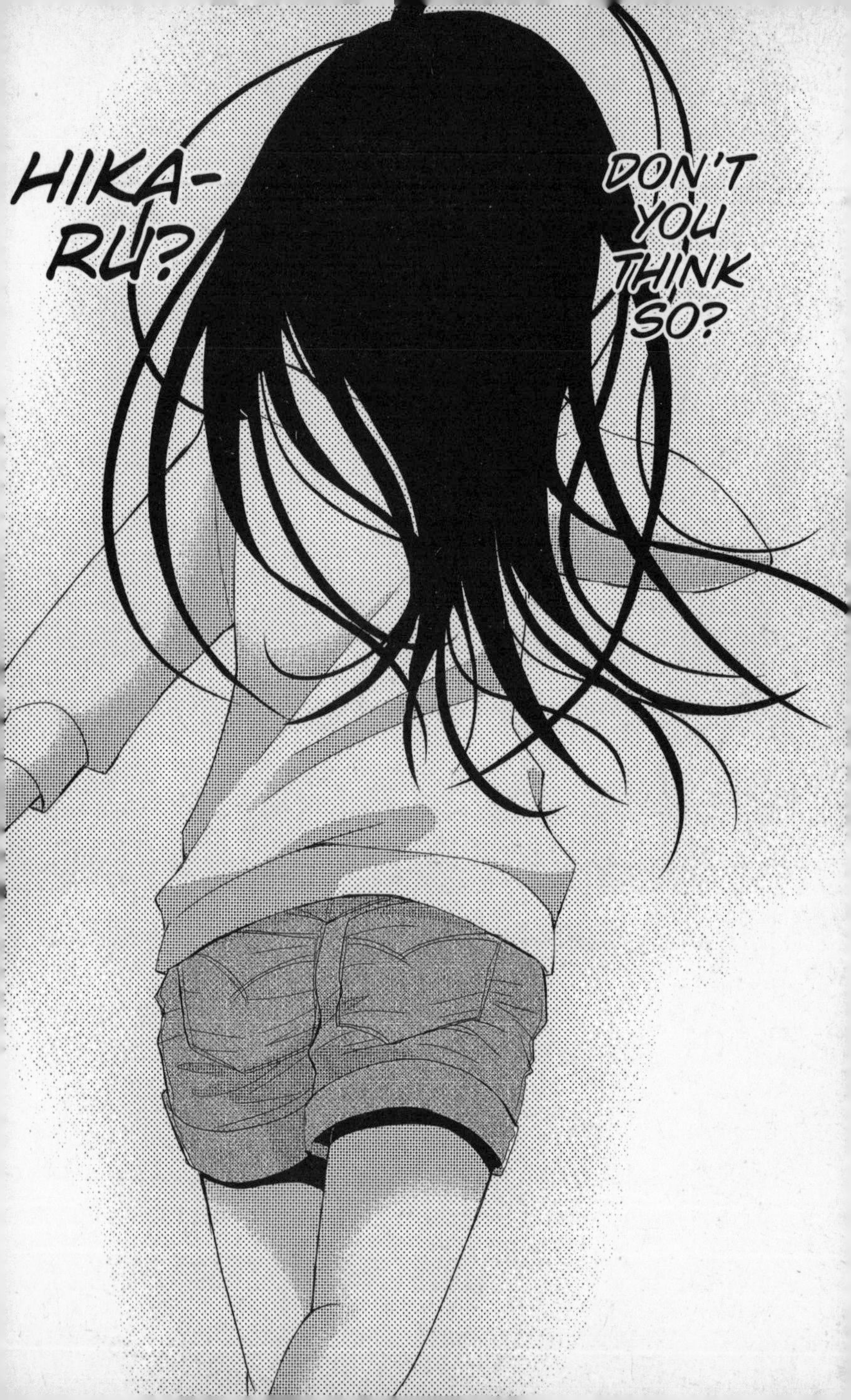
DON'T YOU THINK SO?
HIKA-RU?

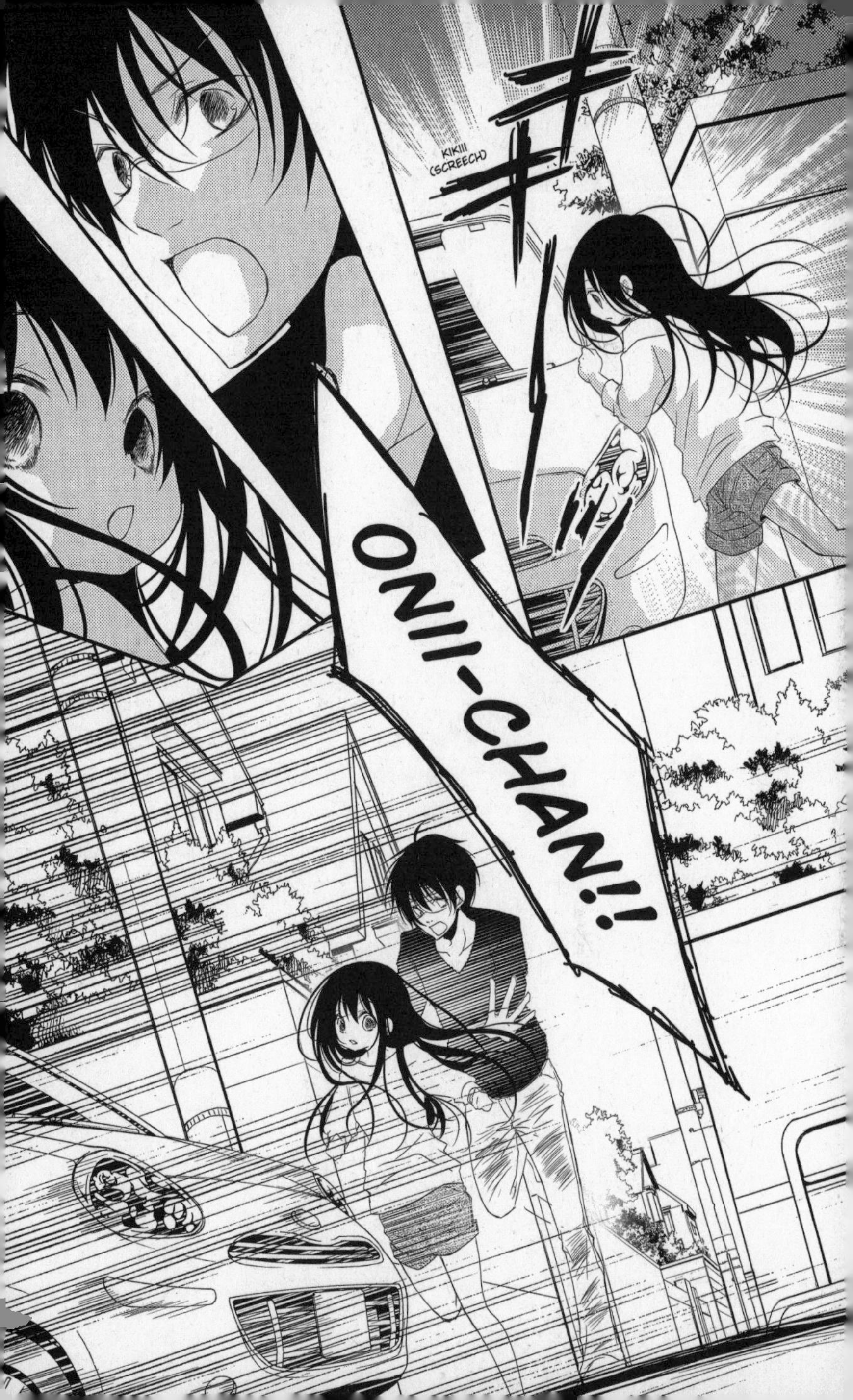
KIKIII (SCREECH)
ONII-CHAN!!

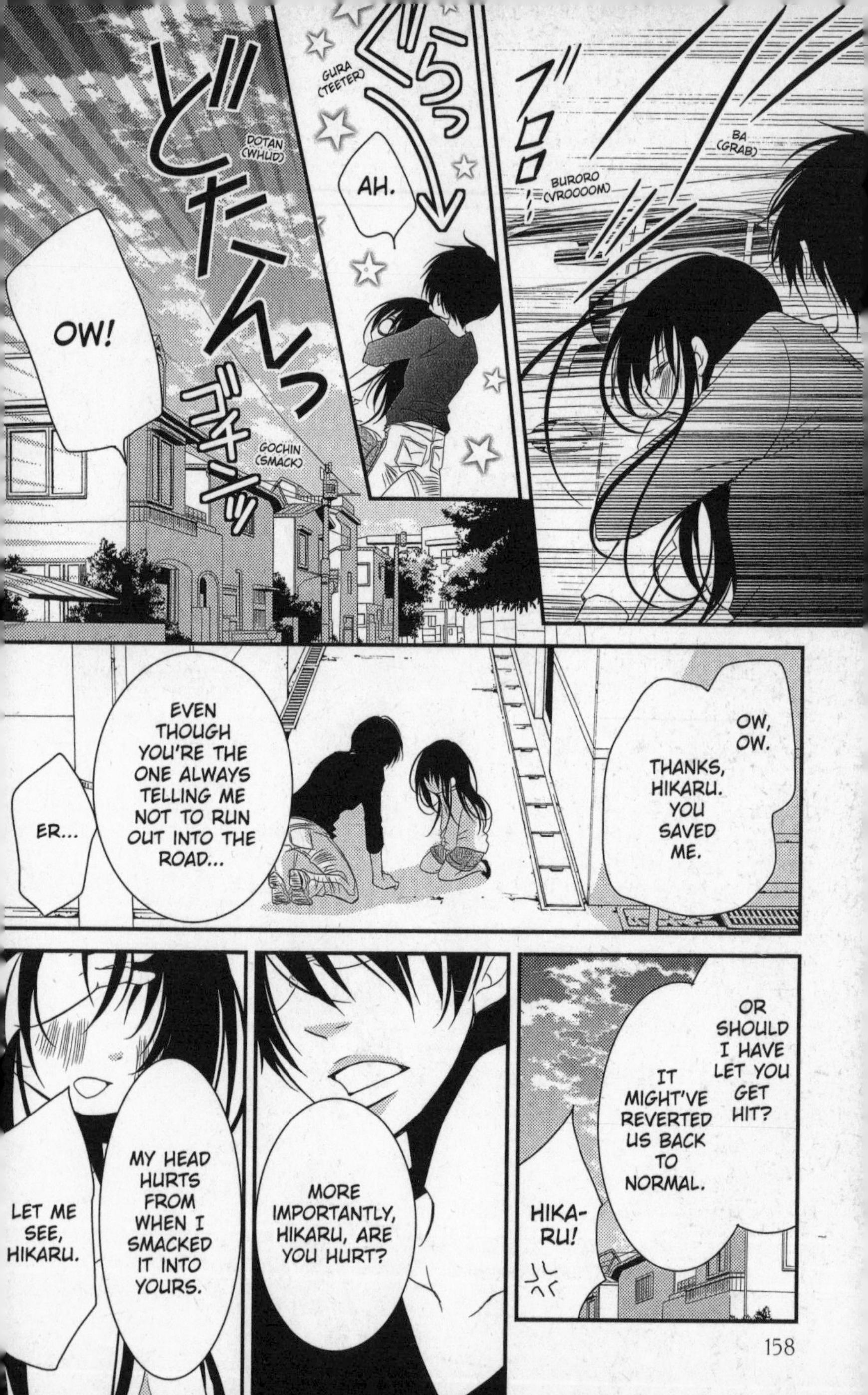
BA (GRAB)
ブロロ…
BURORO (VROOOOM)
ぐらっ
GURA (TEETER)
AH.
どたんっ
DOTAN (WHUD)
OW!
ゴチンッ
GOCHIN (SMACK)
OW, OW.
THANKS, HIKARU. YOU SAVED ME.
EVEN THOUGH YOU'RE THE ONE ALWAYS TELLING ME NOT TO RUN OUT INTO THE ROAD...
ER...
OR SHOULD I HAVE LET YOU GET HIT?
IT MIGHT'VE REVERTED US BACK TO NORMAL.
HIKA-RU!
MORE IMPORTANTLY, HIKARU, ARE YOU HURT?
MY HEAD HURTS FROM WHEN I SMACKED IT INTO YOURS.
LET ME SEE, HIKARU.

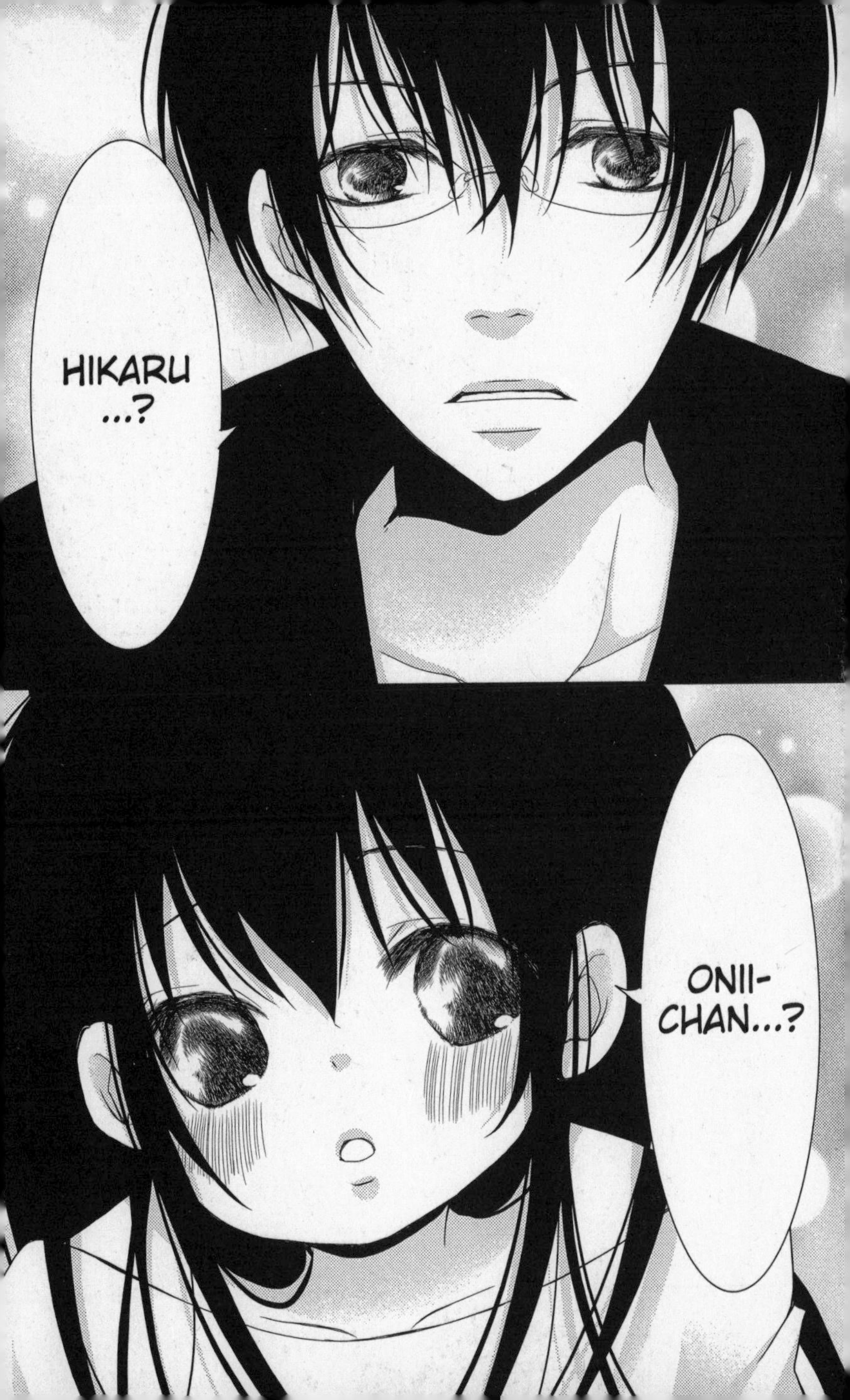
HIKARU ...?
ONII-CHAN...?

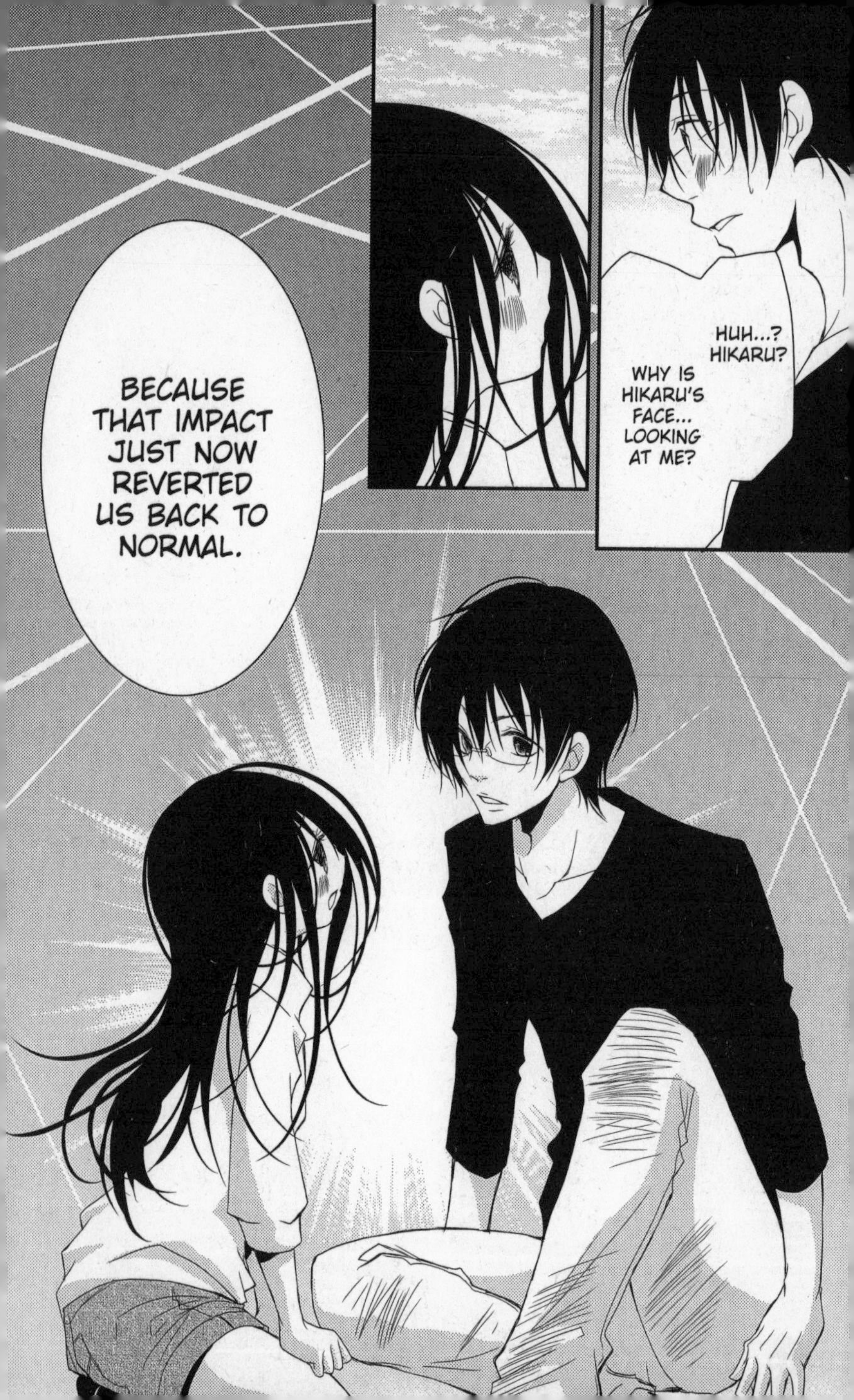
HUH...? HIKARU?
WHY IS HIKARU'S FACE... LOOKING AT ME?
BECAUSE THAT IMPACT JUST NOW REVERTED US BACK TO NORMAL.

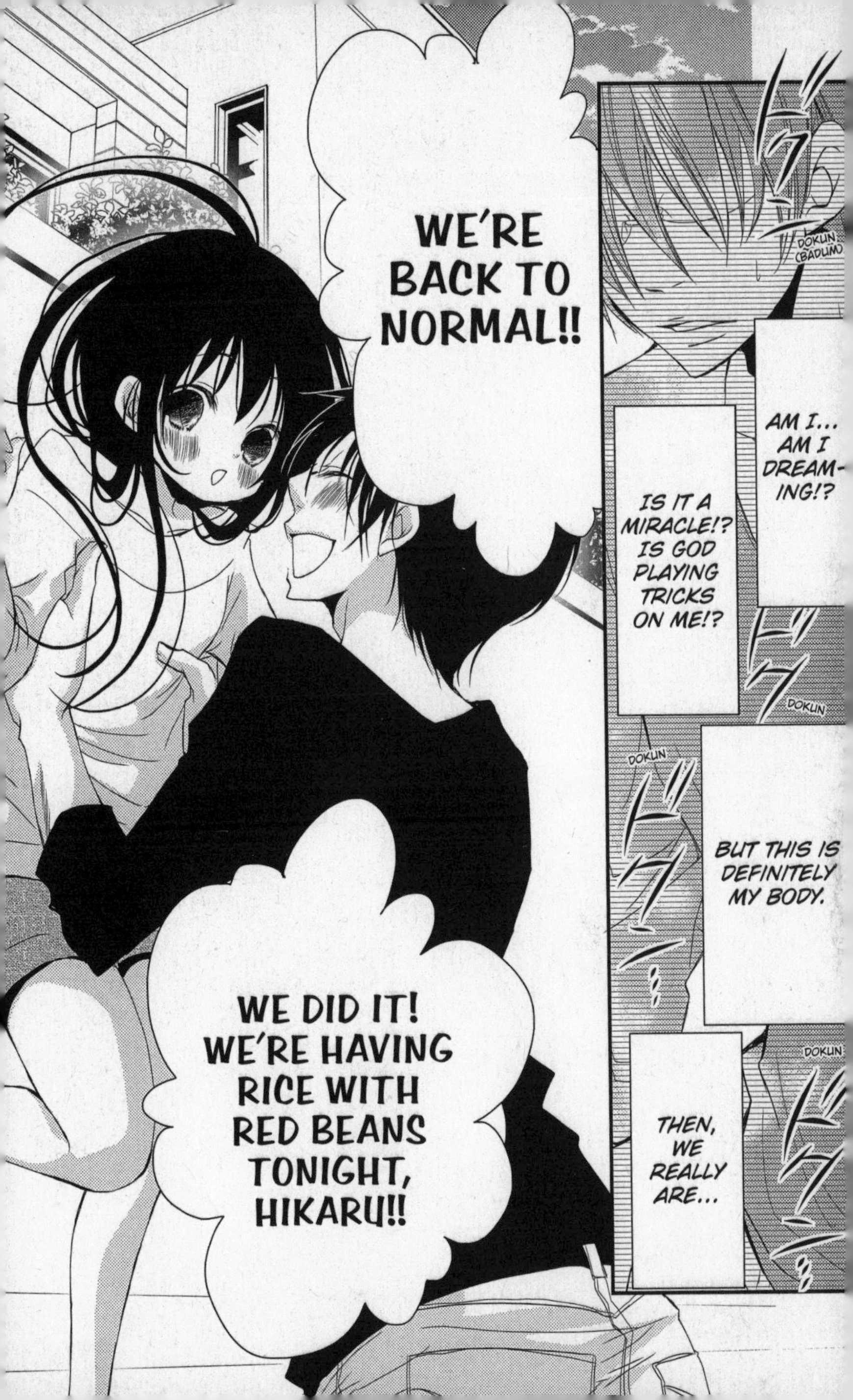

DOKUN (BADUMP)
AM I... AM I DREAMING!?
IS IT A MIRACLE!? IS GOD PLAYING TRICKS ON ME!?
DOKUN
DOKUN
BUT THIS IS DEFINITELY MY BODY.
DOKUN
THEN, WE REALLY ARE...
WE'RE BACK TO NORMAL!!
WE DID IT! WE'RE HAVING RICE WITH RED BEANS TONIGHT, HIKARU!!

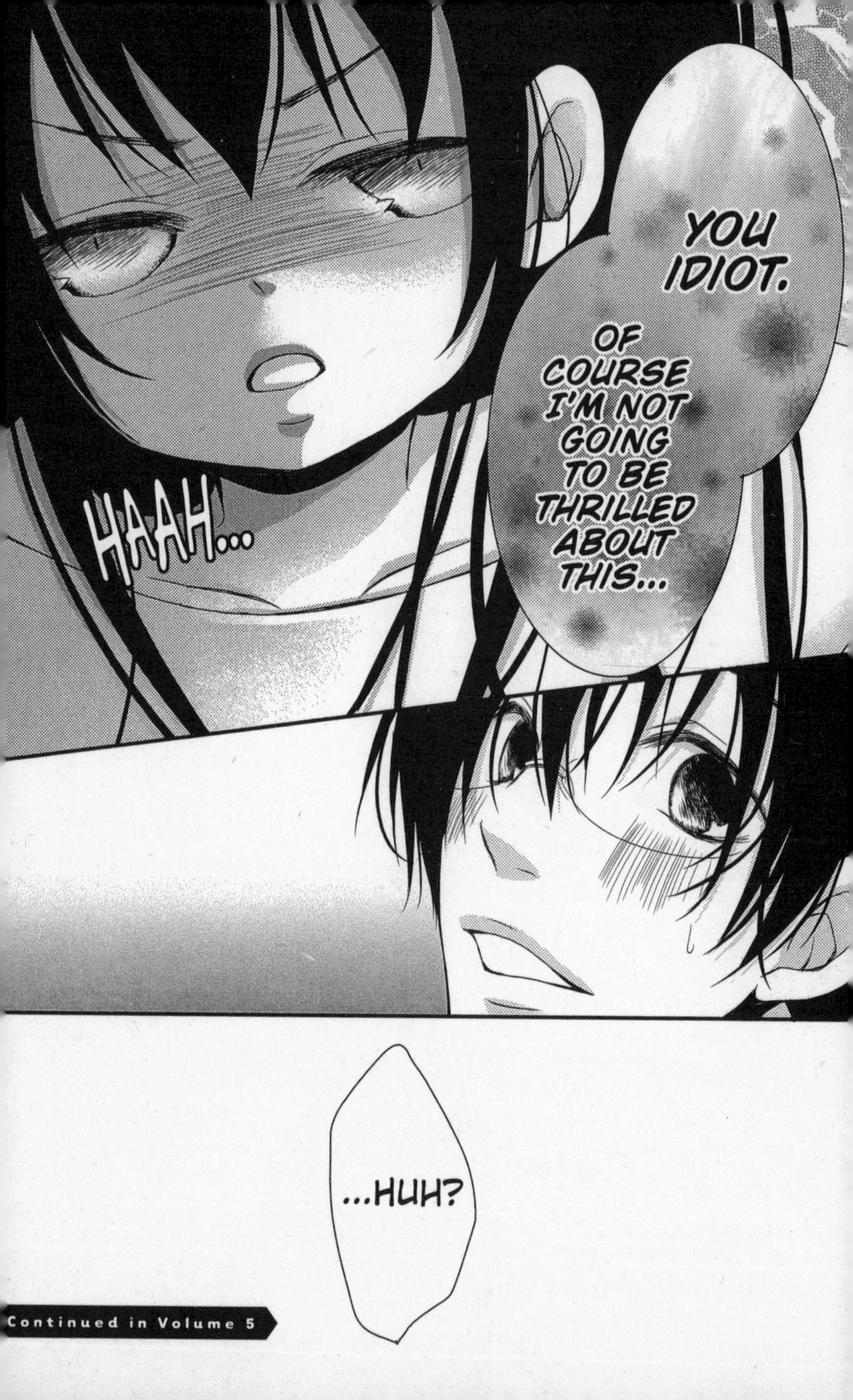
YOU IDIOT.
OF COURSE I'M NOT GOING TO BE THRILLED ABOUT THIS...
HAAH...
...HUH?
Continued in Volume 5

[Ani-Imo]

Big Brother becomes Little Sister;
Little Sister becomes Big Brother.

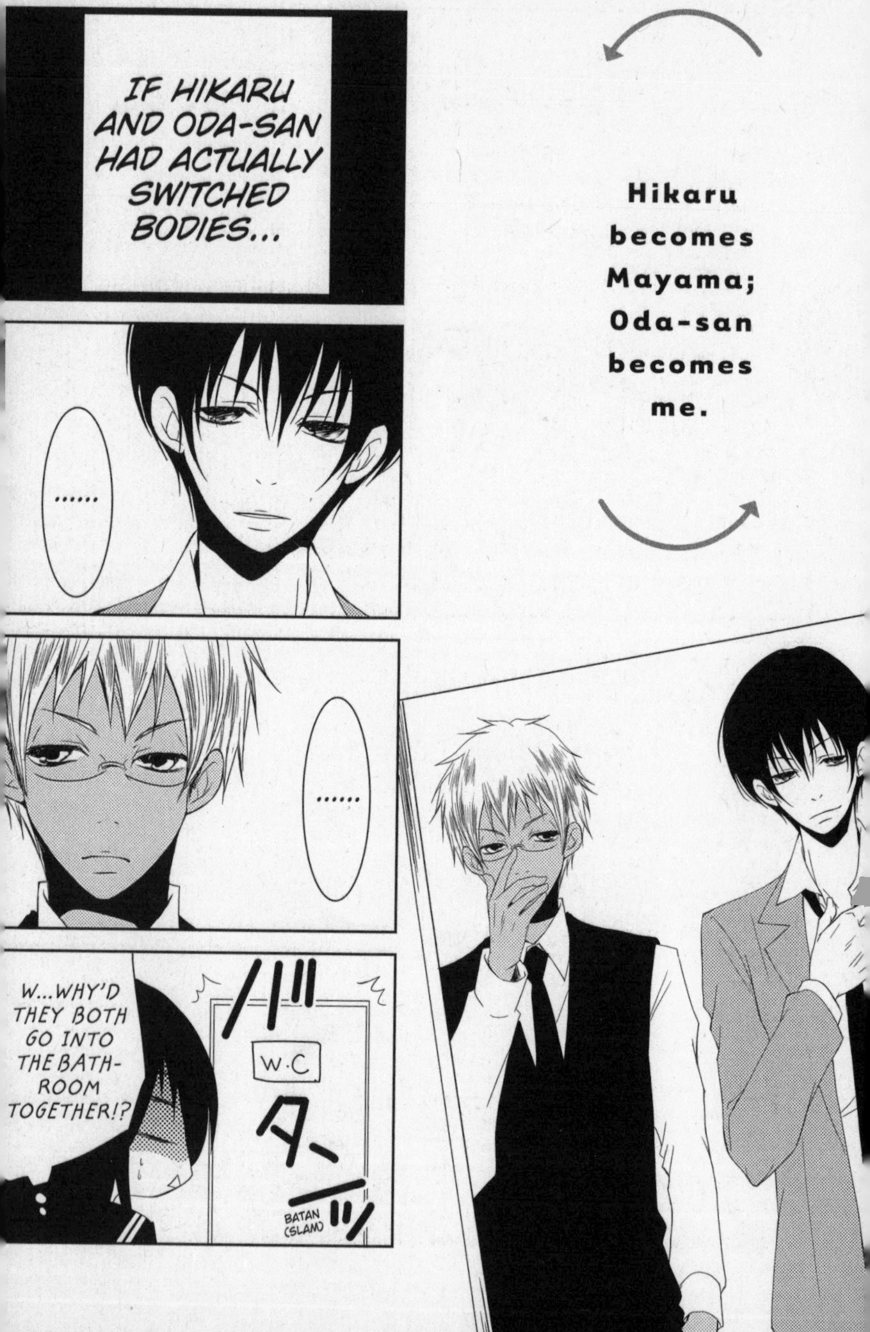
Hikaru becomes Mayama; Oda-san becomes me.
IF HIKARU AND ODA-SAN HAD ACTUALLY SWITCHED BODIES...
......
......
W...WHY'D THEY BOTH GO INTO THE BATH-ROOM TOGETHER!?
W.C.
BATAN (SLAM)

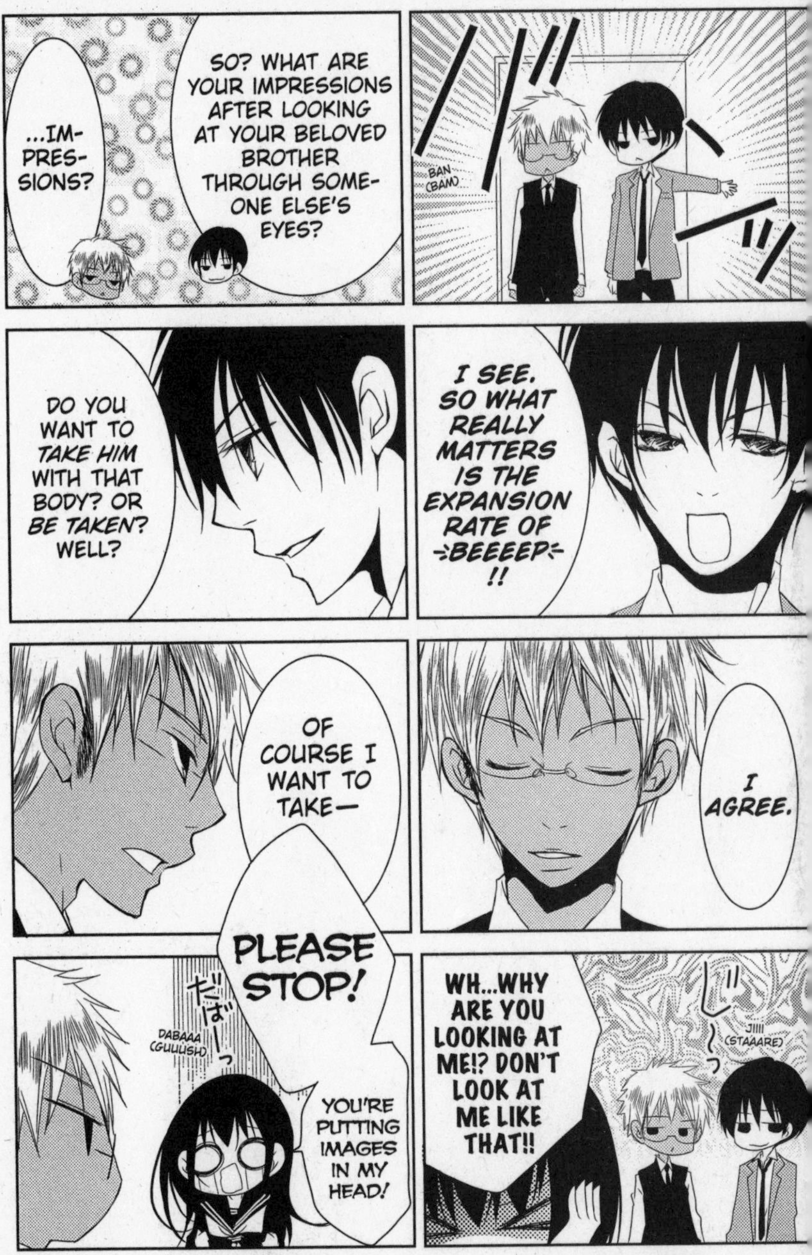
BAN (BAM)
SO? WHAT ARE YOUR IMPRESSIONS AFTER LOOKING AT YOUR BELOVED BROTHER THROUGH SOME-ONE ELSE'S EYES?
...IM-PRES-SIONS?
I SEE. SO WHAT REALLY MATTERS IS THE EXPANSION RATE OF BEEEEP!!
DO YOU WANT TO *TAKE HIM* WITH THAT BODY? OR *BE TAKEN*? WELL?
I AGREE.
OF COURSE I WANT TO TAKE—
じ〜っ
JIIII (STAAARE)
WH...WHY ARE YOU LOOKING AT ME!? DON'T LOOK AT ME LIKE THAT!!
PLEASE STOP!
だばーっ
DABAAA (GUUUSH)
YOU'RE PUTTING IMAGES IN MY HEAD!

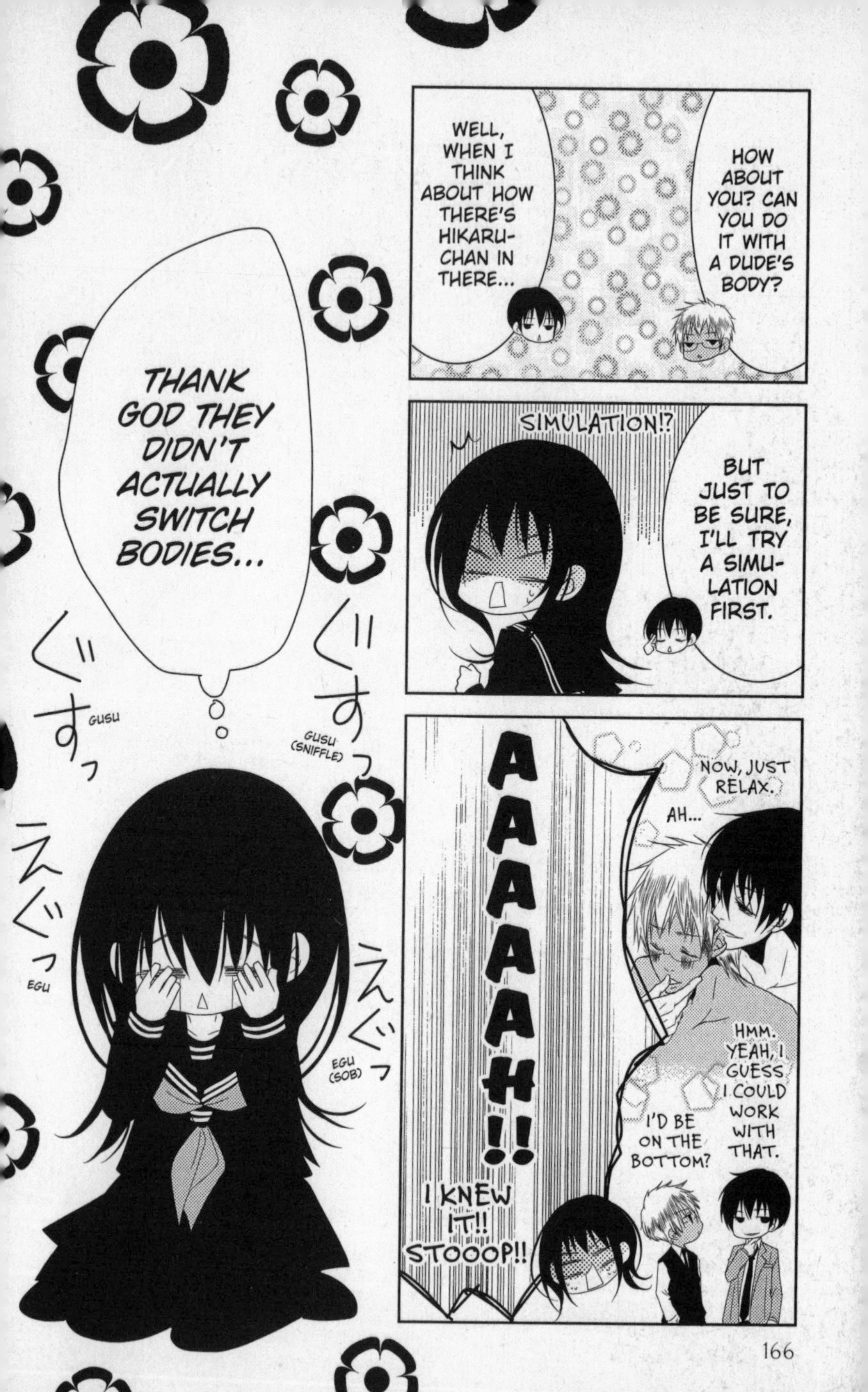
HOW ABOUT YOU? CAN YOU DO IT WITH A DUDE'S BODY?
WELL, WHEN I THINK ABOUT HOW THERE'S HIKARU-CHAN IN THERE...
BUT JUST TO BE SURE, I'LL TRY A SIMULATION FIRST.
SIMULATION!?
NOW, JUST RELAX.
AH...
HMM. YEAH, I GUESS I COULD WORK WITH THAT.
I'D BE ON THE BOTTOM?
AAAAAH!!
I KNEW IT!! STOOOP!!
THANK GOD THEY DIDN'T ACTUALLY SWITCH BODIES...
ぐすっ
GUSU (SNIFFLE)
ぐすっ
GUSU
えぐっ
EGU (SOB)
えぐっ
EGU

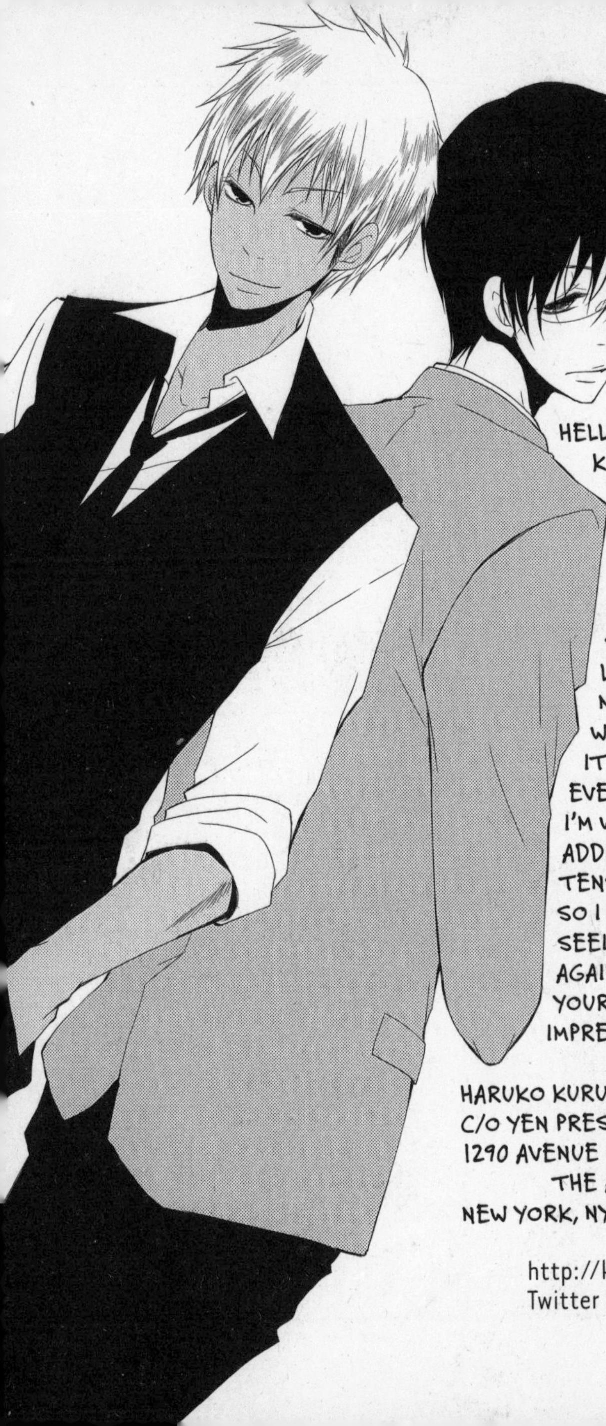

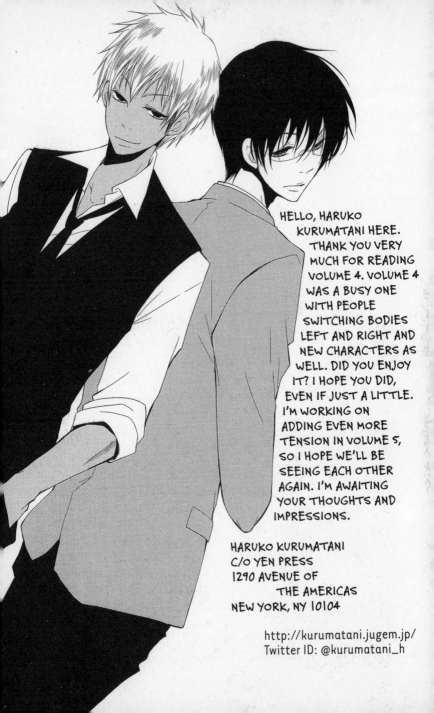

HELLO, HARUKO KURUMATANI HERE. THANK YOU VERY MUCH FOR READING VOLUME 4. VOLUME 4 WAS A BUSY ONE WITH PEOPLE SWITCHING BODIES LEFT AND RIGHT AND NEW CHARACTERS AS WELL. DID YOU ENJOY IT? I HOPE YOU DID, EVEN IF JUST A LITTLE. I'M WORKING ON ADDING EVEN MORE TENSION IN VOLUME 5, SO I HOPE WE'LL BE SEEING EACH OTHER AGAIN. I'M AWAITING YOUR THOUGHTS AND IMPRESSIONS.

HARUKO KURUMATANI
C/O YEN PRESS
1290 AVENUE OF
THE AMERICAS
NEW YORK, NY 10104

http://kurumatani.jugem.jp/
Twitter ID: @kurumatani_h

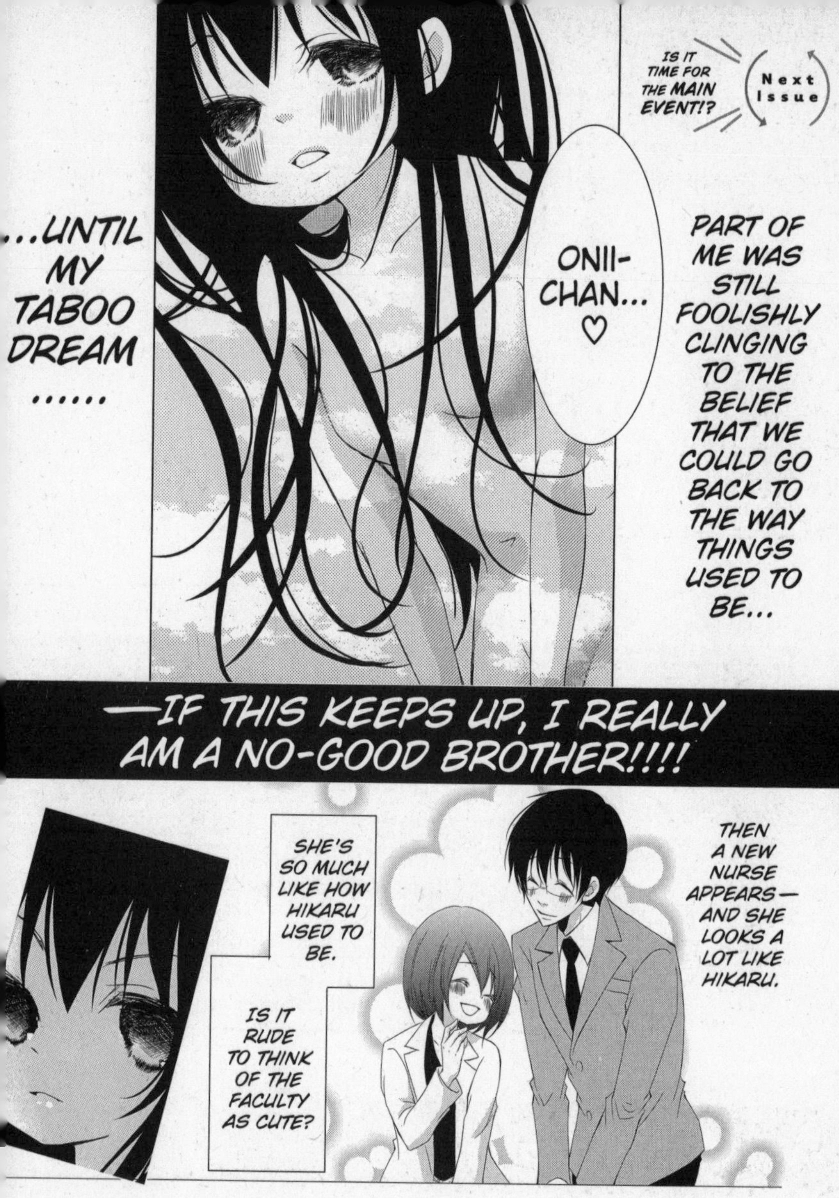
Next Issue
IS IT TIME FOR THE MAIN EVENT!?
PART OF ME WAS STILL FOOLISHLY CLINGING TO THE BELIEF THAT WE COULD GO BACK TO THE WAY THINGS USED TO BE...
ONII-CHAN... ♡
...UNTIL MY TABOO DREAM ......
—IF THIS KEEPS UP, I REALLY AM A NO-GOOD BROTHER!!!!
THEN A NEW NURSE APPEARS—AND SHE LOOKS A LOT LIKE HIKARU.
SHE'S SO MUCH LIKE HOW HIKARU USED TO BE.
IS IT RUDE TO THINK OF THE FACULTY AS CUTE?

Available November 2015

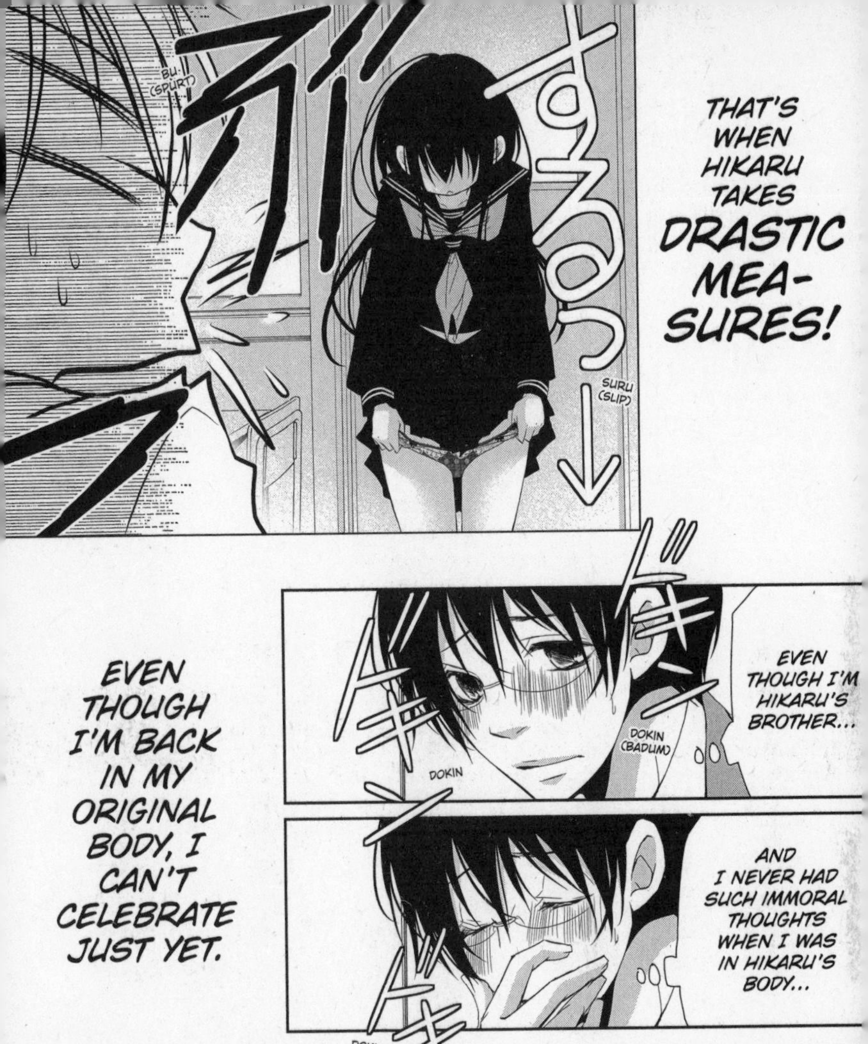
THAT'S WHEN HIKARU TAKES DRASTIC MEA-SURES!
SURU (SLIP)
BU- (SPURT)
EVEN THOUGH I'M HIKARU'S BROTHER...
DOKIN (BADUM)
DOKIN
AND I NEVER HAD SUCH IMMORAL THOUGHTS WHEN I WAS IN HIKARU'S BODY...
DOKIN
EVEN THOUGH I'M BACK IN MY ORIGINAL BODY, I CAN'T CELEBRATE JUST YET.

WHAT AM I SUPPOSED TO DO NOW!!?

Ani-Imo (5)

Translation Notes

Common Honorifics:

no honorific: Indicates familiarity or closeness; if used without permission or reason, addressing someone in this manner would constitute an insult.

-san: The Japanese equivalent of Mr./Mrs./Miss. If a situation calls for politeness, this is the fail-safe honorific.

-sama: Conveys great respect; may also indicate that the social status of the speaker is lower than that of the addressee.

-kun: Used most often when referring to boys, this indicates affection or familiarity. Occasionally used by older men among their peers, but it may also be used by anyone referring to a person of lower standing.

-chan: An affectionate honorific indicating familiarity used mostly in reference to girls; also used in reference to cute persons or animals of either gender.

-senpai: A suffix used to address upperclassmen or more experienced coworkers.

-sensei: A respectful term for teachers, artists, or high-level professionals.

-oniisan, onii-san, aniki, etc.: Terms used to address an elder brother or brother-like figure.

-oneesan, onee-san, aneki, etc.: Terms used to address an elder sister or sister-like figure.

Page 85
Makunouchi

A popular type of Japanese bento (boxed meal) that includes fish and meat, pickled and fresh vegetables, egg, and rice topped with a pickled plum. The name *"makenouchi"* literally means "between acts," derived from a time when boxed meals were served between the acts of theatrical performances.

Page 113
Onsen tamago

Onsen tamago, or "hot spring eggs," are eggs that have been slowly cooked in the waters of a hot spring. The resulting egg has a firmer yolk, while the white becomes soft and custard-like.

Page 161
Rice with red beans

Sekihan, literally "red rice," is a traditional dish of steamed rice mixed with red beans that is served especially on celebratory occasions.

Ani-Imo

Ani-Imo (5)

Sneak Peek

Read on for an early look at Volume 5,
available November 2015.

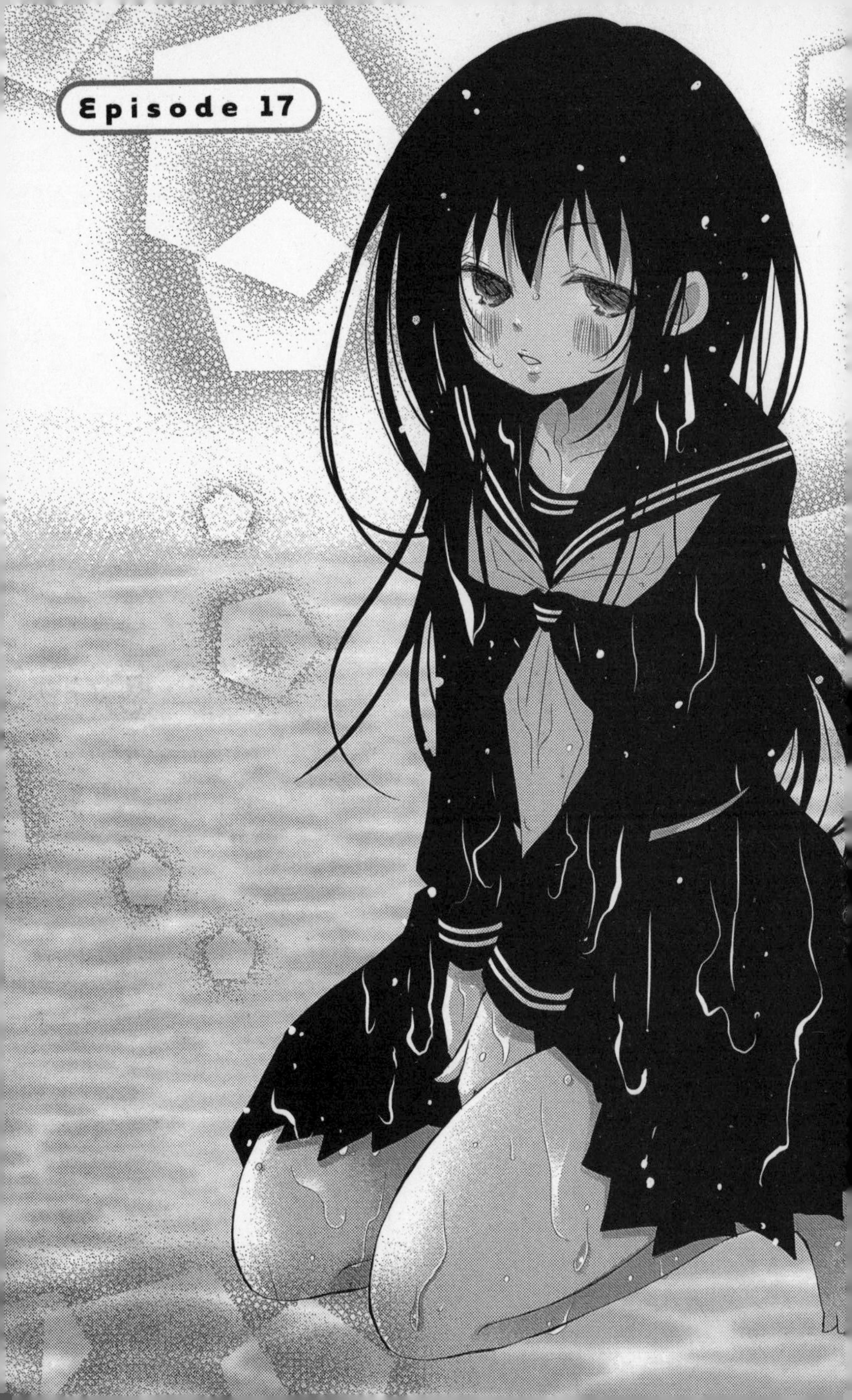
Episode 17

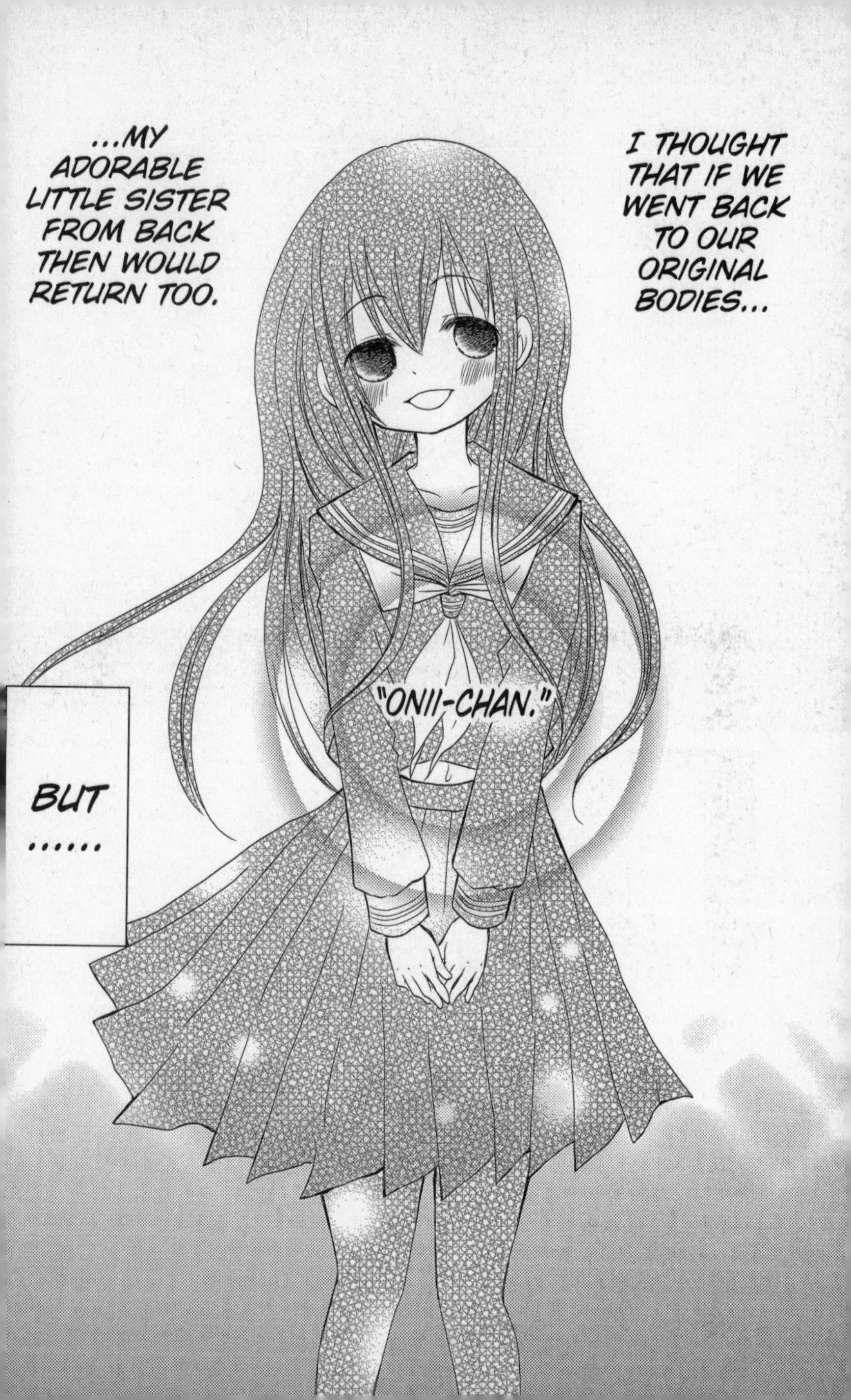
I THOUGHT THAT IF WE WENT BACK TO OUR ORIGINAL BODIES...
...MY ADORABLE LITTLE SISTER FROM BACK THEN WOULD RETURN TOO.
"ONII-CHAN."
BUT ......

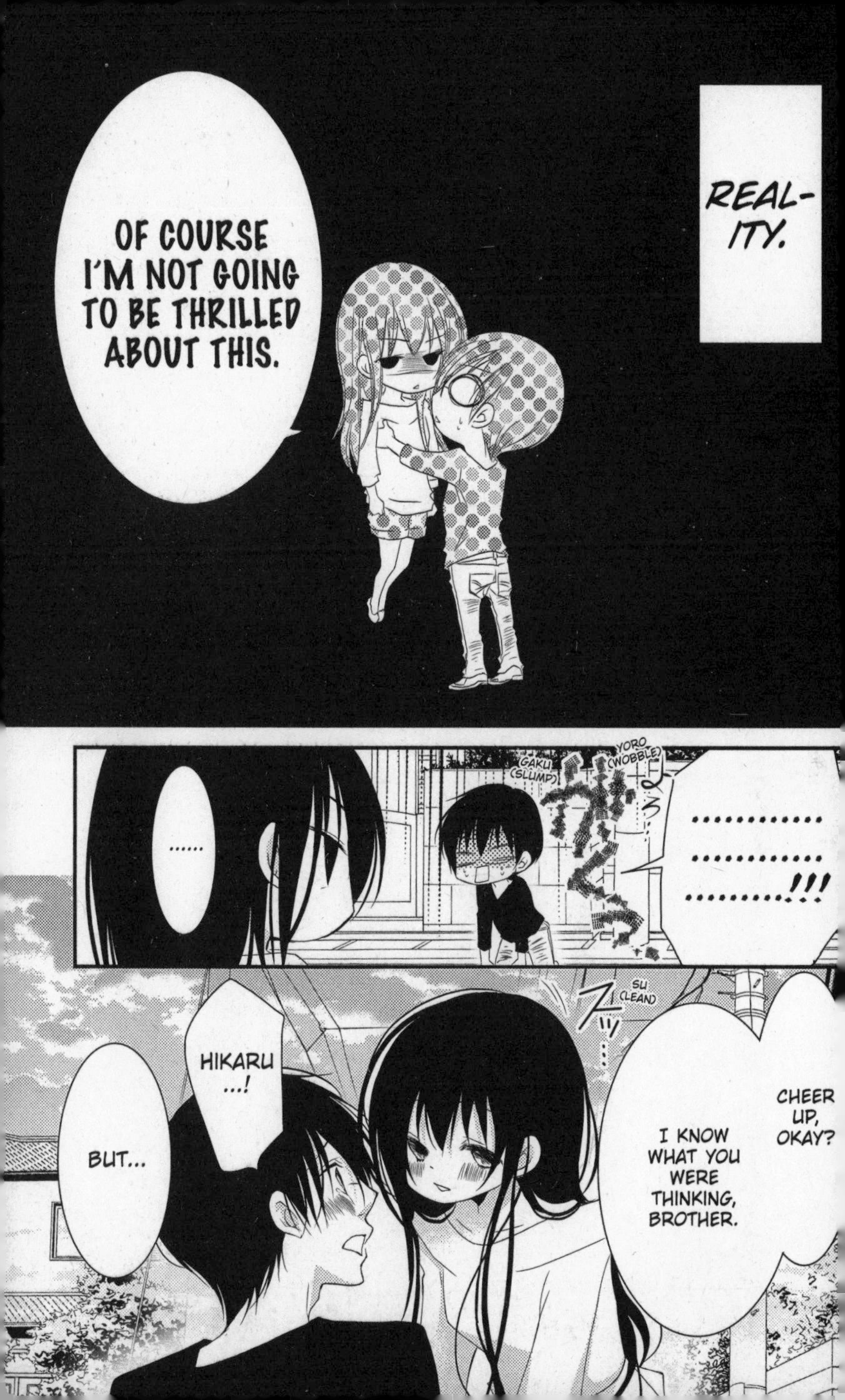
REAL-ITY.
OF COURSE I'M NOT GOING TO BE THRILLED ABOUT THIS.
....!!!
YORO (WOBBLE)
GAKU (SLUMP)
......
SU (LEAN)
CHEER UP, OKAY?
I KNOW WHAT YOU WERE THINKING, BROTHER.
HIKARU ...!
BUT...

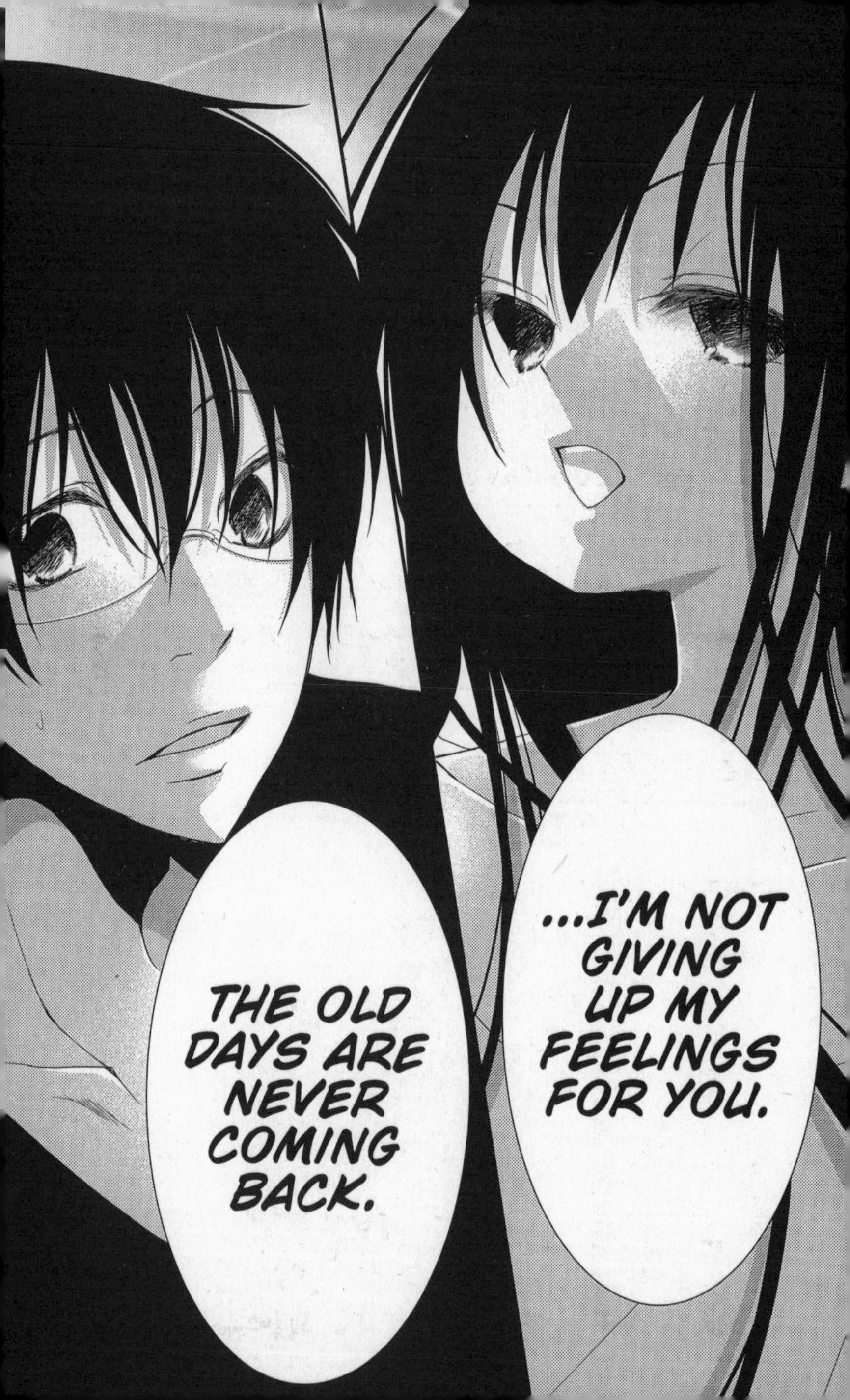
...I'M NOT GIVING UP MY FEELINGS FOR YOU.
THE OLD DAYS ARE NEVER COMING BACK.

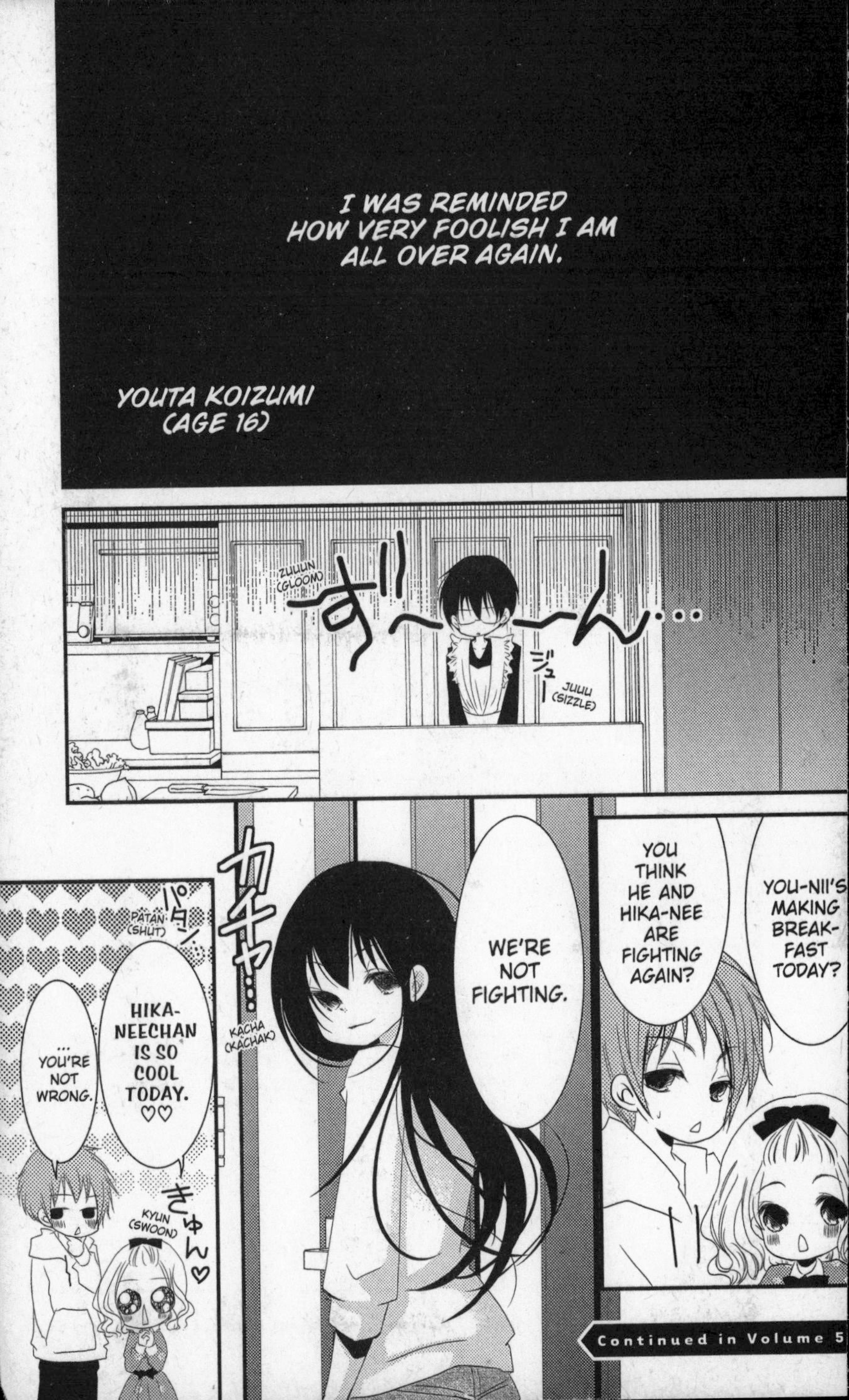
I WAS REMINDED HOW VERY FOOLISH I AM ALL OVER AGAIN.
YOUTA KOIZUMI (AGE 16)
ZUUUN (GLOOM)
すーーん…
ジュー
JUUU (SIZZLE)
YOU-NII'S MAKING BREAK-FAST TODAY?
YOU THINK HE AND HIKA-NEE ARE FIGHTING AGAIN?
WE'RE NOT FIGHTING.
カチャ…
KACHA (KACHAK)
パタン…
PATAN (SHUT)
HIKA-NEECHAN IS SO COOL TODAY. ♡♡
... YOU'RE NOT WRONG.
きゅん♡
KYUN (SWOON)

Continued in Volume 5

ANI-IMO(4)

HARUKO KURUMATANI

Translation: Christine Dashiell

Lettering: Abigail Blackman

ANI-IMO Volume 4
© 2013 Haruko Kurumatani. All rights reserved.
First published in Japan in 2013 by Kodansha, Ltd., Tokyo.
Publication rights for this English edition arranged through Kodansha Ltd. Tokyo.

Translation © 2015 by Hachette Book Group, Inc.

Yen Press
Hachette Book Group
1290 Avenue of the Americas
New York, NY 10104

www.hachettebookgroup.com
www.yenpress.com

Yen Press is an imprint of Hachette Book Group, Inc.
The Yen Press name and logo are trademarks of Hachette Book Group, Inc.

The publisher is not responsible for websites (or their content) that are not owned by the publisher.

First Yen Press Edition: August 2015

ISBN: 978-0-316-30504-4

10 9 8 7 6 5 4 3 2 1

BVG

Printed in the United States of America